THE POLITICS OF THE ANCIENT CONSTITUTION

The Politics of the Ancient Constitution

An Introduction to English
Political Thought, 1603–1642

GLENN BURGESS

The Pennsylvania State University Press
University Park, Pennsylvania

Copyright © Glenn Burgess 1992

First published in 1993 in the United States
by The Pennsylvania State University Press,
Barbara Building, Suite C, University Park, PA 16802

Library of Congress Cataloging-in-Publication Data

Burgess, Glenn, 1961–
    The politics of the ancient constitution : an introduction to
English political thought, 1603-1642 / Glenn Burgess.
        p.   cm.
    Includes bibliographical references and index.
    ISBN 0–271–00903–9 (cloth)
    ISBN 0–271–00926–8 (paper)
    1. Political science—Great Britain—History—17th
century.
I. Title.
JA84.G7885   1993
342.42'029—dc20
[344.20229]
                                        92–17255
                                            CIP

It is the policy of The Pennsylvania State University Press to
use acid-free paper for the first printing of all clothbound
books. Publications on uncoated stock satisfy minimum
requirements of American National Standard for Information
Sciences—Permanence of Paper for Printed Library Materials,
ANSI 239.48–1984.

Copyedited and typeset by Grahame & Grahame Editorial,
Brighton, England

Printed in Hong Kong

For Mandy

Contents

Preface

The idea of the ancient constitution provided the English political nation of the early-seventeenth century with its most important intellectual tools for the conduct of political debate. The common law, from which the ancient constitution derived, had a near-monopoly when it came to the discussion of such issues as taxation, property rights, and the making of law. Many of its central features were described in 1957 by Professor J. G. A. Pocock, in his book *The Ancient Constitution and the Feudal Law*. Since that time there have been many attempts to revise some elements of Pocock's account, as well as his own reflections on these attempts published in a new edition of the book in 1987. The Part I of the present work is an attempt to survey the state of play on this matter, and to contribute new material to the discussion. The heart of it is contained in Chapter 2, where it is argued that Pocock's account of the ancient constitution, though in many respects as valid as it ever was, over-emphasized the typicality of Sir Edward Coke, and (partly in consequence of this) under-played the role of *reason* in the thought of the common lawyers. They certainly thought that the ancient constitution was built on *custom*, but the temptation for us is to conclude from this that – like some later conservative thinkers – they believed the ancient constitution to be good simply because it was old, and (in any case) changing it would be more inconvenient than it was worth. In fact, I argue, custom was always subservient to reason: the ancient constitution was good because it was a rational system. Custom was a tool used to explain its rationality.

It is Part II of this book that justifies its sub-title. The common law was the most important political 'language' of early Stuart England, but it was not the only one. In the second half of the book I examine its relationships with the other 'languages', and thus its place in the overall system of political discourse to be found in the period. The aim of this is to show the basic structures and operation of political debate in the pre-Civil-War period. The account is not in all respects a complete one, and more could certainly be said about divine-right theory than I have said here. Inevitably, my focus is on law. As a result, Part II is effectively a re-examination of what were once considered to be some of the great constitutional high-points on

More reason than custom

ix

Consensus to confusion

the road to Civil War. I have attempted to show that they were nothing of the kind: far from showing an articulate and conscious opposition to the theories used by royal spokesmen, the conflicts of the early Stuart period show a pattern of consensus giving way to confusion, fear and doubt before the *actions* (rather than the theories) of Charles I. By 1640 there was evident a *crisis of the common law*, characterized by the growth of doubts about whether it really could fill the role that the doctrine of the ancient constitution gave it. This role was to protect the lives, liberties and estates of Englishmen. There was not so much a theoretical challenge to monarchy as a growing realization of the inadequacy of existing theories to cope with a new situation. Men in fact found it extremely difficult in the 1640s to construct for themselves a language with which to criticize and justify resistance to royal misgovernment.

I have aimed to address in this book both a student audience, and an audience of colleagues. There are always risks in aiming at more than a single audience, and some comment on the use of this book might help. Chapter 2 is undoubtedly more complex and technical than other parts. It is the place in which I develop my own views about the nature of the ancient constitution. Specialists in the subject will find in it justification for remarks made elsewhere. However, those more interested in my views on the general nature of political debate in the early-seventeenth century will find that Part II is to a considerable degree (if not entirely) able to be read on its own. Similarly Chapters 1 and 3 will also give between them a reasonable portrait of ancient constitutionalism, even without Chapter 2. Finally, Part II of the book forms one single argument: its parts do not really stand alone. It is intended to be accessible enough for an undergraduate audience (in part surveying the findings of recent historiography), while presenting a line of interpretation that will be of interest to scholars.

Throughout the book I have concentrated on *public* debate. There may be value in asking what people said in the privacy of their families, or wrote in the privacy of their studies, but these are not questions that I have chosen to address. I wanted to uncover the rules governing the conduct of political debate in the public arena, and – with a few exceptions – the evidence I cite is evidence from the public domain: pamphlets and books, legal trials, parliamentary debates. Whether people thought things that they were unable to express publically is a separate issue (and for what it's worth some recent work has now suggested that censorship did not weigh so

Public debate

heavily on the expression of opinion in the period than has hitherto been believed). In any case, the structure of public discourse is a subject in its own right.

I have, as a general rule, left quotations as I have found them: punctuation and spelling are unaltered; the same is usually true of capitalization. I have not always followed the italicization and other font styles of the originals, and I have usually modernized the usage of the letters i, j, u, and v. I have, of course, corrected obvious typographical errors on occasion. Throughout, the year is assumed to begin on January 1, though in other repects I have followed normal seventeenth century dating habits. This book does not have a bibliography, but I have tried to indicate the most important further reading in my notes. Such notes have been indexed, so those looking for information on particular subjects should consult the index.

The most pleasant duty that falls to the writer of prefaces is to recall the names of the friends and colleagues who have helped and inspired his or her work. In many cases we do not know the people personally. The names of those in this category will be found in my footnotes. I am particularly indebted to many of the recent scholars of the early Stuart political world whose work has led me to ask the question: if politics was like *this*, then what must political discourse have been like? Part II gives my answer to this question. It focuses on the balance between consensus and conflict, terms central to recent historiographical debate. Prof. Louis Knafla responded generously to my request for help in tracking down some of his own work. Dr Richard Tuck gave of his time and knowledge while I worked on the thesis from which some of this book derives, and Dr Mark Goldie made valuable comments on the completed thesis. During this period I was kept buoyant by the conversations and moral support of friends, notably Dr Jonathan Scott and Mr. Howard Moss. Both have contributed more to my conclusions than they possibly realize. To Dr John Morrill, supervisor of my PhD thesis, and Prof. Colin Davis I have accumulated, and continue to accumulate, debts which I shall never be able to repay. Their friendship and advice at all stages of this project both made it more pleasant and improved the quality of its product.

Ideas alone do not make books. In the process of producing the finished product one gathers a further set of friends and, in a wide sense, creditors. Mrs Dawn Hack and Mrs Judy Robertson converted my MS into typescript. Financial aid was provided, at various points, by Trinity College, Cambridge; the Cambridge

Commonwealth Trust; a Claude McCarthy Fellowship from the
N.Z. University Grants Committee; and by research grants from
the University of Canterbury and its Department of History. I am
grateful also to the staff of the Rare Books Room of the Cambridge
University Library, where much of the research for this book was
carried out, and to the excellent interloans staff at the University of
Canterbury Library. My thanks to all of them, and to my publishers,
Vanessa Graham in particular, for patience with my dilatoriness.

I have been lucky: my parents have always done their utmost to
enable me to fulfil my wish to become an historian (however bizarre
they may have thought such a wish). Without them, it would not
have been possible. My final thanks are reserved for my wife, to
whom the book is dedicated. She did *not* type the manuscript or
compile the index; but without her willingness to value the writing
of this book as highly as I did myself, its progress would have been
much slower. What more can one ask for?

GLENN BURGESS

Part I
Exploring the Ancient Constitution of England

1

Ancient Constitutions –
Politics and the Past

In the past people thought differently. The point is a deceptively obvious one. It is always tempting to interpret ideas from the past in ways that make them more like our own than they really were. No matter how frequently we remind ourselves of the differences between the past and the present, our very habits of mind encourage us to abridge them. The study of past ideas must always be in part a process of defamiliarization. In early-seventeenth century England there were two common ways of legitimating the political rules and arrangements of the present,[1] and both of them are liable to look bizarre to modern eyes. One of these ways involved the employment of the concept of custom, the other the concept of grace. Things were legitimate either because they were customary, or because they were the product of God's grace. In the hyper-rationalistic twentieth century neither of these justifications seems particularly persuasive, and a considerable degree of effort is required for us to rethink the thoughts of people for whom these concepts were of such legitimating power.

This book will consider in detail the thinking that underlay the concept of custom. Many have argued that this forms the basic language for political debate in the early Stuart period,[2] and this is probably so. The language of custom was derived from the practices and attitudes of the common law, and most of the English ruling élite had at least a passing acquaintance with this. In law courts, in pamphlets, in parliamentary debate, the preconceptions of 'the common-law mind'[3] were fundamental to the ways in which political matters were discussed. These preconceptions together formed the concept of the *ancient constitution*. This concept is an inherently ambiguous one, so we must begin with a careful examination of its possible meanings.

3

(A)   THE IDEA OF AN ANCIENT CONSTITUTION

The ideas that make up the theory of the ancient constitution can be resolved into three basic elements: *custom, continuity,* and *balance.* Let us examine each in turn.

Professor Pocock has summarized his understanding of the idea of the ancient constitution in these words:

> The relations of government and governed in England were assumed to be regulated by law; the law in force in England was assumed to be the common law; all common law was assumed to be custom, elaborated, summarized and enforced by statute; and all custom was assumed to be immemorial, in the sense that any declaration or even change of custom . . . presupposed a custom already ancient and not necessarily recorded at the time of writing.[4]

The 'ancient constitution' of England was identified with the common law because that law regulated the relations of government and governed. Even the maker of statute law itself, the institution of King-in-parliament, was also the High Court of Parliament and the highest common-law court in the land. This common law, then, constituted the English polity. Further, the common law, and consequently the ancient constitution itself, were customary. By this was meant two things: first, that English common law was unwritten (*lex non scripta*), not written as the Roman law was. This raised the problem of how it could be law at all (the Roman law term *lex* meant written law), and this problem Bracton resolved by making English common law a customary law. It partook of the features of Roman *leges* (it was general not local), *and* of *consuetudines* (it was unwritten).[5] Thus common law became seen as the national law of England, yet was unusual in being (in origin at least) unwritten. So, where did it come from? how was it known? The answer to this provided the second feature of the customary common law, it was *immemorial*. This indeed was the defining feature of custom – some action performed or rule followed 'time out of mind'. This phrase 'time out of mind' did not mean simply old. It meant what it said: the practice had existed for as long as could be remembered, or (in other words) that no proof could be had of a time when it had not existed. There was no interest in the *origin* of customs. Quite the contrary, for if their origin could be discovered they would not be

unwritten and immemorial

customs. Origin presupposed a time before.

Because the ancient constitution was customary in this sense, believers in it were led to the doctrine of continuity. The ancient constitution was still in place in the seventeenth century, and it had existed 'time out of mind'. This implied that English legal and constitutional history must be a continuous one. If there were any evidence of breaks or sudden innovations then there would also be evidence of a time before current political arrangements were in force – a time when things were radically different. Therefore the idea of the ancient constitution presupposed that English history could be traced back step by step to its earliest documents, with no intervening ruptures. Professor Pocock has argued that this need for continuity committed people to a denial of the reality of conquest (and above all the Norman Conquest of 1066) in English history. This is a matter of some complexity to which we shall return in later chapters.

Finally, it was agreed that the essential political characteristic of the ancient constitution was balance. The fundamental laws of the English polity, as James I remarked early in his reign, gave the king his prerogatives, and gave the subjects security in their liberties and property.[6] They guaranteed the balance of prerogatives and liberties. The point could be formulated in a number of different ways. It could be stated as a balance of prerogative and law (rather than prerogative and liberties), as in Sir Francis Bacon's statement that 'so the laws, without the king's power, are dead; the king's power, except the laws be corroborated, will never move constantly, but be full of staggering and trepidation'.[7] Prerogative and law were mutually enhancing, not contradictory. Where James I balanced prerogatives and liberties, and Bacon balanced prerogative and law, Sir Edward Coke balanced allegiance and protection:

> for as the subject oweth to the king his true and faithfull ligeance and obedience, so the sovereign is to govern and protect his subjects.

Between a sovereign and a subject there is 'duplex et reciprocum ligamen'.[8] What is common to all of these variations is the theme of balance, the idea that the king's authority, while it remained unchallengeable, was to work in harmony with the needs of the subject as expressed in the common law. Balance was harmonious, and so in England the prerogatives of the monarch and the liberties of the subject co-existed in stable perfection. Thomas Hedley summarized the matter in a way that might look self-contradictory in our eyes, but was not: 'This kingdom enjoyeth the blessings and benefits of an absolute monarchy and of a free estate . . . . Therefore let no man think liberty and sovereignty incompatible, . . . rather like twins . . . they have such concordance and coalescence, that the one can hardly long subsist without the other'.[9]

Though these three components are all essential to the concept of the ancient constitution, there are a variety of ways in which they can be made to cohere. These can be reduced to two. Each may be linked to pre-existing approaches to the common law which can be found in fifteenth and early-sixteenth century writings. Later, we shall have to confront the question of the origins of the 'common-law mind', but it can be said in anticipation that at least part of the answer to this question is provided by features inherent to the English common law tradition itself. Nevertheless that tradition points in divergent directions, and each of the directions has a quite different implication for the idea of an ancient constitution.

The first consists of the argument that the English constitution and the common law were, in essentials, *unchanging*. Custom and continuity resulted in stasis, with institutions and laws passed on from generation to generation essentially unaltered. The view may be found expressed in Fortescue's *De Laudibus Legum Anglie* (written c. 1470). Fortescue's argument was summarized by Chief Justice Popham in 1607: that the laws of England,

> had continued as a rock without alteration in all the varieties of people that had possessed this land, namely the Romans, Brittons, Danes, Saxons, Normans, and English, which he imputed to the integrity and justice of these laws, every people taking a liking to them, and desirous to continue them and live by them, for which he cited Fortescues book of the laws of England.[10]

Or, as Fortescue himself put the matter, through all changes of rule, 'the realm has been continuously ruled by the same customs as it is now.'[11]

But this is not the only reading that can be given to the concepts of custom and continuity.[12] The alternative reading saw English constitutional history not as stasis but as continual change. Customs were constantly being refined and modified to fit changed circumstances. In this view English law was a body of rules in constant unbroken evolution, and at any given time was in perfect accord with its context. The classic expression of this reading was given by John Selden, appropriately in his commentary on Fortescue.[13] Selden argued that the customs of the present were not literally *identical* to those of the past yet could be said to be the same, just as

> the ship, that by often mending had no piece of the first materialls, or as the house that's so often repaired, *ut nihil ex pristina materia supersit* [i.e., that nothing of the original material survives], which yet (by the Civill law) is to be accounted the same still.[14]

This view of the meaning of custom and continuity, though considerably elaborated by Selden, was not really alien to English legal traditions. A basis for it may be found in St German's *Doctor and Student* (1523) which was (with Fortescue) one of the most widely read and cited of legal books. It has been said of this book that it argued that, though law was grounded in the principles of reason, nevertheless those principles 'are not necessarily universal and abstract, but may be drawn from historical growth'.[15] The *Doctor and Student* provided an account of custom that both avoided Fortescue's assertion that English customs had existed unchanged since pre-Roman times, and implied that customs were not all of the same age. St German, particularly in the way in which he linked together reason, custom and maxims so that they became almost identical,[16] was clearly aware of the diverse sources from which English law had gradually been accreted over time. For him, custom was a term of art, and the immemoriality of custom not so much a recognition of long immutable existence as of simple ignorance of origin. It was on such a basis as this that an account of legal history such as Selden's could be constructed.

Though we must eventually attempt to decide whether the path provided by Fortescue, or that provided by St German, was the one more commonly followed, we need first to explore some of the general contexts in which the doctrine of the ancient constitution can be seen.

(B)   POLITICS AND THE PAST

Modern attitudes toward the role of the past in settling the political questions of the present are generally coloured by the acceptance of a principle given classic formulation by Hume and Kant in the eighteenth century, the fact-value distinction.[17] This asserts that questions of *value* (that is questions that require moral decisions or commitments) cannot be answered factually. Questions about the best sort of political organization, or about the rightness of political policies or courses of action, in so far as they are moral questions, cannot be answered by saying that in the past things were done in some particular way, and that this ought to be continued. No matter how frequently people have done something, this cannot be considered proof of its rightness. In short, questions of value can only be answered by rational proof of the rightness of the value one wishes to recommend, not by appeal to experience or the past.

But in the period between the Italian Renaissance and the Enlightenment conventional attitudes were quite different from these modern ones. They differed in two ways: first, the distinction between facts and values was blurred, perhaps even non-existent; and, second, the study of the past (or history) was conceived of in ways that made its nature and purpose different from that of modern historical inquiry. For the early modern thinker, values themselves were a sort of 'fact' – they had an objective status and existed, in some sense, even if no one accepted them. Some values were good, some bad, and the judgement between the two was not a subjective one. Rather, God had created the world, and endowed human beings with reason in such a way that objective values were part of the world and human reason could give us access to them. The laws of nature, therefore, not only laid down such things as the principles whereby trees grew and human beings reproduced; it laid down also a basic moral code that was immutable and valid throughout the world. For people who thought in this way values were rather like facts: they were something to be discovered (even discovered empirically), not something of emotional or psychological origin within each subject's mind.

Even more important for understanding the thinking that lay behind the doctrine of the ancient constitution is the conventional attitude to history found during the early modern period. During this period the primary justification for the study of history was not so much the need to seek the truth about the past as the need to seek truths that would be valid in the present. Perhaps, indeed, *seek* is the wrong word; history was more a storehouse of examples that demonstrated, from the record of human experiences, truths already known. One scholar has aptly named this understanding of history 'the exemplar theory of history' because it was, in the famous formulation derived from Dionysius of Halicarnassus, philosophy teaching by examples.[18] Such a view prevailed (at least amongst historians if not among antiquarian scholars) until the advent of the attitudes to historical inquiry associated with historicism. 'Historicism' was a position that, when adopted by historians, tended to result in the idea that the historian should try to understand the past in its own terms (an aim fraught with difficulty and ambiguity), and should place the disinterested search for truth and accuracy above the wish to create a past usable for present purposes. The process by which historicist attitudes came to dominate the modern historical profession is a long and complicated one, spanning the period from the mid-eighteenth to the early-twentieth century.[19]

Against such a background as this the idea of the ancient constitution does not look as silly as it might at first sight appear.[20] Virtually everyone in the sixteenth and early-seventeenth centuries believed that the past contained lessons of direct relevance to the present. William Blundeville, in 1574, expressed the platitudes of an age. He believed that three subjects were central to political knowledge (peace, sedition and war) and that truth in these matters

> is partly taught by the Philosophers in generall precepts and rules, but the Historiographers doe teache it much more playnlye by perticular cxamplcs and experiences.[21]

Amongst the purposes of reading history Blundeville numbered 'that by the examples of the wise, we maye learne wisedome wysely to behave our selves in all our actions, as well private as publique', and 'that we maye be stirred by example of the good to followe the good, and by the example of the evill to flee the evill'.[22]

History was to provide moral lessons for the present, and that was its basic function. But one should not automatically conclude from this that early modern historical scholarship was based on an attitude to the past similar to that held by the makers of modern television commercials, or the writers of politicians' speeches. The past was used to construct general lessons for the present, but this was not thought to detract from the truth of the knowledge acquired from a study of the past. Rather, past and present existed in a continuum so that lessons from the past were automatically transferrable to the present. In short, present-mindedness was not viewed as an obstacle to historical understanding. The enormous energy that early modern antiquarians poured into the examination of the past was in part motivated by the belief that this would be of use in the present – though this need not detract from the view that they were also motivated by a genuine curiosity about the past.

But mention of antiquarianism introduces a complication. In good part English ancient constitutionalism was the product of legal antiquarianism. In the early modern period antiquarianism and history were rather different things. The historian often had no direct acquaintance with the surviving documentation from the periods he wrote about. His aim – as expressed by Blundeville – was to *retell* stories from the past with as much literary elegance as possible and in such a way as to bring out the moral lessons to be derived from them. History was not so much a branch of scholarship as a branch of literature, and it did not necessarily involve detailed research. The antiquarian, on the other hand, was a scholar concerned with collecting, preserving and arranging the primary sources for the study of the past. However, the antiquarian did share many of the general preconceptions about the past of the historian.[23] Antiquarians also believed in the direct value of the past for present-day political concerns.[24] Indeed, it may be argued that it was the fruitful impact of present day concerns that diverted the attention of antiquarians from classical antiquities to the antiquities of England, a process evident from the Elizabethan period onwards. The end result was that antiquarianism became – in the hands, for example, of John Selden – a type of history. It was characterized by an evolutionary model of historical change (perhaps the product of the much greater sense of historical continuity and much weaker sense of anachronism evident in the comparison of the seventeenth century to our own). In the words of one historian, which probably go just a little too far, 'antiquarianism became . . . social history'; but unlike normal humanist historiography it was not just 'the narrative of political action' but dealt with the structural evolution of societies and polities.[25]

Thus the set of attitudes and assumptions that we call ancient constitutionalism arose, in a general sense, from two preconceptions with which early modern intellectual life was deeply imbued. The first was that the past could speak directly to the present, and the historian's job was to enable it to do so. For the traditional political historian this might involve the recounting of the wicked deeds of wicked men (and with any luck the evil consequences of the deeds) as a warning against repeating such actions. A classic example of this was the growing popularity (from the 1590s) of Tacitus as a model for historians to emulate – a popularity that had a lot to do with the belief that Tacitus could give political lessons appropriate to the circumstances of late Elizabethan England.[26] For the antiquarian, on the other hand, it might mean showing that in times past the structure of political action took a particular form, with the implication that this form should be maintained and not corrupted. The past was a storehouse of moral knowledge waiting to be raided. The second preconception, very strong amongst the legal antiquarians most responsible for the doctrine of the ancient constitution, was that the past and present existed in an evolutionary continuum. It was this that both made the past relevant to the present, and formed the basis for one of the central components *Progress?* of ancient constitutionalism, the idea of continuity. There were ambiguities, which we have touched on already and will explore again, in this idea. Were past and present continuous in the sense of being *the same*? Were they linked in a continuous evolutionary process? Or was the continuity more complicated still? Perhaps past and present were continuous in the sense of being governed by the same principles, as in Machiavelli's cycle of construction and decay, or in Vico's more complex theory of historical cycles.

The fact that the idea of the ancient constitution was deeply embedded in the preconceptions of its age raises one more background question about it. To what extent was it a peculiarly English phenomenon, and to what extent was it but the English version of a general European pattern of ideas?

(C)   THE ANCIENT CONSTITUTION OF ENGLAND IN EUROPEAN PERSPECTIVE

In *The Ancient Constitution and the Feudal Law*, Professor Pocock began with a chapter on French historical and legal thought in the sixteenth century. In it he recognized the important role that 'constitutional antiquarianism' played in the political thinking of most early modern European countries.[27] In this sense English ancient constitutionalism was not a unique thing. But Pocock also argued that the English case was, in other senses, unique. Continental theorists were generally exposed to both Roman and customary law, but in England there was a total monopoly of the latter (in the form of the common law). This meant that English legal antiquarians

Pocock saw any as theoretically isolated

and constitutional historians lacked any comparative perspective on the English past. They tended as a consequence to be trapped within their documents, which disguised change by employing various legal fictions.[28] Their view of the past was thus blind to change, at least of some types, and they were encouraged 'to interpret the past as if it had been governed by the law of their own day . . . to read existing law into the remote past'.[29] The English scholars tended to remain unreceptive to the principles of legal humanism that developed amongst Roman law scholars in Continental Europe (France above all). Legal humanists were able to recognize that the laws of the present were the product of historical change and discontinuity, possibly even the result of clashes between rival law codes (especially Germanic customary law and the civil law of Rome), while English lawyers and historians remained committed – at least when they considered their own country – to simple and unhistorical notions of immemoriality.

If this is true then the resemblances between the English idea of an ancient constitution and the myths of ancient French, German and Dutch constitutions that can be found in the sixteenth and seventeenth centuries must be largely illusory. Certainly, such resemblances would have to be balanced against enormous differences.[30] In particular English ancient constitutionalism would need to be seen as being based on a very different attitude to history from that found on the Continent. Sixteenth-century historical thought is now widely credited with preempting the insights of historicism, developing a 'new historical relativism', 'a new awareness of change'. Laws, it was thought, 'had to be understood, as they had once existed, in the context of the society which created them'.[31] But, in contrast to this attitude found in various forms in French scholars like Budé, Hotman and Bodin, the English remained insular. The 'common-law mind' has been described as possessing a fundamentally insular outlook, seeing English history only in English terms, ignoring outside influences, and ignoring change to such an extent that the past came to look very much like the present.[32]

This idea of the insularity of English common law thought has proved highly controversial.[33] This has been in part because the notion of insularity is slightly ambiguous, and has been taken to mean a number of separate things. Consequently, the question of whether or not 'the common law mind' was insular actually conflates several quite distinct issues. These might be separated

Disagreement over common law

by posing a number of more precise questions. The important ones might include:

1. Did English common-law scholars of the late-sixteenth and early-seventeenth centuries know any civil law, and were they acquainted with the methods of legal humanism?
2. Did they apply this knowledge and these methods in their study of English law?
3. Did they end up seeing the history of English law as possessing a unique pattern, or one that exemplified general European historical evolution?
4. Were the attitude to and theories of history held by common-law scholars peculiar to themselves or shared with Continental scholars?

It is this last question that we need to answer here. The first three will be considered later, when the common-law attitude to history has been examined in detail.

It is clear that Pocock and Kelley do consider English ancient constitutionalism to have been insular in this fourth sense. It was out of touch with the most up-to-date thought on legal and historical science being generated by Roman law scholarship in other parts of Europe. However, there are grounds for believing that the insularity of the English common law mind has in this matter been considerably exaggerated. Partly this has been because the 'modernity' of the historical attitudes of legal humanism has been overplayed; partly it is because the lack of 'modernity' in common law thought has also been excessively magnified. The former of these points will be dealt with here; the latter in Chapter 2.

In a series of recent articles Zachary Sayre Schiffman has critically examined the concept of 'Renaissance historicism'.[34] He argues that those who have found the birth of historicism in sixteenth-century France (Pocock, Kelley, Huppert, Franklin) 'have mistaken developments in scholarship for the emergence of' a new historical consciousness.[35] The view of history that underlay the scholarship of sixteenth-century humanists was very different from that of nineteenth and twentieth century historicists. The humanist scholars had little sense of historical *development*. Instead, they tended to see history as a teleological process in which potentialities inherent in an entity were gradually made visible over time. The historical process was not an evolution (or revolutionary leap) from one

History as telos

state to another that was completely different from it. Everything that happened to a nation, let us say, was inherent or potential in that nation from the beginning. Thus historical 'change' was *not* change in the sense of moving away from an initial starting point; it was, rather, a process by which an entity (such as a nation) became more itself over time. All, that in the beginning existed in an entity only potentially, gradually became actual. Thus Schiffman is able to remark, with regard to La Popelinière's history of historical writing, that it 'was less concerned with describing the evolution of that body of literature than with discovering its eternal, unchanging essence'.[36] Essences became more visible as time progressed. This attitude was expressed neatly by Thomas Woods, who translated Hugo Grotius's account of the ancient constitution of Batavia into English in 1649. In Grotius's account, Woods said, it could be discovered

> that that Commonwealth which is at the present among us, hath not had its beginning now of late, but that the very same Commonwealth that in former times hath been, is now made more manifest and appeareth more clear and evidenter than ever before.[37]

If Schiffman is right in believing that this form of teleological historical consciousness underlay sixteenth century legal human- ism, then there would be a reasonable basis for believing also that English ancient constitutionalism was not 'insular' in the sense under consideration here. The ancient constitution of England was an object that remained essentially the same, even though it under- went changes of a sort. Schiffman's model of sixteenth century historical consciousness provides, at the least, one possible way of making sense of this fact. It would explain how the 'ancient constitution' could both serve as a normative paradigm to which the present was supposed to adhere, and yet still be an historical object undergoing evolutionary change. Indeed, going a little further, it would explain why the present *could not but adhere* to the forms of the ancient constitution, and hence automatically conformed to its normative requirements. In short, the ancient constitution was forever changing yet always the same. This, as we shall see, captures exactly the central features of English ancient constitutionalism.

There is, thus, some reason for recognizing that the idea of the ancient constitution of England, and the historical consciousness that underlay it, was not dissimilar to ideas that could be found in other European countries in the early modern era. Since 1957, when Pocock first uncovered the English common law mind,[38] a number of scholars have gradually put together a European context for it. As well as the English, the Dutch, the French, the Scots, and the inhabitants of the Holy Roman Empire had an 'ancient constitution' constructed for them. (No doubt this is a far from exhaustive list.) Though the historical consciousness that underlay these various constructions may have been broadly the same, the European ancient constitutions did differ from one another in other ways. In general, they can be divided into two categories.

The basis for such a categorization lies not in differences of historical understanding but in differences of ideological purpose. One type of ancient constitution was developed by, or on behalf of, groups engaged in political struggle of one sort or another. It was a form of ideologically-slanted political propaganda. This type of theory was found in France, Scotland and the Netherlands. English ancient constitutionalism, however, was of a second-type, to which the theory of an ancient German constitution may also have belonged. The key to understanding the difference between the two types is to be found in a consideration of the political circumstances in which the various theories were developed.

French, Scottish and Dutch ancient constitutionalism was essentially the work of Calvinist rebels. The major purpose behind it was to demonstrate that though Calvinists might be rebels, they were not innovators. The actions they were following were defended as being in accord with the essential nature of the polity, and this in turn was revealed through historical analysis. What distinguished this form of ancient constitutionalism from the English variety is that it used the past to create a highly partisan account of the present. It formed a critique of the present, as it had to if it were to justify resistance to constituted authority. The classic writers in this tradition of ancient constitutionalism all had specific ideological axes to grind. François Hotman, who first turned the 'humanist investigation of the French ancient constitution' into a 'revolutionary ideology',[39] is a case in point. Hotman's *Francogallia* (first published in 1573, during the crucial decade of the French Wars of Religion) was in essence a defence of the power of the Estates General (and hence the French aristocracy) over the crown. The public council of the realm was, according to Hotman, constituted for 'the appointing and deposing of kings; next, matters concerning war and peace; the

public laws; the highest honours, offices and regencies belonging to the commonwealth', and other matters. Indeed, its consent was needed in all 'affairs of state' for there was 'no right for any part of the commonwealth to be dealt with except in the council of estates or orders'.[40] Indeed, the fundamental laws of the kingdom limited the power of French kings. They were 'restrained by defined laws', the chief of which decreed that 'they should preserve the authority of the public council as something holy and inviolate', and 'that it is not lawful for the king to determine anything that affects the condition of the commonwealth as a whole without the authority of the public council'.[41] Hotman's work, in short, was an attempt to construct an ancient French constitution that provided institutional and legal checks on the monarchy – checks that could be exploited by Huguenot rebels.

During the late sixteenth century Dutch and Scottish Calvinists, as well as French, frequently found themselves acting in conflict with civil authority. They too developed ancient constitutionalist theories to defend themselves in this conflict. In Scotland George Buchanan found a 'revolutionary tradition' within Scottish history. Hereditary monarchy was not the essential nature of the Scottish polity. It began as an elective monarchy, and this elective principle was kept alive by occasional depositions. Scottish kings could always, in the last resort, be brought to account.[42] So, of course, could Scottish queens: one of Buchanan's major works was written in defence of the deposition of Mary Stuart in 1567, the *De Jure Regni apud Scotos* (1579).[43] Resistance theory also played its part in Dutch ancient constitutionalism, though it was of a rather different character from that of Buchanan. The Dutch fashioned their theories to defend a national resistance against Spanish rule after 1568, and so needed to do more than others to construct the very image of themselves as a nation.[44] Paramount amongst those Dutch writings that constructed an ancient Batavian constitution, to serve as a precursor and exemplar for the modern Dutch, was Hugo Grotius's *Liber de Antiquitate Reipublicae Batavicae* (1610).[45] Grotius wrote to defend a particular form of constitution for the new Dutch republic, a form which left power in the hands of the provinces rather than in any central authority. It was aimed against absolute monarchy, but it was also aimed at defending a preeminent role for the ruling élite of Holland in the affairs of the United Provinces as a whole. Grotius portrayed the Hollanders as heirs to the Batavians, and was thus (when he had shown that the Batavians had possessed a government of the sort he was recommending) able to argue that experience and antiquity – 'so many hundred years' – attested to the fitness of this form of government for the Dutch (though he was happy to admit that other peoples might suit different forms of government).[46] Schöffer has indicated how Grotius's approach can be seen as an extension of traditional humanist historiographical practice: 'he expanded his *exemplum* [i.e. the object being put forward as an example to emulate] beyond the traditional humanist approach, which had usually been restricted to persons and virtues in a rather vague manner, to the whole structure of a society'.[47] The remark applies, *mutatis mutandis*, to all examples of this first type of ancient constitutionalism. It was fundamentally *normative* in character, setting up a model of the way a particular political community ought to be organized and criticizing the present in terms of that model. Ancient constitutionalism of this sort was generally engaged with the issues of its day. It was thus ideological in character, the intellectual weapon of particular groups and individuals.

English ancient constitutionalism was different in character from this. It corresponded to a second type of early modern European ancient constitutionalist thinking. The closest parallel to the English model seems to have been found in the German Empire.[48] This second type of theory was primarily *descriptive* in character, and was concerned less with criticizing the present and more with explaining how the present, whatever form it took, was to be justified, and why it was to be accepted. It was not the ideology of a party but the shared language of an entire political nation (at least in the English case) – a *mentalité* perhaps. The key feature of this variety of ancient constitutionalist theory was possession of an evolutionary theory of history. It did not assert the identity of past and present, but it did assert that a continuous process had transformed the former into the latter in such a way that they were in essence the same. This process of 'change' was characteristically seen as a gradual refinement whereby the customs and laws of a nation remained always in perfect accord with their environment (i.e. the needs of the nation that they served). The English ancient constitution was not a state to which the English ought to return (as the French was, in a sense, to Hotman); it was a state in which they still lived.

Thus the English version of ancient constitutionalism was of a very peculiar character. It looked like a glorification of the ancient past, but it was in fact a glorification (and a justification) of the present. The key to explaining its peculiar ideological nature lies in the fact that it developed in different circumstances to most continental ancient constitutionalist theories. The French version, for example, was developed as a form of resistance theory, but English ancient constitutionalism took shape during the late sixteenth century when the paramount political need was for a defence of the *status quo* in church and state. Thus it developed, in sharp contrast to most other parts of Western Europe, into a form of political conformism. English ancient constitutionalism explained why the current shape of the English polity was automatically the best that could be achieved. It was thus an antidote to Calvinist resistance theory, not a form of it. There is a very real sense in which the theory of the ancient constitution of England was but the secular portion of the theory contained in Richard Hooker's great defence of the Elizabethan church, *Of the Laws of Ecclesiastical Polity* (Books I–V, 1593–97; later Books not published until 1648 and 1661). Exactly what that sense was we must now discover.

How does Hooker fit in?,

2 *rationality over custom*

The Ancient Constitution of England

The phrase 'the ancient constitution' is a misleading one.[1] It tends to suggest a fixed constitution that had existed sometime in the past, and to conjure up the image of a Golden Age of liberty and constitutional perfection to be found in days of old. But this is not really what was meant by the term. 'The ancient constitution' was not a constitution of the past; it was the present constitution, the constitution of the seventeenth century. This is to say no more than that the ancient constitution was a collection of laws and institutions that had evolved in a continuous process whose beginnings were lost to human memory (including, that is, written records which were a form of collective memory). In short, an ancient constitution was a modern constitution that had ancient foundations.

A study of the ancient constitution of England will, then, be a study of the relations between the past and the present. What sort of a process transformed the Saxon polity into that of seventeenth-century England? Even more important than this was the question of *why* men ever believed that the past could legitimate the present, or (a more answerable question) *how* they believed it was able to do so.[2] For seventeenth-century common lawyers the answer to this question was that they conceived of the process linking past and present in such a way that it was able to explain to them why their law was reasonable, why it was a law of reason. The law of England was good law not because it was old but because it was rational. The theory of the ancient constitution was an explanation for this rationality, and consequently it was also a justification of the law and the constitution. The rational was *ipso facto* the good.

Thus our pursuit of the ancient constitution of England will have to be a study of what Pocock called 'the common-law mind'. It will be a study of the way in which early Stuart lawyers conceived of the rational and historical basis of their own law, the common law

19

of England. This study of the ancient constitution is a study of a process, not of an event.

(A)   INTRODUCTORY: THE PROBLEMS OF LEGAL CHANGE AND LEGAL DIVERSITY

Reason, it can truly be said, was in the eyes of the common lawyers the fabric from which the laws were cut. But to produce from this fabric the finished garments of a legal code was not a simple process. Two concepts were developed by common lawyers to explain why the common law of England was a *rational* system of law. The first of those concepts was *artificial reason*; the second, *custom*. When these concepts have been examined we shall find that the early Stuart lawyers believed in two principles which, on the face of it, do not look to be readily compatible with one another. They believed, firstly, that the law of England was a law of reason; and they believed also that the law of England had undergone a long process of (evolutionary) change. We shall then be able to see how these principles combined to produce a particular attitude to history amongst common lawyers, and a particular view of the nature of legal change.

'History' and 'legal change' might seem odd terms to use of such a reputedly unhistorical group of minds as those of the early Stuart common lawyers. It has been an (unintentional)[3] consequence of J. G. A. Pocock's work on *The Ancient Constitution and the Feudal Law* that it has fostered the view, at least amongst textbook writers, that the common lawyers believed the law to have remained literally unchanged since the time of the ancient (pre-Roman) Britons. Beyond the odd isolated passage in Coke (or Saltern) there is little support for such an interpretation, as we shall see. Furthermore, Pocock's work has also fostered the idea – again this might plausibly be said to be a *mis*reading of the text of *The Ancient Constitution and the Feudal Law* – that early Stuart common lawyers thought not in terms of reason but in terms of history and custom. They believed English law to be good law more because it was old and of long continuance than because it was rational or reasonable. Behind this view lurks an assumed dichotomy between an attitude that sees laws and institutions justified by abstract reason, and one that sees them justified by history and experience. But this dichotomy can only mislead in the present case, for (we shall discover) early Stuart legal thinkers did not see reason and custom/history as alternatives. Rather, custom was one of the means by which the rational essence of the law was made apparent. It was a mode with which reason revealed itself.

On both of these matters (immutability versus legal change; reason versus history) we shall find that an extreme position was taken by Sir Edward Coke. This must raise considerable doubt about Pocock's decision to make Coke the paradigm example of his 'common-law mind'. By the end of this chapter it should be clear that Coke was in fact an eccentric, and sometimes a confused, thinker. The majority of the common law scholars of the early-seventeenth century possessed an attitude to the past and to the law that was closer to the opinions of John Selden, or even Sir Francis Bacon, than to those of Coke.

But even Coke was not totally committed to the idea of an immemorially unchanging law. Like most of his contemporaries, he recognized (at least on occasion) that the common law had undergone change of a sort. At the outset we need to be clear about the attitude that the early Stuart common lawyers had to legal change. It is necessary initially to distinguish between two propositions. First, the proposition that the law ought not to be changed, and that no good would be likely to come from any such change. And, second, the proposition that any alteration to the law is either impossible or utterly illegitimate. Some seventeenth-century common lawyers certainly came very close to asserting the former proposition in its strongest possible sense, but none of them asserted the second. Possibly one of the most interesting of passages stating the extreme version of the first principle was Sir John Davies's brief remark about the relationship of parliamentary statute to the common law. The common law, he says

> doth far excell our *written* Laws, namely our Statutes or Acts of Parliament: which is manifest in this, that when our Parliaments have altered or changed any fundamentall points of the Common Law, those alterations have been found by experience [sic] to be so inconvenient for the Commonwealth, as that the Common Law hath in effect been restored again, in the same points, by other Acts of Parliament in succeeding Ages.[5]

Coke seems to have held views similar to these.[6] Yet the interesting thing about such remarks is not what they say but what they have carefully refrained from saying. Neither Davies nor Coke seems to have particularly liked the idea that parliament could alter the common law by statute, but they were aware that there was no doubt that it could do so. As a consequence their remarks tend to be a little curmudgeonly in tone. Hence Coke's assertion that statutes (and above all Magna Carta) 'were, for the most part, but declaratories of the ancient Common Laws of England',[7] and that innovation in law is a bad thing, seldom to be recommended.[8] However, though Davies and Coke might do their utmost to convey the impression that changing the law is a bad thing they did not suggest that it was not possible or allowable. Indeed the very tone of their remarks shows their awareness of the impossibility of denying that the common law could be altered. In a case where the process outlined by Davies, of change and restoration, is incomplete, so that dangerous innovations remain, Coke can do nothing but accept the legitimacy of the change, albeit with poor grace and in a tone of spluttering irritation. Here he was talking about whether or not inferior judicial officers ought to take money from other people, and remarked:

> But after that [Act of 3 Ed.1] this rule of the Common Law was altered, and that the Sheriff, Coroner, Gaoler, and other the Kings ministers, might in some case take of the Subject, it is not credible what extortions, and oppressions have thereupon ensued. So dangerous a thing it is, to shake or alter any of the rules or fundamentall points of the Common Law, which in truth are the main pillars, and supporters of the fabrick of the Commonwealth, as elsewhere I have noted more at large . . . [9]

One might wonder why it should be that Coke and Davies so disliked the idea of legal change, even though they were forced to recognize it as a fact (and, indeed, in other places their jurisprudence *required* an acceptance of legal change). The first thing to note is that Davies and Coke were untypical in the extent to which they detested innovation. Some common lawyers accepted the theoretical possibility of radical change to the law without the signs of discomfort we have seen in Coke and Davies. Bacon is a case in point, thought he was perhaps untypical at the other extreme:

> if the parliament should enact in the nature of the ancient *lex regia*, that there should be no more parliaments held but that the

king should have the authority of the parliament, or, e converso, if the King by Parliament were to enact to alter the state, and to translate it from a monarchy to any other form; both these acts were good.[10]

And, of course, those lawyers strongly influenced by legal humanism were in no doubt that laws could be altered, by authority, and did not think this a matter for regret. Selden, startlingly, asserted that it could be made law that anyone rising before nine o'clock should be put to death.[11] Lord Chancellor Ellesmere's view, while much less trenchant than the remarks of Bacon or Selden, was that the law was in continual change. All laws were but *leges temporis* and became obsolete or were subtly changed as circumstances changed.[12] One should note also that many of the scholars involved with the Elizabeth Society of Antiquaries were frank about their recognition of the realities of legal change. One anonymous contributor to their proceedings said of parliament that the King called it together 'upon occasion of interpreting, or abrogating old laws, and making of new'.[13]

In general, then, there seems to be no problem in accepting that law is mutable. But this merely leaves the position of Davies and Coke looking even more wayward. Why *were* they so recognizably ill at ease with the idea of legal change? Now, in part, the answer to this question is that contrasts between Coke and Davies on the one hand, and Selden, Bacon, Ellesmere and Spelman on the other, have been overdrawn. While all of this latter group were frank in their acceptance of legal change they could also give voice to remarks rather similar to those of Coke. The reason for this is quite simple: the difficulty and inadvisability of altering laws was one of the most tired of political platitudes in early modern Europe, and derived ultimately from Aristotle. It was a matter on which there was almost universal agreement.

Sir John Doddridge, in a contribution to the debate on Anglo-Scottish Union that took place in the first decade of the reign of James I, wrote the following:

But lawes were never in any kingedome totallie altered without great danger of the evercion of the whole state. And therefore it is well said by the interpreters of Aristotle that lawes are not to [be] changed but with these cautions and circumspeccions: 1. *Raro, ne incommodum;* 2. *In melius, ne periculum;* 3. *Prudenter et censim ne reipublicae naufragium ex innovacione sequatur.* Lawes are to be changed: 1. Seldome lest suche change prove to the danger of the State; 2. For the better, lest it breede danger to the State; 3. Warilie, and by little and little, lest the shipwreck of the commonwelthe and the totall evercion of all be occasioned by such innovacion.[14]

The passage of Aristotle from which these precepts ultimately derived was *Politics*, 1268b–1269a. It is of considerable complexity and subtlety, but one can readily see how it might be read as containing the advice which Doddridge provided. Aristotle pointed out that because circumstances are always changing customs must be altered gradually in order to cope with these changes. And, as regards written laws, he argued that because they must initially be framed in general terms (given that their initial formulator cannot foresee all the particular cases with which they will have to deal) then much fine-tuning will later become necessary. But, he went on to say, even given all this, we should not forget that law depends for its observance upon habits, i.e. upon being customarily observed. Consequently it is dangerous to interfere too lightly with such settled habits. Changes to the law should therefore be made with great circumspection, and in some cases abuses were best left unremedied, for the evil consequences of alteration would inevitably outweigh any minor benefits that might come about.[15] Almost identical remarks are found frequently in subsequent thinkers: Aquinas, Bodin and Machiavelli are all cases in point.[16]

But a more useful example for us to consider is Francis Bacon. We have already seen that Bacon took rather a high view of the capacity of statute to alter even the most fundamental laws of the land, and indeed this accords with the traditional interpretations of Bacon's thought which tend to stress his impatience with lawyers and the law and his willingness to allow strict legality to be overridden in the interests of the state.[17] Yet, whatever his theoretical appreciation of the possibilities and legitimacy of legal change, Bacon shared with Coke, and just about everybody else, the view that such change is often dangerous. In his essay 'Of Seditions and Troubles' he listed 'alteration of laws and customs' as one of 'the causes and motives of seditions'. The essay 'Of Empire' warned rulers that meddling with the customs of the 'commons' is like to bring trouble.[18] But more interesting was the short essay 'Of Innovations'. It did not mention law at all, but much of the essay reads like an attempt to address the same question that Aristotle grappled with in the passage cited above. Indeed Bacon gives an account of the matter similarly complex and balanced. Underlying Bacon's view was an almost Machiavellian awareness of the inevitable alterations brought by time itself – 'time is the greatest innovator' – which alterations often meant that customs were becoming or would become redundant, or even pernicious. So we must remember 'that a froward retention of custom is as turbulent a thing as an innovation'. Even so, 'what is settled by custom, though it be not good, yet at least it is fit'. Great care must, therefore, be taken when introducing alteration. Bacon summarized his position with the following (rather platitudinous) advice:

> It were good therefore that men in their innovations would follow the example of time itself, which indeed innovateth greatly, but quietly and by degrees scarce to be perceived . . . It is good also not to try experiments in states, except the necessity be urgent or the utility evident; and well to beware that it be the reformation that draweth on the change, and not the desire of change that pretendeth the reformation. And lastly, that the novelty, though it be not rejected, yet be held for a suspect, and, as the Scripture saith, *that we make a stand upon the ancient way, and then look about us, and discover what is the straight and right way, and so to walk in it.*[19]

Bacon, like Doddridge, was a contributor to the debate on Anglo-Scottish Union, and in his advice to King James on the matter he made points very similar to those made by Doddridge. Experience shows us 'that *patrius mos* is dear to all men', and any legal changes and innovations cause deep bitterness and discord. Therefore proceed slowly and gradually.[20] The points were reiterated endlessly during the debate, and not merely by common lawyers: the civilian John Hayward made very similar points, and provided two general rules to govern legal change. That change be not great, and that it be gradual.[21] The matter then is clear enough: virtually everyone, common lawyers included, was of the opinion that laws *could* be changed (and in some cases *should* be). But they were equally aware that such innovations were made only at some price: and that price entailed running the risk of instability and subversion. It was never an easy thing to alter laws, and often one might be better off tolerating the existence of inadequate ones. The matter was summarized very neatly, in rather humanistic terms, by another contributor to the debates on Union, Sir Henry Spelman:

> But some will say a Parliament can do anything. I say it may quickly change the lawe but not the myndes of the people whom in this union we must seek to content.[22]

The point was rather like Aristotle's: it is quite possible for the relevant authority to declare that the law is altered, but it is another matter to alter those customary habits of the people on which their obedience to the law depended.

Given this agreed background, what can we now make of Davies and Coke? The first point to emphasize is that this background is not in itself sufficient to account for what they said. For while Aristotle, and all the others whom we have been considering, recognized that in many cases it was *necessary* for the law to be changed, that legal innovation (if we ignore its practical difficulties) was sometimes a desirable thing, this recognition seems lacking in Coke and Davies. Legal change, for them, was no doubt possible, but it could not be said to be a desirable or even (by and large) a useful thing. It is possible to lay down the outlines at least for an explanation of this situation. It must initially be recognized that we are doing Sir John Davies a considerable disservice in linking him with Coke.[23] Davies viewed the common law as essentially customary, and it was of the essence of his theory of custom that customs changed and evolved over time, so that they gradually came to fit the needs of the nation like a hand fits a glove. In this sense is the law 'connatural to the Nation'.[24] There is no trace, in Davies, of the Fortescuean idea that the laws have been continually and unchangingly in existence since the time of the Britons. Therefore, his statement (quoted above) on legal change should be read as saying no more than that in practice alterations to custom have often been found to be harmful. He thus fits neatly into the Aristotelian context analysed above, albeit at one extreme of the possible spectrum of interpretations of the Aristotelian wisdom.

Coke, however, is a different matter.[25] As we shall see, he combined ideas similar to those of Davies on the customary nature of the law with a view of the literal immemorial antiquity of the law derived from Fortescue. The two positions were radically incompatible, and have subsequently caused much confusion to the expositor of Coke's writings. The logic of Coke's position forced him to attempt to reconcile the idea of evolving customs with legal immutability, and part of this attempted resolution is found in the passages we have discussed above. Coke tried, half-heartedly and with a notable lack of success, to pretend that statutes were declaratory of pre-existent law, or at best restored law to its pristine purity. Essentially he was saying that while in theory statutes could alter law and make new law, in practice (as experience and history tells us) they had not done so. But it must be stressed that even Coke did not believe that laws could not be changed, and as we shall soon see he could at times adopt theories that required a belief in legal mutability.

Davies's point, that when 'fundamentall points of the Common Law' have been altered this has proved 'inconvenient for the Commonwealth' and the common law eventually has been restored, was not an assertion of the essential immutability of law (even at face value one should note the restriction of its scope to the fundamental points of the law). Rather it was derived from a widely-shared Aristotelian maxim of political prudence. Only if we assume beforehand that Davies held simple Fortescuean beliefs about the antiquity of the law does it look like anything else. Coke, who did gesture towards such beliefs, was a different matter, and seems (at times) to have wanted to convey the impression that English law had, in some ways, remained unaltered time out of mind. The remainder of this chapter will flesh out the consequences of these points. It will stress Coke's eccentricity and untypicality and demonstrate that the jurisprudence of the common lawyers involved a view of the history of law incompatible with that of Fortescue. And because Coke had a foot in both these camps we will be able to see that his thought was deeply self-contradictory.

The acceptance by the common lawyers (however reluctantly) of legal change poses another broader problem for us. If the lawyers believed that the common law, like all codes of positive law, was a law of reason (as they did), then how could they also have believed that it changed over time? Equally problematic was the question of how laws could differ from place to place. Reason was immutable, both synchronically and diachronically; but law clearly was mutable. It changed over time; it varied from place to place. The problem, in short, is this – how could the common law (mutable) be said to be a law of reason (immutable)?

Professor Pocock captured this problem when he talked of the *paradox* inherent in the common law view of custom (hereafter referred to as Pocock's paradox):

> If the idea that law is custom implies anything, it is that law is in constant change and adaptation, altered to meet each new experience in the life of the people . . . yet the fact is that the common lawyers . . . came to believe that the common law, and with it the constitution, had always been exactly what they were now, that they were immemorial.[26]

The question of immutable reason versus mutable law can, then, be restated as the question of the law as reason versus the law as custom. If it is one, how can it also be the other?

This chapter will build up a picture of the assumptions upon which English ancient constitutionalism rested, but it will – in doing so – be an extended answer to this question. Of considerable help in this is a conceptual distinction inherent in traditional (medieval) natural law theory. This particular formulation comes from St. Thomas Aquinas, but this should not be taken to imply that common lawyers themselves took the idea from this source.

In his discussion of the relationship between positive and natural law in the *Summa Theologiae*, Aquinas wrote:

> But it should be noted that there are two ways in which anything may derive from natural law. First, as a conclusion from more general principles. Secondly, as a determination of certain general features. The former is similar to the method of the sciences in which demonstrative conclusions are drawn from first principles. The second way is like to that of the arts in which some common form is determined to a particular instance: as, for example, when an architect, starting from the general idea of a house, then goes on to design the particular plan of this or that house. So, therefore, some derivations are made from the natural law by way of formal conclusion: as the conclusion, 'Do not murder', derives from the precept, 'Do harm to no man.' Other conclusions are arrived at as determinations of particular cases. So the natural law establishes that whoever transgresses shall be punished. But that a man should be punished by a specific penalty is a particular determination of the natural law.
>
> Both types of derivation are to be found in human law. But those which are arrived at in the first way are sanctioned not only

by human law, but by the natural law also; while those arrived at by the second method have the validity of human law alone.[27]

Some human laws were the formal, demonstrative conclusion of natural laws. Such human laws, as Aquinas indicated, bound with the full force of natural law, and like natural law would be everywhere valid and everywhere the same. Customs and statutes, however, bound only as human laws, but this did not mean they were completely adrift and unrelated to natural law or justice. Rather, they were derived from nature, in the second of the ways indicated by Aquinas, as particular determinations of matters left indifferent (though bounded) by natural laws. Laws of this sort did not have the force of natural law and though, so long as they did not actually conflict with the injunctions of natural law, all such laws were equally legitimate, they need not be seen as equally desirable.

Some laws, then, could be *demonstrated* to derive from the rational principles of natural law, as simple logical deductions. But other laws were rational in a different sense: they *determined* a particular matter from a range of possible choices left open by reason itself. But what guarantee was there that these determinations were in all cases rational and not arbitrary or erroneous? For most laws there could be no simple demonstration of their rationality. Natural reason alone could neither explain nor justify why it was rational for land to be inherited by primogeniture in most of England, but by partible inheritance in Kent (under the customary provisions known as gavelkind).

Two concepts were employed by common lawyers to link particular positive laws to the law of reason. The first, which we will soon be looking at in some detail, was *artificial reason*. Natural reason, the sort of reason with which all human beings were endowed naturally, might not reveal the link between the detailed content of the common law and the law of reason (or nature), but there might be an artificial reason which would do so. The second concept was that of *custom*. The idea that the common law was customary in nature, far from being an alternative to the view that positive law was a law of reason, was in fact parasitic on the idea of the rationality of law. Custom explained how laws were both rational and mutable.

There were at least two possible directions in which the concept of custom could have been taken by early Stuart legal commentators. Each of these directions had historical roots in fifteenth and sixteenth century legal and political thought. Fortescue[28] gave some support to the view that because English law – or at least its basic principles or maxims – was rational, then it must be unchanging. Its customary nature, therefore, might imply that it had been the same since time immemorial. Its origins were lost in the mists of time, but throughout recorded history the law had shown no fundamental alteration. (Whether this is an accurate account of what Fortescue meant to say is a matter we can afford to leave aside.) Other thinkers, however, such as Christopher St German and Richard Hooker,[29] explored the opposite side of Pocock's paradox: for them the customary nature of law meant its continuing evolution not its immobility in time. Pocock's paradox will turn out, upon examination, to be an illusion. It was created by Coke's attempt to combine a theory of custom similar to that found in St German with ideas of legal immutability drawn from Fortescue. But most common-law thinkers did not attempt to follow the Fortescuean path, and so most did not fall into this paradox (a paradox that comes remarkably close to self-contradiction). Indeed, Pocock's attribution of this paradoxical position to 'the common-law mind' in general shows once again the danger of taking Edward Coke as typical.

However, before we can fully comprehend the peculiarities of Coke's position, we need to examine one more preliminary matter: the view of custom found in Christopher St German and its difference from Fortescue's thought. St German believed English law to be a rational law. It contained *within itself* the principles of reason rather than being subject to external measures of its rationality. Human law (according to St German) 'is deryuyed by reason as a thinge whiche is necessaryly & probably folowying of the lawe of reason /& of the lawe of god'. Thus in all true human laws there 'is somewhat of the lawe of reason', though to 'discerne . . . the lawe of reason from the lawe posytyue is very harde'.[30] Of course, if natural reason was to be used to discriminate between positive laws it was first necessary that the dictates of such reason be clearly distinguished from, and knowable independently of, the positive law.

When the student in St German's dialogue came – in chapter v – to examine natural law as one of the six grounds of the law of England (the others being the laws of God, general customs, maxims, particular customs and statutes) he made it clear that this condition was not fulfilled. He said on the matter of the law of reason/nature that:

It is not vsed amonge them that be lernyd in the lawes of Englande to reason what thynge is commaundyd or prohybyt by the lawe of nature and what not: but all the resonynge in that behalfe is under this maner: as when anythyng is groundyd upon the lawe of nature : they say that reason wyll that suche a thyng be don/and yf it be prohybyte by the lawe of nature. They say it is agaynst reason or that reason wyll not suffre that it be don.[31]

Though it is not immediately apparent, what this passage meant was that the law of England contained in itself rules for determining what was and what was not in accord with natural law. To say that a particular thing was not allowable by reason was to say that it was not allowed by a particular category of rules of English law. It was not to say that extra-legal rules prohibited such a thing. Thus Chrimes can say of St German that he 'seems to have known nothing of a law of reason which was not to be found embodied in or rationally derivable from the positive law of the land'.[32] St German, in other words, simply used the terminology of the law of reason to provide categories into which certain parts of English law could be divided. The law of reason primary provided the grounds for certain rules of law necessary to make human society possible: the prohibition of murder, perjury, deceit and the breaking of peace. The law of reason secondary general was a category containing the rules outlining the laws of property which are common to all nations. (For most earlier thinkers these two categories would together form the *jus gentium*.) And the law of reason secondary particular included all laws which the English thought rational but which were not observed in other countries. It was made plain that it was only through an examination of English law itself that we could know what particular laws were included in each of these three categories.[33] There was no rational law – at least not for the lawyer – independent of positive law. Thus the entire body of English law was in one way or another the law of reason, since St German's definition of the law of reason secondary particular seems to cover any law not covered by the two other categories. St German appeared to deny this in the English (but not the Latin) versions of his work where he said that it could not be proved 'that all the lawe of the realme is the lawe of reason', but in fact he was arguing (along lines already outlined) that not all law could be *demonstrated* to be derived from the law of reason. This was largely for practical reasons, or because the particular forms in which rational laws were enforced were not in all their detail necessary logical deductions from rational principles. In other words – as the Latin edition makes plain – English law was all rational but it was not necessarily all *provable* by deductive reason.[34]

So it is clear that St German believed the laws of England to be laws of reason. Could he also have believed them to be customs, or customary laws? Given what has already been said of custom it will come as no surprise to learn that he could.[35] St German believed all laws to be reasonable and in that sense laws of reason. But he did not think that reason alone could tell us why some particular body of laws was in force in a particular place and time. To do this he needed some more specific grounds for the English common law.

These grounds were provided by general customs, and by maxims. This inclusion of maxims amongst the grounds of English law raised some interesting questions. Maxims were, after all, rational principles or axioms that were not in need of demonstration, so were they the same as or different from customs? The answer to this would appear to be that they formed a special sub-class of customs which for convenience sake St German treated separately. It was the close linking of maxims and customs that revealed most clearly St German's belief that reason, and nothing else, was at the core of the law.

St German introduced his discussion of customs in these terms:

> The thyrde grounde[36] of the lawe of Englande standeth vpon dyuerse generall Customes of old tyme used through all the realme: which have been accepted and approuyd by our soveraygne lorde the kynge and his progenytours and all theyr subgettes. And bycause the sayd customes be neyther agaynst the lawe of god/nor the lawe of reason/& have ben alwaye taken to be good and necessarye for the common welth of all the realme. Therefore they have optayned the strengthe of a lawe in so moche that he that doth agaynst them doth agaynst Iustyce and law. And these be tho customes that proprely be called the common lawe . . .   And of these general customes and of certayne pryncyples that be called maxymes which also take effecte by the olde custome of the realme . . . dependyth moste parte of the lawe of this realme.[37]

The remainder of the chapter on general customs indicated that all the major common law courts and all the basic principles of the land law (especially inheritance rules) depended on custom and had no other immediate grounding. But we have just been told that maxims 'take effect' by these customs. This is ambiguous, but fortunately St German dealt with the complex relations between customs, maxims and reason near the end of the chapter and in the two following chapters in some detail. He raised the crucial question of whether or not customs were demonstrably rational.

> And of this that is sayd byfore it apperyth that the customes aforesayd nor other lyke unto them/whereof be very many in the lawes of Englande can not be prouyd to have the strength of a lawe only by reason: for how may it be prouyd by reason that the eldest sone shall onlye enheryte his father & the yonger to have no parte/and that all the daughters together shall share the land if there be no son or that the husbonde shall have the hole of his wife's lande for terme of his lyfe as tenaunt by the curtesye in such a manner as byfore apperyth.[38]

The lesson from this argument was put thus:

> All these and suche other can not be prouyd oonly by reason that it shuld be so and no otherwyse although they be reasonable/& that with the custome therein vsed suffyseth in the lawe. And so a statute made agaynst such general customes is perfectly valid and ought to be obseruid as law bycause they be not merely the lawe of reason.[39]

That last phrase 'merely the law of reason' is an interesting one, and linked St German in one direction to Aquinas and in another to Hooker. Aquinas, as we have seen, thought that all laws derived from natural law, but that they could do so in two ways: either they were logical deductions from natural law, or they were determinations of matters on which the rules of natural law gave only very general instruction. When Hooker took over this idea he expressed it by dividing human law into two categories: mixed human law and merely human law. The first category covered those laws that are also laws of nature (i.e. the deductive conclusions of natural law); the second covered those laws that commanded things which were not in themselves commanded by nature.[40] St German appears to be making a closely related point, but he was looking at things from the opposite direction to Hooker. Customs were not 'mere' laws of reason because reason by itself was insufficient to demonstrate their force. So besides being reasonable, there must be some other element involved to explain why they were in force. This other element would appear to be long continuance and the presumption of their goodness and necessity that this established.

In his two chapters on maxims St German took the discussion a little further. Maxims were rational axioms like those of geometry and were not themselves in need of proof. They were rather the starting-point for legal proofs and arguments.[41] Yet these rational principles could be seen as a sort of custom, and this fact should give us cause for much reflection. If maxims were a category of custom, then clearly at least some customs were rational principles customarily observed. In fact, St German's words tended to imply that customs as such are simply rational principles. Therefore there could be no conflict between saying that all law is reason and that all law is custom. Here are St German's words on the relationship of customs and maxims:

> And though all those maxims might be conveniently numbered among the said general customs of the realm, since the generall custom of the Realme be the strength and waraunte of the sayd maxymes: as they be of the general customes of the realme/yet bycause the sayd generall customes be in maner diffused throughout the realm of England and knowen through the realme as well to them that be vnlernyd as lernyd/and may lyghtly be had and knowen and that with little stodye in English law. And the sayde maxymes be onlye knowen in the kynges courtes or amonge them that take great studye in the lawe of the realme/and amonge fewe other persones (nor can they be known easily). Therfore they be set in this wrytnge for severall groundes and he that lysteth may so accompte them/or yf he wyll he may take them for one grounde after his pleasure/and in that case by his reckoning only five grounds of the law of England ought to be assigned.[42]

The distinction, made in this passage, between two types of custom is an extremely interesting one. It has recently received an interesting discussion from the pen of Professor Pocock, when he talks of 'the problem of determining in what community *usus et consuetudo* were said to operate'.[43] Pocock distinguishes two possible solutions to the problem. Customs could be either the practices of the people in general, codified into law by some gradual process; or they could be rules customarily applied in the courts. In this latter sense customs are the same as maxims, and both become terms of art. St German, whom Pocock does not cite, adds support to Pocock's distinction, but also helps us to solve some of the subsidiary problems that troubled Pocock. In particular, Pocock had some difficulty in deciding what Sir John Davies might have meant in saying that customary law was recorded only 'in the memory of the people' given that he cannot have meant that English lawyers ought to conduct sociological investigations to determine what the content of the law really was.[44] However, we can see from St German's words that the distinction can be read as one between customs *known* to laymen and those *known* only in the courts and amongst trained lawyers. St German's examples of the former category consist primarily of rules of land tenure and inheritance, and there is no difficulty in seeing what he might have meant by saying that knowledge of these customs was widely diffused outside the courts. They were rules that governed the day-to-day practices and behaviour of ordinary people and as such would have been customarily observed without, in general, the need for recourse to legal enforcement. They were the practices that held society together as a functioning whole. Maxims, on the other hand, which form the second class of customs, were more specialized principles not known to or customarily observed by the people at large, but instead used as the basis for deciding cases in courts. This formulation of the problem has the distinct advantage of avoiding all awkward questions (such as those asked by Pocock) as to how it can be that popular practices can become laws. It also forms a useful grounding for the two concepts that we shall soon examine. To the first category of custom can be related the concept of custom found in early-seventeenth century legal writers and scholars; to the second category (i.e. maxims) can be related the concept of artificial reason. This was a form of reasoning or of rationality discernible only to those learned in the law.

In the following chapter St German elaborated on these points. The Doctor asked the Student how it was that customs ought not to be denied when they cannot be proved to be rational. If they cannot be proved by reason then surely it is a matter of indifference whether they be accepted or denied, unless they are backed up by statute or some other sufficient authority. The Student's reply to this question took an interesting form. It maintained the previously-established division of custom into two types, and made plain that the basis of this distinction lay in the ways in which the customs came to be known.

> Many of the customes & maxymes of the lawes of Englande can be knowen by the use and custome of the realme so apparently that it nedeth to have any lawe wrytten therof/for what nedyth it to have any lawe wrytten that the eldest sone shall enheryte his father/or that all the doughters shall enheryte togyther as one heyre . . . The other maxymes and customes of the lawe that be not so openly knowen amonge the people may be knowen partly by the lawe of reason: & partly by the bokes of the lawis of Englande called yeres of termes/& partly by dyuers recordis remaynynge in the kynges courtes & in his tresorye. And specyally by a boke that is called the regestre/& also by dyuers statutis whein many of the sayd customes and maxymes be ofte resyted/as to a dylygent sercher wyll euydently appere.[45]

Thus, there were some customs whose observation was second-nature to the people, and the universality of the assent given to them was sufficient in itself to provide knowledge of them: they were, therefore, *jus non scriptum* in its purest form. But the other more detailed and more arcane customs and maxims were accessible only to learned experts. Here we reach the subject of artificial reason. For, as St German has clearly stated, natural reason alone was unable to give knowledge of such customs. Therefore to know what maxims were customarily enforced in English courts one required an artificial reason that could be gained only from a study of the written records of the English courts. These would tell you what had been enforced as law in the past, and therefore what will continue to be enforced as law in the present and future.

Customs (in the form of customary maxims) thus played in St German's thought a role closely linked to that of what later lawyers will term artificial reason. This was so because custom was not to be understood in his work as having overtones of reactionary romanticism or irrationalistic conservatism (as it does in modern, i.e. post-Enlightenment, conservative thought). Custom and artificial reason both were concepts developed to explain how positive law could be both rational and yet independent of the control of a person or institution drawing upon natural reason alone.

These concepts also helped to explain how the mutable law could be said to be rational. St German's notion of custom, unlike

Fortescue's, had the potentiality to serve as the basis for a complex historical approach to the law. The difference between Fortescue and St German lay in the fact that the former linked custom to a set of immutable maxims, while the latter linked maxims to the mutability of custom. As a result the entire body of positive law (except for those parts of it which were the law of nature) became mutable and, in theory, capable of patterned historical development. It was only to be expected then that there was nothing in St German's works at all similar to the assertion of the immutability of law made by Fortescue: England, claimed the latter, had been ruled successively by Britons, Romans, Saxons, Danes and Normans, yet 'throughout the period of these nations and their kings, the realm had been continuously ruled by the same customs as it is now'. This proved that these customs must have been, from the beginning, the best, otherwise they would have been altered.[46]

The common lawyers of early Stuart England – with the partial exception of Sir Edward Coke – followed the jurisprudence of St German rather than that of Fortescue. They considerably extended the concepts of artificial reason and of custom (that were implicit in St German's work) in ways that we must now consider.

(B)   THE COMMON LAW AS REASON[47]

'Limited law of nature is the law now used in every State'.[48] This dictum by John Selden would have been acceptable to every common lawyer in early-seventeenth century England. It occurred in a passage in which he was commenting on Sir John Fortescue's contention – made in his *De Laudibus Legum Angliae* (written c.1470)[49] – that the laws of England were older than the laws of other nations (and this included Roman law). Selden did not agree with Fortescue, though he tried his utmost to avoid saying so too clearly. Fortescue's view, that the English had been ruled by the same customs continuously since the time of the pre-Roman Britons,[50] was one that Selden preferred to deal with by creatively reinterpreting rather than by contradicting it. At one point, after he had corrected Fortescue, he concluded his remarks with the statement: 'By this well considered, That of the laws of the realm being never changed will be better understood'.[51] Yet these corrections, ostensibly provided to help us better understand Fortescue's utterances, consisted of the argument that conquests (including the Norman Conquest) lead to the alteration of laws. Strictly speaking, there was no contradiction between Selden and Fortescue at this point: the latter merely said that ancient customs remained continuously in force; the former did not deny this but pointed out that new laws and customs were over time added to the original ones. But elsewhere Selden made clear his own view that ancient laws had been frequently *abrogated*.[52] There were two basic reasons for Selden's inability or unwillingness to agree with Fortescue on the antiquity of English law. One was precisely this matter of conquest. England had been successively conquered by various peoples and they had all, except the Romans, contributed to English law. 'But questionless', he wrote, 'the Saxons made a mixture of the British customes with their own; the Danes with old British, the Saxon and their own; and the Normans the like'.[53] The common law as it existed in Selden's own day was a mongrel law, and consequently the tenor of Selden's remarks clearly diverged sharply from the tenor of Fortescue's. The differing tones of the two positions reflected two incompatible legal temperaments.

The nature of this incompatibility is better revealed by the second of Selden's reasons for disagreeing with Fortescue. English law, he argued, cannot be the most ancient, for 'all laws in general are originally equally ancient' since they were all 'grounded upon nature . . . and nature being the same in all, the beginning of all laws must be the same'.[54] That is to say that all law codes were equally grounded upon reason.

All legal systems were derivations from natural law, and could therefore be traced back, through whatever mutations, to the time at which natural law was first promulgated to human beings.[55] Therefore *all* legal systems were of an equal age, and *all* of them were laws of reason. This, in short, was Selden's critique of Fortescue. There are a number of important implications to be derived from such an argument. Attention should be given to that small word, *all*. 'All nations were grounded upon nature, and no Nation was, that out of it took not their grounds'.[56] This meant not only that all legal codes were equally ancient; it meant that they were also all equally valid, equally rational. If one surveyed the legal systems of all contemporary nations one found diversity and variation – often outright conflict – and yet it cannot be said that any one of these systems is better than the others. Diversity did not alter the fact that codes of positive law, including the English common law, were all 'limited law of nature', and thus were all laws of reason. All law codes were also, however, of only local validity because they were all adaptations of the essence of natural law to local circumstance. Selden put the matter at length:

> As soon as Italy was peopled, this beginning of laws was there, and upon it was grounded the Roman laws, which could not have that distinct name indeed till Rome was built, yet remained always that they were at first, saving that additions and interpretations, in succeeding ages increased, and somewhat altered them, by making a *Determination juris naturalis*, which is nothing but the Civil Law of any Nation. For although the law of nature be truly said Immutable, yet its as true that its limitable, and limited law of nature is the law now used in every State. All the same may be affirmed of our British laws, or English, or other whatsoever. But the divers opinions of interpreters proceeding from the weakness of mans reason, and the several conveniences of divers States, have made those limitations, which the law of Nature hath suffered, very different. And hence is it that those customs which have come all out of one fountain, Nature, thus vary from and cross one another in several Commonwealths.[57]

Of particular significance in this passage is the mention of 'the weakness of mans reason'. Human beings, Selden was arguing, may be mistaken in their understanding of the natural law, and they may be mistaken in a variety of ways. Consequently, when human beings – operating to the best of their understanding – set about the process of constructing systems of positive law on the initial base of natural laws (reason) they will construct a considerable variety of such systems. This, as well as environmental influence, explained the variety of positive laws. But, most striking of all, Selden did not say that positive-law systems based on fallacious reasoning were any less valid than other systems. It seems to be implied that there were no criteria by which one could distinguish a valid from an invalid understanding of natural law.

Another noteworthy feature of Selden's argument is that it was of a markedly historical character. Selden, indeed, used the concept of custom rather than that of artificial reason to explain how legal diversity was compatible with the view that the common law (like other codes of positive law) was a rational law. We will pursue this aspect of Selden's thinking later in the chapter. Other common lawyers, however, while agreeing with Selden's starting point (that the common law was a limited law of nature, a 'determination' of natural law, in the words of Aquinas as well as of Selden, and thus a law of reason), moved from it in a rather different direction.

The actual words of the common lawyers of early Stuart England on the matter of reason often bore a striking resemblance to those of St German. Such is the case with this statement by William Noy:

> The Common Law is grounded on the Rules of reason, and therefore we use to say in Argument, That reason Will that such a thing be done, Or that reason will not that such a thing be done; The rules of reason are of two sorts, some taken from Learning, as well Divine as Humane, and some proper to it selfe onely.[58]

But Noy's words, even more than those very similar ones of St German, gave a clear impression that 'reason' was a term of art, a trick of the lawyers' trade and little more. Reason was a synonym for common law, and the common law was simply reason. Thus Noy could talk interchangeably of the law being divided into *laws of reason*, customs and statutes; and into *common laws*, customs and statutes.[59] The underlying maxims or rules of the common law were shown to be rational principles taken from a wide range of disciplines (theology, grammar, logic, philosophy, politics and ethics).[60] But it was the use of reason as a term of art, as found in the passage quoted, that in other writers culminated in a concept of artificial reason, though the concept did not say much that was not implied in Noy's account. For it seemed to be the case that Noy meant by reason not so much ratiocination as following certain rules of law, not so much natural reason as the artificial reason that was contained within the body of the law itself.

Other writers put the matter more plainly. Of a passage from Plato, Sir Henry Finch said:

> it teacheth Common Law to be nothing else but common reason: but what reason? not that which everie one doth frame unto himselfe: but refined reason.[61]

(It is clear from the context that Finch meant by 'common law' all codes of positive law not just that which was in force in England.) John Doddridge, like Noy, believed the law to be a deductive system grounded on a set of rational axioms or maxims. The terms 'grounds, maxims, principles, eruditions, lawes positive, law, rules, propositions' were all the same thing, and what that was was conveyed in this definition:

> A maxime is the foundation of Law, and the conclusion of reason: for reason is the efficient cause thereof, and Law is the effect that floweth therefrom.

This definition Doddridge quoted from Plowden's *Commentaries*. He provided an alternative of his own, which was perhaps more exact but should not be seen as contradicting Plowden's:

> A Rule or Principle of the Law of England, is a Conclusion either of the law of Nature, or derived from some generall custome used within the Realme, containing in a short summe the reason and direction of many particular and speciall occurrences.[62]

The introduction of custom at this point should not surprise us. Customs were themselves valid only because they were rational (as we shall see) and there was no necessary conflict in believing the English common law to be essentially the (or a) law of reason and believing that much of that law was also customary.

Doddridge said that the grounds of the law were either necessary (primary conclusions of reason) or contingent (secondary conclusions).[63] The distinction corresponded to that of Aquinas between demonstrative and determinative derivations from natural law, and was found also in St German. It was because determinative derivations (or secondary conclusions of reason) were not demonstrable that St German said that the laws cannot all be *proved* to be derived from the laws of reason. Because there were a considerable variety of possible determinative derivations from reason (or nature) there must have been some particular way of deciding which of them would be of force in a particular country. The English common law did this partly by custom. In England some rational principles (maxims) were customarily observed; others were not. Therefore, to assert that that part of the law not strictly deducible from reason was customary was not to say that the law was not common reason. A law, to be a valid law, had to be rational, but it need not have been customary.

Thus Doddridge could say of these secondary principles that they 'are not so well knowne by the light of Nature [i.e. natural reason], as by other meanes'. And although they were so probable as not to require much proof,

> yet many times are they, at the first shew, not yeelded unto without due consideration: and are peculiarly knowne, for the most part, to such onely as professe the study and speculation of Lawes.[64]

This led naturally on to, and provides another context for, the idea of the artificial reason of the law.

> The efficient cause of Rules, Grounds, and Axiomes is the light of naturall reason tryed and sifted upon disputation and argument. And hence is it, that the Law (as hath bin before declared) is called reason; not for that every man can comprohend [sic] the same; but it is artificiall reason; the reason of such, as by their wisedome, learning, and long experiences are skilfull in the affaires of men, and know what is fit and convenient to bee held and observed for the appeasing of controversies and debates among men, still having an eye and due regard of justice, and a consideration of the commonwealth wherein they live . . . [65]

Artificial reason was necessary to any account that wished to identify the common law with laws of reason (and therefore in some never-too-carefully defined sense with the law of nature). Because, as Aquinas, Fortescue, and St German all agreed, deductive reason alone could not account for the derivation of positive law from natural law, therefore, if one wished to identify the law of reason (i.e. of nature) with positive law (and in so doing remove positive law from the control of any higher law and its interpreters) then it was necessary to find some means of supplementing deductive or natural reason – necessary, in other words, to find some sort of artificial reason. Natural reason could explain how positive law might incorporate the law of nature (or reason) primary (and for Aquinas this part of positive law was the *jus gentium*), but it could not explain how the remainder of the law (*jus civile* for Aquinas) could be said to *be* the law of reason. Doddridge provided an answer: artificial reason. Artificial reason was the reason of those learned in the law (and other relevant subjects, perhaps), and those who had gained it would automatically realize that the common law as a whole was the law of reason, a collection of rational rules.

As such, of course, it could hardly be in conflict with the law of nature which was itself also the law of reason. There was therefore no way in which any higher law outside the body of the common law itself could be used to control the common law. So that when Finch said that positive laws 'direct contrarie' to the laws of nature and reason (by which he meant the laws of reason primary and secondary, in St German's terms) 'loose their force, and are no lawes at all',[66] this could be of no clear practical force. By definition the laws of England were the laws of reason, and therefore they either were, or contained, the laws of nature.

On this latter point it was possible for some variety of expression to exist. The writers we have already considered – and most especially Doddridge – called all positive laws the laws of reason because they argued that even those laws derived by determination from reason (i.e. St German's laws grounded on the law of reason secondary particular) were still ultimately laws of reason, in that it was their rationality that enabled them to be considered true laws, even if that rationality could not fully explain why some and not others of them were in force in any particular place. But other writers restricted the term 'reason' to the laws of reason primary and secondary general. The final effect however was much the same. For example, witness Francis Bacon's statement, in *The Maxims of the Law*[67] that:

The law hath many grounds and positive learnings, which are not of the maxims and conclusions of reason, but yet are learnings received, which the law hath set down and will not have called in question: these may be rather called *placita juris* than *regulae juris*. With such maxims the law will dispense, rather than crimes and wrongs should be unpunished; *quia salus populi suprema lex*, and *salus populi* is contained in the repressing offences by punishment.[68]

A little later he added to this

But if the rule be one of the higher sort of maxims, that are *regulae rationales* and not *positivae*, then the law will rather endure a particular offence to escape without punishment than violate such a rule.[69]

The point Bacon appears to be making is that, while it was quite possible for there to be a conflict between rational (or natural) and positive rules, this conflict occurred *within* the common law. In other words the possible conflict between natural and positive law found in Aquinas and other medieval theologians has here been internalized within the body of English law. And therefore, of course, such conflict was resolved by common lawyers themselves, following principles – which the law also contained and Bacon adumbrated – laid down in order to achieve such resolution when it was necessary. So, though Bacon did not go so far as Doddridge in identifying common law and reason, he did indicate that the law itself contained the laws of reason (or nature), and this was sufficient to rule out the possibility of common law being in practice controlled by any higher law, or by anyone except common lawyers. The judgement on whether a particular law did, or did not, conflict with reason was one for the common law itself, and the common lawyer, to decide.

There were two common lawyers who, one might think, did not readily fit into the thesis being advanced here: Sir John Davies and Sir Edward Coke. Davies, it is commonly believed, thought that the common law was not reason but custom.[70] But in fact Davies's view was not substantially different from the views of those writers whom we have already encountered. It is certainly true that he stated, bluntly enough, that 'the *Common Law* of *England* is nothing else but the *Common Custome* of the Realm.'[71] But what did he mean by this? To understand his meaning there are two key passages that need to be taken into account. The first was this:

> Therefore as the *Law of Nature*, which the Schoolmen call *Jus Commune*, and which is also *Jus non scriptum*, being written onely in the heart of man, is better then all the written Laws in the world to make men honest and happy in this life, if they would observe the rules thereof: so the *Customary Law* of *England*, which we do likewise call *Jus Commune*, as coming nearest to the Law of *Nature*, which is the root and touchstone of all good Laws, and which is also *Jus non scriptum*, and written onely in the memory of man . . . doth far excell our *written* Laws . . . [72]

And the second passage is this:

> Certain it is that Law is nothing but a Rule of Reason, and humane Reason is *Lesbia Regula*, pliable every way, or like a Cup with two eares, as the French proverb is, which may be

taken up on either side, as well with the left hand as with the right: so that not onely the knowledge of the Law, but all other rationall Sciences that are subject to Argument and Discourse, must needs be subject to uncertaintie and to errour.[73]

So, Davies agreed that law was reason, but the problem for him was: how do we know what reason is? That is how do we know what is truly rational rather than what is merely considered rational by individual human minds? The answer was custom. Custom fulfilled the same function for Davies that artificial reason did for Doddridge. In both cases there was a need to bridge the gap between the particular rules in force in particular places and the law of reason (or nature) – a gap which all admitted could not be closed by natural reason considered simply as ratiocination. But again, it must be emphasized, in this context, that the passages (especially the second) from Davies show that this use of custom did not conflict with the view that law was primarily reason. The first passage shows in addition how very close Davies came to identifying the common law with natural law.

Exactly how custom performed this function, and how both Davies's and Doddridge's formulations of the links between positive law and reason fitted into the common framework of a jurisprudence derived from St German, are matters that will be discussed in detail in the next section. But it is necessary to treat briefly Davies's ideas on reason and custom at this point because it has been into the context they provide that Coke's ideas on artificial reason have been placed by Pocock. Now, strangely enough, as has been indicated, custom and artificial reason do serve similar purposes, and to this extent Pocock's contextualization is useful. Yet the primary context for Coke's ideas on this matter was the same as for Doddridge's, that is the identification of law with reason.[74]

Coke's clearest presentation of the idea of artificial reason was in a passage in *The First Part of the Institutes* (i.e. 'Coke on Littleton') where the function of the concept is quite apparent when seen against the background presented above:

For reason is the life of the Law, nay the common law it selfe is nothing else but reason, which is to be understood of an Artificial perfection of reason, gotten by long study, observation, and experience, and not of every mans natural reason, for *Nemo nascitur artifex*. This legal reason *est summa ratio*. And therefore if all the reason that is dispersed into so many several heads were united into one, yet could he not make such a law as the Law of England is, because by many succession of ages it hath been fined and refined by an infinite number of grave and learned men, and by long experience grown to such a perfection, to the government of this Realm, as the old rule may be justly verified of it. *Neminem oporlet esse sapientiorem legibus*: No man (out of his own private reason) ought to be wiser than the law, which is the perfection of reason.[75]

As with all the other thinkers we have considered, Coke used the idea of artificial reason to bridge an embarrassing gap between immutable reason and mutable law. Coke's solution was to develop the concept of artificial reason and assimilate it to the idea that law was customary. 'Customes are either generall or particular; generall, which are part of the Common law, being currant through the whole Commonwealth, and used in every Towne, and every Manor'.[76] Custom and reason: the law would appear to be both. This is because, for Coke, custom was itself artificial reason; the process Coke described in his passage on artificial reason, the process of slow refinement and development over long periods of time, was the process by which customs grew and were transmitted. Coke brought the two concepts, custom and artificial reason, together. In this he differed from Doddridge for whom artificial reason was the reason possessed by trained lawyers: this formulation was more obviously aimed at defending the common law from meddlesome laymen.[77]

But Doddridge like Coke did possess a theory of the common law as custom, even if he kept it separate from his theory of artificial reason. In fact, the early Stuart common lawyers all possessed a jurisprudence that began by identifying law (common law) with reason. Their theory of custom was a functional component of this jurisprudence, and was required in order to reconcile the idea that the common law was, or contains, reason and can therefore be identified (in what sense is never very clear) with the laws of reason and/or nature, with the observed fact that all codes of common law or positive law differed and none could be proved rational by deductive reason alone. The links between reason and custom in common law thought were plainly apparent in Thomas Hedley's speech on impositions (1610).[78] Hedley was aware that the common law was a rational system in that once it was explained to someone their natural reason would enable them to perceive the logical links that held it together, otherwise, he argued, it would be unjust to say that ignorance of the law was no excuse for transgression of it.[79] Nevertheless, it was not sufficient simply to *define* the law as 'common reason', for though reason was the 'genus or matter' of law it did not constitute its essential form. Not all reason was law, so it was necessary to know why in any particular place some rational principles in particular, and not others, had the force of law. This information was provided by *time*.[80] '[T]he common law was somewhat more than bare reason, . . . [it] was tried reason, or the quintessence of reason'. Time, Hedley said, was 'the trier of truth, author of all human reason', and it was 'such time whereof the memory of man is not to the contrary, time out of mind, such time as will beget a custom'. Thus the common law could be defined as:

> a reasonable usage, throughout the whole realm, approved time out of mind in the king's courts of record which have jurisdiction over the whole kingdom, to be good and profitable for the commonwealth. But here because I make custom a part in my definition of the common law, I would not be mistaken, as though I meant to confound the common law with custom [i.e. local customs], which differ as much as artificial reason and bare precedents.[81]

Hedley could also describe common law reasoning as being secondary reasoning grounded ultimately on 'some primitive maxim, depending immediately upon some prescription or custom'.[82] Thus, as for St German, rational maxims were given force in a particular place by being used customarily. Maxims, therefore, 'cannot be proved by reason alone . . . but by custom and reason conjoined'. In the last resort, law was constructed out of rational principles, but only custom explained why some principles and not others were used as law in England. Thus law was 'artifcial reason', reason tried by time; or, in Hedley's words, 'reason tried and allowed by the wisdom of time for many ages together to be good and profitable for the commonwealth'.[83]

Two conclusions that Hedley drew from this argument are worth noting. Artificial reason was distinguished from natural reason by the fact that it was an accumulation of the reasoning and wisdom of many generations, for this reason even a Parliament, drawing on the wisdom of the entire nation in the present, could not build from scratch a law as wise as the common law.[84] Only artificial reason, reason plus time, could do that. Secondly, Hedley was clear that one consequence of his position was that law must be always changing. If previous decisions could not be altered,

> then the common law could never have been said to be tried reason grounded upon better reason than the statutes, for it should then be grounded merely upon the reason or opinion of 3 or 4 judges, which must come short of the wisdom of the parliament.[85]

Thus the idea of artificial reason had two uses. It was able to support the conclusion that the law embodied a rationality superior to that of any individual or institution, even parliament itself perhaps. Therefore, it could be concluded, no one could claim superior wisdom to the law, and it could not be found wanting by outsiders. Its wisdom was always superior to theirs. Secondly, the idea served to bring together custom and reason, and thus to demonstrate how the law could be a rational system while also being unwritten and customary. Some emphasized the rationality more than the custom, but all saw the law as defined by both of these things. In some cases, indeed, the idea of custom was elaborated to a degree of sophistication that left reason trailing in the distance. Yet, trailing or not, it remained in the race. It is to these elaborated theories of custom that we must now turn.

(C)   THE COMMON LAW AS CUSTOM

The jurisprudence of the early Stuart common lawyers followed, in general, the model provided by St German rather than that provided by Fortescue. Like St German they argued that though the law was a rational system it was also a body of customary rules. They did, however, go much further than St German in developing the historical possibilities of the concept of custom. Some of them were decisively influenced by humanist thought – both legal humanism and more general humanist ideas – and consequently pushed this development of the idea of custom to considerable lengths. Yet in doing so they were not simply adopting Continental ideas and discarding the ideas of the common-law mind. There was in fact no necessary incompatibility between English and Continental ideas for there were features of common-law thought that made the reception of at least some humanist ideas quite undisruptive. These same features may also explain why it was that so few common lawyers seem to have been deeply influenced by humanism: they had little need for what it provided.

But before we look at the role of custom in the thought of humanist-influenced lawyers we need to know how their less *avant-garde* contemporaries made use of the term. William Noy followed St German closely in identifying customs with maxims:

> Customes are of two sorts; General Customes in use throughout the whole Realme, called Maximes, and particular Customes used in some certaine County, Citie, Towne, or Lordship, . . . [86]

Noy did not develop his theory of law very clearly, but as he had already analysed legal maxims as a set of rules of reason[87] it would seem that he was similar to St German also in thinking that 'general customs' and 'maxims' were equivalent entities, which is to say that general customs were rational principles. Henry Finch moved matters a little further, however. He defined the common law as being of customary nature: 'The Common law of England is a law used time out of mind, or by prescription throughout the Realme'.[88] But like a number of other writers Finch reserved the term 'custom' for particular local customs so that he could also say that 'that which is currant throughout the Realme, is Common Law, not custome'.[89] This distinction would appear to be purely technical. In defining customs as 'speciall usuages time out of mind altering the common law'[90] Finch was not just making customs completely local but also mirroring his definition of the common law itself, which we have just quoted. We saw in the previous section that Finch thought the law to be made of reason, but by adopting a notion of custom that combined both reason and immemoriality he was able to accept the existence of diversity and historical change without this being a threat to his rationalistic view of law. He said:

> Positive laws are sundrie and divers, according to the seuerall and diuers constitutions of particular places and Countries. Such among the Jewes were their Politicals, deliuered by Moses, which so farre as they been positive, binde us not unto them. Such were the antient law of the Grecians, the xii tables, & civil lawes of the

Romans, and *Such are the Common Lawes of England.* And almost
so many people so many lawes. And as those lawes are divers
one from another, so one and the self same laws may be altered
and changed in themselves. So long as no alteration is permitted
against the two maine Lawes, of Nature and Reason.[91]

This appreciation of diversity and change goes beyond anything in
Fortescue or St German, but it is not theoretically incompatible with
the ideas of the latter. Accepted notions of the relationship between
(customary) law and reason meant that there was no difficulty in
combining the ideas of law as reason and law as mutable custom.
What is reasonable depended to a degree on circumstance, and it
was precisely this act of determining exactly what is reasonable *in
given circumstances* that custom performed.

John Doddridge's *The English Lawyer* gave very thorough treatment to the idea that law is reason, and his book was an attempt
to demonstrate that English law could be taught as a deductive
Aristotelian science. Yet he too believed that much of the law
was customary. He appears to have shared St German's idea that
maxims and customs were very closely linked, and also the idea that
customs were as much to do with courts of law as popular practices.
At the beginning of his discussion of custom he remarked that 'every
Court of Justice hath his Customes and courses of proceedings
sometime different from others'.[92] The remark was not developed,
but it should be kept in mind when reading some of Doddridge's
other statements about custom. Customs he defined as 'either
generall throughout all the Realme, and so doe they constitute
that part of the Common Law which is grounded upon the generall
Custome of the Realme', or particular and local customs.[93] Customs
'ought to bee reasonable and agreeable to common right without
absurdity'.[94] In a passage which we have already examined once
Doddridge said of legal maxims (which are the axiomatic grounds
for all legal reasoning) that they were

a Conclusion either of the Law of Nature, or derived from some
generall custome used within the Realme, containing in a short
summe the reason and direction of many particular and speciall
occurrences.[95]

He thus reconciled the view of the law as reason with the customary
nature of the common law in a way similar to St German: custom

provided knowledge of what was reasonable in a particular place. And, in addition, by equating general customs with legal maxims Doddridge brought custom into the sphere of his 'artificial reason' and made of it a term of art. The artificial reason of the lawyer consisted in good part in the ability to discern the rational core possessed by customs.

More than any of the above writers, Charles Calthrop, in a discussion primarily of local customs, revealed some of the historical potentialities of the term, and some of its subtleties. He also believed that customs were grounded upon reason,[96] but he also said this of them:

> Some say that men have their mind affected according to the constitution of their bodies: As so have Countries their Customes, according to the constitution of the places; as in Kent, and in North-Wales, because those Countries have been most subject to forraign invasions, (that every man there, may be of power for resistance,) the inheritance for the most part descends in Gavel kind (*viz*) to every brother alike; but in the middle parts of the Realm for whose government least equality is best, the inheritance wholly descendeth to the eldest brother: And in Borough English which is in divers Boroughs, because their substance commonly is lands; and in such Townes, lands may be better preserved then goods, therefore their youngest sons shall onely have their lands: and as it is in those great parts of the Realme, so it is in divers private parts and Mannours, and divers private and speciall Customes, as some Mannors have Coppy-hold of inheritance, some for life or lives: in some Mannour the Coppy-holders surrender in one manner, and in some in another sort. In some the Fine is arbitrable: and in some certain, *et sic in similibus.*[97]

This passage opens up a splendid vision of a complex hierarchy of custom. Each community had customary rules to inform it of what were the rational solutions to their particular problems. Those rules developed gradually in relation to the historical vicissitudes through which all communities pass. The rationality of a custom derived from that fact that it evolved to fit the needs of a particular environment.

Ideas similar to these were applied to the common law itself by Sir John Davies in his now-familiar definitions of the customary nature of that law. The common law, he said, 'is so framed and fitted to the nature and disposition of this people, as we may properly say it is connatural to the Nation, so as it cannot possibly be ruled by any other Law'.[98] This natural fit between nation and law came about because of the process of historical evolution that gave birth to customs. Customs were matters of fact not record, they consisted 'in use and practice', and so 'can be recorded and registered no-where but in the memory of the people'. Their genesis occurred in the following manner:

> When a resonable act once done is found to be good and beneficiall to the people, and agreeable to their nature and disposition, then do they use it and practise it again and again, and so by often iteration and multiplication of the act it becometh a Custome; and being continued without interruption time out of mind, it obtaineth the force of a Law.[99]

Laws developed in this way were best fitted to the needs of the nation. Written laws 'are imposed on the Subject before any Triall or Probation made, whether the same be fit and agreeable to the nature and disposition of the people'. This is not true, though, of customs, for a custom does not become law 'untill it hath been tried and approved time out of mind, during all which time there did thereby arise no inconvenience'. If the custom had been found detrimental, then 'it had been used no longer, but had been interrupted, and consequently it had lost the virtue and force of a Law'.[100] But Davies did not lose sight of the fact that the law was also rational. It was custom itself that explained why and how it was rational, for customs themselves are 'full of reason and convenience'; and the fact that the common law was a tradition – 'delivered over from age to age by Tradition' – ought not, we are warned, obscure the fact that 'no humane law . . . hath more certaintie in the Rules and Maximes, more coherence in the parts thereof, or more harmonie of reason in it'.[101] Davies's conception of custom was thoroughly historical. There is no sign in his thought of Pocock's paradox of a theory of mutable custom being used to support a theory of the immutability of law. For that we have to look elsewhere.

There would appear then to be no conflict between viewing the law as both rational *and* customary. In fact its customary character explains how it could be rational at all. But it must never be forgotten that for all these thinkers it was reason that had the last *reason ultimately before custom* (handwritten marginalia)

word, not custom. No custom could make a law valid when it was in conflict with reason; custom was a means of discovering rational principles, or axioms, not an alternative to them. As Finch put it, positive laws 'directly contrary' to the laws of reason or nature 'loose their force, and are no lawes at all'.[102]

Diff w/ Foc. (handwritten marginalia)

A number of humanist-influenced lawyers developed these historical ideas of custom rather more fully.[103] The influence of humanism on the law is a complex matter. One influence it could have had – and this is apparent in both Finch and Doddridge, as well as more obviously in Bacon – was to create a concern with methodological questions. In particular it could lead to a wish to portray the law as a coherent ordered system – a science – and to reduce it to a code more readily accessible to human minds.[104] But more important was the development during the Renaissance of the study of legal history.[105] Particularly among the French humanists, the practitioners of the *mos gallicus*, this took the form of developing ways of talking about the law in terms of its almost infinite mutability. They were interested in examining the evolution of the various types of positive law (civil, canon and feudal) as a comprehensible process, and examining it largely without reference to the immutable certainties of nature. Most political institutions, including property and government itself, they tended to treat as part of the *jus gentium* and as such malleable to fit particular conditions. The English lawyer who best fitted into this tradition was John Selden.[106] Most other lawyers may have picked up bits and pieces from humanist sources, but seldom did this have such a deep influence on their view of things as it had on Selden.[107]

Amongst some civil lawyers there was, from quite early on, some reception of humanist ideas about the law. Thomas Starkey, for example, spent much time discussing how it is that law is both mutable and yet based on an immutable natural law common to all nations.[108] Sir Thomas Smith engaged in the more obviously humanist practices of providing a comparative analysis of common law and civil law (on more historical and less xenophobic grounds than Fortescue).[109] Common lawyers did not go this far, but it is likely that what knowledge they might have had of humanist work would encourage them to push the historical tendencies in their idea of custom further than they might otherwise have done. Humanists tended to see the whole body of the law as customary and therefore mutable. For the (non-lawyer) humanist, Sir Henry Savile, law and custom were interchangeable, for *patrios mores* . . . I take to contain both, there being no difference between them but written or not written, *consuetudo* (custome) being *lex non scripta* (an unwritten law), and lex (law) nothing else but *consuetudo scripta* (a written custome).[110]

One trained common lawyer, whom we know to have been influenced by humanist ideas, Lord Chancellor Ellesmere, said a rather similar thing. For him,

The common Law of England is grounded upon the Law of God, and extends itselfe to the originall Law of Nature, and the universall Law of Nations.[111]

We can know what the common law is because 'it is the common custome of the Realme', and these customs rested on two sources: established maxims and precedents.[112] Ellesmere then said

that some lawes, as well Statute Law, as common Law, are obsolete and worne out of use : for all humane Lawes are but *Leges temporis* . . . By this rule also, and upon this reason it is, that often times ancient Laws are changed by interpretation of the Judges, as well in Cases criminall as civile.[113]

Notable in all this are two things that relate to the themes we are discussing here. First by reducing 'customs' to maxims and precedents, Ellesmere reduced custom to a term of art, and hence linked it to the specialized knowledge of a lawyer (i.e. artificial reason). And, second, it is clearly implied that a law that was entirely customary was also to be seen as constantly changing. It was therefore eminently a subject for historical investigation.

Another English lawyer with a good knowledge of continental humanism, a man who was himself one of the great Renaissance intellectuals, was Sir Francis Bacon. And he too possessed a deeply historical understanding of custom and law. It is an interesting exercise to compare the section on law in Book VIII of his *De Augmentis Scientiarum* (1623), a book aimed at an international learned audience, with what he said in 'A Proposition touching the Compiling and Amendment of the Laws of England' (c.1616) which was written for James I and aimed at an audience familiar with at least the basic principles and shape of the English common law. The two works were both pleas for the reform of the law, and both said very similar things, but they said them in quite different ways. Bacon's aim, as far as English law was concerned, was to reform without innovating; his idea of reform 'is rather matter of order and explanation than of alteration'.[114] The plan of reform that he advocated was essentially one of reordering the law so as to make it easier to use, and it entailed no substantive alteration to the law. But there are some curious features to the type of ordered system Bacon believed the law to be. These curious features in his jurisprudence arose from the fact that for him custom was the paradigm for all law. He raised the question of whether or not the most useful reform of the law might consist in converting it to a 'text law', that is a written law. And his reply was

> It is too long a business to debate whether *lex scripta aut non scripta*, a text law or customs well registered, with received and approved grounds and maxims, and acts and resolutions judicial from time to time duly entered and reported, be the better form of declaring and authorising laws. It was the principal reason or oracle of Lycurgus, that none of his laws should be written. Customs are laws written in living tables; and some traditions the Church doth not disauthorise. In all sciences, they are the soundest that keep close to particulars; and sure I am there are more doubts that rise upon our statutes, which are a text law.[115]

Given this preference for *lex non scripta*, Bacon naturally did not wish to simply reorganize the common law into a written code. His proposal consisted (in so far as it was concerned with common law and not statute) of three steps. Firstly, 'ancient records' were to be collected in a book *De antiquitatibus juris*. Secondly, there was to be compiled a complete series of Year-books covering the years from the reign of Edward I to the present. Obsolete and irrelevant cases, repetitious argument and other unnecessary things were to be purged, while cases of contradiction were to be especially noted and set apart from the rest. Thirdly, there were to be several auxiliary books comprising 'Institutions; a treatise *De regulis juris*; and a better book *De verborum significationibus*, or terms of the law'.[116] The most important thing to note about this plan is that it was designed to preserve the historical structure of the English common law. The collections of case reports on which knowledge of what has been treated by the courts as custom and law was based remained at the heart of things. These collections were to remain chronological and were not to be arranged topically like Justinian's *Digest*. In other words Bacon's plan was for a more coherent arrangement of the sources of law, not for a rearrangement of the laws themselves.

The reasoning behind this becomes much clearer if we examine what Bacon had to say in the *De Augmentis Scientiarum*. The eighth book of this work contained a partial example of a 'Treatise on Universal Justice or the Fountains of Equity, by Aphorisms'.[117] This work contained, amongst other things, an account of the rationale underlying Bacon's view of the law. Law he believed was a science based on axiomatic maxims which were to be derived from experience by induction. That is to say they were essentially customs. In this way the reasoning underlying the law was, we might say, historical rather than logical. A number of maxims made this quite plain. Bacon repeatedly urged his reader to look to the historical circumstances in which laws were made in order fully to understand them. Laws made for particular circumstances – laws which 'spring out of a temporary emergency of state' – ought not to be distorted so as to apply to more normal times. The character of a period in which 'examples' occurred was to be examined before the example was followed: they 'are to be sought from good and moderate times, not from such as are tyrannical, factious, or dissolute'. Examples from such latter times 'are spurious in their origin, and rather injurious than instructive'.[118] In the new digest of laws that Bacon proposed the old volumes containing the original records of the law ought not to be cast away because where laws are very difficult to interpret one might need to examine their history: 'in important cases it will not be amiss to examine and consider the successive changes which have taken place in past laws'.[119] A little later came a key statement that related closely to the ideas of the 'Proposition' discussed above:

> Let these judgements be digested in chronological order, and not by method and titles. For such writings are a kind of history or narrative of the laws. And not only the acts themselves, but the times also when they passed, give light to a wise judge.[120]

Bacon was talking here of what in an English context were called Year-books, the chronological record of judicial decisions, and he explained why they ought not to be arranged topically: because law was fundamentally an historical artefact that could only be apprehended when this fact was recognized.

The aphorisms that explained Bacon's idea of maxims took this matter a little further. Although Bacon referred to maxims as 'the general dictates of reason'[121] this should not be taken as a denial of their customary nature. For Bacon, as for so many others, maxims were rational customs, that is they had the character both of reason and of custom. This is clear from Bacon's statement of how knowledge of maxims was to be gained.

> It is a sound precept not to take the law from the rules, but to make the rule from the existing law. For the proof is not to be sought from the words of the rule, as if it were the text of law. The rule, like the magnetic needle, points at the law, but does not settle it.[122]

Thus maxims were to be induced from laws themselves: they were the reason immanent in the body of the common law, or the rational principles that underlay the changes of a customary law. On this basis Bacon was able to view English law as constantly evolving in a passage very reminiscent of what Selden said in his 'Notes' to Fortescue. Our laws, he writes, in a passage directly critical of Coke (and indirectly of Fortescue himself):

> are as mixt as our language, compounded of British, Roman, Saxon, Danish, Norman customs. And as our language is so much the richer, so the laws are the more complete : neither doth this attribute less to them, than those that would have them to have stood out the same in all mutations; for no tree is so good first set, as by transplanting.[123]

All of the writers whom we have discussed had a deeply historical view of law – that is to say they viewed law as an historical artefact, the product of circumstance and subject to evolution and change – whilst also having an idea of the law as being rational. English jurisprudence at least from St German onwards was perfectly compatible with the view that law was in a state of constant evolution, indeed its development of the idea of custom provided a potent theoretical basis for such a view. Some legal scholars build on this basis substantial accounts of the history of English law. An examination of them can serve both to clinch the argument that English common-law jurisprudence was fundamentally evolutionary in character, and to demonstrate finally the eccentricities of the position taken up by Sir Edward Coke.

(D)　CONCLUSION: VIEWS OF THE HISTORY
OF ENGLISH LAW

In this concluding section we will develop two main themes. The first is that there was in the early-seventeenth century a 'standard model' for the history of English law. Its two most sophisticated (and therefore least typical) exponents were John Selden and Henry Spelman, but its basic features were shared by a good many other legal antiquarians. The second theme is that the attitude to the history of English law expressed by Sir Edward Coke was both untypical and confused. The confusion arose because Coke shared the St German-style jurisprudence of all the other figures we have examined while at the same time he tried to graft on to it ideas that were incompatible with it, ideas that he derived from Fortescue.

Implicit in the case argued here is the view that John Selden – humanist intellectual of European stature though he was – serves as a better paradigm for the 'common law mind' than Coke. It is perhaps the major weakness of Pocock's account of English ancient constitutionalism that it treats Coke as the norm rather than the exception.

Selden's work on the history of English law and institutions was amongst his earliest published writing. As with Bacon it is impossible to tell whether his early historical writing owed more to the English common-law tradition or to his early acquaintance with the works of the Continental humanists, a number of whom are cited in these early works. The point to note, however, is that there was nothing in Selden's account that broke radically with common-law ideas, and the background we have established above shows how common-law ideas could serve as a theoretical basis for Selden's ideas on English legal and constitutional history. There are several key features present in both the 'standard model' of the history of law found in early Stuart England, and in Selden. These are: (a) Gothicism, (b) immemoriality; and (c) continuity. We shall examine them in turn.

By Gothicism is meant the view that English laws and institutions derived in the last resort from those of the Germanic tribes that invaded the collapsing Roman Empire – in the case of England, the Saxons.[124] This view was quite widely accepted in early Stuart England, but its acceptance was a fairly recent phenomenon achieved largely by English antiquarian research.[125] The antiquarian movement can be said to commence with the publication in 1576 of the first history of an English county, William Lambarde's *Perambulation of Kent*. Lambarde originally intended this work to be the first instalment of a county-by-county survey of English antiquities,[126] but after the appearance of Camden's *Britannia* (which Lambarde read in manuscript the year before its first publication) Lambarde felt that he had been pre-empted and moved on to delve into other matters, in particular legal antiquarianism. He returned Camden's manuscript to its author, saying how sad he was that he 'may not nowe . . . dwell in the meditation of the same things that you are occupied withal'.[127] However Lambarde was not unusual in spending a large amount of his time on legal records. The link between common lawyers and the Society of Antiquaries (the institutional embodiment of antiquarianism) was a very close one: the bulk of the Society's members were lawyers and most of the questions it debated were in some way related to the history of English law.[128] Indeed, it can be said that it was the growth of antiquarianism that led to the writing of recognizable histories of the law (as opposed to the historical *obiter dicta* and myths that common lawyers had previously been content with). A theme common to both the antiquarian movement as a whole, and legal antiquarianism in particular, was the destruction of the myth that the English polity and nation could be traced back to the Britons, who were thought to be a people of Trojan origin.[129] This myth owed much to the twelfth-century writings of Geoffrey of Monmouth, and was widely-held in Tudor times. The first generation antiquarians tended to reject these sorts of ideas. The greatest of them, William Camden, firmly but tactfully rejected the idea of a Trojan origin for the Britons and instead saw them as one of a group of similar peoples inhabiting Western Europe.[130] The earliest works of the antiquarian movement, such as Lambarde's *Perambulation* and Camden's *Britannia*, were rather vague on early English history; and because they were not concerned with tracing the continuity of English laws and institutions over time they did not see any problem with accepting the reality of the Norman Conquest. Lambarde, after discussing the laws of the Saxons, went on to remark (against a marginal note that read 'The Lawes of our time') that

Al these laws, king William the Conqueror collected together, and (after a discrete view had) by advise of his Counsell allowed some, altered others, and quite abrogated a great many, in place of which he established the lawes of Normandie his owne countrey.[131]

And Camden – interestingly relying not on legal sources but upon contemporary chroniclers – talked of a violent and bloody conquest, remarking that

> William the Conquerour, in token as it were of a Trophee for this conquest, abrogated some part of the ancient positive lawes of England, brought in some Customes of Normandie, and by vertue of a decree, commanded, That all causes should be pleaded in the French tongue.[132]

However when legal antiquarians came to examine the history of English law in and for itself they seem to have come to different conclusions. One of the first scholars to write on legal antiquities in particular was Lambarde himself. And in his legal work he developed ideas different from those contained in the *Perambulation*. These are especially to be found amongst the material on the history of parliament in his *Archeion*. He treated parliament as the centre-piece of the English legal system, and his history of it not only contrasted with his earlier views, but also neatly encapsulated the three features of the standard common-law model of history. It is therefore a useful place to begin.

Although the word 'parliament' was obviously French and so presumably post-dated the Norman arrival, nevertheless the thing itself, the assembly of the Estates of the Realm, was known to the Saxons, under the terms '*Micel-Gemot, Witena-Gemot, & Ealrawitena-Gemot*'.[133] As for the origins of the institution, the sum total of Lambarde's remarks on this subject were:

> The beginning of which manner of *Consultation*, and namely with Us of this Realme, I see not how I can derive it from any other time, than from that, in which the *German* or *English* did set their first foot on this *Land*, to invade it. For *Cornelius Tacitus* writing of the manners of the ancient *Germans*, sayth thus: *Nec Regibus infinita potestas, de minoribus rebus Principes consultant, de majoribus omnes.*[134]

There are some important implications to be derived from this passage. First, the origin of this institution was derived from the Saxon conquest of England – that is what has been termed Gothicism. But

it is important to note (and this is the second important implication)
that there is a degree of vagueness to the passage. We are not told
on what authority, or by which person, Parliament was founded. It
is this fact that enabled Gothicism, or Saxonism, to be compatible
with a theory of immemoriality. Gothicism essentially postulated
that each group of peoples had its own customs peculiar to itself
(and this matches nicely all the language we have come across above
about customs being most 'fit' and natural to a people), and that
existing English laws and institutions derived, as a matter of contingent fact, from the customs of one particular people, the Saxons,
implanted on English soil at the time of the collapse of the Roman
Empire. This did not conflict with the idea of immemoriality, partly
because the origin of the customs themselves was still unknown
(immemorial) and could presumably only be found in the German
forests; and partly because the Saxon Conquest was itself immemorial in that it predated the existence of any substantial written
records (and especially of legal records). This of course is why it was
quite possible to accept that English law was founded on the Saxon
Conquest and impossible to accept its foundation on the Norman
Conquest. The latter was a conquest by a single king recorded in a
good number of documents; the former was a conquest without a
conqueror and beyond record. The Saxon Conquest, therefore, did
not run the risk of introducing into the English constitution a law-
giver or law-maker outside and above the body of the law itself; the
Norman Conquest did. From Saxon times onwards the continuity of
written records necessitated a continuity in the history of the laws.

That Lambarde believed the Parliament of England to be
immemorial as well as Saxon is plain from his treatment of the
history of the institution in Anglo-Saxon times. Having postulated
its origin in the Saxon invasion he then quoted a number of examples
of assemblies amongst the Saxons, and finally remarked,

> Now as these written *authorities*, do undoubtedly confirme our
> *assertion* of this *continuance* of this manner of *Parliament* : So
> is there also unwritten *Law*, or *Prescription*, that doth no lesse
> infallibly uphold the same.[135]

In other words written records demonstrated the continuance of
a custom. It is nowhere said that they told us anything about
its detailed origins, for as far as the records were concerned it
would give the impression of being born fully mature. In addition

other customs or unwritten laws survived into the present, such
as the custom by which certain decayed boroughs sent burgesses
to Parliament, and these could be shown to have a continuous
history that stretched back to pre-Conquest times, thus indicating
that parliament was an immemorial Saxon institution.[136]
   This continuity across the Conquest was of course the third
feature of our model of the history of the law. Lambarde adopted
one of the several possible strategies for dealing with the problem
of the Conquest. (His solution to the problem is similar to the one
found in Selden's *Historie of Tithes*.)[137] It consists in the argument
that although there was indeed in 1066 a violent conquest of the
country, nevertheless it did not in fact interrupt the continuity of
English history. It was a conquest of no effect. Thus Lambarde could
open a chapter entitled 'The Continuance of the Parliament After the
Conquest' with the words:

> To looke for a *Parliament* assembled of the *English Nobilitie*, and
> *Commons*, soone after the *Conquest*, were but to *labour* without
> expectation of *good speed*; for, *Silent Leges inter arma*: And during
> all the reigne of the *Conquerour*, eyther the *Sword* was not put up
> into the *Scabbard*; or, if it were, the *Hand* was alwayes upon the
> *Hilt*, readie to draw it.

At this time, '*Obedience* was to bee *compelled*, [rather] than their
Opinions to bee *consulted*'.[138] But, Lambarde explained, the Norman
Yoke was of brief duration. William II, in word rather than deed
admittedly, pretended to moderate the severity of government; and
then Henry I 'did not onely at this *Coronation* promise restitution of
St. Edwards Lawes' but also 'acknowledgeth, that hee was *Crowned*
by the *Common Councell* of the *Barons* of the *Realme* of *England*'. This
latter body was Parliament and the same institution as the Saxon
witenagemot.[139] And so the continuity of English institutional and
legal history was restored, or rather preserved.
   Lambarde made all these points about the history of the legal
system as a whole in a passage that summarized the points made
above. He examined briefly the legal institutions of the Gauls of
France, and then continued:

> After which order also the *Britans* of this *Iland* did make their
> like meetings as it might be well gathered out of *Caesars*
> *Commentaries*, where he plainly writeth, that those *Druydes*

(which then were the *Iudges* amongst the *Gauls*) had fetched that their manner of *Discipline* out of *Britaine*, where wee now dwell: Yet neverthelesse, the *Saxons* our Ancestors, (which succeeded them in this Countrie) they (I say) retained the manner of the old *Germans*, their own Elders, who (as *Tacitus* writeth) *Iura per pagos vicosque reddebant . . .* And truly, the *Normans* (that invaded the posteritie of the same *Saxons* here) did not so much alter the substance, as the name of the *Saxons* order, which they found at their coming hither.[140]

Lambarde was the pioneer amongst English legal historians. The greatest of his successors, John Selden, followed his lead on all three of the points we are examining.[141] Selden's earliest works were on the history of English law. These include the *Annalecton Anglobrittanicon* (written 1607), the *Jani Anglorum Facies Altera* (1610), *England's Epinomis* (written c.1610), and – the culmination of this early work – the 'Notes' on Fortescue (1616). During the 1610s he began to publish work based on a much wider variety of sources than the purely English ones used for the above works, in particular *Titles of Honor* (1614) and *The Historie of Tithes* (1618). Beyond 1620 his interests moved away from English legal history towards comparative jurisprudence and especially Hebrew studies. But in 1647 he published the finest of his works on the history of English law, an introduction to an edition of Fleta known as the *Ad Fletam Dissertatio*. Though Selden's opinions on points of detail changed during the course of his scholarly career, nevertheless all of his works on English history shared the basic themes that have been isolated above, the themes of Gothicism, immemoriality and continuity.

In 1647 Selden was mainly concerned with the history of Roman law in relation to English common law, and the extent to which Roman law had influenced English legal development. But in examining this question he was forced to summarize his views on the history of English law itself. The Saxons he portrayed as bringing their own laws with them, so there was no continuity with either the Britons or with the laws used by the Romans when they ruled England as a conquered province. 'The Anglo-Saxon invaders of England used neither this nor any similar code, but only their native Germanic customs'.[142] A little later he wrote that 'the Anglo-Saxons, the Danes and the Normans had in succession, during a period of about 740 years, used their own laws (*i.e.* our English common law) without any Roman admixture'.[143] The English, in fact, had proved over time to be quite exceptionally unwilling to have much to do with civil law. One of the major reasons for this was 'the remarkable esteem in which the English or common law was held, and our constant faithfulness to it as something immemorially fitted (*antiquitate adaptata*) to the genius of the nation'.[144] These passages form a very neat sketch of English common law seen as originating amongst the customs of the Saxons and having a continuous history therefrom (in spite of subsequent invasions and conquests). This law was rationally defensible as good because it had evolved in tandem with the nation itself, and therefore was ideally designed to serve its needs. These were the historical principles contained in the English lawyer's concept of custom: customary law was rational precisely because it was 'immemorially fitted' to the needs of its environment. It was a 'determination' of natural law suited to one particular people.

In his earlier writings Selden was both more detailed and more guarded. He minimized, so far as possible, his break with the myths of England's British origins, and gave a complex account of the Norman Conquest.[145] For example Selden was willing to recognize that there may have been some continuity between British and Saxon law: some laws in existence in the seventeenth century 'have been carefully enough kept up from the time of the Saxons, and perhaps from an earlier date'. And he was even able to talk of 'our English British Law'.[146] Yet his own treatment of the Saxon invasions was, in spite of this, essentially a statement of Gothicism. The Saxons, he said,

> in process of time, contrary than the Britains first hoped, established to themselves in divers parts of what we now call England, several Kingdomes, extruding Vortigern's posterity, and their subjects, into the Western parts, where to this day they remain. And how can we but conjecture that of particular Customes of Law-government in their own Countrey, they made requisite use in this their part of the Island? What those were, until Christianity made some abolition, may best be observed out of *Tacitus de moribus Germanorum*; who relates divers of their Customes and Rites Religious.[147]

Recent work done on Selden's idea of feudalism (largely as contained in *Titles of Honor*) has strengthened this view of Selden as a Gothicist. This subject has been well discussed by others, and I propose only to summarize their conclusions.[148] Selden saw feudal institutions as developing amongst the Germanic tribes that overran the Roman Empire. This of course included the Anglo-Saxons, who developed their own forms of feudal tenure. The Normans also developed feudal tenures; and consequently in 1066 there was some alteration in the exact forms in use, but the fact remained that feudalism as such was a 'Gothic' institution. Not many other legal scholars of early Stuart England can be said to have possessed a developed idea of feudalism, apart from Spelman (whom we will glance at in due course). But one who does seem to have had at least some understanding of the matter was Sir Roger Owen. Like Selden he viewed feudalism as a Gothic institution, though he went much further in stressing that it was introduced to England as a result of a catastrophic Saxon conquest of the country. For example he wrote

> That all Tenures in the foundation of the English Monarchy arose out of the Crowne upon the Conquest of the Brittons by the English Saxons. The King haveing all the South side of this Island gave unto A many Thousand Acres And gave unto B some hundred of Acres To Hold of him by knights Service and Soccage, and to come unto his Courts And B againe subdivided and gave out some of his lands upon the same Tenures and Condicions unto C . . . [149]

But – to return to Selden – the history of Parliament was also fitted into a Gothicist framework. As with Lambarde, Parliament was deemed a Saxon institution with a Norman-French name.

> These Assemblies were termed by the Saxons, *Wittena gemotes*, i.e. Meetings of the Wise Men, and *Micil sinodes*, i.e. the Great Assemblies. At length we borrowed of the French the name of *Parliaments*, which before the time of Henry the First, Polydore Virgil sayes, were very rarely held. An usage, that not without good reason seems to have come from the ancient Germans.[150]

Again, this was a view widely shared amongst legal antiquarians,[151] though there was a much stronger tendency in relation to Parliament (as opposed to other institutions or laws) to trace its history back to the Britons.[152] But they tended to be much vaguer on British assemblies than on Saxon ones. Camden, for example,

origins of Britons or Saxons

said that 'some gather' there were parliamentary bodies amongst the Britons, and he talked of the 'Kifrithin' as a 'parliament-like' assembly.[153] But Arthur Agarde followed the Lambarde/Selden line exactly in ignoring the Britons and saying that the word 'Parliament' was French but that the institution could be found amongst the Saxons.[154]

From the time of the Saxon Conquest continuity was provided, according to Selden, by the fact that English kings began the practice of confirming the laws of their predecessors. In this way the continuity of law was preserved. Laws were handed on from one king to another like the baton in a relay race.

> There are a great many laws of King Ina, Alfred, Edward, Athelstan, Edmund, Edgar, Ethelred, and Knute the Dane, written in the Saxon language; which have lasted till these very times. 'For King Knute gave order ('tis William of Malmsbury speaks) that all the Laws which had been made by former Kings, and especially by his Predecessor Ethelred, should under pain of his displeasure and a Fine, be constantly observed: For the keeping of which, even now in the time of those who are called the Good, people swear in the name of King Edward; not that he appointed them, but that he observed them.[155]

This continuity from Saxon times not only provided some mechanism for the transmission of customary law (as well as obscuring the distinction between the making of law and the observance of it) but also explained how the Conquest could be bridged. The Conqueror reasonably agreed to let the conquered people retain the use of their old laws. Consequently,

> to refer the original of our English Laws to that Conquest (as some make bold to do) is a huge mistake; for as much as they are of a far more ancient Date. For it is a remark amongst Statesmen, That new acquired Empires, do run some hazard by attempting to make new Laws: and the Norman did warily provide against this danger, by bestowing upon the yielding conquered Nation the requital of their ancient Law.[156]

Now, clearly this sort of view of things was likely to produce a rather knowing interpretation of ideas of immemoriality and continuity. Selden was aware that these things were legal fictions, applicable to the realm of law but not to the wider realm of facts. He was therefore able to add to this initial statement the remarks that William's allowance of the preservation of the Saxon laws was rather 'for shew than use'. William was able to alter their real meaning 'by sly interpretations against the sense and meaning' of the original laws, and to make new laws himself, 'for the times on this side of the Norman entrance, are so full of new Laws, especially such as belong to the right or Tenancy or Vassalage'.[157] Elsewhere Selden said that 'although one may truly say . . . that the English Empire and Government was overthrown' at the Conquest, nevertheless the new laws introduced did 'take their denomination from the English, rather than from the Normans'.[158] The preservation of continuity here was strained to the limit, but was, all the same, maintained.

It is easy to see how these early studies in English history could culminate in the theory of customary law that was found in Selden's 'Notes' on Fortescue, and which we examined earlier. Present in both was the view of law as a body of rules in continuous evolution, transmitted from generation to generation as custom, and – except for statutory law – immemorial, in the sense that its beginnings were unknown.

It will be noted from this account of Selden's legal theory that he derived his assessment of the nature of the English constitution from an examination of the positive laws of the realm. He showed how the various parts of the constitution had come together over time – Parliament in Saxon times, the laws of land-tenure substantially after the Conquest, the various legal officers and local courts at various times [159] – but there had never been a time in the past when the English constitution was exactly what it was in the present. So Selden cannot be said to be offering a theory that defended present political and legal arrangements simply by saying that things were thus at some previous time, and thus things ought to remain. To the extent that his theory was prescriptive it must be understood that prescription meant justification of the present, nothing more. And immemoriality functioned as a way of saying that the origins of things were unknown and hence irrelevant. If we place Selden's view of English legal history into this theoretical context we can see just how fully the English common lawyer, Selden, resembled the English divine, Hooker. Selden assumed that government, monarchy especially, existed to serve certain ends. He further assumed that institutions widely accepted in fact, or accepted for a long time, best served those ends. Hence customary laws and institutions best ensure the attainment of society's rational goals. This was so not because there was any merit in antiquity as such but because human affairs were so structured that long continuance was proof of rationality and fitness. He thus developed a view of prescription that in effect asserted that the present state of things is as good as human capacity allowed it to be, for we can only derive knowledge of what human beings ought to do from an assessment of what they have found it convenient to do. Hence the value of custom – for Selden and for Hooker.

The central ideological task of Hooker's *Laws of Ecclesiastical Polity* (revealed particularly in his Preface) was to defend the existing church polity against claims that it ought to be altered. One component of the arsenal of weapons that he deployed for this purpose was the use of a concept of custom very similar to that employed by the common lawyers. (Indeed there has been some, rather inconclusive, speculation that Hooker's work 'was a product of the law schools' in that much of its essence 'derived from his study of British institutions and the laws of the land').[160] The concept underlay, for example, this most characteristic passage:

> if they [puritans] think that we ought to prove the ceremonies commodious which we have retained [i.e. since the Reformation], they do in this point very greatly deceive themselves. For in all right and equity, that which the Church hath received and held so long for good, that which public approbation hath ratified, must carry the benefit of presumption with it to be accounted meet and convenient. They which have stood up as yesterday [i.e. the puritans again] to challenge it of defect, must prove their challenge.[161]

Custom – the long continuance of institutions, laws or ceremonies – provided a presumption of rationality. This rationality consisted in the development of particular regulations compatible with abstract reason but 'meet and convenient' for particular circumstances. Hooker, in Sheldon Wolin's words, 'insisted that individual reason must often bow before a kind of historical reason [artificial reason?] shaped by the experience and wisdom of other ages.'[162] But – and again this was very similar to the common lawyers – Hooker was not blindly opposed to change. Things evolved and, as a good Aristotelian, Hooker was capable of seeing things becoming more and more themselves over time as their potentialities became actual.[163] Indeed, as we have been seeing, the concept of custom required an acceptance of evolutionary progress of a sort. The present state of things, which was not identical to any past state, was always good, both because it was the product of refinement over time (i.e. customary) and because it contained the potential for future improvement: 'all things that are, are good'.[164] However, Hooker also warned against the dangers of change, of human meddling with the process of customary evolution.[165] And a final point of contact between Hooker and the common lawyers was Hooker's primary emphasis that the laws should be laws of reason before they were customs. Some customs could be bad, irrational, and these were not to be followed: there were such things as 'lewd and wicked customs'.[166] Yet, in the last resort, the presumption in favour of the rationality of custom was strong and not easily overriden:

> The things which so long experience of all ages has confirmed and made profitable, let not us presume to condemn as follies and toys, because we sometimes know not the cause and reason of them.[167]

Thus, the central features of Hooker's theory of custom were identical to those of 'the common-law mind': customs provided a presumption of rationality; they required an acceptance of change, though most also warned of the dangers of *deliberate* alteration of customs; and they were linked to a type of rationality that was 'artificial' or in some way different from natural, abstract, or deductive reason.

There were two modifications of the 'standard model' of legal history that could be found amongst early Stuart common lawyers and scholars learned in the law. The first of them was based on a denial of the principle of continuity, the second of them on a strengthening of it. The former is generally associated with Henry Spelman; the latter with Edward Coke. We shall examine these two alternatives in turn. Spelman is well-known as the earliest English historian of the feudal law and for seeing feudalism as imposed on England at the Norman Conquest. I do not propose to reiterate what is already known about him.[168] However I would like to point out that Spelman's views were not quite as innovatory as they have sometimes been portrayed – that his views were, indeed, a *modification* of the standard model and not a rejection of it. The difference between him and Selden or Lambarde was one of degree

rather than kind. Like most common lawyers Spelman had a view
of the law that saw it as in constant gradual evolution from Saxon
times:

> To tell the Government of England under the old Saxon Laws,
> seemeth an Utopia to us present; strange and uncouth: yet can
> there be no period assign'd, wherein either the frame of those
> Laws was abolished, or this of ours entertained; but as Day
> and Night creep insenibly, one upon the other, so also hath
> this Alteration grown upon us insensibly, every age altering
> something, and no age seeming more than what themselves
> are Actors in, nor thinking it to have been otherwise than as
> themselves discover it by the present.[169]

It was amongst the Saxons that English common law originated.
This happened when England became united under one monarchy,
at which time it was decided 'that no part of the Kingdom should
henceforth be goven'd by any particular law, but all alike by a
Common Law'.[170] In his brief sketch of the history of Parliament
Spelman added further to this picture. He said of the feudal law
that it was the place 'from whence all that Part of our Common-law
that concerneth Fee and Tenures hath Original, and which our
Common-law also affirmeth'.[171] This clearly manifests the extent
to which the continuity of law from Saxon times was, for Spelman,
a convenient fiction. If by common law he meant only law common
to the whole nation then it became a matter of indifference what the
content of that law was: it was infinitely malleable. There is nothing
in this incompatible with the views of Selden or with accepted
notions of the idea of customary law. But Spelman was a little more
unusual in admitting of complete discontinuity at the Conquest. He
admitted that in Saxon times laws were made by consent, but denied
any continuity between this practice and the Norman parliaments,
for at 1066 we 'come to the Times of the Conqueror, wherein *Novus
Seclorum nascitur ordo*; and from whence, as from a new Period, we
must now take all our Projections'.[172] From this point he gives a
summary of his view of the historical evolution of Parliament that
has been well-analysed by others.

   We can say of Spelman, then, that although he developed a
more discontinuous model for English history than many others,
he developed it within the framework of older ideas about the
continuity of an evolving law having existed from Anglo-Saxon

times. His break with older ideas was less than catastrophic. A number of other writers share his more discontinuous view of things without fully abandoning the 'standard model'. A fine example is William Hakewill's paper (read to the Society of Antiquaries) on the antiquity of English law. He remarked that Fortescue's authority, or his love of his country and profession, seem to have 'drawn some late writers also to publish the same opinion'. But, Hakewill wrote, this view cannot be maintained, because

> the laws of the Britaines were utterly extinct by the Romans; their laws again by the Saxons; and lastly, theirs by the Danes and Normans much altered.[173]

This appealingly realistic vision of English history should not obscure the fact that Hakewill fits the standard model constructed above in that he (1) said that the Saxons were a new beginning for English law; and (2) implied at least some continuity from Saxon times, since he said Saxon laws were altered not abrogated. These points are borne out by the remainder of his tract in which he said that the Saxon Conquest was as 'absolute' as any in history and caused a complete change in the law and constitution,[174] that the Danes altered these a little,[175] and that the Norman Conquest was not such a catastrophe as might be thought. This last point was defended on two grounds: first, English and Norman laws in 1066 were in any case rather similar (thanks partly to the common influence on both of the Danes); and, second, Henry I restored the laws that existed before the Conquest in any case.[176] In spite of Hakewill's language of catastrophism, his view of legal history fits into the paradigm provided above. Indeed of major accounts of English legal history there are few that do not. An example, though, is provided by the anonymous *Use of the Law*. This work derived the entire judicial system (including – uniquely I think – the administrative division of the country into shires) from the Norman Conquest. It cannot be said that this tract was based on much historical scholarship but it did show the advantages of the perspective it adopted in that it was able to give an extremely neat and easily-comprehensible account of the origin of feudal tenures in the military needs of William the Conqueror.[177]

These discontinuous models of history are, at least, models of historical *change*. As such they reinforce the central theme of this chapter, which is that the common lawyers habitually saw the

common law as a set of rules that was constantly changing. Historical evolution was at the heart of the common law. Historical
evolution provided the major ground for the defence of English law
in terms of its being immemorially fitted to the needs of the nation.
Fortescue, as we have seen, provided the outlines of an alternative
model which saw English law as immutable from the time of the
Britons. This was a view that Sir Edward Coke tried to adopt,
with sad consequences for the overall coherence of his writings.
Coke's views seem to have struck most people around the turn of
the century as being either novel or foolish (we have already heard
Hakewill on this). The civilian Hayward said in 1604 that he would
not spend much time on the idea of English law as being unchanged
since British times 'because it is not commonly received'.[178] Bacon
was dismissive of the idea.[179] And an anonymous contributor to the
Society of Antiquaries' debates thought the view highly unsound:

> Mr Attorney General in his third report hath made a very learned
> discourse of the antiquity of the laws of England, where he
> maketh mention of British laws . . .   But of those laws of this
> day I think there remaineth few or none, except they were
> preserved among the Britons, that fled into Wales: for the Saxons
> having made a full conquest, did alter as well the laws as the
> language . . . [180]

Pocock, Ferguson and Sommerville have all assumed that Coke's
ideas were typical, though none of them has cited a major work
on English legal history or on the nature of the law that supported
Coke's views.[181] Given what has been shown above, it is apparent
that Coke's (or Fortescue's) argument actually runs counter to a
wide body of opinion, and is incompatible with generally accepted
views of the common law as a changing, adaptive customary law.

The paradox is, of course, that Coke himself accepted the idea that
English law, as well as being a law of reason, was also customary.
This much we have already seen. It was inherent in the way he
explained his idea of the 'artificial reason' of the law. One of his
statements of this idea was quoted earlier in this chapter (from the
first part of the *Institutes*), but he said much the same thing in his
remarks on Calvin's Case:

> First, on our own part, 'hesterni enim sumus et ignoramus, et
> vita nostra sicut umbra super terram'; for we are but of yesterday,

(and therefore had need of the wisdom of those that were before us) and had been ignorant, if we had not received light and knowledge from our forefathers and our days upon the earth are but as a shadow, in respect of the old ancient days and times past, wherein the laws have been by the wisdom of the most excellent men, in many successions of ages, by long and continual experience, the trial of right and truth, fined and refined, which no one man, being of so short a time, albeit he had in his head the wisdom of all the men in the world in any one age could ever have effected or attained unto.[182]

This statement of Coke's was eloquent and powerful. But it was also, like many of the views we have examined above, dependent upon a view of law as evolving. English law had been tested by several generations of fine minds, added to and altered, so that the end product was perfectly fitted to the needs of the nation. In addition the laws themselves embodied a wisdom superior to the natural reason of any individual human mind. There was nothing paradoxical in such a view of law as evolving custom, and when Pocock says that the common lawyers view of custom was paradoxical in that it implied both evolution and immutability he mistook the fact that Coke tried to graft Fortescue's historical simplicities onto the complex historical views that he espoused elsewhere for a more universal problem. In fact Pocock's paradox was really just Coke's confusion.

Coke first advanced his peculiar historical views in the 'Preface' to the Third Part of his *Reports*, which was published in 1602. The 'Preface' to the Second Part, published the same year, had said that though England had been conquered several times, the conquerors had never altered the laws because they realized how good they were.[183] But this was as nothing compared to what was to follow. One must be careful not to caricature Coke: his views are not as clear-cut as is sometimes indicated. To assert that some of the laws of the Britons survive to this day or that the Norman Conquest did not alter the law was not incompatible with the historical views we have outlined above. What caused problems was any assertion that the law, or at least its basic framework, was immutable, and hence had not changed significantly since the Britons.

So, when Coke wrote that 'the rules and principles of the science of the common law . . . do manifestly prove that the common law of England had been time out of mind of man before the conquest', and was not altered by the Conqueror the remark might be taken as a platitude.[184] But Coke moved on to discuss the opinion held by some

> that Brutus the first King of this land, as soon as he had settled himself in his kingdom, for the safe and peaceable government of his people, wrote a book in the Greek tongue, calling it the Laws of the Britons, and he collected the same out of the laws of the Trojans.[185]

Acceptance of this view would not only have meant that the law was not really immemorial (since a beginning was being found for it) but would (more seriously) introduce a law-giver above and outside the law into English constitutional history. Not surprisingly Coke never signalled his acceptance of the view. He said, in fact, that 'I will not examine these things in a quo warranto; the ground thereof I think was best known to the authors and writers of them',[186] which sounds like a dismissal of the matter. Immediately following it Coke embarked on a long discussion of whether the ancient Britons used the Greek language for their judicial records. Once again, the discussion was inconclusive (and meandering) and seemed to culminate in the remark 'that hereby as I think it is sufficiently proved that the laws of England are of much greater antiquity than they are reported to be, and than any the constitutions or laws imperial of Roman Emperors'.[187] There followed a few more remarks on the laws of the Britons and then Coke concluded his discussion of this particular matter by quoting Fortescue:

> And throughout the period of these nations and their kings, the realm has been continuously ruled by the same customs as it is now, customs which if they had not been the best, some of those kings would have changed for the sake of justice or by the impulse of caprice, and totally abolished them, especially the Romans, who judged almost the whole of the rest of the world by their laws.[188]

What did all this amount to? The answer is far from clear. The citation of Fortescue, and perhaps the passage quoted just before that, seem to indicate that Coke wanted to share Fortescue's view that the Britons' laws had been preserved through subsequent history. Yet in fact he said nothing very definite on the matter and always pulled back from making any bold assertions about the Britons. It was perhaps the case that he wished to show how old English law was (as Fortescue did) but was unwilling to assert its immutability since the time of the Britons, presumably aware of the difficulties in such a view. To have fully committed himself to the opinion he quoted from Fortescue, Coke would have had to contradict the principles he had put forward under the guise of artificial reason. In several of the 'Prefaces' to later parts of his *Reports* Coke elaborated on particular aspects of his historical views. These elaborations confirmed the points we have made here. The 'Preface' to the Sixth Part of the *Reports* defended Coke's claim that English laws had remained unchanged through all conquests against the objections of civil lawyers.

> And . . . some of another profession are not persuaded that the common laws of England are of so great antiquity, as there [i.e. 3 Rep. Pref] superlatively is spoken. True it is, that the said period was my own opinion, but not out of my own head: for it is the judgment of that most reverend and honourable judge, Sir John Fortescue, knight . . .

And hereupon Coke proceeded to quote entire Chapter XVII of Fortescue's *De Laudibus*.[189] But when he became more specific it was clear that Coke was totally reliant on Fortescue for his belief in the British sources of English law, and had no coherently developed theory of his own. He examined four particular points of law in order to show 'that the common law in these four particular cases was before the Conquest, as now it is'.[190] In other words, when it came to matters of detail Coke tacitly dropped his claims for the British antiquity of the law and undertook only to prove its continuity since Saxon times, the standard view. Similarly, the remarks that introduced the Eighth Part of the *Reports* undertook to provide documentary support for Coke's beliefs only in part. There was no mention at all of Fortescue or the Britons, and what Coke did was to show

> that it doth appear most plain by successive authority in history what I have positively affirmed out of record, that the grounds of our common laws at this day were beyond the memory or register of any beginning, and the same which the Norman conqueror then found within this realm of England.[191]

In support of this Coke examined 'historians' rather than legal documents, and by 'historians' he meant essentially the medieval chroniclers. He showed that they all agreed in saying that all of the kings since Edward the Confessor had preserved the continuity of the law by agreeing always to rule according to the ancient laws of the realm. And it was the surviving laws of the Saxon kings that formed the earliest texts of the ancient laws.[192] So here, where Coke has dropped his reliance on Fortescue, he seemed to be claiming no more than that English law was both Gothic and immemorial. We have already seen that there was no necessary contradiction between these two things, and that this was a widely-held belief.

Like many of the other legal scholars whom we have examined, Coke discussed the antiquity of Parliament. He did this in the 'Preface' to the Ninth Part of the *Reports*. Interestingly, he was again led astray by putting overmuch reliance upon the testimony of one document, so that his use here of the *Mirror of Justices* was analogous to his earlier use of Fortescue. According to Coke the *Mirror* gave a full account 'of the laws and usages of this kingdom, whereby this realm was governed about 1100 years past'.[193] He thought it an accurate picture of the judicial system as it was during the reign of King Arthur, that showed

> the great antiquity of the said courts of the common law, and particularly of the High Court of Parliament ever since the time of King Arthur, who reigned about the year of our Lord 516, not that this court and the rest were instituted then, but that the reach of this treatise extendeth no higher than to write of the laws and usages of this realm continued since the reign of that king.[194]

Having thus linked Parliament to pre-Saxon times, Coke went on to show that it continued to function in its normal way through both the period of the Heptarchy and the Norman Conquest.[195] Like many others Coke said that William I gave the name 'Parliament' to the institution, 'yet manifest it is . . . that he changed not the frame or jurisdiction of this court in any point'.[196] So, Coke seems to have taken the opportunity afforded to him by the *Mirror of Justices* to make wild claims for the antiquity of Parliament, just as he made extreme claims for the antiquity of the common law by using Fortescue. Yet the evidence shows that when he came to discuss more detailed matters and to base his arguments on wider documentation he often tacitly abandoned his more extreme claims and accepted an historical account widely held by other legal scholars.

Coke's views were therefore less resounding and more hesitant and confused than is generally allowed. It is not surprising. No work by a well-informed legal scholar would appear to accept Fortescue's notion of the immutable persistence of British laws. Certainly there are a few passing remarks that reflect the view, possibly reflecting the influence and prestige of Coke's own writings. Such were the remarks of the Speaker of the Commons, Edward Phelps, in his speech at the close of the 1604 session (July 7). He said the laws of England were of three kinds: the common law drawn from the laws of God, reason and nature, which is 'not mutable'; positive law, 'founded, changed, and altered by and through the occasions and policies of times'; and customs and usages 'without known beginnings'.[197] Or, another example, Michael Dalton's opening paragraph to his *Countrey Justice* which said that the common laws were 'those whereby this Realme was governed many hundred yeares before the Conquest',[198] thus tending to suggest immutability. But neither of these examples is easy to interpret, and it is simply not clear what exactly was being implied or stated in them.

There is at least one substantial work that did explore the path of Fortescue in some detail, George Saltern's *Of the Ancient Lawes of Great Britaine* (1605). It is interesting in showing the sort of company Coke was in danger of keeping. Saltern's aim was to show that the laws of England were genuinely Christian, and more particularly that the laws of the Britons, 'appering yet in the bodie of our common lawes' had as their basic principles 'the verie Lawes of the eternal God'.[199] He cited in his support the same passage of Fortescue that was used by Coke.[200] Saltern viewed all law as being a 'covenant made by God with the societie of men', and nothing contrary to divine law could be allowed, even 'though all the world in a joynt Parlament confirme it'.[201] His point in showing that English law went back to the time of the Trojan Britons was that this enabled him to link it to Japhet and hence to that 'first age' in which the laws of God and nature were more fully and properly observed.[202] He not only argued that the form of the English constitution was settled in the days of the Britons,[203] but in a discussion of the law of outlawry he was able to trace a principle of English law backwards through Bracton and Caesar to the outlawing of Cain in Genesis 4, showing that the law in each case was the same.[204] Now the upshot of this argument was quite antipathetic to the idea of 'artificial reason'. It opened up the law to examination by divines who could assess its conformity with the laws revealed in Scripture. It is perhaps the final irony that one of the few of his contemporaries to share Coke's interest in the British origins of the law should take such a very 'unprofessional' view of it. Saltern was a most untypical legal writer. He viewed the law as immutable in order to make it subservient to *natural* reason. Lawyers, on the other hand, tended to make the law the province of an *artificial* reason possessed only by themselves, and to this end saw it as mutable. Only they could perceive the rationality beneath the change.

With respect to Pocock's study of the common-law mind in *The Ancient Constitution and the Feudal Law* we can now draw two conclusions. Firstly, Pocock exaggerated the typicality of the thought of Sir Edward Coke, and this distorted the conclusions that he reached. In particular, he underestimated the degree to which common lawyers were prepared to accept the considerable historical mutability of the law (and the degree to which they were able to do so without falling into paradox). And, secondly, Pocock's analysis of the common lawyers' crucial conceptual tool, custom, needs to be supplemented by an analysis of the concept of reason.[205] Custom was, at least logically, subordinate to reason, and the function of the common law theory of custom cannot be fully appreciated without a full discussion of reason.[206]

The wider implications and historiographical conclusions of this re-evaluation of the common-law mind are the subject of Chapter 3.

3

Problems and Implications

Tidying up loose ends can be an untidy business. In consequence this will be an untidy chapter. It is required to perform three separate tasks which together will both flesh out our portrait of English ancient constitutionalism and lay a foundation for the second part of this book (which places the theory of the ancient constitution into the background of early-seventeenth century English political discourse). The first of the three tasks will involve a consideration of the historiographical debates surrounding the nature of ancient constitutionalist thought. Of these there are two: the question of its insularity; and the question of its relationship with the idea of conquest. For both of these matters the findings of the previous chapter have clear implications. The second of our tasks will be to determine the political implications of English ancient constitutionalism. What sort of political theory could be raised upon the foundations that it provided? Did it have a 'radical face', as some historians have argued? Our third and final task – the most difficult of them all – will be to examine the chronology of the theory of the ancient constitution. What were its origins and sources? When did it begin? When did it end? We shall then discover that the theory, in its 'classic phase', lasted only from the reign of James I (though it had deep Tudor roots) to the Civil War (though it had also a lengthy aftermath).

(A)   TWO CONTROVERSIES: INSULARITY AND CONQUEST THEORY

(I)

The question of the 'insularity' of the common law has already been broached (in Chapter 1).[1] At that point, the problem of insularity was resolved into a number of separate, though overlapping, component questions:

1. What knowledge did English common lawyers have of Continental jurisprudence and its methods?
2. Did they use this knowledge in the study of English law?
3. Did they think this history of English law possessed a unique pattern or one shared with other European legal codes?
4. Were their attitudes to history peculiar to themselves or shared with Continental scholars?

The material presented in the previous chapter suggests some answers to these questions.

Critics of the insularity thesis, advanced by Pocock and Kelley, have demonstrated conclusively one point: English lawyers were *not* ignorant of either civil law or humanist jurisprudence. Whatever insularity they may have shown, it did not come from ignorance of laws other than their own. Nor did it come from an ignorance of the sort of legal scholarship being carried out elsewhere in Europe. Hans Pawlish, for example, has shown that Sir John Davies – one of the two paradigm figures in Pocock's account of the common-law mind – made extensive use of civil law principles in his attempt to import English common law to Ireland and 'was thoroughly familiar not only with the Roman and canon laws, but also with the literature of French legal humanism'. The same is true, also, of the other of Pocock's paradigm figures, Sir Edward Coke, whose library catalogue betrays his knowledge of both civil law and legal humanism.[2] With other legal writers and scholars there is even less doubt: Lord Chancellor Ellesmere was well educated in humanistic and civil law matters, and the scholarly methods of John Selden were as up-to-date as those of any European scholar.[3] Other common lawyers, most notably Sir John Doddridge, displayed their knowledge of Renaissance learning through their concern with the methodological debates between Aristotelians and Ramists, one of the key features of sixteenth-century intellectual life.[4] On a more general level, it has been shown that the English common lawyer of the sixteenth and early-seventeenth centuries remained in touch with European intellectual trends, and made use of a broad knowledge that extended beyond the common law itself to civil law, canon law and humanistic method.[5]

Nevertheless, in spite of all this there remains a sense in which it can still be maintained that the English common law mind was indeed insular. The fact that common lawyers had some knowledge of civil law and legal humanism, and that they used that knowledge in certain contexts, does not demonstrate that it affected their view of English legal history.[6] Does this point us towards a type of insularity possessed by the common lawyers? It has already been shown (Chapter 1) that, in broad outline at least, the attitude to history of the common lawyers was not too different from that of Continental scholars: our answer clearly does not lie in that direction. That leaves us with the matter raised by questions (2) and (3) above: was there something in the particular accounts given by common-law writers of the historical development of English law that we can call insular?

There was, though its exact definition is elusive. Perhaps the best way of putting it is to say that the insularity of the common-law mind was not a product of its ignorance; insularity was a carefully-developed principle. This point is a straightforward consequence of the argument presented in Chapter 2. The English common lawyers developed a strong sense of the historical mutability of the law. Central to this was a concept of custom, the sources of which were in St German but which was developed and elaborated – possibly with some humanist influence – over the later sixteenth century. Inherent in the historical picture erected around this concept was the idea of separate national codes of customary law. Each nation had a body of customs appropriate to its circumstances and needs. National law codes were particular determinations of reason (or the law of nature) designed to make general rational principles appropriate to a particular environment. Thus the laws of any nation – at least their customary as opposed to their enacted laws – could be understood only with reference to their 'insular' history, the way they had developed over time. Only thus could their inherent rationality be discerned (and only then after painstaking effort). In the case of England we have seen that common lawyers generally saw its law as evolving from a Saxon base, with some limited room allowed for the addition of Danish and Norman customs.

Thus, the common lawyers' view of English law was insular because of the concept of custom that underpinned it. But they were also aware that other nations might have similarly 'insular' legal histories (though the presence of Roman law on the Continent could complicate matters). Norman customs, for example, were a development of Danish ones; and French customary law evolved from the customs of the Gauls. England was unusual, perhaps, in that a greater body of its law was customary than was the case in other parts of Europe. But the principle that customary laws were inherently insular because they evolved in particular environments could in theory be widely applied. England, as John Selden demonstrated at length in his *Ad Fletam Dissertatio*, had been relatively free of the influence of Roman law: but this was a judgement based not on ignorance (quite the contrary). Rather it reflected the view that the bulk of English law was, as a contingent fact, of customary origin without much admixture of civil law. Once that point was accepted, then the insularity of English legal history followed as a matter of course.

Insularity, then, was not a product of the ignorance of other law codes. It was a product of a sophisticated view of how customs developed and of why they were justifiable. It follows from this also that the common-law mind was not insular because of its primitive views about historical change. The insularity arose from its well-developed awareness of legal change, and of the mechanisms that underlay it in the case of customary law (which English law primarily was). In short, insularity should be taken as proof of the sophistication of common-law thought rather than as proof of its backwardness.[7]

(II)

A second controverted matter raised by Pocock's portrait of the common-law mind has been the role that conquest theory played in it. This is part of a wider debate over the role of conquest theory in English political thought in general.[8] The debate originated in Pocock's claim that English writers did not admit the reality of conquest in English history because to do so would disrupt the continuity of the law. Consequently, Englishmen were highly reluctant to derive the rights of their king from conquest.[9] Both Wallace and Skinner attempted to modify this thesis. Skinner showed that a large number of chroniclers did admit the reality of the Conquest as a true conquest, and Wallace pointed to a number of Royalist writers of the 1640s who did derive the King's rights from the Conquest.[10] Recently J. P. Sommerville has produced an incisive critique of all three of these writers. He argues that large numbers of early Stuart theorists were prepared to accept the fact of genuine conquest occurring in English history. They were able to do this because their political thought was not as fundamentally historical as Pocock, Skinner and Wallace all agreed that it was. This latter trio believed that political theorists in early-seventeenth century England derived their political principles from their views of the history of the English constitution and common law. That is, they believed political theory in this period to be primarily prescriptive in character, a matter of history not abstract reason. Sommerville completely rejects this. Political theory under the early Stuarts was, he argues, seldom purely historical. It generally derived its basic features from theory, which is to say from philosophical principles outside the historical process. Hence an acceptance of conquest did not necessarily pose problems for them since their theories were not dependent on mere facts.

There is much to be said in favour of Pocock's original position on conquest. Two distinctions must be kept clear: first, between conquest in general and the Norman Conquest; and second, between common-law thought and other intellectual traditions. Common lawyers were prepared, as we have seen, to admit the reality of conquest in English history – *but* they admitted it within the guidelines laid down by the basic structural features of their view of the past, namely immemoriality and continuity. To avoid allowing a place in English legal and constitutional development for institutions outside of the body of the common law itself, they were required to ensure that there was no *discontinuity* since the beginning of good legal records. Thus, common lawyers were quite happy with the Saxon conquest, and some members of the Elizabethan Society of Antiquaries saw conquest as a basic feature of English history. But the conquests they allowed were themselves immemorial, and did not provide a warrant for the introduction into the English constitution of a sovereign lawmaker outside of and superior to the law itself. The Norman Conquest, though, was a different matter. Admitting that William the Conqueror refashioned the laws of England would have meant admitting discontinuity. It would also have suggested that English law was not immemorial but the product of a royal will. Might that not suggest that all law could be remodelled by kings at their pleasure? Perhaps – and then again perhaps not: but common lawyers were not inclined to take the risk. In consequence, common lawyers tended to preserve the continuity of English law across the year 1066, either by denying that a conquest had occurred at all, or by admitting that it had but arguing also that it had not disrupted the continuity of the law. The old laws were preserved as the customs proper to the English nation.[11] Both Selden and Coke, for example, were prepared to accept that the Norman Conquest was a genuine conquest while arguing that it did not break the continuity of the law.[12] Indeed, of those who did adopt a basically common-law perspective Robert Mason was one of few who were prepared to envisage any real discontinuity at the conquest. But even he, in order to ensure that he did not 'set at liberty the claim of the sovereign power of a conqueror which is to be limited or restrained by no laws', was forced to argue that Statute (above all Magna Carta) did 'limit that sovereign power' claimed at the Conquest. (He did, however, remain reticent about whether or not William really had the power of a Conqueror).[13]

The second distinction we need to make is between the thought of common lawyers (and others working within the common-law framework) and the thought of those who belonged in other intellectual traditions. The second part of this book will show that common lawyers, civil lawyers, and clerics used separable political languages in early Stuart England. We should not conflate these separate languages. Pocock's argument was about the common-law mind. To say that he was wrong by pointing to things said by clerics or civilians, as Sommerville does, is to confuse two issues. These are: (1) the question of what role conquest played in common-law thought; and (2) the question of how, in the early Stuart period, common-law thought was related to other intellectual positions (some of which might allow a much greater role to conquest theory). The first question can only be answered with reference to common-law writings themselves. This we have done, showing that common lawyers were unwilling to recognize the *Norman* Conquest as a true conquest, or (at best) were prepared to concede that it had been a genuine conquest only with the proviso that it had no disruptive effects on legal continuity because William and his immediate successors reconfirmed the existing institutions and laws. The second question requires a broad analysis of the structures of political discourse in early Stuart England. This will be provided in the second half of this book. The result of this will be to show how the common-law mind was one of several 'minds' to be found in the period. In the present context, however, it needs to be stressed that demonstrating that the possessors of these other minds believed that the Norman Conquest introduced new laws to England in fact tells us *nothing whatsoever about the common-law mind*. And that, after all, was the subject of Pocock's book.

Consequently, Somerville's discussion of the theories of conquest found in such civilians and clerics as John Cowell, Sir John Hayward, Hadrian Saravia, David Owen and Calybute Downing, while interesting in itself, need not lead to any revision of Pocock's portrait of the common-law mind. There is certainly no doubt that members of these professions, intense rivals to the common lawyers in many cases, were indeed prepared to take a stance critical of the common-law tradition on the subject of conquest. Sir John Hayward, for example, bluntly asserted that William the Conqueror 'changed the greatest part' of the law, and 'brought in the customes of Normandie in their stead'. Elsewhere, he was explicitly critical of the common-law doctrine of the immemorial continuity of the law.[14] William Fulbecke (who was, it seems, half common lawyer and half civilian) was less blunt than Hayward, but said much the same thing. 'The law of this Realme', he commented, 'as the Realme it selfe suffered chaunge by conquest'. But, qualifying this, Fulbecke remarked that 'rather reason then soveraignety, and consent rather than commaund' were responsible for the alterations. All the same, William the Conqueror did change the laws of England, albeit with considerable circumspection.[15] These were not isolated voices,[16] but it should still be remembered that the questions they raise for us concern, not the role of conquest in common-law thought, but the place of common-law thought in the general pattern of political thought to be found in early-seventeenth century England. This is the subject of Part II of this book.

Sommerville's wider argument, that political thought in early Stuart England was based on reason and theory rather than history, is of fundamental importance, but takes us some distance from our subject. In so far as it applies to the common lawyers, this particular distinction (reason versus history) is one that has been central to the previous chapters. Sommerville has rightly perceived that it is wrong to deny that the common lawyers argued from reason, and wrong to think that they relied solely on history. But if we transform his reason/history distinction into our distinction of reason/custom, then it becomes apparent that the distinction is one without a substantial difference. For the common lawyers (and Hooker) argument from history (or custom) was a means of arguing from reason, and it is impossible sharply to distinguish the 'rational' from the 'historical' elements in their thought. When they examined the history of English law they were examining a rational process, but this reason was an immanent reason (i.e. the rationality of the law and its history could not be determined by comparison with *external* rational principles but was discernible by (or as) the artificial reason inherent in lawyers (or customary law)). This conception of things made possible a complex fusion of rational and historical arguments.

(B)   COMMON LAW, POLITICAL THEORY AND RADICALISM

The common law view that the body of the English common law possessed an inherent rationality – a view we have just sketched – is the best starting place for a consideration of the political consequences of common-law theory. The one essential political conclusion of that theory was that the common law (and hence the English constitution) was an entirely self-contained entity, requiring no interference or amendment from either general rational principles or other legal systems. This was a position that sixteenth-century lawyers worked out with reference to the relationship between common law and equity, and it became an essential feature of early-seventeenth-century common-law jurisprudence.

Equity and its relationship with English law was the chief subject of St German's *Doctor and Student*. The purpose of the book was to demonstrate that the Englishman ought to govern his conscience by the positive law of the land and not by an abstract reason lying outside it.[17] Equity was not something outside the law, but something within it.[18] It was to support this claim that St German developed the theory – examined in the previous chapter – that English law *contained* the law of reason, and was not to be judged by principles or reasoning external to itself. In his *Replication of a Serjeant at the Laws of England* St German was able to draw the remarkable conclusion:

> Me thinke that the lawe aughte not to be lefte for conscience yn no caas; for the lawe commaundeth all thing that is good for the common welthe to bee doon, and prohibitithe all thing that is evill and that is againste the commen welle . . . [T]he lawe of the realme is a sufficiente rule to ordre you and your conscience, what ye shall do yn every thing and what ye shall not doo. Yf

ye therfore follow the lawe trewly, ye cannot do amys, nor yet offende your conscience, for it is saide, *quod implere legem est esse perfecte vertuosum* (to fulfill the lawe is to be perfitely vertuouse).[19]

Conclusions very similar to St German's were also reached in another major common-law treatise on equity, Edward Hake's *Epieikeia* (written late in the reign of Elizabeth I). This work had as its purpose the refutation of the view that 'Equity and the Common lawe weare distincte things & dissevered the one from the other'.[20] Equity was not a set of principles apart from the law: it was inherent in the common law itself, 'a parte or vertue attributory to the lawe'. When maxims of the common law are subject to equitable construction it does not mean that they are being rejected but rather they are being 'expounded by the hidden righteousnes of those growndes and maximes'.[21]

These claims on behalf of the common law were made, in part, from professional self-interest. St German's work was part of a sustained attack on ecclesiastical jurisdiction. Hake was attempting to argue that the equitable jurisdiction of the Court of Chancery did not create a body of equitable principles to be administered separately from (and possibly over) the common law.[22] Undoubtedly one reason for asserting the self-sufficiency of the common law was to aid its battle with the non common-law courts. Be that as it may, the effect was to develop the view that the common law provided a complete, perfectly rational way of dealing with all domestic political matters.

From this was derived a peculiar political theory that stressed the 'insularity' of English law and constitution. These formed a body of principles hermetically sealed from outside influence or meddling. These principles had developed, over time, to become perfectly fitted to the current needs of the English nation. Consequently, the doctrine of the ancient constitution (considered as political theory) consisted in the argument that the *present* laws and constitution were perfect – not, that is, abstractly perfect, but perfectly fitted to English circumstances. This we have seen in Chapter 2. Ancient constitutionalists worshipped the present more than they ever worshipped the past.

This, then, was the political core of English ancient constitutionalism. Its real peculiarity can only be seen in comparison with other political positions. It is possible to delineate three broad categories that between them cover the range of viable opinions on the relationships between natural law, positive law and political practice. The first of them is the classic position of natural law theorists: political practice was legitimate only when it was in accord with positive and natural law; positive law could not be in conflict with natural law, and (where it was) it could not be considered true law. This position made positive law (and political life) subject to the judgement of the natural law and its authoritative interpreters. A second position, much discussed in relation to the Engagement Controversy (1649–52), was that of *de facto* theory.[23] This was really a complex variety of theories, but the essential feature they had in common was the employment of arguments that severed legality and legitimacy. Even illegal political acts could be legitimated, whether by providence, self-interest, or the need to maintain peace. The political theory of the common-law, however fell into a third category, separate from both of these other ones, but also sharing features with them both.

First, like the natural law theorist, the common lawyer believed that political life should be governed by the law – including both the laws of nature and reason. But, whereas the former saw reason as something external to positive law, by which it could be measured and declared wanting, the common lawyer saw positive law as *inherently* rational (for reasons we have already considered). Therefore, it formed a self-contained system for giving political guidance. And, second, like the *de facto* theorist, the common lawyer found the measure of political legitimacy in the facts of the present not in abstract and timeless reason.[24] Both recognized the need to fit action (and law) to circumstances; both recognized the mutability of the law in changing situations. But the common-law thinkers found the guidance for political life in a particular category of present fact: the law. What was right and what was wrong were questions best answered in terms of whether they were or were not conformable to the law of England. Or, in St German's words, 'to fulfill the lawe is to be perfitely vertuouse'. To fulfil the law meant also to act in accordance with reason and nature (as the natural law theorist demanded) and to act in a way best suited to dealing with the political problems posed by your community (as the *de facto* theorist required). The common law of England was the law of reason; it was also a customary law as well fitted as was possible to bringing peace and stability to the English nation. Obeying it ought to satisfy the political requirements of both Aquinas and Hobbes.

It might be thought that the consequence of this would be that those who held the idea of the ancient constitution would inevitably believe in a form of *constitutionalism*, and inevitably be opposed to the politics of *absolutism*. (By constitutionalism, in this sense, is meant a political theory that required all political action, including that of kings, to be in conformity with the law, and which provided legal remedies for dealing with actions that were not.) Such a conclusion would be much too simple. It is true that for problems that fell clearly within its purview the common law believed itself to provide sufficient answer. It had no need of the help of either a (conquering) king with rights outside the law, or of rational and legal principles external to itself. But not all matters did fall within the purview of the common law, as even common lawyers recognized. Within its own sphere the common law was self-sufficient, but its sphere was not universal. Thus kings could claim to be acting *outside* the common law – in which case their actions could be defended using political languages other than that of the common law. In such situations the king might be able to justify a right to act arbitrarily without this being any threat at all to the common law. The crucial question, then, was: what were the boundaries of the common law? It was quite possible for the same person to believe that within those boundaries the king was to obey the common law (e.g. with respect to property rights), but outside them he had greater latitude for action based on his absolute authority. This points to the urgent need for us to gain some idea of what the boundaries of the common-law (and of common-law political thought) were in early Stuart England.

Another way of putting these points would be to say that in so far as kings were seen as *part* of the ancient constitution they were assigned a limited role in a complex system. But kings were not generally seen *just* in these terms. They had an ordinary, legal prerogative – this they exercised through the common law because it was part of that law. But they also had an absolute prerogative, they were also God's lieutenants on earth, and in these capacities they could act outside the common law. Most people accepted both of these things. (Does this mean that most people were *both* constitutionalists *and* absolutists?) And what mattered to them most, what they argued about, was the exact scope of the king's legal and his extra-legal powers. What could the king do only through the law? What could he do in areas where he was free of the law? These matters will be the subject of Part II.

There is one final aspect to the political complexion of common
law thought worth considering: was it capable of supporting a
radical political theory? The general view has been summarized
by one recent historian: 'modern scholars often characterize historical argumentation as essentially conservative, while deeming
argumentation from natural law inherently radical'.[25] On this standard view, ancient constitutionalism could not be deployed for
radical ends. So when, in the 1640s, radical theories were needed,
those who developed them abandoned the language and attitudes of
ancient constitutionalism. Instead, they built their theories on a base
of abstract reason and natural law. There is a large element of truth
in this standard view, though (as some recent work has shown) it
does require qualification. These qualifications involve two matters,
the rhetorical and propaganda value that ancient constitutionalist
ideas could have for radical writers, and the possibility of using the
language of the ancient constitution to defend a constitutional right
of resistance. (The problem with this latter point, however, is that it
is not at all clear that a resistance theory of this type really deserves
the label radical.)

The rhetorical function of ancient constitutionalism in the 1640s
is best appreciated with respect to the Levellers. The accepted view
of the Levellers has been that they were critics and subverters of the
common law.[26] This view of them could be reached in one of two
ways. Firstly they could be pictured against the context of the large
number of early-seventeenth-century proponents of law reform.[27]
Here they appear as rebels against the professional obfuscation of
the lawyers and against a law which they saw as reflecting and
serving the interests of the wealthy.[28] An alternative approach was
through the theory of the Norman Yoke (anti-Normanism) which
has been given classic treatment by Christopher Hill.[29] From this
theory the Levellers and others derived arguments to demonstrate
that English common law and the existing constitution derived from
an alien imposition upon a conquered nation in 1066. They were a
form of bondage and should be overthrown and replaced by the
good and true laws of the Anglo-Saxons. Norman law enslaved the
people of England, who in Saxon times had been free. This theory
has been seen as a complete opposite to the typical common-law
view of history in that it accepted fully the reality of the Conquest
and so denied the ideas of continuity and of the immemorial origin
of existing law.

More recently R. B. Seaberg has attempted to revise what he

considered to be the oversimplifications of this approach to the Levellers' view of the common law.[30] Seaberg advances two claims. Firstly, he says that the Levellers made *positive* use of legal scholarship and that their view of legal history influenced their political demands. And, secondly, he argues that their acceptance of the reality of Conquest in 1066 did not necessarily require them to deny the idea of the continuity of the law.[31] Central to his case is the view that when the Levellers appealed to equity or reason they were not shifting from the historical language of the common law to the rationalistic language of natural law and natural rights. Reason and equity were essential features of the common law tradition: common lawyers and Levellers were agreed that laws and customs were invalid if they were not in accord with reason.[32]

There can be no doubt that the Levellers could employ common law language to support some of the positions they advocated. But the significance of this fact can only be appreciated when the fundamentally *rhetorical* nature of much political writing in the 1640s is recognized.[33] The Leveller writers, like others in the period, sought to *persuade*; and the audience that they were seeking to persuade was one inherently hostile to their demands. So they did their utmost to turn the best arguments of their enemies into their own rhetorical weapons. People on all sides sought to exploit the language of mixed monarchy (the king because it enabled him to look moderate and respectful of the ancient constitution; parliamentarians because it provided a toe-hold for resistance theory). The languages of natural rights, common law, and counsel were all bandied about for various ends. It is along these lines that the Leveller use of appeals to the common law – quite extensive[34] – should be understood. Indeed, John Lilburne in particular made a speciality of using what should have been his enemies' most valuable weapons for his own purposes, as witnessed by his use of Parliament's own *Book of Declarations* in his attacks on the parliamentary positions and actions.[35]

Examples of Lilburne's rhetorical deployment of common law sources abound. Witness, for example, the 'Plea' against the House of Lords that opens his *Legal Fundamental Liberties*:[36] the point of the plea was to demonstrate that Lilburne's arrest on a warrant from the Lords was illegal on Parliament's own definition of legality. Indeed in his long campaign against the House of Lords Lilburne's main point was to show that their jurisdiction over himself and other commoners was contrary to English law: 'they have by the Law, no authority at all to make me dance attendance upon them, in the present case, or to try me a Commoner, in any Criminall cause whatsoever'.[37] It was a central rhetorical ploy for Lilburne to be able to show up the Lords' actions as contrary to the law that Parliament claimed to be defending.[38] In these rhetorical contexts – and here we must agree with Seaberg – Lilburne could argue from continuity. For example, Lilburne used pre-Conquest parliamentary precedents to show that a 'perpetual' parliament (such as the Long Parliament) was illegal.[39] Here he was clearly arguing that since time immemorial frequent short parliaments had been the customary English practice, an argument fully concordant with the ideas of the common-law mind. Similarly, in this same place, Lilburne could adopt an attitude to the Norman Conquest identical to that of some common-law scholars (Selden, for example): a conquest had occurred but the continuity of laws and institutions was maintained by William's promise to respect the old existing laws.

But Lilburne's use in certain contexts of arguments based on the continuity of English law since Saxon times should not obscure the fact that his anti-Normanism was in essence (as Pocock originally asserted) fundamentally opposed to common law thought.[40] Lilburne believed, basically, that all law had to be in accord with both reason and nature, and was quite prepared to override any positive laws that did not in his view meet this test. His arguments from the continuity of this law were purely tactical; they gained him rhetorical advantage. But, unlike the common lawyers, Lilburne did *not* believe that immemoriality was in itself a guarantee of the inherent rationality of the law. He was always prepared to subject laws to an external test of rationality – and by this test some laws were found to be irrational because imposed on the English as a mark of bondage at the time of the Norman Conquest.[41]

The rationalistic basis of Lilburne's anti-Normanism makes a marked contrast with the principles underlying the theories of the common lawyers.[42] He believed that positive laws ought to be 'agreeable to the law Eternall and Naturall, and not contrary to the word of God'. Laws that failed this test 'are not the law of the land: nor are to be observed and obeyed by the people'. Furthermore, 'that which was not grounded upon good right, and sound reason; is not made good by continuance of time'.[43] In theory, as Seaberg has observed, there may be nothing in this that a common lawyer would have objected to. However, the practical difference between Lilburne and the common lawyers was enormous, for he lacked their view that long continuance was itself a proof of rationality. For him 'Reason is demonstrable of it self, and every man (less or more) is endued with it'.[44] Consequently Lilburne did not see English law as a self-contained rational system. It was, rather, subject to simple external tests of its rationality: law could be judged by the Golden Rule, 'To teach a man to do as he would be done to',[45] or by other rational tests of right and wrong (such as whether it had been consented to).[46] Lilburne was therefore quite happy to argue (citing Coke on Bonham's case) that particular laws were contrary to 'Common Right', and therefore void.[47] So, though they agreed that laws needed to be rational, Lilburne and the common lawyers disagreed on how that rationality was to be judged. The lawyers thought that the customary nature of English law guaranteed its inherent rationality, or that (in any case) only those possessed of 'artificial reason' were capable of seeing the rationality of English law; Lilburne judged the law of England on the basis of simple rational tests of its morality, and often found it wanting, not least because of the taint of conquest that it bore.

Other theorists of anti-Normanism show the divergence of this position from that of the common lawyers even more clearly. Edward Hare, for example, in *St Edwards Ghost* demonstrated the glorious Saxon pedigree of English customs and institutions, but went on to show how they had been overwhelmed at the conquest. On the conquest itself he was a little coy, arguing that William was allowed to rule because he promised to accept the Saxon laws, but that he broke this promise so that the English found 'their ancient honour, Lawes, Libertie, and Language . . . overwhelmed and buried in . . . Normanisme'.[48] Of the effect of the Norman Conquest, Hare remarked: 'the evidency of this wee may descry in our owne Lawes'. To remedy this, Hare urged that the continuity of the law should be restored by ensuring that the title to the Crown of England not be based on conquest and that all laws introduced by the Normans be abolished and replaced with Saxon laws (or by civil law). He even suggested that William might be adjudged a lawful successor of Edward the Confessor, so that (once his innovations were abolished) the Conquest would disappear altogether.[49] Thus, far from seeing the present laws of England as well-nigh perfect, Hare wanted them pruned of Norman innovation. This wish for a return to an ideal Saxon past (which he spent the first pages of his tract establishing) was the complete opposite of the principles held by the common lawyers.

Perhaps the clearest expression of the incomparability of anti-Normanism with the common-law mind is in a pamphlet by John Warr.[50] Warr accepted like many common law scholars that England had been conquered many times, and 'that several alterations have been made of our laws, either in whole or in part, upon every conquest'.[51] He added, however, that if conquerors did ever preserve the ancient laws they did so only to ingratiate themselves with and deceive the people. Warr went on to quote Fortescue's verdict that English conquerors always confirmed the laws of their predecessors, thus preserving the continuity of the law. When Fortescue said that the same laws continued through several conquests he must (according to Warr) be understood as meaning this, for we must suppose that conquerors retained only those laws 'which made for their own interest'.[52] This was true even of the Saxons. Thus Warr turned the accepted picture of conquest followed by confirmation of existing laws against the whole body of the law: 'And yet this is no honour at all to the laws of England, that they are such pure servants to corrupt interests that they can keep their places under contrary masters'. This really meant only 'that the notion of fundamental law is no such idol as men make it'. The term meant no more than those customs that were the oldest and had existed the longest,[53] which meant those most useful to conquerors. The continuity of English law was for Warr evidence of its inherent irrationality: if it survived repeated conquests this was only because it served the interests of successive conquerors.[54] This was indeed an extremely clever attempt to turn upside down one of the common law's central doctrines, continuity. It is eloquent testimony to the diametrically opposed positions of the common lawyer and the anti-Normanist: the former believed the customary nature of English law to be *prima facie* proof of its rationality; the latter found existing law to be, in one way or another, corrupt. Some, like Lilburne, accepted that what laws had survived since the Saxons were good; but others, like Warr, thought continuity just another proof of corruption.

It might seem at this point that we are firmly committed to the view that the common-lawyers' key political belief (that the law was a self-sufficient rational system) was incompatible with any radical political theory. For obvious reasons, this was essentially true. Radicals were committed to the view that the existing constitution and law needed to be undermined; the doctrine of the ancient constitution asserted their perfection. There is, however, a second qualification to be made to this position: ancient constitutionalism could be combined with resistance theory. What this suggests is perhaps less the radical potential of the ancient constitution than the very limited extent of the radicalism of resistance theory.

The ancient constitution and resistance theory could be reconciled only by incorporating the institution of monarchy entirely within the framework of the ancient constitution. That is it required a development of the view that the king had no powers that could not be analysed and discussed in the language of the common law. By these means a constitutional right to resist (under limited circumstances) could be identified as part of the ancient constitution itself. Such a theory hardly deserves the name radical:[55] it allowed for the clinical removal of the king but left the laws and institutions of the ancient constitution otherwise intact. Probably the greatest ideological value that a theory of this type had was to *minimize* the degree of radicalism that a solution to England's problems would require. In the context of the late 1640s and early 1650s there was much use for a political theory that could: (a) defend the removal of Charles I from authority, and if necessary, his execution, while (b) assuring the nation that in all other respects business would be as normal.

Hints of a possible combination of ancient constitutionalism with resistance theory can be found in the political opinions held by John Selden in the 1640s. Throughout this period Selden consistently upheld the view that the issues at contention between the King and the two Houses could be decided by an examination of the state of the law. Before civil war itself occurred, Selden had rejected the excesses of both sides, and condemned both the Militia Ordinance and the Commissions of Array as illegal. 'It would be much better', he said, 'if both were rejected, than if either of them should stand, and remain uncontrolled'.[56] Ultimately Selden opted for supporting the Lords and Commons against the King on the grounds that he was certain that the King was breaking the law of the land, but was not certain that his opponents were. This position was reached only on the basis of a detailed examination of the actions of both sides.[57] For the rest of the decade, so far as can be discovered from the scattered remarks in his *Table Talk*, Selden remained of the same opinion. This was most clearly stated in the following remarks

> *Quest.* What law is there to take upp Armes against the prince in Case hee breakes his Covenant?
> *Answer.* Though there bee no written law for it yet there

is Custome which is the best Law of the Kingdome; for in England they have allwayes done it.[58]

Thus resistance could be seen as a legal remedy in certain cases, and so looking to positive law could help the subject to decide on what course of action to take, even in civil war. There was a customary right to resist the crown in some circumstances. Even if this was exercised then, presumably, the rest of the constitution would remain unaffected. (Admittedly, there are also hints in Selden's *Table Talk* of an alternative theory of resistance based on the idea of original contract and natural rights – 'Where the Contract is broken, & there is no Third person to judge, then the division is by Armes . . . betwixt the prince & the subject'.[59] The idea here would appear to be that where the constitution failed the subject could fall back on a natural right of self-defence. The language of original contracts and natural rights is totally alien to ancient constitutionalism: an original contract contradicted the doctrine of immemoriality,[60] and the ancient constitution functioned to make the use of natural rights unnecessary. It substituted for natural rights a perfect set of legal or constitutional rights.)

However, the use of ancient constitutionalist thought-patterns as the grounding for a theory of resistance reached its fullest development in two later works by Nathaniel Bacon and John Sadler.[61] Bacon's *Historical Discourse* was a notable achievement, the English *Francogallia*. It was a work of considerable scholarship as well as a piece of political propaganda (as was its French predecessor) – indeed it was claimed in the 1689 edition of the work that Bacon had compiled it on the basis of manuscript notes of John Selden's.[62] The *Historical Discourse*, though it begins with a discussion of the Britons, saw the English polity originating amongst the Saxons whom it described as 'a free people'. Bacon showed 'how the influence of these old principles [of the Saxons] doth worke in the fundamentall government of this Kingdome to this present day'.[63] The Saxons established a fundamental paradigm for the English constitution which later changes and developments only reinforced. Kingship was, essentially, elective, and 'this election was qualified under a stipulation of covenant' by which the people promised to defend the king, and he to govern by the law ('unto which not onely the people, but also the King must submit'). To this contract (which was not an original contract, but part of the body of positive law) the kings bound themselves by oath, with the result that the obedience of the Saxons to their monarchs was always conditional. 'The Saxons fealty to their King was subservient to the publique safety.'[64] Bacon then drove the message home: 'Nor was this a dead word, for the people had formerly a tricke of deposing their Kings'.[65]

The remainder of the *Historical Discourse* was designed to show that the conditional kingship of the Saxons and the polity of which it was a part (a polity which 'affarre off it seems a Monarchy, but in approach discovers more of a Democracy')[66] remained in operation through the rest of English history. The major obstacle to doing this was, of course, the Norman Conquest. Not surprisingly, Bacon discussed it at great length. Indeed, he indicated that the motive for writing the work was supplied by 'a private debate concerning the right of an English King to Arbitrary rule over English Subjects as Successor to the Norman Conquerour'.[67] Bacon had no illusions about the motives that impelled William towards the Conquest, but he argued nevertheless that he was a king by election and not be conquest. William voluntarily accepted the kingship on 'Saxon' terms:

> Thus this mighty Conquerour suffered himselfe to be conquered, and stooping under the law of a Saxon King he became a King by leave: wisely foreseeing that a title gotten by election is more certaine then that which is gotten by power.[68]

The case was clinched by Bacon's examination of William's coronation, 'the same with that of the Ancient Saxon Kings'. At the coronation William entered into the same covenant to obey the law as his Saxon predecessor had done, and the subjects promised obedience on the same terms as the Saxons had done. The 'fealty' of William's subjects was 'the selfesame in substance' with that of the Saxons to their kings:

> the allegiance of the English to the Norman Kings was no other then what might stand with brotherhood, and tender regard of the publique above all: and differing from the Saxon fealty onely in this that that was in one oath, & this in two.[69]

Thus the continuity of the Saxon-English polity was ensured: the Normans, and all English kings, held office on the conditional terms originally found in Saxon kingship. The form by which this was signified at the coronation may have changed, but underneath the essence persisted.

Bacon's Saxonism and his stress on continuity since time immemorial show his acceptance of the main features of English ancient constitutionalism. He built into this portrait of the ancient constitution a conditional kingship that enabled him, implicitly at least, to justify a sort of resistance theory. Recognition of that fact, however, should not lead us to forget that in other respects Bacon's work followed the path of asserting that the English polity was a self-sufficient system, which could deal satisfactorily with all political problems (perhaps even by deposition, if necessary). A very similar thought pattern was to be found in John Sadler's *Rights of the Kingdom*, an historical defence of the regicide. Sadler defined the allegiance owed by the subject to his or her king as conditional since time immemorial, conditional in that it was an oath to preserve the kingdom more than the king.[70] This effectively conditional allegiance to the crown persisted across the divide of the Conquest. Like Bacon, Sadler characterized English kingship as primarily elective.[71] When kings broke the conditions upon which they were elected (i.e. broke the law), the ancient constitution provided, in Sadler's view, the constitutional means for bringing them to justice. This was the institution of Parliament.[72] Sadler was able to trace the Parliamentary exercise of judicial authority over the king across the entire span of English history.

Bacon and Sadler considered the monarchy entirely as an institutional fragment of the ancient constitution. This enabled them to subordinate kingship to the workings of the constitution as a whole, and thus develop a defence of resistance theory. In this regard they moved as far as possible in developing the radical potential of ancient constitutionalism, which was not far at all. The basic message they both put forward was that bringing the king to justice was an act that could be (or was) performed within the normal operation of the ancient constitution. Consequently, it did not threaten the integrity or survival of that constitution. But Sadler and Bacon differed from most pre-Civil-War ancient constitutionalists. Before 1642 the accepted view was that the king was more than just a part of an ancient constitution. That constitution was a self-sufficient entity within its own sphere, but the king's sphere was wider than it. For this reason, the political thought of early Stuart England cannot be understood just in terms of the common-law mind, or in terms of the simple opposition of common-law thinking with other modes of political discourse. It is necessary instead to understand how ancient constitutionalism interacted with other modes of political argument – and to remember that interaction does not necessarily mean outright rivalry. This we shall do in Part II.

(C) THE CHRONOLOGY OF ENGLISH ANCIENT CONSTITUTIONALISM: ORIGINS AND COLLAPSE

There is one final aspect of ancient constitutionalism that needs consideration before we move on to consider its place in a wider intellectual context: its *history*. When and how did it originate? What can be said of the process of its decline? These are extraordinarily difficult questions to answer. In Pocock's account of ancient constitutionalism there was no discussion of its origin, though it seems to be implied that the common-law mind was formed over the late-sixteenth century. The lack of any adequate studies of the developments in sixteenth-century English jurisprudence and political thought means that there can still be nothing but a tentative answer to the question of origins. In this section I will sketch an account of the origins of ancient constitutionalism that seems most probable to me, but it must be admitted that future research may well require revision of this account.

The collapse of ancient constitutionalism is easier to pinpoint, if only because the history of seventeenth-century political thought is more fully known than that of the sixteenth century. The 'classic phase' of the doctrine of the ancient constitution lasted quite briefly, from around 1600 until the Civil War. It ended when the political discourse of the 1640s began to show that writers no longer believed the common law provided a self-sufficient language for the discussion of *domestic* political issues. This process of destruction will be examined in detail in later chapters. After the 1640s, the ancient constitution never regained the form it had possessed before Charles I fell into war with his subjects. After 1660 appeal to the past, *via* antiquarian scholarship, remained a central feature of English political thought, but the particular attitudes of ancient constitutionalism analysed in this and the previous chapter no longer formed a coherent and identifiable whole. Immemoriality tended to give way before the idea of an original contract, laying down the terms on which power was distributed within the English polity. Others fused ancient constitutionalism with ideas drawn from the thought of James Harrington. This fusion of 'classic' ancient constitutionalism with other discursive modes destroyed its central political doctrine: no longer was it a defence of the *present* English polity as a perfect self-contained system. (Again, this matter will be covered in more detail in the final chapter.)

That leaves us with the question of origins. What were the sources of English ancient constitutionalism? Professor Pocock, though not discussing the matter in *The Ancient Constitution and the Feudal Law*, has not left us entirely without guidance on this matter. He has suggested two general sources for the common law mind: humanism and English ecclesiology.[73] These do seem to be crucial areas to which we need to direct our attention, but to which we also need to add an additional item, namely the intellectual tradition of the common law itself. In essence, ancient constitutionalism was an intensification of trends already apparent within the common law; and this intensification was governed by antiquarianism (a sort of humanism, perhaps), and by the need to defend the Elizabethan settlement.

Many of the ideas and concepts crucial to English ancient constitutionalism were central to common-law thinking well before the late-sixteenth century. These must provide the bedrock for any explanation of the rise of the doctrine of the ancient constitution. In their different ways, both Fortescue and St German are evidence of how much this doctrine owed to the professional discourse of English lawyers. The sense of the continuity of English legal and institutional development owed much to the (admittedly still far from rigid) doctrine of precedent, by which present decisions could be made with guidance from past ones.[74] In addition, the idea of English law as customary has an intellectual history that goes back at least to the time of Bracton.[75] Ancient constitutionalism can be viewed as little more than an elaboration of these ideas. In Fortescue we already see the idea of English law as without any historical discontinuity, though it was expressed in a form that was to be outmoded by late-Elizabethan antiquarian scholarship. We see too in Fortescue the crucial role of customary law in England.[76] In St German's work even more of the ideas characteristic of ancient constitutionalism are to be found, largely as a product of the way in which St German brought together the concepts of custom and reason (rational maxims). In his work there are firm hints of the idea that customary survival was itself a proof of rationality, and of the common-law idea of artificial reason. It can sometimes be too easy (for us) to forget that we need to remember continuity as well as change in history, but it would be ironical indeed if we forgot this when talking about common lawyers. The ideas of custom and continuity were much elaborated in the Elizabethan and Jacobean periods, but their application to English law was scarcely a new thing.

The elaboration of the concept of custom after St German's time occurred in two broad areas: scholarship and politics. (Of course, given the very close links between antiquarian scholarship and political ideology in the period, the distinction is largely a heuristic one.) In the first of these areas change was guided by the impact of antiquarianism.[77] The antiquarian movement (discussed in passing in the previous chapter) and its findings made it very difficult by about 1600 to believe literally in the account of English history to be found in Fortescue. In particular, it cast serious doubt on the supposed pre-Saxon (British) origins of English law, and the mass of detail it unearthed on Saxon laws made it difficult to believe that they were identical with the law of the seventeenth-century. The destruction of the myth of British origins can be conveniently dated from 1605, the year in which Richard Verstegan's *Restitution of Decayed Intelligence* was published.[78] It portrayed the English constitution as originating amongst the Saxons: they brought their laws with them when they invaded Britain, and from that base the present constitution had evolved. Scepticism of British origins for the law was a central feature of ancient constitutionalism. It is at its most notable in Selden, but in practice even Coke never really undertook to demonstrate in detail that English law was any older than the Saxons.[79] Saxonism became the standard scholarly opinion in the early-seventeenth century.

Recognition of the devastating extent of the Saxon conquest of the Britons introduced the idea of change into the account of the law inherited from Fortescue. This could only have been reinforced by knowledge of Saxon law, increasingly detailed following the pioneer work of William Lambarde in *Archainomia* (1568).[80] The base provided by Lambarde was built upon by many others including Camden, Selden and many members of the Elizabethan Society of Antiquaries.

The challenge posed by this increasing knowledge of the past (and of its difference from the present) could easily have been antagonistic to the ideas of custom and continuity inherent in the common law. As it turned out, this antagonism did not develop, perhaps because so many of the antiquarians were also common lawyers. Ancient constitutionalism was in part a synthesis of basic common-law concepts with the new learning of the antiquaries. It did not assert the identity of past and present, but rather their connection by an evolutionary continuum. It accepted the reality of the Saxon conquest, and the role that various invaders played in bringing a diversity of laws into England; but it also, by a variety of means, carried the continuity of the law across the gap of the Norman Conquest, even when sometimes recognizing that a real conquest had occurred. This was a complex fusion of the growing knowledge of change with the persistent idea of continuity. The English constitution remained immemorial, if only because the origins of the Saxon polity were themselves immemorial; but in good part those origins were also freed from a myth of British-Trojan foundation and placed instead amongst the Germanic peoples of the Continent. The idea of custom that underlay this view of the English past was, thanks to antiquarian scholarship, not a piece of simple-minded myth-making. It was a complex and subtle piece of historical imagination, capable of recognizing change while seeing the basic form of the constitution (the nature of kingship, the role of parliament) handed down from generation to generation since the Saxons.

Ancient constitutionalism also possessed by about 1610 at the latest a built-in political ideology, the self-sufficiency of English laws and constitution. The sources of this should be looked for in Elizabethan ecclesiology, perhaps reinforced after 1603 by fears of the impact that Anglo-Scottish Union might have on English law.[81] John Guy has remarked that 'St German did for English common law what, a generation or so later, John Jewel and Richard Hooker did for the Anglican church'.[82] There is no doubt much truth in this, but it might be as true to say that Hooker and the other defenders of the *ecclesia Anglicana* did for the ecclesiastical polity what Coke and Selden, a generation or so later, did for the civil. It is worth remembering that many works about the ancient constitution of England also included proofs of the early Christianization of Britain, establishing a pedigree for the Church of England that antedated the growth of the see of Rome.[83] Furthermore, it is clear that religious concerns provided the major impetus behind the development of antiquarian research. From Archbishop Matthew Parker's *De Antiquitate Britainnicae Ecclesiae* (1572) to Archbishop James Ussher's massive *Britannicarum Ecclesiarum Antiquitates* (1637) enormous energy was poured into ecclesiastical antiquarianism – energy that tends to be downplayed in modern surveys of the subject.[84]

However, when we compare legal antiquarianism (ancient constitutionalism) with ecclesiastical antiquarianism, there appears initially to be a sharp contrast between them. The basic pattern that emerged from the study of the history of English Christianity resembled more that of the Norman Yoke theory than it resembled ancient constitutionalism proper. England (or, rather, Britain, for ecclesiastical antiquarianism maintained a strongly British focus, for reasons that would probably repay further examination) was properly Christianized and part of the primitive church, and – in particular – its church was properly under the control of an 'imperial' monarch, in the beginning.[85] This pristine state was destroyed by the gradual usurpations of the Bishops of Rome, who extended their own power, and clerical jurisdiction generally, at the expense of the English crown. The Reformation and events subsequent to it constituted the throwing off of this 'Roman yoke'. This sort of argument was most useful for rejecting the Catholic claim that the Church of England was in a state of schism from the true church, and was given classic expression in John Jewel's *An Apology of the Church of England* (1564),[86] though here Jewel's contrast between the true primitive church and its corrupt Romish form was not drawn with specific reference to Britain. In particular, Jewel needed to rebut the charge that 'they [the Catholics] will have their own, whatsoever they are, to be praised as things of long continuances' while they 'condemn all our matters as strange and new', a charge which led him elsewhere to prove the pre-Roman antiquity of English ecclesiastical customs and institutions.[87] It was the Church of England, not that of Rome, that followed the true primitive church.[88]

The matter should not, however, be left here. In two crucial respects the Elizabethan defences of the *ecclesia Anglicana* explored themes that were essential features of ancient constitutionalism a generation or so later. Firstly, the Elizabethans were primarily responsible for elaborating the concept of custom. Perhaps they provide the 'missing link' between St German and Selden or Coke. In works such as Thomas Bilson's *True Difference between Christian Subjection and Unchristian Rebellion* there was developed a strong sense of the legitimate diversity of political and legal systems, and the need to settle the political problems of each individual polity with references to its own laws and customs, and not with reference to universal principles. This was particularly evident in Bilson's proof that in some places (e.g. England) it was always wrong to resist the prince, while in others it might be acceptable.[89] This was a principle useful in explaining why the English owed unconditional obedience to their Godly Prince, while they could still aid the Dutch in their rebellion against the King of Spain.[90] This sense of the diversity of national customs, and of the need to refer political questions in any nation to its own customs, reached its fullest development in Richard Hooker, as we have seen. It was a central theme in his work that any Christian commonwealth had its own customary ways for the administration of civil and ecclesiastical affairs which it would be folly to try to alter. It is possible, then, to see the central conceptual nexus of ancient constitutionalism given its first full examination in Elizabethan ecclesiology. We should recall at this point the fact, noted in Chapter 1, that the English ancient constitution, in contrast to the French and some others, did not develop as an adjunct to resistance theory. It developed under conditions which demanded defence of the established polity.

A second area, closely linked to this, in which ancient constitutionalism might be seen to draw upon earlier ecclesiological thought is its very constitutionalism. Notwithstanding the Elizabethan glorification of the Godly Prince (associated particularly with John Foxe),[91] it is now apparent that many in the Elizabethan establishment also held to the view that England was a law-governed polity. Their attitude to monarchy remained ambivalent: they had good ideological reason to distance themselves from the Calvinist resistance theories advanced before Elizabeth's reign (and in Scotland more recently); but they could not necessarily forget the circumstances that had called forth those theories. Nor could they forget that outside England those circumstances still pertained in many areas. The result was, in a sense, a recognition of the peculiarities of the English (insularity once more!). The customs of England were not only different from those of other nations; they were such as to render resistance to the magistrate unnecessary. This argument was apparent as early as 1559 in John Aylmer's reply to Knox's attack on female rulers. Aylmer argued, in part, that the law-governed polity of England was sufficient to prevent misgovernment, even by a woman.[92] This view persisted in the writings of Bilson, Bridges, Hooker, and others. Monarchs were not always Godly, as many had cause to remember, and a persistent undercurrent of Elizabethan thought was its reliance on the rule of law as well as on the rule of the prince.[93]

There was thus implicit in Elizabethan ecclesiology a view of the 'insularity' of the English polity, its reliance upon customs and institutions peculiar to itself, but also peculiarly fitted to its needs. There was also an awareness that in other places things were (quite rightly) done differently: the diversity of laws and customs was a product of the different circumstances, in which nations and communities found themselves. This vision underlay English ancient constitutionalism also, and it is hard to believe that this fact is purely coincidental. It is especially hard when we remember that most of the early Stuart writers on the ancient constitution had close knowledge of ecclesiastical antiquarianism and issues of ecclesiology.

In these brief remarks upon Elizabethan thought there is apparent a degree of tension between the faith put in the Godly Prince (monarchy by divine right, essentially), and the continuing vision of England as a law-governed polity. Was there perhaps a contradiction between these things? In the early Stuart period did divine-right monarchy and constitutionalism, things kept in a tense but fruitful partnership under the Tudors, go their separate ways? Perhaps ancient constitutionalism was one result of the separation, and the theory of the divine right of kings the other. To answer these questions we need to turn to a broader context, the full range of political discourse found under the early Stuarts, and to consider the place of ancient constitutionalism within it. Only then can we appreciate the degree of continuity between Elizabethan and Jacobean thought. This wider context will be the subject of Part II.

Cultural
relavance ?
Montaigne

Part II
The Commmon Law Mind and the Structure of Political Debate

4

Some Historiographical Perspectives

Though the common law provided early Stuart Englishmen with what was probably their fundamental set of assumptions and concepts for thinking and talking about politics, even a cursory glance at the period would make it apparent that there were other competing theoretical modes available. If we wish to understand the political debates of the pre-Civil-War period it is not enough to understand ancient constitutionalism alone. It is also necessary to understand how ancient constitutionalism compared with other ways of thinking about politics, and how these rival languages of political discourse interacted with one another.

This task is a more wide-ranging one that it might appear at first sight. It has important implications for a whole range of issues currently being debated by historians of the early Stuart period. Was it a period of consensus or of conflict? Were early Stuart Englishmen ideologically polarized, or did they agree on most fundamental issues and share a 'consensus culture'? Can a study of the political conflicts of the 1610s and 1620s help us to understand the outbreak of civil war in the 1640s? The historian of political discourse cannot provide full answers to these questions, but his or her conclusions will have their contribution to make to these more general discussions. In what follows here, it will be apparent that answers to all of these questions are being suggested. As a result, the following chapters can serve not only as a general introduction to the structure of political debate in early Stuart England, but also as a contribution to the assessment of the impact of 'revisionism'[1] on the historiography of seventeenth-century England.

In spite of the considerable growth that work in the history of political thought has shown in recent decades, there has been surprisingly little of this work done on the early Stuart period. Dr J. P. Sommerville's recent book *Politics and Ideology in England,*

1603–1640 is the first and only general history of early-seventeenth century English political thought since the classic works of Margaret Judson and J. W. Allen.[2] Compared to the work done in the field for the period after 1640, even specialist articles and narrower monographs are thin on the ground. This has had a very curious effect. The 1970s and 1980s have seen the development of a broad-based challenge to older ways of understanding the period 1600–1640, and this challenge has certainly had its implications for the history of political discourse and thought. Yet there has been no attempt to work through some of these implications. There has been no 'revisionist' history of political thought. Sommerville's excellent book is, in fact, a powerfully-argued and meticulously-researched attempt to reassert the viability of older approaches to the subject. So far as the historian of political thought is concerned, the revisionist challenge might never have occurred.

There is one obvious way of explaining this pattern. We might say that if historians like Conrad Russell and Kevin Sharpe were as familiar with the history of political thought as they were with other branches of the subject, then they would never have written the books they did. No one, we might go on, who is familiar with the passionately principled political debates of the early Stuart period could ever commit themselves to revisionist claims about the absence of ideological division in pre-Civil War England.[3] The view is a tempting one, but – as so often – temptation ought to be resisted. It ought to be resisted both because it would be a pity to close off the debate before seeing in more detail than we have so far if a revisionist history of political thought is viable, and because there are problems with an argument of this sort even on its own terms. Both of these points will become clearer as we go on.

If the simple way of dealing with the historiographical pattern will not do, we need to develop a more complex one. That requires us, first of all, to be clear about exactly what is at stake in the debates of the last decade or so, especially as they relate to political ideas.

One basic organizational move has long-dominated the study of early Stuart political thought. It entails the idea that the period was marked by a growing conflict between two sets of principles. One set, which we can label 'absolutist', held that kings had their authority directly from God (which meant that it was not conferred on them by their people), and that subjects were never justified in resisting the commands of their rulers (though on rare occasions they might be justified in passively refusing to obey). The other set of 'constitutionalist' principles (also labelled a 'contractarian' position) committed people to the belief that authority resided originally in the people as a corporate entity and was conferred on kings by their people for certain purposes only. A largely *unspoken* implication of this might be that under some circumstances the people might choose to revoke the authority they had granted away in order to discipline an erring ruler.

These two opposed sets of principles have structured most general accounts of our subject. The most recent of these accounts, Sommerville's, serves, if anything, to make the contrasts sharper. It is indeed another curious feature of the historiography in this area that the nearest thing to a 'revisionist' attempt to break down these dichotomies is in the opening chapters of Margaret Judson's *The Crisis of the Constitution* (originally published in 1949) where much stress is laid on the elements of consensus in early Stuart political thinking. In those chapters Judson shows how common attitudes to monarchy, Parliament and the law served to unite many men in agreement on fundamentals, whatever other differences they might have had. In the later chapters of her book Judson does bring back the old dichotomous organizing categories, but even so she has usefully suggested how fundamental agreement and deep division can co-exist.

With this one exception there have been few attempts to break out of the pattern. For a long time this was quite understandable. The conflict between 'absolutist' and 'constitutionalist' theories fitted in well to a historiography that assumed that there was a series of constitutional conflicts between the King ('absolutists') and his Parliament ('constitutionalists') in the early-seventeenth century. Furthermore, this view nicely served to connect the reign of James I with the Civil War. The struggles of the 1640s were but the climax of a long crescendo, and the constitutional principles that lay behind earlier phases of the conflict also lay behind it. Once again 'constitutionalists' did battle against 'absolutists', only this time they began to speak the unspoken implications of their positions. One group defended their right to resist their king on behalf of the free-born people of England; the other advanced the case for the irresistibility of a divine-right monarch.

More recently, though, much doubt has been cast on all of this. We are now told by some that there were no conflicts between king and parliament because kings were part of parliament, and because parliaments lacked the desire, initiative or means to be a serious threat. We are told also that the Civil War was not a war of opposing constitutional theories, but a conflict over religion and the church. By 1642 the constitutional grievances that Charles I had stirred up had all been satisfactorily settled. But *beneath* all of this, revisionist historians have implied (or stated without ever demonstrating in detail) that, in fact, the idea that Englishmen in the first decades of the seventeenth century were divided by two opposing political theories, the absolutist and the constitutionalist, is just plain wrong. These Englishmen shared a common set of political assumptions, so that consensus on theoretical issues was a more striking feature of the period than conflict. Certainly squabbles and arguments occurred, in and out of parliament. But they were not principled, not caused by ideological divisions. They were pragmatic disputes over organizational or administrative issues, rating disputes, attempts by localities to avoid taxes or soldiers, attempts by individuals to avoid the same. They were of very limited constitutional or political significance.

In the face of this challenge it will not really do merely to reiterate the old dichotomies. This is so because the challenge is more subtle than it looks (and more subtle than the summary just given here might imply). The revisionist position – in particular the position of Conrad Russell, the historian whose work is most relevant in this context – is (or at least, can be) compatible with the mere existence of deep theoretical disagreements amongst early Stuart Englishmen. The questions raised by the work of Russell, and others go deeper than this. Professor Russell has written, for example, that:

> [an] ideological gulf between 'government' and 'opposition' is impossible to find in Parliament before 1640. There were many disagreements on policy, often profound ones, but these were decisions which split the Council itself. On none of the great issues of the day did Parliamentary leaders hold any opinions not shared by members of the Council.[4]

What seems to be at issue here is not the question of whether there were or were not principled conflicts, but rather how any such conflicts meshed with the operational structures – the institutions and less formal groupings – of practical political life. In the (practical) conflicts between supporters of government policy and opponents of it the issues dividing the two groups were not theoretical. Such theoretical differences as existed were manifest *within* government (i.e. the Privy Council). (Also implicit here is the matter of exactly what *types* of theoretical disagreement there actually were, a matter to which we shall return.) Such an argument need not deny the existence of competing theories of politics. It states just that *if* there were any such competing theories they did not form the basis for a split between government and opposition,[5] whatever else they might have done. Because the issue at stake is the meshing of structures of political practice with structures of ideas, the debate cannot be resolved by looking at the structure of ideas alone. Sommerville has shown without doubt that it is possible to discern sharply different political theories in early-seventeenth century England, but it remains open to consider whether categorizing theories in this dichotomous way tells us much about how ideas *operated* in the political society that was early Stuart England. If the placing of ideas into neat boxes labelled 'absolutist' and 'constitutionalist' is to tell us anything about the *past* we need to know if such categorization itself would have made sense to the past. If it would not, then our use of such categorization runs the risk of becoming a form of sterile idealism.

Besides this basic issue about how ideas *functioned*, in debate and argument there are two other questions thrown up by recent historiography that are worth identifying. One is the concept of a 'consensus culture',[6] and what might be meant by that term. The 'consensus-versus-conflict' debate is misleading not only for the reason just given (i.e. supporters of conflict have not given sufficient credit to the subtlety of their opponents' position); but also because the debate has never fully examined what consensus might mean. Clearly no complex society is free of conflict, and for that reason consensus and conflict should not be seen as opposites. Rather, the two occur at different levels. Consensus on certain principles need not mean that there is no conflict over how those principles are to be implemented or achieved. In what follows here a complex understanding of the nature of consensus and conflict in early Stuart England will be developed. This will show how it is correct to talk of 'consensus' in the Jacobean period, even though this was in some ways a period of conflict as well. We shall also see both the persistence after 1625 of consensualist assumptions and the growth of a feeling that they were being undermined in the reign of Charles I.

A second question worth looking at, though seemingly narrower, has important implications for our understanding of early Stuart politics. It may be labelled the issue of 'move versus *mentalité*'. In response to some criticisms of his *The Ancient Constitution and the Feudal Law* Professor John Pocock has remarked that the work of his critics tends to share a common tendency:

> it seeks to transform what I said were assumptions into asser-
> tions, and essentially contestable assertions at that, made by
> identifiable actors in identifiable circumstances for identifiable
> reasons. It seeks, that is, to transform a *mentalité* into a series of
> 'moves' – a historiographical strategy typical of our times.[7]

The issue raised here by Pocock is central to our major theme of assessing how ancient constitutionalism and other languages of political discourse functioned in the wider political world. Were they sets of linguistic tricks to be exploited by political actors as needed – that is, used as 'moves' – or were they a series of *mentalités* that shaped men's assumptions and thinking, that told them what moves to make? The question puts once more one of the hoariest of historians' chestnuts: the relationship of thought and practice. An answer to this question, move versus *mentalité*, must therefore be a central feature of our account of the structures of political debate. Was there a 'common-law mind' in any sense stronger than the obvious truism that there was a set of words and concepts associated with the common law and its practice?

5

The Elements of Consensus in Jacobean England

The history of political discourse in early-seventeenth century England divides into two phases. The difficulty is in knowing where to draw the dividing-line between them. It was perhaps not until the end of the 1630s or later that changes in political debate became unmistakable, yet it is also arguable that a new mood of political reflection was making itself felt as early as the 1590s.[1] Perhaps when all considerations are taken into account the best year to single out as important in marking a change remains 1625, when Charles I succeeded his father. Before that date James had managed, more or less, to keep going a stable consensual system. And though change might initially be visible only in retrospect, it seems clear that crucial to the change that did occur was the person of Charles himself. But before we can understand the nature of those changes, and their significance (if any) for the Civil War, it is necessary that we understand the structure of what went before. It must be remembered that what we are examining here is not the structure of languages or theories. We have already examined one of these structures (the language of common law), and a general survey of others is available in the work of Dr. Johann Sommerville.[2] What matters here is the structure of *debate*, how ideas were used, not the internal logic of ideas themselves. How, then, did political debate function in Jacobean England?

(A)   THE BASICS: LANGUAGE, PROFESSION, AUDIENCE

The account of early Stuart political debate that will be developed here is based on three crucial concepts. The three concepts are language, profession and audience. They each require careful explication.

The term 'language' is currently rather a vogue word in the history of political thought. This may well be because historians have become dissatisfied with the concept of a *tradition* of ideas.[3] Traditions have come to seem dangerously anachronistic. However the replacement of 'tradition' with 'language' is sometimes a dubious gain, since some historians use the latter term as if it were interchangeable with the former. Much of what is now written about languages could as well be written about traditions. Nevertheless, one advantage that the concept of language can have over that of tradition is that it requires less self-consciousness. Traditions tend to be willed, with ideas being passed on and taken up deliberately; languages are just there. A language, because it need not be at the front of its users' consciousness, is more genuinely a *mentalité*. It is in this sense that the term is used here, to denote a set of conceptual assumptions not a tradition of theorising.[4]

We ought also to insist that a 'language' have some degree of coherence and some degree of self-containment – the latter can never be total of course. If it is to be identified and, in some sense at least, to exist, a language needs to possess terms and concepts not employed by other rival languages; and it needs to be able to address all relevant problems entirely in its own terms. This is obvious when comparing, let us say, English with French: each is a different but *more or less* complete way of describing the same world and talking about the same problems. But the languages that we are concerned with are only parts of these 'natural languages' and this can make them difficult to think about. Perhaps we can imagine them as specialized sets of words and concepts designed for dealing with special areas of debate. We are concerned with those languages that can be used in *political* debate, and in the early-seventeenth century two of these can be identified – the language of the law, which talks about politics using such concepts as custom, precedent, rights and liberties, prerogatives and so on; and the language of theology conducted through such terms as God, providence, grace and order. Presently, it will be possible to make this picture more precise and more complex.

Though historians of political thought have used the concept of a 'language' quite freely, an obvious difficult exists. What is the ontological status of such entities? Too often languages can appear to be disembodied abstractions with an existence that is quite independent of the persons who use them. At this point the second of our concepts, that of *profession* might be introduced. If we want to find a social group to which a language of the sort we have identified can be attached, then the most likely place to look in the seventeenth century is amongst the learned professions. The languages of law and theology clearly derive from professional discourse. In fact we can probably identify *three* broad languages of political discourse produced by professional groups in early Stuart England:

1. that studied in previous chapters of this book, 'the common-law mind', which derived from the language of common lawyers;
2. the language of civil or Roman law, attached to a small group of civil lawyers; and
3. theological languages produced by various groups amongst the clergy of the Church of England.[5]

Before a little more is said about each of these, two caveats need to be made. First, in early modern Europe intellectual life tended to be much more international than it has since become, with philosophers and writers able to communicate across national boundaries through the use of a common language, Latin. This meant that, at least in some circles, English thinkers were open to traditions of political thinking developed in continental Europe (for example reason of state theory, or classical republicanism). Nevertheless, though such European ideas might occasionally crop up in English writings, it needs to be emphasized that the major institutions and structures of English government in the early-seventeenth century were controlled largely by the professional groups identified above, who conceptualized their workings in ways that owe more to their professional training and the linguistic resources that it provided than to European traditions of political philosophy.

The second caveat requires the introduction of a (rough and ready) distinction between the makers or generators of a language and its users or consumers. Clearly, much political discourse in our period was conducted by people who were not members of any of the learned professions. In particular, the political world of early Stuart England was dominated by the aristocracy and the gentry. The gentry spoke not only in their localities, as Justices of the Peace or landlords, but also in the House of Commons as representatives of their communities. Nevertheless, the language that they spoke, when it is of significance for the history of political thought, was not of their own devising. Most often, indeed, they spoke in the terms of the common law, for many gentlemen had a smattering of legal knowledge acquired from the Inns of Court.[6] On the other hand some may have used a language that derived from Puritan preachers or Calvinist writers. But whatever theoretical language they used, it was one provided by the intellectual labours of others. The most characteristic political attitude of the gentry may have been localism, but there was no language of localism that can satisfy the criteria of self-containment and coherence laid down above. The gentry were the users not the generators of language.

In the early-seventeenth century each of our three languages had a recognized range of applications, and could be used to address particular types of political question without arousing controversy. Here can be introduced the third key term that we need, that of *audience*. It is easy to discover that in the early Stuart period different people say what *seem* to be incompatible things about, for example, the nature of monarchy. Some might say that the king has authority by God's grace and that all his subjects have a duty to obey him; others might say that kings are bound to obey the laws of the land. When juxtaposed in this way the statements *appear* antagonistic. Yet James I himself could make both of them, as we shall see. This is because the statements are made in different contexts, to different audiences. Many claims about the absolute nature of English monarchy for example, are aimed more at the claims of the Papacy to temporal supremacy than at the monarch's own subjects. Statements appropriate to an international Catholic audience were, however, less appropriate for a domestic audience, and so in the debate on impositions James produced a defence of his position in terms more compatible with common law.

The point of this is that if we simply bring together pieces of political theory understood out of context it is quite easy to pit them against one another and produce a 'debate' or disagreement that never took place. In fact, claims and principles addressed to different audiences might be rather like ships that pass in the night, and their supposed conflict a fiction. Such differing claims were the product of different languages being used for different purposes. There were, in other words, accepted *conventions* in Jacobean England governing the use of the available political languages. Indeed this is where consensus in the period resides – not in the absence of conflict, but in a shared set of conventions for the theoretical resolution of conflict, and for the non-controversial employment of a variety of languages. To understand this, however, we must know more about the three languages and their range of accepted uses.

(B)   THE THREE LANGUAGES (I): COMMON LAW

The language of common law is something of which much has already been heard in this book, and it can therefore be treated more briefly here. In the *political* world of Jacobean England the common lawyers were probably the dominant professional group, and the language of the common law was (even more probably) the dominant language for the discussion of political issues (at least for a domestic audience). In 1600 Sir Thomas Wilson was able to note the dominance of common lawyers over other professions, which had occurred 'since the practice of civil law hath been as it were wholly banished and abrogated, and since the clergy hath been trodden down'.[7] Of note here are both the implicit assumption that these three professions are valuable categories of social analysis for this period, as well as the explicit statement of the common lawyers' dominance. It does not much matter whether Wilson was correct in his analysis of the causes of this dominance, it is the dominance itself that is important.

During the early-seventeenth century there were something under 2,000 attorneys practising at the Westminster Courts, and something under 500 barristers.[8] This compares with just a little over 200 civil lawyers practising in the Court of Admiralty or the ecclesiastical courts (though this figure excludes those men trained in civil law who held posts as chancellors of dioceses, officials of archdeacons, and other minor ecclesiastical posts).[9] The numerical superiority of the common lawyers was reinforced by their tighter and more coherent institutional and educational structure, and by the greater control they had over their own professional activities.[10]

As we have seen, perhaps the most important feature of the ideas held by this numerous and well-organized professional body was the claim that the common law, its principles and institutions, formed not only a necessary but a sufficient means for dealing with all *domestic* political problems that might be generated by the English political nation. Common lawyers certainly were aware that other types of law were in use in England, but they believed that the common law had a controlling jurisdiction that defined the limits of other jurisdictions, and that in the High Court of Parliament the ancient constitution provided an institution that could make laws superior to any others.

Central to this claim for a controlling jurisdiction of the common law is the idea that the common law itself embodied the moral principles of nature and reason, and that it embodied them in such a way as to ensure that they had become formulated in just the manner necessary to make them most useful for English needs. The ancient constitution and the common law were rational principles fitted by customary evolution to particular circumstances. They therefore made unnecessary any resort to a natural law or a law of reason that lay outside the common law. Further, because only those educated and trained in the 'artificial reason' of the common law could discern its full rationality, it followed that only the person with full knowledge of the common law was properly equipped to deal with questions of political right in a domestic context.[11]

For the moment we can postpone any discussion of the ways in which the language of common law functioned in political debate, except to make the simple point that it was indeed the most prominent way of discussing political issues in a practical context. This is most clearly seen in parliamentary debates, often dominated by lawyers, and in particular debates over taxation and finance. This is scarcely surprising, because property law was at the heart of the common law. We find that the words and concepts of the common law dominated the debates on impositions, forced loans and the Petition of Right.[12] Yet, equally clearly, there were areas in which common law needed supplementing, and this was recognized by most people. It was a law that was English, and hence was not well suited to dealing with matters that had an international dimension (hence the fact that Admiralty was staffed by civilians). Before the Reformation the church had been administered by canon law, and so here too the common law had no competence. Consequently, when the study of canon law was abolished in England it was the civil and not the common lawyer who replaced the canon lawyers.[13] These limits to the common law's jurisdictional capacity are carried over into its capacity for political debate. We shall see that for issues involving an international audience, as well as for some political issues with a theological dimension, other languages were more appropriate than that of common law.

(C)   THE THREE LANGUAGES (II): CIVIL LAW

During the early-seventeenth century civil lawyers had two main functions in England: they served the Court of Admiralty (which by this time had considerable powers in matters of shipping and mercantile commerce),[14] and they staffed the ecclesiastical courts. In addition to this civilians were, thanks to their knowledge of international law, sometimes employed as ambassadors or on various diplomatic missions.[15]

Just as they were limited professionally to a small number of lesser tasks, so too their theoretical writings tended to be limited in scope. While common lawyers, and gentlemen with knowledge of it, wrote about English constitutional history and antiquities, and addressed themselves to analysing the ancient constitution and the liberties and prerogatives that it allowed to subjects and kings, civilians addressed such matters only indirectly. This they could do in two ways: firstly through general analyses of the principles of politics as derived from the principles of natural law, and secondly through comparative analyses between English common law and civil law.

There has been considerable debate amongst scholars about whether or not Roman law propagated a particular set of political values. Most who have answered this question in the affirmative would probably point to its inherent absolutism, and the way in which continental rulers during the early modern period used it to foster their acquisition of absolute authority. They might contrast Roman law and English common law, the latter being seen as placing obstacles in the path of the development of absolute sovereignty.[16] This is not a debate in which we need to become involved, other than to issue a general warning that nothing as diverse and protean as the *Corpus Juris Civilis* and its subsequent commentators is likely to be of simple ideological thrust.

Rather more important for us is to understand some of the general characteristics of the language of civil law (as it is found in the writings of seventeenth-century English civilians). This will help us to understand the uses that could be made of such a language, and the audiences and problems that it could address without raising controversy. Three features of civil law writing in particular serve to contrast it with the writing of common law commentators:

1. it was conducted at a higher, more philosophical, level of
    generality;
2. it was predominantly rationalistic rather than historical, and
    took its shape from logical rather than historical principles of
    organization; and
3. it judged the adequacy of codes of positive law by measuring
    them against an *independently-known* set of laws of nature or
    reason.

All of these points have important implications, and therefore
require some elaboration. As a consequence of the first, we find
that civil lawyers are able to write about English institutions and
laws, the English constitution, with a detachment and an attention
to first principles that is not found amongst common lawyers.
Probably the most significant intellectual achievement resulting
from this was Sir Thomas Smith's *De Republica Anglorum* (1583),
of which it has been said that 'Smith could never have written
[it] . . . if he had not been a civil lawyer'. Only his studies in
the civil law gave him 'the ability to consider English institutions
from the outside'.[17] This same ability was seen in the writings
of those English civilians who produced comparative studies of
civil law and English common law. Smith himself did this in
De Republica Anglorum where the discussion of the English legal
system in Books II and III maintained a constant awareness of
the differences between England and other European countries. In
the early-seventeenth century a number of writers attempted more
elaborate comparative surveys, most famously John Cowell's effort
in *The Interpreter* (1607), of which we shall be hearing more. But
there were other attempts, much less contentious than Cowell's:
William Fulbecke's *A Parallele or Conference of the Civil Law, the Canon
Law, and the Common Law of this Realm of England* (1601, 1602); Sir
Thomas Ridley's *A View of the Civil and Ecclesiastical Law* (1607); and
Cowell's earlier work the *Institutiones iuris Anglicani ad methodum et
seriem institutionum imperialum compositae et digestae* (1605).[18] These
writers were able to address the question of how far English law
was similar to other laws, and therefore raise questions about the
extent to which English law could be judged by the adequacy with
which it embodied moral principles external to itself. The English
civilians were all respectful of common law, they wrote in its praise
not in criticism, and they tended to argue that it did indeed come
to much the same moral points as Roman law. But, all the same,

unlike their common lawyer colleagues they developed ways of assessing English law by seeing it from the outside rather than the inside. And they found the first principles of law to be not something inherent in the common law, but something contained in rational natural laws known independently of any particular code of positive law.

Coupled with this, is the greater analytical clarity of the civilians. The most obvious effect of this was their supposed concern with the concept of *sovereignty*.[19] It is this feature of their work that has given the civilians the reputation of favouring absolute authority. But to make this leap from the civilians' analytical clarity to attributing to them a particular ideological position is surely a mistake. It confuses an intellectual technique with a political disposition. The concept of sovereignty was developed – and this is particularly clear in Jean Bodin's *Six Books of a Commonwealth* – to provide an analytical concept that could be used in the analysis of all legal-constitutional systems. Bodin and other sixteenth century humanist and Roman law scholars were much exercised by the problem of the diversity of laws and institutions – ultimately by the problem of relativism. This made it difficult to talk about political or legal matters in general terms. One way of doing so was to search for what underlay the diversity of laws and institutions. From this search came the concept of sovereignty, which was for Bodin (as it was for Hobbes) not a normative recommendation but an analytic characteristic of all stable polities.[20] The comparative and philosophical approach of the civilians made them open to concepts of this sort – any comparative study of law and politics required a terminology applicable across national boundaries, and this is what a concept such as sovereignty provided.[21] Clear, rational analysis of the issue of sovereignty can be found in the writings of a whole succession of Regius Professors of Civil Law: Sir Thomas Smith, John Cowell, Alberico Gentili, and Richard Zouch.[22] To take just one example, Smith's *De Republica Anglorum*, we can see that the analytical precision that Smith gains from his humanist-civilian background was a tool of understanding rather than an ideological weapon. The aim was to give clear and succinct descriptions, and we can see Smith's analytical precision in his analysis of English monarchy, and the fact that the king had no superior (I, 9; & II, 3); his analysis of parliamentary supremacy (II, 1); and his reconciliation of the two (II, 4). What we end up with is a precise description of the 'absolute' nature of royal authority in England that avoided 'absolut*ism*' – it avoided it because some of the absolute powers could only be exercised with the consent of the realm assembled in Parliament.

As should now be apparent, the high level of philosophical abstraction at which civilians were able to work, as well as their employment of the comparative method, was made possible by their willingness to judge different law codes with reference to natural law. Concepts of natural law were a built-in foundation of the *Corpus Juris Civilis* itself. They formed, in particular, philosophical introductions to both the *Institutes* and the *Digest*, and made it apparent that all law, Roman or otherwise, depended for its legitimacy on the neatness of its fit with the moral principles of natural law. Common lawyers, as we have seen, showed almost no interest in the content or sources of natural law: it was contained in all existing codes of national laws, particularly if those codes had undergone a long process of customary refinement. The rational customs of the common law were in accord with the principles of the natural law simply because they were rational customs, with all that that implied.

But the view of the civilians was very different, as we can see from an examination of the way in which one leading civilian, John Hayward, made use of natural law theory. Hayward argued that, though the *Digest* defined the law of nations (which Hayward took to be part of the law of nature) as consisting of those laws observed everywhere,[23] it should not be imagined 'as though all nations have at any time observed one usage alike'. The Fall, and the consequent corruption of human reason, meant that there was no agreement amongst individuals or nations about what was and what was not naturally just; and, in any case, it had never 'bin brought into knowledge what customes all nations have held in use'. The fact that many transgressed the laws of nature did not alter the fact that it contained the principles of natural right.[24] This ruled out any possibility of knowing natural law simply from looking at its embodiment in any one code of positive law (such as the common law), because there was always the possibility that such laws were corrupted and contrary to natural reason. Thus Hayward, unlike the common lawyers, allowed that natural and positive law might actually (as opposed to just theoretically) be in disagreement, and consequently that the moral validity of the common law (or any other positive law system) could only be determined by assessing *from the outside* its accordance with natural reason. This was quite different, of course, from the beliefs associated with the common lawyers' ideas of 'artificial reason', which enabled those trained in the law to discern its rationality from the inside.

Hayward proceeded to discuss how knowledge of the natural law could in fact be obtained. There were three rules governing the matter. The first two (where there *is* universal consent to certain propositions, or where there *are* customs universally observed, then it is a sign that such propositions or practices are in accord with natural reason and thus allowable by natural law) do not get us far, because Hayward had already denied that universal agreement is either necessary or important as an indicator of natural right. His third rule is 'to observe what hath bin allowed by those who are of greatest both wisedome and integrity, in whom nature doth shew her selfe most cleere'. There were three categories of such wise men: first, the compilers of scripture, plus the ancient councils and fathers of the church; second, philosophers, historiographers, orators and the like; and, third, there were the authors of the civil law, plus their interpreters 'of most approved note'. The civil law, Hayward added for good measure, 'hath bin these many hundred yeers, admired by many, approved by all, and is at this daie accepted for lawe, almost in all states of the christian common wealth'.[25] The effect of this was to make the civil lawyer (and other interpreters of Roman law) into a controller of the common law. The fact that the civil lawyers who wrote about common law in fact used their external perspective to point out its *congruence* with Roman law[26] should not hide the fact that they were implicitly claiming the right to judge its soundness from the outside.

Of the three features of civil law thinking identified above, we have examined the close connection between the first (its high level of abstraction) and the third (its claim to measure positive law against standards external to itself). The second feature remains in need of elaboration, the reliance upon logical rather than historical organization. This was one feature of civil law thought that had considerable impact on common lawyers, and led to demands for the codification of the common law along simple, rational lines.[27] The demand was not new in the early-seventeenth century: it had been made by those earlier Tudor humanists who were attracted by continental jurisprudence and Roman law and appalled at the barbarities of the common law.[28] The most distinguished advocate of codifying and reorganizing English law in the early-seventeenth century was Sir Francis Bacon. While Bacon may have been influenced in this direction by his humanist (which is to say in this context, his Roman law) learning, it is instructive to see the limits he wished to draw around the process of codification. Bacon was a trained common lawyer and, though he became much else besides, he remained devoted to the historical organization of the common law. While a civilian such as John Cowell in his *Institutes* might be prepared to fit the common law into the rational categories of the *Corpus Juris Civilis*, Bacon's proposals were not. Cowell, as a glance at his contents pages shows, proposed to fit the common law into a series of topics derived from the *Institutes* of Justinian.[29] Bacon, as we saw in Chapter 2, proposed a reorganization of the law that preserved its matter in the historical form that it had acquired over time.[30] In these proposals for rationalization – and especially in any comparison of them with the writings of such civilians as Fulbecke and Cowell – we can see clearly the difference between the primarily historical orientation of the common lawyer and the more rationalistic one of the civilian. For all the impact of legal humanism on Roman law studies, the discipline remained wedded to a systematic arrangement of law that was inappropriate for a country such as England, where the law in force was a customary one and where unwritten custom remained the paradigm of a good law.

These three features of civil law that we have examined together determined its range of acceptable use. There were obvious political situations in which the language of the common law would be inadequate, and they shared the common feature of involving an international dimension. When there was a need to address political problems that were not purely English this had to be done in terms of legal first principles, natural law, and the law of nations. Much of this was of Roman law origin, and had to be talked about using Roman law traditions if an international audience was to be persuaded, or even engaged with. One civilian, Calybute Downing, explicitly argued that because European international relations were conducted largely in civil law terms, this fitted the civilians for a role in the conduct of international politics above all other groups.[31]

For Englishmen after 1603 it is probable that the most important arena for the employment of Roman law ideas and terms was in discussion of 'the British problem', that is the relationship between the English polity and those of Scotland and Ireland. Already when James came to the throne, he inherited an 'Imperiall Crowne', 'the Imperiall Crowne of England'.[32] The designation of the English crown as 'imperial' was a product of medieval ideas about public law, not an English common law one, and was initially made common usage to assert the independence of the crown and realm from papal control.[33] James I later used the same term to cover his proposal for a union of the Scottish and English Crowns 'under one Imperiall Crowne'.[34] Thus in both the 1530s and the 1600s the Roman law term 'imperial' was used to describe the English (or British) crown in an international context that ascribed to it sovereign independence.

In both the debates on Anglo-Scottish union and the legal arguments of Calvin's Case (1608) we find natural and civil law principles unusually dominant. Indeed, it is in this context that we can meet with the most unlikely spectacle of Sir Edward Coke grounding allegiance to the Crown in natural law.

The Parliamentary and pamphlet debates on James I's proposal to bring the English and Scottish crowns together saw contributions from both common and civil lawyers. It needs to be stressed that the issue was both one on which civilians were felt to be qualified to judge, and one on which even common lawyers would resort to civil law principles in order to discuss the matter adequately. On the question of whether or not those Scotsmen born after 1603 were aliens in England (the question at issue in Calvin's Case), the House of Commons itself made much of a civil law maxim which stated (in Francis Bacon's paraphrase) that 'when two rights do meet in one person, there is no confusion of them, but they remain still in the eye of the law distinct'.[35] In the pamphlet debates on Union there was much discussion of comparative law and politics, even in the contribution of a practising common lawyer such as John Doddridge.[36] Further, much of the discussion of legal union was based on a civil-law distinction between public and private law, and some even proposed that the civil law and its basic principles should be used as a foundation for the union of English and Scottish law.[37] The point is not, of course, that English common lawyers wanted to import civil law into England in any way; it is rather that when forced to discuss legal issues of more than English scope they had to use the language of civil and natural law, even if they used it to defend English common law from supposed impurities.

It is scarcely surprising also that, even though something like English common law was administered in Ireland, when they came to discuss and to practice law in an Irish context common lawyers had resort to principles of Roman law. Ireland was a conquered nation, and any justification of conquest would require resort to the *jus gentium*. Consequently, Sir John Davies made selective use of Roman law conquest doctrine to justify the replacement of Irish customs with English law.[38] Furthermore, in his actual practise of law in Ireland Davies showed himself ready to supplement common law with civil and canon law where the need arose. Usually (as in ecclesiastical matters) this was in areas where English common law had little to offer; but it seems also that Davies's use of civil law had an imperialist function, 'to justify and consolidate English sovereignty over the island'.[39] It is clear, then, that when operating in this 'British' context even common lawyers would be willing to resort to Roman law traditions. Naturally, there remain differences in the degree to which various individuals were prepared to do this. For example, in Calvin's Case both Bacon and Coke grounded the allegiance owed by subjects to their sovereign on the law of nature. In Bacon's case this led to the argument (much misunderstood as a form of 'absolutism') that though the rule of kings had subsequently been made 'regular' and 'limited by law' – or 'perfected' as he said more ambiguously – royal dominion began with one man governing arbitrarily. Bacon would appear not to be saying that the king's *prerogative* derived from this original arbitrary rule, but rather that the duty of allegiance alone did so. Allegiance to kings 'is more natural and simple' than allegiance to any other form of rule. This is because allegiance to a king is to a *natural* body, whereas allegiance to a republic (for example) is to an artificial body that must first be constituted 'by a law precedent'. The argument was a clever way of saying that, although the power of kings had subsequently been defined and limited by law, allegiance to them retained a natural simplicity. Thus subjects could be shown to have a *natural* (and not just a legal) duty of submission to the king, without this altering the fact that the way in which the king could govern was now shaped by law.[40] Bacon could thus argue the case he was expected to argue as Solicitor-General (that allegiance was due by natural law to the person of the king) *without* undermining the political status of common law. He specifically indicated that the argument in a case of this sort was to be conducted in terms of 'reason' not in those of any 'municipal law'.[41]

Coke accepted much of this – but with one significant qualification. He agreed that 'ligeance or obedience of the inferior to the superior, of the subject to the sovereign, was due by the law of nature many thousand years before any law of man was made', and that 'it remaineth still due by the law of nature'.[42] Such a view seems scarcely compatible with what Coke said elsewhere, in his more Fortescuean moments. There he seldom showed much willingness to contemplate a period before the laws of men were made. It is not surprising, then, to find that Coke sought to ease his discomfort by a demonstration that 'this law of nature is part of the laws of England'.[43] In his discussion of natural law Coke certainly referred to such sources as the scriptures, Aristotle and Cicero. But repeatedly he added 'and herewith doth agree . . . ', and proceeded to show that the great oracles of English law also accepted such principles as part of the law of England. He cited in this context Bracton, Fortescue and St German.[44] The effect is curiously to suggest that there might be some doubt in the matter, that English law might not contain the natural law, and that if it did not do so, so much the worse for natural law! It was the willingness of the law of England to recognize natural law that gave it force in England. However, though Coke tried to get around the problem, it remained true that when forced to confront the issue of allegiance in a context that was British and not just English, he had to move outside the common law of England and rely on the natural law of civilian traditions. As Bruce Galloway has pointed out, it is easy to be misled by Coke's verbiage into missing the point that, here, even he accepted 'the picture of a king ruling by law of nature, over and above common or municipal laws'.[45]

Beyond the British dimension of English politics there was also a European dimension. This was most obviously the case with the long debate, that ran through James's reign, in which King James and his supporters defended the kings of Europe against papal pretensions to an indirect deposing power.[46] (The theory of indirect deposing power held that the Pope had no direct authority in temporal matters, but that the exercise of his spiritual authority could have indirect temporal consequences, including deposition.) The vast bulk of this debate was linked in one way or another to the Oath of Allegiance which was required initially of those suspected of Catholicism, but extended in 1610 to virtually everybody over the age of eighteen. The Oath required subjects to swear that James was the lawful king, to deny outright the theory of the indirect deposing power, and to swear allegiance to James even in the face of any papal excommunication of him.[47] The debate over the Oath became a European one, conducted in Latin, though there was also a subsidiary English debate aimed at a more local audience. It was conducted mainly by clerics, and we shall hear more of it when we discuss theological languages of politics below.[48] But in the present context it is worth noting that the international anti-Catholic slant of the Oath of Allegiance defence made it a suitable context in which to espouse basically medieval-law theories of 'Imperial' independence from the papacy. It should also be remembered that the main catalyst of the theory of the divine-right of kings was the need to defend the independence of kings against papal interference.[49] While the problem was one with a substantial medieval pedigree, it remained a live issue in Jacobean England.

Without doubt, then, civil law traditions and language had a place in the political discourse of England in the reign of James I. Problems that could not be addressed through the common law, and in particular problems that needed to be tackled from an international perspective, could make use of the ability of civil law concepts to work from first principles or through comparative methods. This was an accepted sphere of operation for civilian traditions, as is demonstrated by the fact that even common lawyers used such traditions when they were working in this area. More problematic, however, was the capacity of civilians and the civil law to speak on domestic political issues, a matter that will be discussed more fully below. Nevertheless, we can say here that although civilians might write or speak on domestic issues, there was no challenge from them to the principle that it was the common law that defined the liberties of Englishmen. They might be impatient with the disorganization and mythology of the common law, but they accepted its pre-eminence in England.

(D)   THE THREE LANGUAGES (III): THEOLOGY

After the Reformation had pruned the numbers of the clerical estate in England from about 35,000 to 15,000, and educational change had improved clerical standards over the late-sixteenth and early-seventeenth centuries, it became possible to see the Church of England clergy as a *profession* in ways that were not possible before the 1530s. By the Civil War the clergy were, like the common lawyers, a relatively cohesive and well trained group attempting to maintain their professional standards in the face of not always adequate remuneration.[50] Though there were considerable differences of opinion on many issues within the clergy, there was probably no time between the 1530s and the 1660s when they were as united in basic theological beliefs as they were during the reign of James I. For the purpose of the broad delineation of a theological language of politics that is being attempted here we can, for the moment, leave aside any differences amongst the clergy. Theology was in many ways as important and fundamental a language for political discussion as the common law during the early-seventeenth century, but the two usually operated in quite separate fields. What we need to do here is to delineate the areas of the political sphere in which theological ideas were used appropriately. Such areas are delimited both by the nature of theological language, and by the audiences that it might address. Three of them can be put forward for further discussion.

First, and probably most commonly, the closest that most early Stuart Englishmen would get to hearing statements of political *philosophy* would probably have been while listening to sermons (especially Assize sermons) or homilies. In this context the subjects of James I were frequently reminded of the duty of submission to their ruler and the divine right by which he and all legitimate powers exercised their authority. Second, very similar views of the power of kings could be put forward not to assert monarchical rights over their subjects but to assert monarchical independence of the papacy. This area of anti-papal rhetoric, therefore, constituted an alternative field for the expression of theories of the divine right of secular authority. A third area has attracted much recent attention: the use, especially during the 1620s, of the image of the godly prince to teach kings their duties. This area was really a continuation of the second in altered circumstances: after the initial Catholic successes in the Thirty Years War writers began to explore the *duties* imposed upon Protestant rulers by their possession of divine right. God guaranteed their independence of the Pope and of their subjects, but he also required them to do his work. In this last context theological language took on an obviously millenarian edge, as could any theories put forward in an anti-papal context (James I himself spent some time in his defence of kings against the indirect deposing power demonstrating that the Pope was Antichrist). The first area, however, was primarily dominated by order theory and patriarchalism.

So we have a picture that looks like this. There are three main components (or sub-languages) of the theological language of political debate (order theory, patriarchalism, millenarianism); and they are employed in three fields of discussion, which is to say, are used to address three different audiences. There is the domestic preaching of the duty of subjection, relying mainly on order theory and patriarchalism; there is an international debate over the relations between kings and the papacy, which uses a variety of languages including both millenarianism and ideas derived from medieval jurisprudential political thought; and there is a domestic context in which millenarian ideas play a role, especially in discussion of foreign policy in the 1620s.

The most obvious example of the uncontentious use of order theory to put forward a powerful statement of the divine origin of royal authority and the need for unchallengeable subjection of the multitude is the Elizabethan homilies, which were 'thought fit to be reprinted by Authority from the Kings most excellent Majestie' in 1623.[51] The homily on obedience to rulers began:

> Almighty God hath created and appointed all things in heaven, earth, and waters, in a most excellent and perfect order. In heaven, hee hath appointed distinct and severall orders and states of Archangels and Angels. In earth hee hath assigned and appointed Kings, Princes, with other governours under them, in all good and necessary order.[52]

All rulers are established 'by Gods goodnesse', and the homily instructed subjects (citing Romans 13) that they must obey rulers, not only for fear of punishment, 'but also because of conscience'. Disobedience to Kings is disobedience to God.[53] Even evil rulers must be obeyed: 'all Subjects are bound to obey them as Gods ministers, yea, although they be evill'.[54] All resistance or rebellion is contrary to God's command, indeed 'the violence and injury that is committed against authoritie, is committed against God, the common weale, and the whole Realm'.[55]

These points were the commonplaces of early Stuart political thought, and were reiterated endlessly in sermons and pamphlets. In 1610, Lancelot Andrewes, preaching before the king, took as his text 1 Chronicles 16, 22: 'Touch not mine anointed'. This text, Andrewes argued, was the 'great Commandment touching the safeguard of Princes', a commandment that taught subjects their duty towards their rulers: 'to do them no hurt'.[56] Furthermore, this duty of subjection and obedience arose *solely* because princes were God's anointed, and had no dependence on the qualities and capacities the ruler displayed (or failed to display). The anointing of kings gave them 'the right of ruling'; it did not require 'the ruling right'. 'Allegiance is not due to him, because he is vertuous, religious, or wise; because, He is *Christus Domini'*. Obedience is due to all anointed princes, even when they are 'as evill a Prince as might be'.[57] The divine authorization of kingly rule was also a common theme of assize sermons. Magistracy, Samuel Ward announced in Bury St Edmunds, was the 'creature and ordinance of God', and was instituted primarily so that kings could do God's work.[58] Rather more emphatically, Thomas Scot (of Ipswich) told the same audience in 1633 that 'what Almighty God is in his great monarchy of the world, that (in his proportion) is every absolute King in his own dominion: for he is in Gods place unto his people, to nourish and protect them'.[59] For Edward Reynolds, princes were God's 'deputies and Vicegerents', and consequently must be honoured 'with cheereful obedience, and with willing Tribute'.[60] And finally, John White of Dorchester seems to have made similar points in a sermon of 1632. White's own text has not survived, but in 1648 (by which time White was preaching in support of Parliament) his sermon was published from the notes taken of it by one of his audience. The point of the publication was to demonstrate White's inconsistency, for his sermon of 1632 was a powerful (though not unequivocal) condemnation of resistance. 'Magistrates are Gods', White argued. Any rebellion or failure to give them due reverence 'is not a trespasse against men, but a sin against God himselfe'. Our obligaton to obey is an obligaton not to the person whom we obey but to God himself.[61]

These sermons all made use of a direct and simple verson of *order* theory. The theory held, to put it as simply as possible, that God created an ordered universe in which all things had their pre-determined place in a complex hierarchy. Within the general hierarchical structure of the universe (macrocosm), were subordinate bodies (microcosms) whose internal arrangement mirrored that of the macrocosm. One of these was the body politic, the commonwealth, the structure of which 'was held to reflect the gradational form characteristic of the universal scale of creation: society was a hierarchy of social degrees and ranks'.[62] The attempt by individuals to move from the place that God had assigned them in the hierarchy was sinful. This sin covered rebellion, the attempt to take from the monarch, God's appointee, his role of deciding all public issues. Quite literally, this was having ideas above one's station. Historians have generally thought that the political implications of this system of ideas were the legitimation of something close to arbitrary monarchy because 'the duty of inferiors was always and only to obey'.[63] More recently, though, others have pointed out that the theory placed limits on kings as well: they were unchallengeably superior to their subjects, true, but it was equally true that a king's position in the divine hierarchy subordinated him to natural law and divine purposes. The royal office – like all offices and callings – was designed by its divine creator to serve certain purposes, and God required kings to fulfil those purposes. Indeed, though rebellion and resistance were ruled out, subjects might still have a duty to refuse to perform any commands by their rulers that were contrary to God's laws. Subjects were always subjects, but they were the subjects of God as well as of the king. And, on the other hand, though the will of the sovereign might well be the creator and guarantor of civil order, it might equally well be the case that the *untrammelled* sovereign will could be disruptive of order.[64]

Whatever the niceties, however, order theory was a statement of the immutably hierarchical nature of the political world. The position was maintained using arguments that were often analogical in character: the king's position in the microcosm of the common-wealth was analogous to the position of God in the macrocosm. But other analogies were available. Perhaps the most common was the comparison between king-in-commonwealth and father-in-family. This gave rise to an important sub-language closely attached to order theory, namely patriarchalism.[65] For some, the analogy between kings and fathers was *just* an analogy and did not imply that monarchy developed from patriarchal origins, or that patriarchal and royal authority were in essence the same thing. An example might be Edward Forsett, a man capable of finding all imaginable analogies (and some others). Forsett claimed that 'the Prince is *Pater Patriae*, the Father of the Countrey', and that this relationship was a 'similitude in Nature'. Subjects therefore had a natural subjection to their rulers 'out of the resemblance of these two paternes' (i.e. of monarchy and patriarchy).[66] Other writers, however, went beyond simple analogy. The most famous of these was, Sir Robert Filmer in his *Patriarcha* (which may have been written in the 1620s, or even earlier),[67] in which it was argued that kings, though 'not the natural parents of their subjects', nevertheless 'either are, or are to be reputed, as the next heirs of those progenitors who were at first the natural parents of the whole people'.[68] In short, monarchy was nothing but the continuation of the rule of the patriarchs found amongst the descendants of Noah.[69] Such a view did not originate with Filmer,[70] but was indeed adopted by Convocation in 1606. God,

> did give to Adam for his time, and to the rest of the patriarchs and chief fathers successively before the flood, authority, power, and dominion over their children and offspring, to rule and govern them.

This power can 'be called either patriarchal, regal, and imperial' for *potestas regia* and *potestas patria* mean the same thing.[71] Much the same situation prevailed after the Flood. During this period Noah exercised a 'patriarchal, or in effect, regal government', and subsequent civil authority was (in some sense) derived from this original rule of Noah. His sons, for example, became 'three great princes'.[72] In versions such as this, patriarchal language went beyond analogy to the assertion that patriarchal and regal authority were the same thing, with common origins. The point of it was to confute those who thought that regal authority 'did not proceed originally from God'.[73] Patriarchy was a natural institution dependent immediately on God's providence. If civil rule was the same thing, then it too was an immediate outgrowth of the divine will.

These theological languages of politics were found also in the anti-papal writings of the Oath of Allegiance controversy. In so far as that controversy was an international debate, we can afford to leave it aside. But it did provide as well an alternative context for the presentation to a domestic audience of ideas similar to those discussed above. It would be tedious to go over this ground again, but we can use the most important of tracts aimed at a domestic audience to draw some conclusions about the basic characteristics of divine-right languages of political discussion. The work in question is Richard Mocket's *God and the King* (1615). On the 8 November 1615 the King issued a proclamation commending the book to the youth of the nation as a way of settling their minds on the truth and saving them from any foolish inclination to refuse to take the Oath. The proclamation indicated that the King had ordered the bishops to ensure 'the universall dispersing' of Mocket's book.[74] *God and the King* was, then, an official epitome of approved religious doctrine (the proclamation recommended it as a religious, not political, treatise). The content of the work is unremarkable (as one would expect) and it excited no controversy. This is a point worthy of some note: the many statements of divine right theory discussed here excited no controversy or opposition. And yet a few writers, putting forward much the same ideas, got themselves into some trouble (as we shall see). Why the difference? The answer seems to be this: that in order to be used uncontentiously theological languages of politics needed to be unspecific. As general statements of the divine right of authority, and the duty of complete subjection (or possibly passive obedience), sermons and religious pamphlets were expressions of the commonplace. *But they properly functioned only at a high level of generality.* Any attempt to use divine-right language to deduce the particular prerogatives of kings or the particular duties of subjects was a different matter. This was the sphere of law not of religion, and so to defend (let us say) the king's right to non-parliamentary taxation in terms of his divine warrant to rule was a mistake akin to a category error.

These points will be elaborated shortly. Here what needs to be stressed is the highly-generalized non-specific nature of the political claims normally made in theological language. Let us return to Mocket's *God and the King* for illustration. Much of the book is an account of popish machinations against Elizabeth I and James (in spite of the latter's 'rare and admirable' 'clemency' toward them early in his reign),[75] and a defence of the King's right to impose an Oath of Allegiance (partly on the ground 'that there is a stronger and higher bond of duetie betweene children and the Father of their Countrie, then the Fathers of private families').[76] The political principles underlying the oath (excluding those that concerned the powers of the papacy) were, then, resolved into two points: first, that the King 'receiving his Authority only from God, hee hath no superior to punish or chastice him but God alone'; and, second, 'that the bond of his subjects in obedience unto his sacred Majesty is inviolable, and cannot be dissolved'.[77] These two points neatly encapsulate the major thrust of religious languages of politics – and their *vagueness*. Everyone can agree that kings rule by divine right and the duty of subjection is inviolable, *provided* that this does not commit them to agreeing that kings can murder or steal as they like. Indeed, the very effectiveness of Mocket's argument was reliant upon its inherent ambiguity: his platitudes could mean all things to all men. Almost nothing is said about the actual duties of kings, about their relationship to the law or to parliament, and so on; because at the level at which Mocket was operating these were inessential matters. His work was, it must be reiterated, primarily a *religious* instruction in the duty of allegiance required of subjects by God. To argue that this makes Mocket an 'absolutist' theorist is simply to mistake the sort of task upon which he was engaged. Who didn't think that allegiance was a duty?

Of course, in the 1620s theological languages of politics came to be used in attempts to pressure the king into anti-Catholic policies at home and abroad, and in particular to push for English involvement in the Thirty Years' War (as it was subsequently to be known). Pamphleteers like the notorious Thomas Scott, reminded their king of the need to enforce recusancy laws, to avoid the wiles of the Spanish, and (in general) to make sure they were on the right side of the war with Antichrist. The arguments employed for this end were various. The King, it might be argued, should follow the example of good Queen Elizabeth; he had a duty to perform the office of a godly prince and to fulfil the ideals of Foxean apocalyptic.[78] Yet, whatever the political significance of these developments of the 1620s, their theoretical significance should not be exaggerated. Peter Lake has written of Thomas Scott, that he 'was operating within what he and certainly most of his contemporaries assumed to be an ideological consensus'.[79] Scott did not import the language of religious war into English *domestic* politics,[80] where his advice (though forceful) was in the language of counsel not that of resistance. Like most of his contemporaries Scott believed in the divine backing given to royal authority ('God hath appointed Kings and Judges to bee life tenants and Deputies in his steade');[81] he believed, too, that decisions of the king-in-parliament were to be 'obeyed for conscience sake';[82] and that if the king should command something contrary to God's wishes the subject must (of course) obey God rather than man, but should 'suffer what is injoyned by him [i.e. the king]', so that:

> thou obayest God and Caesar too; God actively, doing what he wills; and Caesar passively, submitting thy will to Gods holy ordinance, and obaying the Magistrate for conscience sake.[83]

In accepting the due punishment from the King, one is obeying in a sense, thus the duty of obedience is complete and unconditional. Certainly, Scott emphasized the need for laws to be made in Parliament, and the need for kings to be bound by law;[84] but these were commonplace opinions. It should not be forgotten that Scott, like many others, combined opinions such as these with conventional ideas of divine right and unconditional subjection. Indeed there is virtually no one in the 1620s who expressed in domestic debate the view that subjects could resist their kings.[85]

We can conclude, then, of the theological language of politics (made up primarily of the sub-languages of order theory, patriarchalism, millenarianism) that it possessed an uncontested capacity to make statements of *moral* duty, but that in *political* matters was vague and unspecific. It could be used to tell subjects of their duty to obey, or to tell kings of their duty to resist Antichrist; it could be used to give instruction on the need to love kings as one loved one's father; or on the importance of kings ruling for the common good and not selfishly. It was much less suited to the task of indicating how these goals were to be achieved. In short, theology provided the purpose, politics and law the means. The usual statements made with a theological language of politics were aimed at an audience that often included many from outside the political élite (the auditors of sermons, the general populace), and were aimed at instructing them in their role as subjects. It would be a mistake to think that most of the statements were intended to make particular political or ideological points. In fact they were generally compatible with a wide range of political positions. We need now to consider how this compatibility was effected.

6

Making Consensus Work

It is a striking feature of the 'Jacobean consensus' that it co-existed with sharp disagreements over political policy and action, and with a range of seemingly quite different theoretical approaches to politics. To explain this situation we need to answer two questions:

1. How could 'consensus' exist in a world in possession of the variety of languages and theoretical traditions examined in Chapter 5?
2. If there was indeed ideological 'consensus' of some sort in the Jacobean period, then why was this also a period one in which at least some level of political conflict was evident? How did consensus survive, or even generate, conflict?

The first question, then, raises the problem of the compatibility of consensus with ideological, theoretical and linguistic diversity; the second, the problem of the compatibility of consensus and conflict.

(A) CONSENSUS AND LINGUISTIC DIVERSITY

The place to begin any discussion of this problem is with the subject of the royal prerogative. It is around the issues of the scope, nature and limits of royal prerogative that the most significant political debates and disagreements of Jacobean political theory cohere. An examination of the ways available for talking about the royal prerogative will therefore serve well to indicate the nature of 'consensus' in the period.

One thing needs to be emphasized: the conventional early Stuart understanding of the royal prerogative was a *duplex* one.[1] The power and authority of the king could be viewed in two quite different ways. But – and this is the crucial point – most people at the time

139

did not see these two views as contradictory, even though in our eyes they might appear quite irreconcilable.

Kings, it was widely agreed, possessed both an *ordinary* and an *absolute* prerogative.[2] 'The King's power is double, ordinary and absolute', as Chief Baron Fleming put it in 1606.[3] Fleming's remarks were made while giving judgement for the crown in Bate's case, and much of the subsequent debate on impositions (particularly in the Commons during the 1610 and 1614 sessions) explored in detail the distinction between absolute and ordinary prerogative. The 1614 Commons Committee on Impositions – whose report was delivered by Sir Edwin Sandys on May 5 – argued that if the king could impose,

> it must be either by legall power, or out of absolute auctority; if by the former, then aither as a matter of fact or law, itt was never dun w[ith]out assent, then noe matter of fact and being never dun then not lawfull . . . . If out of absolute auctority then hath he noe law to governe him, which is a case very miserable and against the grownd of the common la[w].[4]

Earlier in the 1614 session it was stated by Sir Herbert Croft that the king possessed both an absolute and a legal/ordinary power. The general theory of prerogative that Croft proposed seems to have been accepted as a basis for the debate. He argued

> that the king if he have power to impose thes new impositions, itt must be either by his lawfull power or absolute power. Touching his lawfull power, itt was never soe iudged by the common law before this judgment in the exchecer [i.e. the judgement in Bate's Case, 1606]. Thearfore not the opinion of antiquity, for absolute power the king had none to make any law touching the prejudice of his subject aither for life, liberty, or goods, but either by laws inacted or to be inacted. For England obeys noe laws but such as themselfs make.[5]

Subsequent debate was over the crucial question of whether or not the royal action of imposing new custom duties could properly be said to be within the sphere of the absolute prerogative, or not.

The same distinction between ordinary and absolute prerogative played a substantial role in the debates of 1610 as well. Though the conflict over impositions has been seen as being sparked off by opposition to demands of the crown that were 'based on principles which would lead to the extinction of English liberty',[6] this judgement is difficult to support. The central issue was not the ability of the common law to preserve Englishmen's property rights against the royal prerogative; it was the matter of the limits to the reach and scope of the common law that provided fuel for debate. This comes through most clearly in the debates of 1610. When it became apparent to James that the Commons were going to insist on including impositions in their list of grievances he assured them that he would follow the habits of his predecessors in the matter, 'neither would he meddle with any property of *meum* and *tuum*; neither would he impose upon any of his subjects lands or goods, but onely upon merchandises exported and imported, and that in Parliament'.[7] Both in 1606 and in 1610 the crown's case clearly rested on the argument that impositions on imports were not a threat to the property rights of the king's subjects. Indeed, they had nothing to do with English property rights, which *were* protected by the common law. The king's right to impose customs duties was a matter of *absolute* prerogative, not because this gave the king rights over or against common law, but because it gave him rights outside it. When Bates's goods were taxed, they were Venetian not English, as Fleming made apparent in his original judgement:

> That the King may impose upon a subject, I omit, for it is not here the question if the King may impose upon the subject or his goods. But the impost here is not upon a subject, but here it is upon Bates . . . and at the time when the impost was imposed upon them, they were the goods of the Venetians and not the goods of a subject, nor within the land . . . .[8]

Both Fleming and the king himself were careful to argue that impositions by prerogative were not a threat to common law because they were only applied in areas beyond the territorial jurisdiction of English common law. In such areas (i.e. the high seas) the law of nations held sway, and here the king could use his prerogative to impose duties for the common good. As Yelverton put it, defending the prerogative in 1610, 'the merchants of England trade not by the common lawe of the land, but by the lawe of nations'. In international trade 'wee are where the common lawe cannot judge. The merchant . . . is not under the protection of the lawe, thoe under the protection of the King'.[9] Francis Bacon, attempting to clarify the issues before a Commons that preferred them muddy, said that there was no one claiming that the king could alter the law, or impose duties upon subjects within the realm. Impositions involved 'the government of the kingdome as it hath relation to forrayne parts'; in this area it was not positive law but God and nature that provided remedies.[10]

Between the competing sides in the imposition debate there was substantial *theoretical* agreement. Everyone agreed that the common law protected property, within England at least, and that the king could not infringe upon property rights without his subjects' consent. Most agreed also that the king had both an ordinary and an extraordinary (or absolute) prerogative, the latter properly used not to *contravene* the common law (through which the king exercised his ordinary prerogative) but to supplement it. It provided a basis for royal action in areas where the common law had no force, whether geographical (possibly the high seas) or institutional (possibly the church). The dispute was not primarily theoretical at all, but more about whether impositions were *in fact* properly a matter for the absolute prerogative and thus of no concern to the common law. Thomas Hedley, responding to Bacon, simply denied that there were limits to the reach of the common law. He was reported to have said: 'this question determinable onely by the common lawe of England, for lawe of State he knowes not. This lawe holds allwayes except in tyme of warre'.[11] Martin made much the same point against Yelverton, arguing that 'the common law extends as farr [as] the power of the Kinge extends'.[12] In consequence, the king had no authority by the law of nations that was not also controlled by the common law. This applied to international commerce as much as anything else. William Hakewill, with considerable verbal ingenuity argued that because the impositions dispute was about the king's right to impose *customs* duties it must be a matter for the common law. The fact that these taxes were called customs was proof enough: 'it is of the very essence of a Custome to have his only beginning by allowance of the common-law'. 'Thus you see, that the very name *consuetudo* [custom] proves Custome to bee a dutie by common-law'.[13] Therefore, because taxes on international trade were in the same category as any other tax on property or wealth, the king could not impose customs duties without the consent of the realm.[14] Other opponents of the crown position might accept that the matter was one which could be discussed in terms of the law of nations, but would then deny that the law of nations allowed the king the right to impose duties at will. Sir Roger Owen, in defence of his claim that 'it is contrary to the lawe of nations to take away the property of mans goods' examined the practice of ancient and modern rulers to show that the claims of James I were not in accord with usual international practices.[15]

But perhaps the most important of the speeches against the royal position, and the one that seems to have structured the terms of the 1614 debate, was that of James Whitelocke. Whitelocke accepted the view that the king had a 'duplex' prerogative, ordinary and absolute (though he did not employ those terms). He argued that in every state there was a sovereign power (*potestas suprema*), 'a power that can controule all other powers, and cannot be controuled but by itself'. This power lay in the king,

> but in the king is a two-fold power; the one in parliament as he is assisted with the consent of the whole state; the other out of parliament, as he is sole, and singular, guided merely by his own will . . . . It will then be easily proved, that the power of the king in parliament is greater than his power out of parliament; and doth rule and controule it.[16]

The power of king-in-parliament, therefore, was the *suprema potestas*, or sovereign power. Though Whitelocke wished to argue that the king's absolute prerogative was subordinate to his ordinary prerogative (i.e. his will exercised through parliament and the law) this was not the point that carried the weight of his position. He still ended up arguing that, though some things were properly the business of absolute prerogative ('denization, coynage, making warre'), taxation of any sort was not amongst them. All actions that amounted to the removal of subjects' property could only be done by the king-in-parliament; here also lay 'the power of erection of arbitrary government'. The distribution of tasks between absolute and ordinary prerogative was a matter of custom that could not be explained in simple rationalistic terms. Some absolute powers 'the king hath time out of minde practised, without the gainsaying and murmuring of his subjects'. 'No man ever read any law whereby it was so ordained; and yet no man ever read that any king practised the contrary'. [17]

We arrive here at a point where we can clearly see the fundamental theoretical agreement between Whitelocke and his king. For while they might disagree on the particular place to be assigned to

impositions, they did agree that the king had an absolute prerogative, that it was not used to govern in domestic politics, and that the
king could not tax his subjects at will. The question that remained
was whether imposing customs duties amounted to taxing his subjects, or whether it was a prerogative based on the law of nations.
Thomas Crew, speaking against impositions, was also clear that 'the
King of England in some cases hathe an absolute power, as in tyme
of warre'.[18] He also thought that it did not apply in this case.

What does all of this tell us about the nature of 'consensus'
in Jacobean England? The answer is complicated. Consensus in
the period arose, fundamentally, from the recognition by all par-
ties of shared rules for using a duplex notion of kingship. All
agreed that the king's prerogatives included a number of rights
that were not exercised through law and parliament, as well as
many that were. Certain matters could appropriately be assigned
to the legal prerogative, and consequently talked about through a
language of common law. Other matters might possibly be outside
the purview of the common law, matters of absolute prerogative,
and thus discussable through the languages of natural law, the law
of nations, or even civil law (all three tending to become much
the same thing). There was also agreement on the crucial issue:
English property rights were protected by common law and not
subject to the incursions of the absolute prerogative. What made
impositions a difficult issue was that there were good reasons for
treating it in terms of both legal and absolute prerogative, and the
basic dispute was over which of these the matter belonged to. On
the one hand impositions looked like a tax on property: but were
they a tax on *English* property? On the other hand, impositions
were an international, not a domestic, matter: but might it be that
the common law did extend to the high seas?

The Jacobean consensus worked, in spite of linguistic diversity,
because there were agreed rules governing which languages applied
in which situations. The debates on impositions broke out over a
matter where the rules gave no simple answer. It was a debate that,
in the true sense, was an exception that proved the rule (or rules, in
this case). Striking, over the whole period from 1606 to 1614, was
James's care to avoid breaking the rules. He believed that he inherited the right to impose customs duties from his predecessors, and
he was careful to convey messages that emphasized the moderation
and legality of his actions.[19]

To put the matter in the terms we have been developing, the

Jacobean consensus was based not on uniformity of opinion (or even of theory), but on a recognition by most players in the political game that there were a variety of languages of politics, each appropriate in some areas and for some audiences. Of course, most would not have put the point with this clarity. We might put the matter more informally by saying that the working of consensus required political agents not to use political languages in wildly inappropriate ways. As we shall see, it was the fact that James recognized this and Charles did not that was one of the key differences between their kingship.

More can be said about these rules. Two works written in James's reign employ them with a visible dexterity that merits close analysis. The first of these was Sir John Davies's mature reflections on the subject (significantly enough) of the king's right to levy impositions, written in the last years of James's reign. The second is a speech delivered by the king himself in 1610, though it was not concerned with the impositions question.

Davies's *The Question concerning Impositions* has been a much misunderstood book. J. P. Sommerville has cited it to show that Davies believed that 'prerogative . . . was not limited by law'.[20] But Davies was more careful and more subtle than this judgement allows. Like Chief Baron Fleming, Davies did not believe impositions to be a domestic matter. 'The King of *England* doth make use of this Prerogative only, in laying Impositions upon Merchandizes crossing the Seas'. He was emphatic that 'neither doth he by his absolute power alone, impose any Tax upon Lands or *Capita hominum*, or *Capita animalium*, or upon other things innumerable'.[21] Once again this distinction was grounded in a 'duplex' understanding of royal authority. Originally kings had 'an absolute and unlimited power in all matters whatsoever' by the law of nations, but 'then came the positive Law, and limited the Law of Nations'. This, in many matters, altered the nature of royal power: 'by the positive Law the King himself was pleased to limit and stint his absolute power, and to tye himself to the ordinary rules of the Law, in common and ordinary cases'.[22] But some powers, which made up the prerogative, were excluded from this process of limitation, and so

the King doth exercise a double power, *viz* an absolute power, or *Merum Imperium*, when he doth use Prerogatives onely, which is not bound by the positive Law; and an ordinary power of Jurisdiction, which doth co-operate with the Law, & whereby he doth minister Justice to the people, according to the prescript rule of the positive Law.[23]

But it was not the case that the absolute prerogative could be used to contravene positive (or common) law; it was a right to act in areas *outside* the jurisdiction of English common law, as Davies's examples indicate. It did not give the king the authority to take the property of his subjects, because within England in most matters the king had bound himself to govern through the law. As Davies himself explained,

> the King doth establish the Standard of Money by virtue of his Prerogative only, for the Common Law doth give no rule touching the matter, or form, or value thereof; but when those Monies are dispersed into the hands of the Subjects, the same do become subject in respect of the property thereof, to the ordinary rules of the Common Law.[24]

Davies grounded his analysis of the dual nature of royal authority on an examination of the various contexts in which the king operated. In these chapters of his book he clearly accepted the standard positions of the common lawyers (that the common law was a customary law of the English peoples, suitable for solving all matters of domestic politics, and that it exercised a controlling jurisdiction over other legal codes). And yet he also found space for an absolute prerogative operating outside, but not above or against, the common law. His approach was to examine in turn the law of nations, the law merchant, the civil law and the canon law, and to demonstrate what role they were allowed in England by the common law. He was then able to show that while in many matters the king had tied himself to following the rules of the common law, in a few things he could operate through these other legal systems which did give him a number of absolute prerogatives.[25] There is nothing in this that contradicted Davies's famous remarks, made in the Preface to his Irish Reports, about the nature of the common law.

It is important to note that Davies was careful to stress the customary basis of common law, and its supremacy in most matters. The jurisdictions he allowed to the law of nations, and other lesser law codes, were entirely *interstitial* in character. They filled in the gaps over which the common law had no purchase. These other law codes were as much part of the law of England as the common law, though it was 'Native and peculiar to our Nation' while they were 'common to other Nations as well as us'.[26] Davies was careful to specify both the confines in which these non-common-law jurisdictions were exercised and the fact that their role was recognized by the common law itself. For example, with reference to the law of nations, he said that it was 'in force in such cases, especially wherein the King himself, or his Subjects, have correspondence or commerce with other Nations who are not bound in those cases by the Municipall Laws of *England*'; and he demonstrated 'that our Common Law doth acknowledge and prove the Law of Nations in most of these cases'.[27] Similarly, the common law itself left certain *specific* cases to be dealt with by the law merchant. On the matter of Roman or civil law Davies was clear that it was but a specific law code, 'rejected in most of the Kingdoms in *Europe*', but left with a certain role in international affairs (as shown by the fact that it was employed in the Court of Admiralty). He took some pains to ensure 'that I may not be mistaken here, and in other places where I cite the Text of the Imperiall Law, as if I intended that Law to be of force in *England* generally'.[28] On this basis Davies was able to conclude the law of nations, law merchant and civil law could all be used to assess the king's right to levy impositions because the king and people had both allowed them a role in matters of international trade.[29]

It would, thus, be misleading to see Davies's *Question concerning Impositions* as an attempt to give the king an absolute prerogative of a sort that would enable him to override the requirements of the common law. In fact the book was an attempt to utilize a consensual position in order to defend the king's position on impositions. The consensus lay in the recognition that there were a variety of legal languages that could be used for analysing royal authority. Certainly, the dominant one in most matters was the language of the common law. But in certain areas the king's power could appropriately be discussed in rather different terms of the law of nations and the civil law. In consequence – again this is a consensual position – the king's authority was duplex in nature. The question that was difficult to resolve was not a theoretical one, but the factual one of whether or not customs duties were a matter entirely to be dealt with through the common law. At the level of theory, consensus prevailed. The essential point of this consensus was that *domestic* property rights were within the sphere of the common law, and could not be infringed by the absolute prerogative.

If Davies's work was a belated attempt to show that the Crown's case on impositions was compatible with consensus principles, King James I (in contrast) produced a broadly similar, if less developed, argument in advance of the 1610 debate on impositions. On 21 March 1610, James addressed the members of the Lords and Commons, assembled together to hear him. Historians have found his remarks (both here and in general) rather difficult to get to grips with, some accepting that he genuinely sought compromise, others thinking that he merely paid lip-service to the prejudices of his subjects in favour of limited government while actually maintaining an absolutist position.[30] But at least one of James's contemporaries did take the speech as a defence of limited monarchy, believing that its message was that 'howsoever the sovereignty of kings was absolute in general, yet in particular the kings of England were restrained by their oath and the privileges of the people'.[31] Furthermore, the speech was widely cited later in the seventeenth century,[32] often to defend the idea that English kings exercised a limited power only. Perhaps the most famous example of this was Locke's use of James's speech to establish the distinction between true kings and tyrants.[33] The reason why James's remarks of 1610 could in future decades be cited both by those wishing to elevate the absolute power of kings, and by such defenders of the people's right to act against tyrants as John Locke, was that they exemplify the consensual duplex understanding of royal authority that dominated Jacobean political thought. One could choose whether to cite remarks relating to the king's absolute powers, or to cite those relating to his legal powers.

James's speech needs to be understood not as a set of empty concessions, not even as a genuine attempt at conciliation, but as an appeal to consensus – that is to an agreed theoretical framework. In order to understand the work as consensual it must be placed in context. James himself identified the occasion of his remarks: his subjects doubted his intentions in two matters. They wondered whether he would continue to govern within the frame of the ancient constitution or whether he would alter that frame 'by the absolute power of a King'; and they wondered whether he would preserve the common law, or attempt to replace it with civil law.[34] These two doubts amounted to much the same thing. Although the speech was delivered in 1610, the doubts to which James referred were not raised primarily by the issue of impositions (debate on this subject did not begin until June 23). Rather, there were a number of other specific issues that lay behind the fears of members of parliament. The most immediate of these was the furore that followed the publication of John Cowell's legal dictionary, *The Interpreter*, which may have fed into fears generated by proposals (made at various times from 1604 onwards) for Union with Scotland. James had previously attempted to explain that such a Union would not imply complete legal union or the destruction of the English common law.[35]

John Cowell was a civil lawyer who had a longstanding interest in using his civilian training to organize and clarify English common law. To this end he published, in 1607, his *The Interpreter: or booke containing the signification of words*. The book then became the object of criticism by some members – mainly common lawyers – of the House of Commons in 1610.[36] Almost certainly some of the motivation behind the attack on Cowell was provided by the fact that it was 'a means of embarrassing the king' in the middle of debate on supply.[37] Had there not been this tactical advantage to be gained from the pursuit of Cowell, it may well be that the book would never have been attacked so openly. Yet the matter cannot be reduced simply to one of tactics. Certainly, for the most part *The Interpreter* was a politically innocuous work designed to serve a real need of legal students and lawyers. But undoubtedly Cowell's search for strict definitions did lead him to make a number of statements that could be interpreted as being contrary to common law principles.

Cowell is a good example of someone who infringed the unspoken conventions structuring consensus, and his carelessness enabled the king to display his own understanding of them. The problem with Cowell's book was not so much that it put forward outrageously eccentric opinions on the nature of the royal prerogative,[38] but rather that it confused several separate views of the prerogative. James's decision to condemn *The Interpreter* does reveal a consensus of opinion amongst himself and his more articulate subjects. But that consensus was not – as Elton has it – that prerogatives were a 'precise' set of legal rights, in part summed up in statute, and 'governed by the law'.[39] This was true of the ordinary prerogative, but so far as the prerogative in general was concerned the consensus that prevailed held it to be duplex. James explained this in his speech of 21 March 1610. He had first announced his disapproval of Cowell's opinions earlier, on 8 March. Cowell's simplistic approach to the relationship of law and prerogative left him in the position of saying things derogatory to both. His arguments tended to bring the king's absolute prerogative within the purview of the language of common-law and this was unpalatable both to James and to the common lawyers in the lower House.

Most of what was objectionable in *The Interpreter* was contained in a few brief remarks in four of its entries, those for 'Subsidie', 'King', 'Prerogative of the King', and 'Parliament'.[40] Two passages in particular reveal the problem that Cowell's ham-fistedness posed. Cowell said of the king:

> he is above the Law by his absolute power. *Bracton lib. pri. cap. 8. Kitchin fol. 1.* and though for the beter and equall course in making Lawes he doe admitte the 3. estates, that is, Lords Spirituall, Lords temporall, and the Commons unto Councell: yet this, in divers learned mens opinions, is not of constreinte, but of his own benignitie, or by reason of his promise made upon oath, at the time of his coronation. For otherwise were he a subject after a sort and subordinate, which may not bee thought without breach of dutie and loyaltie. For then must we deny him to be above the lawe, and to have no power of dispensing with any positive lawe, or of graunting especiall priviledges and charters, unto any, which is his onely and cleare right.[41]

Cowell's search for conceptual clarity has led him close to asking the question: which is superior, the king or the law? Unfortunately the simple answer he has given produced not clarity but confusion. For, as the opening sentence of this passage indicates, Cowell conflated the king's ordinary and absolute powers, effectively subordinating the former to the latter. But, as we have seen, the relationship between the two was not generally thought to be of this simple hierarchical kind, not even by those who wished to invoke the absolute prerogative for particular purposes. Cowell's statements about the king's absolute authority were not in themselves contentious: many others could say similar things without arousing any controversy. But Cowell did not perceive that this aspect of royal power, approachable through the languages of civil law and divine right, was outside not above the ordinary (legal) prerogative. Nor did he realize that the languages of absolute prerogative could be safely employed only in a number of contexts, particularly with regard to international matters or with reference to the subject's duty of obedience. This led Cowell to suggest that the king had the right to 'alter or suspend any particular lawe',[42] and even to suggest in his article on 'subsidie' that parliamentary consent for taxation was something owed to the king as a duty. What was most objectionable in Cowell is neatly indicated by the second crucial passage, his definition of the royal prerogative:

> Praerogative of the King (Praerogativa Regis) is that especiall power, preeminence, or privilege that the King hath in any kinde, over and above other persons, and above the ordinarie course of the common lawe, in the right of his crown. And this word (Praerogativa) is used by the Civilians in the same sense.[43]

Cowell does not seem to have been aware that 'prerogative' could mean not just this (absolute prerogative), but also a collection of common-law or customary rights. And in many matters, crucially those involving the subject's property rights, absolute prerogative had no role. Further he was fatally ambiguous about the relationship between prerogative (as he defined it) and common law, again suggesting that the king had a right to override the course of law as he saw fit.

Speaking through his Lord Treasurer, Salisbury, (on 8 March 1610) James condemned Cowell's book on three grounds. It was 'too bold with the Common lawe of the Land'; it 'utterly mistooke the fundamentall and originall grounds and constitucions of the Parliament'; and 'in the poynt of prerogative . . . he hath waded further then was fyt for a subject'.[44] James promised to suppress the book by proclamation, a promise kept on 25 March.[45] Though it is no doubt the case, as most accounts of the matter indicate,[46] that James's decision to suppress *The Interpreter* had much to do with gaining tactical advantage for himself, there is no reason to doubt the sincerity of his remarks, or of his attempt to find common ground with his subjects in the Commons.

As well as reprimanding Cowell for his remarks on the prerogative, James agreed with the Commons that there were worrying things in Cowell's remarks on the common law. In collapsing the duplex understanding of prerogative into a simple one *The Interpreter* gave the impression that James's absolute monarchy was in fact an arbitrary monarchy.[47] James said in reply that, while 'for his Kingdome he was beholden to noe elective power, neither doth he depend upon any popular aplause', nevertheless 'the lawe did set the Crowne upon his head, and he is a Kinge by the common lawe of the land'. Further, 'he did acknowledge that he had noe power to make lawes of himselfe, or to exact any subsidies *de jure* without the consent of his 3. Estates'. In short, 'there was such a marriage and unyon between the prerogative and the lawe as they cannot possibly be severed'.[48] Cowell was wrong to suggest that the king could ignore the law at will; and he was wrong to attempt to pin down the prerogative with simple definitions.

The latter point was a crucial one. James indicated that 'yt was dangerous to submit the power of a kinge to definition'.[49] This theme he took up at length in the great speech of 21 March. In doing so, the king laid down his understanding of the 'Jacobean consensus' – an understanding that, like the one given here, was presented in terms of languages and their proper use. It can be used to supplement the understanding of the subject that we have already gained from the work of Sir John Davies. The language of the common law defined – literally – English kingship:

> But the maine point is, That if the fundamental Lawes of any Kingdome should be altered, who should discerne what is *Meum & tuum*, or how should a King governe? It would be like the Gregorian Calender, which destroyes the old, and yet doeth this new trouble all the debts and Accompts of Traffiques and Merchandizes: Nay by that accompt I can never tell mine owne aage; for now is my Birth-day remooved by the space of ten dayes neerer me then it was before the change.[50]

By fundamental law James seems to have meant either all, or the most important part of, the common law.[51] The law defined what kings ruled over, and how they did so. A king who destroyed the law destroyed himself, for concepts like 'king', 'subject', 'property' needed definition. Before there could be a King James I there needed to be a defined office of kingship.[52] 'And for a King of England to despise the Common Law, it is to neglect his owne Crowne'. The common law provided that definition, and hence (as James had said on 8 March) he was king by the common law. This was not an admission of his *subordination* to law; but a recognition that, unless it was legally defined, royal authority could not exist. James said that given a choice he would prefer (in England) the common law to the judicial law of Moses, because it was naturally fitted to English circumstances.[53] Of course the common law was not the only law in use in England. James said that he had great admiration for the civil law, but its use in England lay in the fact that it 'maintaineth

Intercourse with all forreine Nations'. He then added: 'but I onely allow it to have course here, according to those limits of Jurisdiction, which the Common Lawe it selfe doeth allow it'.[54]

If the common law was the 'base' language for English politics, defining the very nature of kingship and property and the terms on which they were held, and if civil law had a role in certain specific areas only by permission of the common law, what then of the language of divine right? How did it fit with these other languages. James has of course been most famous as an exponent of the theory of divine-right monarchy, especially in two works written while he was King of Scotland but not yet King of England, *The Trew Law of Free Monarchies* (1598) and *Basilikon Doron* (1599). In the 1610 speech he did not abandon this position, but rather attempted to show its place in a political world of linguistic diversity. 'Kings are justly called Gods, for that they exercise a manner or resemblance of Divine power upon earth',[55] James wrote. But this did not mean that the King could in practice rule arbitrarily, for over time the monarch had bound 'himselfe by a double oath to the observation of the fundamental Lawes of his kingdome'. In settled kingdoms the divine power of rulers had become institutionalized in such a way that it was normally exercised through legal means, thus 'every just King in a setled Kingdome is bound to observe that paction made to his people by his Lawes'.[56]

Nevertheless, kings retained, in a sense, their original absolute authority, even in settled states. In a crucially important passage James wrote:

> I conclude then this point touching the power of Kings, with this Axiome of Divinitie, That as to dispute what God may doe is Blasphemie; but *quid vult Deus* [what God wishes], that Divines may lawfully, and doe ordinarily dispute and discusse; for to dispute *A Posse ad Esse* is both against Logicke and Divinitie: So is it sedition in Subjects, to dispute what a King may do in the height of his power: But just Kings wil ever be willing to declare what they wil do, if they wil not incurre the curse of God. I wil not be content that my power be disputed upon: but I shall ever be willing to make the reason appeare of all my doings, and rule my actions according to my Lawes.[57]

The point made here was not that kings were above the law in any simple sense. Indeed, James specifically said that 'the King *with his Parliament* here are absolute . . . in making or forming of any sort of Lawes'.[58] But kings did have an absolute power, essentially mysterious, that was not legal in nature. While kings normally operated through their legal prerogative (which was, of course, tied to the forms of common law and could be discussed through the language of common law), they did have in essence an absolute power. This it was not the business of lawyers to discuss. Furthermore, this absolute prerogative could be exercised in the present, though only in areas where the common law had no purchase.

Thus, James was quite sincere in portraying himself as a legal monarch, tied (by his own consent) to the forms of the common law in most matters of domestic politics. But it is important to be clear about the fact that in saying this James was *not* saying two other things. He was not saying that his prerogative was *subordinate* to law; and he was not saying that all of his actions should not 'be disputed on'. His authority was not subordinate to law because (a) he had an absolute prerogative that was not definable in legal terms at all; and (b) even his legal prerogative was legal in the sense of *defined by* law, but not necessarily in the sense of *subject to* law. (In fact, he would probably have agreed that in many matters his power was controllable by the law, while in a few things the law gave to him powers that it could not control).

With the matter of disputing what kings could (and could not) do, we return to the problem of languages and their use. A king's power in essence could not be disputed, above all disputed in terms of law, because it was not legally defined. James, in fact, wished to prevent such discussion of his power in the abstract, but was quite willing (as, most of the time, with regard to impositions) to allow particular actions and exercises of prerogative to be tested legally. Once his will was exercised, it became defined by the forms through which it was being exercised, and could then be discussed in appropriate language. In his proclamation condeming Cowell's *Interpreter* James put this point by drawing an analogy, of the sort of which he was so fond, between God and kings:

> For from the very highest mysteries in the Godhead, and the most inscrutable Councels in the Trinitie, to the very lowest pit of Hell, and the confused actions of the divels there, there is nothing now unsearched into by the curiositie of mens braines; Men not being contented with the knowledge of so much of the Will of God, as

it hath pleased him to reveale; but they will needs sit with him in his most privie Closet, and become privie of his most inscrutable Councels: And therefore it is no wonder, that men in those our dayes doe not spare to wade in all the deepest mysteries that belong to the persons or State of Kings or Princes, that are gods upon Earth: since we see, (as we have already said) that they spare not God himselfe.[59]

The distinction between the mystery of the Godhead and God's revealed will mirrored that between the king's absolute authority and his ordinary authority, 'revealed' in his laws. The latter could be discussed, analysed and interpreted; but not the former. Hence it was that James could conclude that some men, notably John Cowell, 'goe out of their element, and meddle with things above their capacitie'.[60] James maintained this position throughout his reign, issuing a Proclamation in December 1620 against 'excesse of Lavish and Licentious Speech of matters of State' (and another in July 1621 to back up the first),[61] and in 1623 issuing Directions to preachers that commanded 'that no preacher . . . shall presume . . . to declare, limit, or bound out, by way of positive doctrine, in any sermon or lecture, the power, prerogative, jurisdiction, authority, right or duty of sovereign princes'.[62] Royal authority, in its essence, was a mysterious matter beyond the reach of human words.

Underlying James's claims was an acceptance of the duplex nature of kingship, and a willingness to operate with that concept in ways attuned to the thinking of his subjects. He did not, in 1610 or at any other time, assert that he could override the common law at will. What he did assert was that the authority which he exercised through the law did not exhaust his power. He had, in addition to his legal or ordinary prerogative, an absolute power which might be conceived of in terms of natural law, or (more commonly with James himself) in terms of an analogy with the mysterious absolute power of God. The former conception might have practical consequences in a limited sphere; the latter was for use mainly in stressing the duty of subjection, and the irresistibility of kings. This double view of royal authority was widely held – it was a consensual position – and was not seen as threatening to the supremacy of King-in-parliament, or to the position of the common law, *provided* that the king was able and willing to maintain a clear distinction between his authority in essence, and his actual legal authority in domestic matters. This James did, supremely well. His son did not. Yet, consensual though the position may have been, the whole matter of the king's absolute authority remained a tricky one. The distinction between absolute and ordinary prerogative originated in the medieval theological distinction drawn between God's absolute and ordinary power.[63] In the writings of James I himself this origin remained quite visible, but in other statements of the position this was not the case. Even so, the fact that the concepts originated outside the legal sphere made them difficult to employ in a political world dominated by the common-law mind.

The problems can, rather artificially, be divided into two. There was, firstly, the difficulty of drawing the boundary between legal and absolute prerogative, a problem that also involved considering whether the boundary was one between law and theology or between common law and natural law. And, secondly, there was the problem of what content could be given to the king's absolute power. This problem was made worse by the tendency to view such power as essentially mysterious and indefinable. Common lawyers did not know quite what to do with the king's absolute prerogative, a situation that was to worsen after 1625.

The difficulty is readily apparent if we consider a typical statement of the nature of royal authority, this one from Forsett's *Comparative Discourse of the Bodies Natural and Politique.* Forsett made clear the analogy between God and the king:

> For as we rightly conceive of God, that albeit he worketh efficiently, and (if I may so say) naturally, by the mediate causes, yet his potencie is not so by them tied or confined, but that he often performeth his owne pleasure by extraordinarie meanes, drawne out of his absolute power, both *preter & contra naturam.*[64]

The same was true of kings, who possessed a

> Soveraigntie: which (besides that which is regular in regiment, and from his power and goodnes imported unto the people) hath still, and reteineth to it selfe certaine prerogative rights of most ample extentions, and most free exemptions, whereof true reverence (filled with all submissive acknowledgements, and contented with that portion and interest which it receiveth from regalitie) admitteth no questioning disputes, and whereof just governors do not so farre inlarge the lists, as to do what they lust, but do so moderate the use (as God in the world, and the

Soule in the body) not to the impeach, but to the support of justice; not to the hurt, but to the good of subjects.[65]

What the practical implications of this might be are uncertain, and there lies the problem. Forsett's account was vague and ambiguous. Was the extraordinary (or absolute) prerogative a right to break the law as the king chose? Was Forsett paying lip-service to the idea of royal divinity while attempting to ensure that the king *in practice* was tied to the exercise of his legal prerogative? Was the king a non-accountable sovereign, or was he (by his own consent, perhaps) enmeshed within structures of consent and law?

The vagueness was what made Forset's statement uncontentious. But it was also what made the whole idea of absolute prerogative difficult to handle. The doctrine threatened, as James Whitelocke noticed in 1610, to rend asunder the fabric of law by introducing into it an essentially indefinable regal power. Whitelocke's claim that the legal prerogative ruled and controlled the absolute prerogative was an attempt to reduce the latter to definition,[66] though it scarcely dealt with the issues raised by the impositions debate. Others tried various strategies to bring the absolute prerogative under some sort of control (in the sense of bringing definition and clarity, rather than in the sense of limiting it directly). The normal way – partially followed by James in 1610, and by defenders of the royal line on impositions, including Davies – was to confine the king's extra-legal power to a few well-defined areas. But there were difficulties in doing this. In the 1610 speech for example there was an unresolved tension between the claim that the royal office was defined by the law (though not subject to it) and the claim that the king possessed a mysterious absolute authority that was essentially indefinable. The latter could remain undefined only if it was never used, and this seems to have been what happened. James did not claim to actually employ this mysterious power, just to possess it. Actions that he performed by absolute prerogative (such as imposing customs duties) were outside the common law, but still defined by natural or civil law. Thus there was implicit in the 1610 speech a three-fold understanding of royal power (corresponding roughly to our three languages): the mysterious essential power of kings (theological), an absolute prerogative (natural and civil law) and an ordinary prerogative (common law). The first two of these were conflated in James's 1610 speech, and the conflation produced a degree of incoherence.

But, for most purposes, royal power was seen as duplex. Though the theological concept of God's absolute power lay behind the distinction, there was a strong tendency to convert the theology to law, even if only natural law. The normal view of the prerogative in political discourse was that it had both absolute and legal parts, and the absolute (extra-legal) prerogative was confined to a few specific areas. Within those areas the king was able to rule by the direct exercise of his will. This path was followed, for example, by Sir Edward Coke speaking in the Commons in 1621:

> There is prerogative indisputable and prerogative disputable. Prerogative indisputable, is that the king hath to make war: disputable prerogative is tied to the laws of England; wherein the king also hath divers prerogatives, as 'nullum tempus' &c.[67]

This was perhaps the standard view that confined the absolute prerogative for all practical matters, to a few areas beyond the reach of the common law. Here the king exercised authority by natural law and divine right unmediated by human positive law. It was his contravention of this doctrine that resulted in John Cowell's condemnation. No doubt unintentionally, Cowell failed to respect the convention whereby the absolute prerogative was not brought to bear directly on such contentious matters as the property rights of the subject. As we have seen, the debate on impositions took place *within* those conventions and did not challenge them, though the discomfort of some members of the Commons with the concept of absolute prerogative remained evident.

Various statements of the consensual position can be cited. Sir Francis Bacon presented the picture of a king who was beneath the law's directive power but above its corrective power (a very old, and very commonplace idea). Monarchs had an absolute power to call upon the nation's resources in time of war, but clearly the exercise of this right was limited to certain special circumstances. For the rest, Bacon conceived of the prerogative not as a single entity but as a list of particular rights given to the king by law. He summarized this conclusion by describing a 'two fold power in the king'; first 'his absolute power, whereby he may levy forces against any nation', and (second) 'his limited power, which is declared and expressed in the laws, what he may do'.[68] In contrast, William Camden developed a much more complex argument than Bacon's. As one might expect, it was an argument primarily historical in nature.

Camden's basic point was one made also by James I in 1610: that the law *defined* the nature of the royal office so that a king who undermined fundamental laws was destroying his own position. The exact nature of royal prerogative differed from place to place as different systems of law defined regal authority in different ways. In words reminiscent of James's own, Camden said that 'the declaring of *meum* and *tuum* . . . is the very object of the laws of England', and that 'the King is limited to punish according to the course of the law *for such offenses as the law taketh notice of* [stress added]'.[69] Because the law laid down basic definitions of property and rights, it followed that royal prerogatives varied from place to place:

> for every particular kingdom hath a several prerogative, and though the government of some kingdoms be so far regal that the kings will in some things be law, yet is it not so in all things.[70]

Kings, Camden argued (following Fortescue), may be either 'regal' or 'politique', or they may be 'mixt'. The kings of England were of the latter variety, which exists 'when a king may in some things make laws without the knowledge of his people, in others not without their assent and consent'. To understand the power of such kings one must be clear about what they can do through their 'regal' power and what through their 'politic' power.[71] But in addition to this distinction between 'regal' and 'politic' power (which here, at least, corresponded to that between absolute and ordinary prerogative) Camden also indicated that *all* kings (whether 'regal' or 'politic') possessed 'some general privileges without which there can be no king'. These included 'the inviolability of his person', 'the disposing of honours', the 'power of coining money', and 'the making league or war with any foreign Prince or State'.[72] For Camden the duplex nature of English royal authority was a product of the particular characteristics of the English legal system and its development. While kings did have various powers essential to the very nature of kingship, their prerogative was primarily defined by English law – though, clearly, it was *not* in all matters subordinate to that law. We can say, then, that Camden avoided the tensions in James I's 1610 speech by stressing the role of law (and custom) in defining kingship, and downplaying the theological view of monarchy.[73] Nevertheless, he still held a view of the royal prerogative that was compatible with the consensual understanding of it as duplex in nature.

A slightly different variation on the theme was provided by Lord Chancellor Ellesmere. Ellesmere, a faithful royal servant, had an elevated view of the royal prerogative, but he wrote about it in terms very different from those employed by Cowell. He accepted that the king possessed a double prerogative, but referred to *both* of its parts as an 'absolute prerogative'. The monarch of England had, firstly, an 'absolute prerogative . . . revealed by his lawes'; and, secondly, an 'absolute prerogative which is in Kings according to therie private will and Judgment'.[74] Ellesmere was careful to delineate exactly this latter type of prerogative in such a way as to ensure that it did not become muddled with the realm of law. It was a prerogative that could not properly be delegated at all – if it was the official to whom it had been delegated was bound to follow normal legal methods, because the law was the only reliable guide he had to the king's will. This prerogative of 'private will' was tied to the natural body of the monarch and was incapable of becoming institutionalized or of operating through settled legal channels.[75] In consequence it was likely to remain a peripheral feature of English governance, at least in practice.

Thus it was that even the king's absolute prerogative was felt to need some definition. There were two main motives for seeking such definition. Firstly, the need was felt (as in Ellesmere) to keep the extra-legal prerogative clearly separated from the normal course of law. Any confusion of the two might lead to a threat to the common law, and above all to its ability to protect the property rights of the king's subjects. But, secondly, it was also the case that unless it were *defined* the absolute prerogative could not be *used* for anything. Hence, James could talk of his absolute prerogative in terms of an analogy with God. But whenever, as in the impositions wrangle, it was necessary to base any practical claims on such a prerogative, discussion left the realm of theology and moved to that of natural law (which tended to mean, in practice, civil law). A mysterious, indefinable prerogative, approachable only in the vaguest of theological language thus became converted to a prerogative defined (and, hence, in a sense limited) by the law of nations. In addition, this prerogative was also bordered by the legal prerogative, and could only operate where the common law was (for one reason or another) unable to reach.

Therefore it can be concluded that the competing languages for discussing politics – common law, civil law, and theology – were held together by the duplex understanding of royal authority. This amounts to the same thing as saying that the Jacobean consensus was held together by this same duplex theory. On the face of it things said by John Cowell (or for that matter Roger Manwaring and Robert Sibthorpe, whom we shall encounter presently) do not seem particularly outrageous. Nor do they seem particularly unusual: how, for example, did Cowell's opinions differ from those accepted by Convocation in 1606?[76] Though James refused to accept the 1606 Canons, they did not appear to raise the outrage in his subjects that Cowell's *Interpreter* did. This is explicable if it is realized that Cowell, unlike the still-born 1606 Canons (or for that matter the opinions of a whole raft of supposed supporters of 'absolutism' from Bacon to Davies), inadvertently failed to respect the conventions that governed the structure of the Jacobean consensus. Those conventions were most fully revealed in such works as Davies's *Question concerning Impositions* and James I's speech of 1610, and we are now in a position to say what they were.

Royal authority was normally seen as duplex in nature. Different writers used different terminology to formulate this distinction, but we have generally employed the terms absolute (or extraordinary) prerogative and legal (or ordinary) prerogative. The relationship between these two types of prerogative was not generally conceived as hierarchical (one ruling the other), or as one between different functions (a power of 'government' versus a power of 'jurisdiction'). Rather, the distinction was based primarily on sphere of operation. The king's ordinary prerogative was coterminous with the common law; his absolute prerogative was exercised in spheres where the common law did not hold sway (the church, international affairs) or where the common law left room for the king to act of his own will (the power of coining money, for example). In practice, however, absolute prerogative did need some sort of legal definition, and this was provided by judicious employment of civil law.

To this duplex view of kingship were fitted three languages of political discourse. Two of them related to the absolute prerogative (theology and civil law), the other to the ordinary prerogative (common law). In addition, the common law was usually thought responsible for constructing the overall framework that assigned some matters to one sphere, and others to a different one. Consequently, it could function as a sort of 'master language', which laid down the place that the other languages could have (as James acknowledged in 1610).

The implications of all of this for political discourse are complex, but a summary can be attempted. The essential point is that, given this framework, political statements that look to our eyes contradictory were not necessarily so perceived by contemporaries. Statements could be made about kings being like Gods, possessors of divine authority and the source of all law without their being read as statements of the king's right to contravene positive law. Provided a clear separation was kept between absolute and ordinary prerogative controversy could be avoided. This was best done by following the rules for language use that we have already examined. Theological statements of divine right, and so on, were quite uncontroversial provided that: (a) they were vague statements about the essence of kingship, not particular statements about particular royal prerogatives; and (b) they were not aimed at the wrong audience, in which case they might contain an *implicit* practical message (for example about the king's right to tax at will) that might arouse opposition. On the other hand natural or civil law statements could be made reasonably uncontroversially if they were clearly linked to the absolute prerogative and not the legal prerogative. This entailed ensuring that these languages were not used (except perhaps incidentally) to settle domestic political disputes, and that they were not used to argue that the absolute prerogative could *override* the legal in ordinary circumstances. Spokesmen for the king's position on impositions, for example, were careful to follow these conventions.

In this way consensus arose from ideological, theoretical and linguistic diversity. James I and his articulate subjects were bound together into a community of discourse. The laws of this community were conventions for the use of various political languages. It is possible to set these languages, and statements made within them, against one another, and to see them as inherently antagonistic – but it is also highly misleading. To do so is to pull apart the structure of the past.

(B)   AN EXCURSUS ON THE ROYAL PREROGATIVE

There are two slightly peripheral matters concerning the duplex theory of the royal prerogative that deserve further treatment. They concern, firstly, its *sources*; and, secondly, the extent to which its ideological functions changed in the early-seventeenth century. Historians of medieval and early modern political thought have found, as well as the absolute-ordinary distinction, two other sets of dichotomous terms used to discuss the nature of royal authority. The first of these was the contrast drawn between the king's natural body and his politic body (the theory of the king's two bodies);[77] and the second the Fortescuean division between the regal and politic capacities of a king.[78] Historiographically, the terminology of Fortescue has possibly been most influential through the particular interpretation of it given by C. H. McIlwain. McIlwain linked Fortescue's phrase *regimen politicum et regale* to a distinction that he claimed to have found in Bracton: 'his adjective *politicum* applies to Bracton's *jurisdictio*, his *regale* to Bracton's *gubernaculum*'.[79] The contrast Fortescue drew was really between two aspects of royal authority *jurisdictio* (jurisdiction) and *gubernaculum* (government). 'Acts of government strictly defined are in the hands of the king alone . . . . There is here a separation far sharper than we make in our modern times between government and law, between *gubernaculum* and *jurisdictio*', McIlwain wrote. Within the sphere of government the king had 'an autocratic and irresponsible authority', but government 'does not include jurisdiction in our narrower definition of the latter word'.[80] At the heart of McIlwain's conceptual dichotomy was a distinction, that (as he admitted) was difficult to draw clearly in the feudal middle ages, between 'matters of public administration' and 'private right'.[81] In the former sphere the king was absolute, but in the area of private property rights (falling under the heading *jurisdictio*) he was obliged to follow legal forms. McIlwain understood Fortescue to be reformulating just this point.[82] The details of McIlwain's interpretation no longer stand, in good part because his distinction between *gubernaculum* and *jurisdictio* just cannot be found in the texts that he examined.[83] But McIlwain's portrait of Fortescue, showing how he argued that in some spheres kings ruled with absolute authority acquired by conquest, while in others they were limited by law and could act only with the consent of their people, has had a continuing influence, notably in the writings of Pocock.[84]

Undoubtedly both of these pairs of terms (natural/politic body; regal/political dominion) can be found in early-seventeenth century writings about royal authority. But they were, at least by this time generally used as subsidiary grounding for the more general distinction between a king's legal and his extra-legal powers. Holdsworth has worked out some of the historical relationships involved. He argued that the initial distinction, inherited from the middle ages, was 'between the natural and politic capacity of the king'. During the sixteenth century this was built upon by developing the idea that some prerogatives were *inseparable* from the natural person of the king, and by applying to the resulting division between inseparable and separable prerogatives the distinction between absolute and ordinary power.[85] No doubt this is broadly true, but by the seventeenth century it was the end result of this process (the absolute/ordinary distinction) that was foremost in people's minds. When the older concepts were employed they were used to draw a rough distinction between prerogatives that the king could exercise at will and prerogatives that were law-bound. We have already encountered Camden's use of Fortescue to draw this contrast. Ellesmere made use of the two bodies theory in arguing that some prerogatives were inseparably annexed to the natural person of the king.[86] Other examples abound.[87] It is even possible to find something like McIlwain's *gubernaculum-jurisdictio* contrast. Sir John Eliot, for example, writing in the early 1630s distinguished two types of royal authority. First, there was 'that supreame power of Judicature & Justice', which 'must be reguleted by lawes & not arbitrary & at large'.[88] There existed a second power also, 'that of Goverment & rule'. This, unlike the power of judicature, had no 'rules & directions . . . prescribed', and consequently 'has noe guidance but the vertue' of the king himself. But, because individual kings were fallible, they were provided with a 'senate' to advise them and to give counsel.[89] Counsel was to the king's power of government what laws were to his power of jurisdiction (though, of course, the king was not bound to follow the advice he got from his counsellors).[90] Once again we have a distinction between a power exercised through law and a power exercised outside (not over or against) it. In the latter sphere the king's will was – in the last resort – unchallengeable.

So whatever the historical roots, and in spite of the fact that there were a variety of different ways of putting the matter, the duplex theory of kingship found in the seventeenth century is best seen as a (rather vague) distinction between absolute and ordinary prerogative, but one that could incorporate a number of other conceptual dichotomies. Even McIlwain, when looking for evidence of his *gubernaculum/jurisdictio* division in early Stuart writings was actually forced to cite passages which seldom, if ever, mentioned those terms but which do use the absolute/ordinary terminology.[91] McIlwain was right about the duplex nature of political thinking in

Jacobean and Caroline England, but was wrong about the nature of the duplexity. Pocock, who has suggested that some might classify him as a 'closet McIlwainian',[92] does seem to preserve some of McIlwain's vision in his own view of early Stuart political thinkers struggling to reconcile two familiar ideas, that of a king ruling *politice* and that of a king ruling *regaliter*. For Pocock this amounts to a distinction between kings ruling by compact and those ruling by conquest. Early modern Englishmen, he believes, tended to follow Fortescue in seeing their kings ruling *politice et regaliter*, combining rights acquired by compact with others acquired by conquest.[93] This may well be an echo of McIlwain and his reading of Fortescue, but it is a muted echo. And in so far as it takes up McIlwain's idea of the duplexity of medieval and early modern English political theories, while abandoning McIlwain's analysis of that duplexity in terms of government and jurisdiction, it would appear to be a harmless echo. Indeed it is as compatible with the dichotomies that we have advanced here as it is with anything in McIlwain. After all, James I in his 1610 speech also drew a distinction between consent or compact and conquest which mirrored (albeit complexly) his distinction between ordinary and absolute powers.[94]

The second matter that needs further consideration, closely related to the above, is the extent to which the duplex theory of kingship underwent change in the early-seventeenth century so that it came to support a political theory different from that which it had supported in Tudor times. A number of historians have, in different ways, advanced claims of this sort.[95] In particular, Brian Levack has argued that a number of common lawyers with knowledge of the civil law were instrumental in developing theories of royal absolutism during the early Stuart period. In doing so they applied ideas from the civilian tradition to English law, and thus brought significant alteration to English ideas of the royal prerogative. Both Berkowitz and Levack see the duplex theory as expressed by Fleming in 1606 as something new: it converted the king's emergency prerogative into 'more general, abstract terms' (Levack), 'to an abstract general principle' (Berkowitz).[96] This was achieved by the application to the prerogative of the new civilian concept of sovereignty. Thus the royal prerogative was converted from a bundle of legal rights and privileges into a general theory of the sovereign supremacy of the absolute prerogative. The ordinary prerogative remained a collection of legal powers; but the absolute prerogative became a discretionary power to act outside and contrary to the law.[97] As such it could be talked of as *sovereign* – a general regal power not subject to legal control – or it could be talked of in terms of 'reason of state' – a power to do whatever the interests of the nation required.

This view, particularly as it has been presented by Levack, tells us much. Undoubtedly civil law influences did work in the direction of *clarifying* the question of the relationship between monarchy and law. But it might also be argued that the use of civil law ideas by such common-law theorists of monarchy as Sir John Doddridge, Sir Francis Bacon, Sir John Davies and (of course) Sir Thomas Fleming, was as much evidence of the *compatability* of some civil law concepts with common-law traditions as it was of the erosion of common-law ideas under civilian influence. There is no doubt that early-seventeenth century writers gave the duplex theory of prerogative greater elaboration than earlier writers had done. There is no doubt that they made use of ideas drawn from Continental jurisprudence to do so. But the theory itself had deep common-law roots. Even for Fortescue the crucial distinction was between kings who ruled 'regaliter' and those who reigned 'politice et regaliter' (such as those of England): 'it was bettir to the peple to be ruled politekely and roialy, than to be ruled only roialy'.[98] In other words, even limited monarchs ruled *both* politically and regally. Such kings could not alter the laws of their country at will, but they had absolute powers in spheres that lay outside the law, and even with regard to their powers of pardoning and dispensing.[99] One of the difficulties in seeing the continuity between these ideas and those of Fleming and others has been the tendency to take the work of Sir William Staunford as a *full* account of the prerogative as seen by Tudor thinkers. His book gives the impression that the prerogative was *nothing but* a collection of very specific legal powers. It is a misleading view. Staunford's work was explicitly an incomplete account of the prerogative. It was framed as a commentary on the apocryphal medieval statute, *Prerogativa Regis*, which confined it to a discussion of prerogatives that were basically legal rights. Nevertheless, Staunford's definition of the prerogative 'as a privilege or preeminence that any person hath before another' which in the case of the prince means that 'the lawes do attribute unto him all honour, dignitie, prerogative and preeminence', arguably implies more than is ever delivered in the text.[100] In any case, as we have seen, Holdsworth and others have adequately demonstrated the duplexity of royal authority in Tudor England.

Undoubtedly, however, Tudor thinkers saw the prerogative (all of it) as *defined* by law. One should not confuse definition with total subjection. Legal definition of the prerogative did not preclude the possibility that it might be defined as including some powers of absolute discretion in limited spheres.[101] The early-seventeenth century writers discussed by Levack should not be seen as breaking out of this Tudor framework. Their theories were elaborations of the old distinction between the king's ordinary legal prerogatives (in the plural) and his emergency prerogative. In some cases, above all Francis Bacon's account of the prerogative, the continuity is very apparent. Bacon provided a long list of particular legal rights, to which he coupled an 'absolute power', *limited* (this is not noted by Levack) to the levying of forces for foreign war.[102]

Indeed, the important point to remember is that the greater conceptual elaboration and clarity of the early-seventeenth century theories of prerogative (compared with sixteenth-century ones) did not necessarily mean that they had changed their ideological character by becoming absolutist. As we have seen at some length, the normal Jacobean position was that the king's absolute prerogative was *not* a sovereign power over the law but a supplementary power, outside it in the sense of not operating through it, though within it in the sense of having its boundaries defined by law. This view is continuous with earlier theories. The intellectual elaboration that it underwent in the early-seventeenth century was made possible by the tools provided by civil law jurisprudence; but the elaboration was not at first fundamentally inconsistent with accepted common-law thinking. That inconsistency would not arise until the king's power outside the law came to be *used* (it was more a matter of use than of theory) as a power over the law. This was a feature of – as Oscar Wilde might have said – the general carelessness that lost Charles I three kingdoms (and a head).

(C) CONSENSUS AND CONFLICT

Now that we have examined the nature of consensus in Jacobean England we are better able to understand the nature of conflict in that period (the second of the two matters raised at the beginning of this chapter). Conflict there undoubtedly was, but the foregoing discussion should indicate that it did not arise from ideological polarization. Early Stuart Englishmen did possess a variety of theoretical perspectives on monarchy, but they also possessed an intellectual framework that united those perspectives into a broadly consensual 'world view'. The occasional disagreement between divine right monarchy and contractual kingship was not the clash of irreconcilable opponents but a tension within a single intellectual system. The degree of tension varied, but the system held.

But, if ideological polarization does not explain political conflict during the reign of James, then what does? It is an obvious truism that all political societies are marked both by elements of consensus and by elements of conflict (a truism that some early Stuart historians have shown signs of forgetting). We have examined and explained the consensus, what of the conflict?

The existence of conflict, by itself, is surely an unremarkable phenomenon. We really need some way of categorizing *types* of conflict if our analysis is to have any degree of precision, or stand any chance of telling us anything useful. A crude but adequate typology might identify three types of (political) conflict:

1. *Practical conflict* over access to power or wealth, or immunity from policies detrimental to one's power or wealth;
2. disputes over *policy*, including goals and strategy; and
3. *theoretical disagreements*, which should be defined as disputes generated (at least in part) by differences over the justification for and extent of political authority, above all disagreements over theories of political *obligation*.

All three categories are found in the early-seventeenth century (as they no doubt are in most communities). But, while category (1) forms the bedrock of political dispute, categories (2) and (3) show interesting fluctuations over time. These patterns need to be examined and explained.

Conflict of our first-type – practical conflict – is of little interest for the history of political thought. Consequently, it can be dealt with rather summarily. This category of conflict is one that has figured prominently in recent writing about the early Stuart period. We have become familiar with the image of a world in which political conflict in central government (at court, in the privy council, or in parliament) is seen as the product of faction, and in which opposition to new forms of taxation is thought to reflect not principled rejection of the tax but an attempt to avoid paying it. It was a world not of high-minded politicians acting for the public good but of aristocrats and courtiers seeking access to office or the royal ear, and of local gentry engaging in endless rating disputes and other actions designed to protect themselves from the financial and other exactions of royal government.[103]

Whatever verdict is reached on the degree of adequacy of such a portrait of early-seventeenth century political life, it surely cannot be doubted that self-interest and other less-than-principled motives were behind at least some of the conflict that was evident. The real question at issue in the historiographical debates is whether or not these sorts of motives, were the *only* precipitants of conflict. During the reign of Charles they certainly were not; but during James's reign, while other types of conflict occurred, it is probable that practical disagreements formed the vast bulk of political disputes.

It is possible that one particular sub-category of practical disputes deserves more attention than it has received. Attacks on men like Cowell seem to have been led by common lawyers in the lower House, and it is possible, though difficult to demonstrate, that one motive for the attacks was the realization that any importation of the language of civil law into domestic politics could ultimately be a challenge to the professional interests of the common lawyers. In other words, our three languages were in part professional languages, and clashes between them might represent defences of professional privilege, or challenges to the privileges of others.[104]

While most of this sort of conflict falls below the threshold of interest of the historian of political thought, there is one difficult issue that deserves some attention. How does one distinguish between: (a) practical disputes for which people provide theoretical or ideological rationalizations; and (b) theoretical and ideological disagreements themselves? Admittedly, for the early-seventeenth century this problem is not as pressing as it could be, for the dominant tendency seems to have been to disguise ideological and theoretical disputes as practical ones rather than *vice versa*. But the real answer to the question is that we need not make such a distinction at all. Rationalizations are as much a part of the fabric of discourse as any other sorts of reason, and it is not a profitable task to attempt to judge the sincere and insincere uses of a theory. The political world is at least as much a world of rhetoric as a world of philosophy.

However one important point can be made. Generally speaking, early Stuart Englishmen, when they did seek for theoretical or ideological justification for their actions, sought it in such a way as to place their actions in category (2) rather than category (3).

That is to say that conflicts of ideas tended to be over policy rather than over first principles (by which is meant the nature and extent of political obedience). Recently, Thomas Cogswell has remarked, with regard to the 1620s, that 'Johann Sommerville has pointedly reminded us of the existence of an extended and frequently sharp intellectual debate over the early Stuart constitution, and Cust explained how this discourse could be conducted and disseminated across the realm'.[105] Yet it was not the sorts of philosophical issues analysed by Sommerville that formed the main fare of newsletters, diaries and the popular press.[106] The main concern of the political nation was with the question of whether or not political authority was being exercised for the right *ends* (i.e. for the victory of the forces of Christ over the forces of Antichrist). The fact remains that what we are still inclined to call 'puritanism',[107] for all its acceptance of consensual positions on *political* theory, contained powerful means for the criticism of royal policy. We have recently been reminded – from two quite different perspectives – that the disruptive power of puritanism has been considerably underestimated in recent historiography.[108] Accepting the point should not lead us into an acceptance of the old Whig idea that the 'puritan party' possessed not only religious coherence but was also made up of men with *constitutional* beliefs that led them to support a Parliamentary struggle against royal absolutism.[109] The immense subversive potential of puritanism arose, in the first instance, not because puritans held different opinions from their contemporaries about the sources or extent of royal authority. It arose because they had very firm ideas indeed about the ends, or goals, for which authority existed, and which it *must* therefore serve.[110]

The implications of this are worth considering. When in the 1620s there was considerable political conflict in England, most of it generated (sometimes indirectly) by dislike of the foreign policy being pursued by James or Charles, this should not necessarily be taken as evidence for the breakdown of theoretical consensus. The rhetorical conflicts of the 1620s primarily concerned policy. Was the crown pursuing policies that would further the Protestant interest, at home and abroad? Was it sufficiently firm in its dealings with the cancer of Catholicism? These sorts of questions, which fall within the second of our three categories, were the substance of the rhetorics of conflict that are found in the 1620s. Conflict of this ideological kind was compatible with the existence of consensus at the third level, that is consensus on matters of political theory narrowly defined.

The period after 1618 (i.e. the beginning of the Thirty Years' War) was, in England, a period of political conflict. That conflict was largely generated (in one way or another) by European affairs. To some extent it was a matter of practical issues revolving around the question of how English involvement in a war perceived as the battle against Antichrist was to be organized and financed.[111] But, as historians are now demonstrating in some detail, there were also ideological aspects to the conflict, which led to the belief that royal policies were not sufficiently protestant.[112] Yet, for all the intensity of this sort of conflict, which fluctuated in response to perceptions of such things as the direction of royal policy and the general European situation, it should not be forgotten that it did *not* imply disagreement over such questions as the duty of subjects to be obedient, the sinfulness of resistance, or the nature of the royal prerogative. Indeed in the 1620s (as in the 1640s – though this claim would take rather a lot of defending) it was the existence of basic consensus that made conflict so threatening. Those who were advocating a more interventionist foreign policy could plausibly point to assumptions shared even by those who disagreed with them in support of their position. Consequently, it was very difficult to dismiss critics of the royal position as wayward eccentrics out of touch with the bulk of the political nation. In fact those critics provided an interpretation of England's role and duty as a protestant nation as compelling as that provided by the king and his favoured advisers of the moment. Critics and criticized could each appeal to a common store of consensual opinions – but then derive different implications about policies to be pursued from them. They could agree, that is, on the value of strong government for the common good – and the common good included, of course, following the paths of godliness.

Two of our three categories of conflict have now been dealt with. Practical struggles are of little interest to us, though they are common enough. Conflict over policy turns out to be as much based on consensus as inimical to it, for it reflects widely held conceptions about the divine purposes of government. Conflict at this level certainly *need* not imply any deep fissures over matters of political philosophy. This leads us to our third category and raises the question: were there any such fissures in early Stuart England? We have already seen that for the Jacobean period, though there were various languages and theories available for talking about politics, these were not antagonistic towards one another.

Rather, they were parts of a consensus world view held together by conventions that determined the boundaries of and relationships between the languages. In Chapter 7 we shall be examining how this consensus began to break down, and the implications of this for the types of political conflict present in English society.

This Jacobean consensus was, as we have already seen, compatible with widespread disagreement over particular policies. The impositions debate was one example of this; debates over foreign policy in the last years of James's reign are another example.[113] When the theoretical consensus did break down it was not the development of contentious policy choices in the 1620s (whether over foreign policy or the church) that caused the breakdown. Conflict over *policy* is not in itself evidence for deep theoretical polarization; nor need such conflict be a cause of polarization.

In order for us eventually to come to understand how consensus became impaired it will be useful to examine how it was that even in the Jacobean period some conflicts of our third type could occur. These conflicts were peripheral, testament to the power of consensus not its weakness; but they do provide a clue to future developments. In these conflicts we can see that it was the re-assertion of consensus when it was challenged that created theoretical disputes within a consensus culture. There were two ways, short of outright theoretical polarization, in which people might (advertently or inadvertently) challenge the prevailing consensus. They could misuse the *general* rules of political discourse, thus confusing and muddling the three political languages; or they could misuse the *particular* rules for the use of a particular language, especially by employing it in inappropriate contexts or addressing it to inappropriate audiences.

A nice example of the first of these situations we have already encountered in the matter of Cowell's *Interpreter*. Cowell was condemned not just by the (common lawyer) members of the Commons but by the king as well. Together they asserted and defended the consensus position against Cowell's muddling. Cowell's error was, in essence, to fail to maintain sufficient distinction between the languages of civil law and common law. As a result he implied a relationship between the absolute prerogative and the common law that was highly controversial. In addition, Cowell probably irritated James by treating the prerogative entirely as a matter of law and playing down its mysterious theological elements. It is not surprising that Cowell's carelessness led others to reassert the agreed position; nor is it evidence for deep constitutional polarization in the Jacobean period.

The second of the means by which theoretical conflict could be generated is harder to illustrate. Perhaps the best way to do so is to encroach a little on the subject of the next chapter and explain why Caroline England saw more of this type of conflict than Jacobean England.[114] We have already established that rules for using theological languages of politics (divine right) demanded that such languages be non-specific. When these rules were followed then statements of the divine right of monarchy, whether uttered by James I, read as a Homily, or preached in a sermon, aroused little comment or controversy. Quite early in Charles's reign, however, a number of divine-right sermons did arouse considerable debate – and they did so by breaking the rules we have adumbrated. The political language and theory contained in these sermons was not new, but the purpose for which it was being deployed was.

It is well known that in the years 1627–28 two clergymen, Robert Sibthorpe and Roger Manwaring, found themselves embroiled in controversy as a result of sermons they preached in support of Charles's forced loan of 1626.[115] A little less well known is the fact that the three sermons concerned (Manwaring preached and published two) were but a subset of a larger group of sermons preached in support of the loan.[116] From these facts it has been argued that Sibthorpe and Manwaring were expressing opinions that were held by a substantial group. The 'absolutism' of these theories, similar to that of some Jacobean divines, was starkly pitted against the anti-absolutist views of many members of the political nation, especially the views of the provincial gentry and members of the lower House.[117] But a question worth asking, before we accept this interpretation, is why it was that the sermons of Sibthorpe and Manwaring aroused controversy while other, seemingly similar, sermons by Matthew Wren and Isaac Bargrave did not. The answer will reveal that it was not really for their political *theory* (narrowly defined) that Sibthorpe and Manwaring were attacked but for the way in which they presented it and the implications that they drew from it.

The sermons preached by Wren and Bargrave, though possibly timed to serve as encouragements to pay the loan, were not at all specific in their message. In this sense, not only was their political theory similar to that found in many Jacobean sermons, but they also followed standard conventions for the uncontentious presentation of theories of divine-right kingship. Wren, preaching before the king at Whitehall on the 17th February 1627, went little beyond a forceful reiteration of 'these Duties of *fearing* God and King', linking these two duties together with the argument that 'it is impossible for him that *feareth* not the *King . . .* to *feare God'*. Kings bore the image of God, 'the lively Image of his Divine Power, and Glory both'.[118] Isaac Bargrave preached his sermon before the king just over a month later, on March 27. His subject matter was the wickedness of rebellion. 'If obedience be the *best* of vertues', he argued, 'then rebellion is the *worst* of sinnes'. In the most traditional manner, he emphasized that just as subjects owed a duty of obedience to their kings, so kings owed a similar duty to God.[119] In neither of these sermons was there any explicit mention of the forced loan, nor was there any mention of the practical implications of the political theory (if such it deserves to be called) that they contained. The theoretical stance they adopted was summarized in Bargrave's words as the belief that

> *Kings* are *Gods Christs on earth* (as the Psalmist cals them,) They are neither from *Pope* nor people, as some would have it; but hold in *Capite* immediately from *God: By me Kings raigne.*[120]

It was a position that aroused no controversy, because (as we have seen) it had an accepted place within the 'Jacobean consensus'. Both Wren and Bargrave seemed, at least at this time, to be prepared to operate within that consensus.

The same cannot be said for Manwaring or Sibthorpe. In terms of basic theory there seems to be little to distinguish this pair from numerous other employers of the theological language of politics. But what does distinguish their statements from those of most earlier seventeenth-century ones was that they flouted the convention requiring vagueness. In consequence they fell into the same category as John Cowell: all three of them confused law and theology in ways alarming to their contemporaries. Sibthorpe's very title gave cause for alarm: *Apostolike Obedience: Shewing the Duty of Subjects to pay Tribute and Taxes to their Princes, according to the Word of God, in the Law and the Gospell, and the Rules of Religion, and Cases of Conscience.* His whole purpose was to apply divine-right conceptions of kingship to solve what most thought was a legal not a theological question, namely whether or not the king could tax his subjects at will. On this matter Sibthorpe was explicit, and he gave his answer without any substantial attention being devoted to the common law, thought by most to be the protector of individual property rights.

> If a Prince impose an immoderate, yea an unjust Taxe, yet the subject may not thereupon, withdraw his obedience and dutie. Nay hee is bound in conscience to submit, as under the scourge of his sinne.[121]

Sibthorpe grounded the king's right to tax as he liked on divine and natural law, and argued that even elective kings possessed this right.[122]

Manwaring was, if anything, even more explicit than Sibthorpe. He made use of the idea that the will and mind of a king, like that of God, was unfathomable, and consequently to be obeyed on trust alone.[123] But Manwaring was also very specific about some of the implications of this. 'To Kings . . . nothing can be denied' – not even when what is asked 'be not correspondent in every circumstance, to Lawes Nationall, and Municipall'. The function of parliaments in the matter of taxation was not 'to contribute any Right to Kings' but rather 'for the more equall Imposing, and more easie Exacting of that, which, unto Kings doth appertaine, by Naturall and Originall Law'.[124] The last pages of the first sermon then applied these ideas to the specific matter of the forced loan, and left no doubt that Manwaring was saying that this money was due to the king in conscience – *in spite of* any doubts about its legality (in the narrower sense of conformity with the common law).[125]

Thus, both Sibthorpe and Manwaring went much beyond the accepted rules for using a language of divine right. They used vague theological doctrine (which might have been acceptable had it been used to preach a *general* message about the duty of subjection) to answer specific legal questions. Not surprisingly, this upset many people. Archbishop Abbot refused to license Sibthorpe's sermon, against the clear wishes of Charles. In his statement of his reasons for refusing, Abbot made clear that it was its encroachment on the domain of law that bothered him most about the sermon. Its argument, in Abbot's summary, was that kings 'had power to put Poll-money upon their Subjects heads'. What Abbot objected to was the use of vague theological doctrine to override the law. He summarized his opinion in the argument that 'there is a *Meum* and a *Tuum* in Christian Common-wealths, *and according to Laws and Customs*, Princes may dispose of it'.[126] Abbot reports that the sermon was shown to John Selden, who commented, 'What have you done? You have allowed a strange Book yonder; which, if it be true, there is no *Meum* or *Tuum*, no man in England hath any thing of his own'.[127] In mixing theology and law Sibthorpe had (like Cowell before him) effectively subordinated the ordinary, legal prerogative (which, by operating through the common law, did not threaten the property of the subject) to an absolute prerogative based on divine and natural law.

Manwaring's words proved even more controversial than Sibthorpe's: he was impeached in the parliament of 1628.[128] Francis Rous, speaking to the charge that Manwaring intended 'to alter and subvert the frame and fabric of this estate and commonwealth', argued that the doctrine preached 'robs the Subjects of the Propriety of their Goods', and 'labours to infuse into the conscience of his majesty, the persuasion of a Power not bounding itself with laws, which king James of famous memory, calls, in his Speech to the parliament, Tyranny'.[129] The Commons' Declaration against Manwaring also made it clear that the really obnoxious thing in his work was the destruction of the opinion that 'the free subjects of England do undoubtedly inherit this right and liberty, not to be compelled to contribute any tax, tallage, or aid, or to make any loans, not set or imposed by common consent'.[130] The other things objected to in Manwaring's sermon were incidental to this central matter: he used the language of divine right not in its proper place but to undermine the role of the common law.

Controversy was aroused, in fact, not by what Manwaring said about kings being like Gods; it was aroused by what he implied about the law. The charges against him were not related to his theology so much as his jurisprudence. In this way there was a clear difference between the likes of Manwaring (or Cowell) and the more consensual uses of a theological language of politics found in Wren and Bargrave, to look no further. While it is tempting to see the hostile reaction to Sibthorpe and Manwaring as evidence of a fear of divine-right absolutism, or of the existence of men implacably opposed to the theory of the divine right of kings, the reality is that these men were disliked not for their commonplace philosophies but for their use of them at the wrong time and in the wrong way. As Pym said of Manwaring's sermon, it was even worse that 'it was preached in the heart of the Loan'.[131] One might go beyond this and claim that the acceptance of the sermons of Wren and Bargrave, and the rejection of those of Sibthorpe and Manwaring, is proof of the persistence of the ideals of the Jacobean consensus. Like Cowell, Sibthorpe and Manwaring were eccentric, but eccentric not in their beliefs and doctrines so much as in the way they employed them in public discourse.

But times were a-changing by 1628. The eccentricities of Cowell, Sibthorpe and Manwaring showed signs of becoming more acceptable in some circles. Whereas James in 1610 condemned Cowell's *Interpreter* at some length, Charles – probably bowing to parliamentary pressure for purely tactical reasons – suppressed Manwaring's *Religion and Alegiance* with a poorly concealed ill-grace. The key statement in the Proclamation of 24 June 1628 said of the sermons that

> although the grounds thereof were rightly laid, to perswade obedience from the Subjects to their Soveriegne, and that for conscience sake; Yet in divers passages, inferences & applications thereof, trenching upon the Lawes of this Land, & proceedings of Parliaments, whereof hee was ignorant, hee so farre erred, that hee hath drawn upon himselfe the just Censure of Sentence of the high Court of Parliament.[132]

Scarcely a ringing endorsement of the parliamentary judgement! Two weeks after Manwaring had submitted to the Lords, Charles ordered that Attorney-General Heath prepare a pardon for him, and in subsequent years royal support gave him a substantial ecclesiastical career.[133]

The opinions of Manwaring and the actions of Charles can provide us with a clue to the way in which the Jacobean consensus was seen to be threatened after 1625 (or thereabouts). Before that time there was very little conflict generated by disagreement over political theory, and what little there was was proof of the desire for consensus rather than proof of ideological polarization. Whether the conflict was over Cowell's civil-law view of absolute prerogative or – just beyond the Jacobean period – Sibthorpe's theologically-oriented view of the king's power to ignore legal property rights, its outbreak was an attempt to reinstate the consensual position. In each case the objections raised were not to the assertion of the king's absolute powers as such, but to the way in which these absolute powers had been related to the domain of common law. In 1610 James made sure he was on the side of consensus; in 1628, however, his son made at best a perfunctory attempt at this. It was perfunctoriness of this kind, as well as a number of other actions by Charles, and his government, that helped to produce a growing feeling that the Jacobean consensus was under threat. This is the key to the changing pattern of English political discourse over the period from the late 1620s to the early 1640s, and we need now to examine its ramifications.

7

Towards Breakdown: 'New Counsels' and the Dissolution of Consensus

Gradually after 1625, under the impact of a king who operated very differently from his predecessor, the pattern of English political discourse began to alter. Whereas in the Jacobean period the three chief modes of political discourse were of clearly recognized compass and incorporated into a coherent overall framework (albeit one with some tensions within it), Caroline England saw the development of implicit disagreement about the scope of the three modes, which disagreement ultimately threatened the framework itself. For our purposes the most significant aspect of this process was a crisis in the confidence which people were able to repose in the common law. A consequence of this was the dissolution of that *mentalité* which has been referred to as 'the common law mind'.

Much recent historical work – both the avowedly revisionist and the avowedly post-revisionist – is of great help to us in explaining and understanding these changes. We might begin with some important remarks by Conrad Russell.[1] Russell argues that the experience of the 1620s gave to many of the members of the House of Commons a growing sense of the contestability of the common law. Whereas, hitherto, it had been assumed that the common law was certain and knowable (and therefore a firm and reliable barrier against any attacks on the liberties of freeborn Englishmen), by 1628 this was no longer the case. Men like Coke and Selden were forced to confront the possibility that the law was uncertain. They were forced to realize that their opponents could claim the shelter of law as readily – if not in their own eyes, as justifiably – as themselves. To alleviate these doubts about the law, common-law theorists in the lower House needed to convince their fellow members that the common law *was*, after all, adequate to its task of defending English liberties. As a result there was what we might call a hardening of the theory of the ancient constitution. There developed 'a growing cult of the rule of law'; Coke made increasingly absolute demands for the authority of the common law; and in general a theory about the relationship between law and prerogative, different from the theory current in parliamentary circles in 1610, was developed.

This account, confined as it is to the language of parliamentary debates, can be extended and adapted to provide a full account of changing patterns of political discourse over the whole period 1625–1642. The experience of the governmental policies of Charles I proved a disturbing one for many of his subjects, as much because of the theoretical incoherence of what he was doing as because of the policies themselves. This experience induced not self-confident and articulate opposition but bewildered incomprehension. Charles came to be a distrusted king more because he played by different rules from those followed by his subjects than because he was personally a liar. They consequently found it difficult to understand what he was doing and it is little wonder that in their eyes he looked simply mendacious. Perhaps the central lesson that Charles's subjects learnt from all this was that the common law and the rules of the Jacobean consensus were inadequate protection for their lives, liberties and estates. The early-seventeenth century may or may not have seen 'the crisis of parliaments',[2] but it certainly did see an equally important crisis of the common law.

A simple view of the political history of Caroline England might portray it as a clash between a monarch content to pursue policies justified solely by reference to the prerogative powers of the crown, and his subjects who believed that the king should rule by following the common law and the principles of the ancient constitution. It is undoubtedly true that after 1625 the prerogative powers of the crown were being exploited more thoroughly, and were being talked about in new ways. All the same, this simple view is a little bit too simple. Because prerogative and law were thought to be intertwined entities in the seventeenth century, no straightforward clash between them was possible. A more accurate way of putting the matter would be to say that the crown and its spokesmen utilized commonplace components of the accepted Jacobean understanding of prerogative in order to subvert some of its other components. They exploited tensions within the Jacobean consensus but did not conduct a frontal assault upon it. It may indeed be that Charles's misuse (or, less judgementally, idiosyn-cratic use) of the linguistic conventions of this society meant that his actions and motives were constantly misinterpreted by his subjects: he always gave them the wrong signals. Perhaps this also explains why Charles has remained one of the most enigmatic of English kings.

Recently, historians have attempted to capture the innovatory characteristics of Charles's reign in the phrase 'new counsels'.[3] The phrase is designed to express the fact that Charles, very soon after his accession, began to listen to and act upon advice encouraging him to abandon traditional policies and to find 'new means . . . for supplying the King's necessities'. On 12 May 1626 Sir Dudley Carleton, at the time a Privy Councillor, warned the Commons that should they fall out with the king 'he should be enforced to use new counsels. Now I pray you to consider what these new counsels are and may be. I fear to declare those that I conceive'. Afraid or not, he went on pointedly to indicate the general pattern throughout Christendom whereby kings 'began to stand upon their prerogatives' and overthrow their parliaments.[4] Before long, in the aftermath of the 1626 Parliament, Charles did indeed take heed of new counsels, particularly with regard to his right to demand non-parliamentary taxation.

What was the nature of these 'new counsels'? Richard Cust has remarked that 'the "new counsels" can be seen in a very real sense as the secular counterpart of the rise of Arminianism'.[5] Perhaps there is an element of truth in this claim, but it is only an element: the statement seems, in general, a bit too neat. It is, of course, accepted by all historians that there was no inherent linkage between Arminian *theology* and any particular sort of pol-itical theory. Arminian theology was as compatible with resistance theory as it was with divine-right absolutism.[6] But the development of Laudianism/Arminianism was not just (according to some his-torians, it was not at all) the rise of a new theology that rejected Calvinist predestinarian doctrine. It was, at least in part, also a result of the demand for 'order and discipline' within the church. Because this demand was shared by Charles, who wished for order and discipline in the state as well, and by his 'Arminian' bishops and clergy, the result was the influx of the clergy into positions of influence around the king.[7] One historian has identified as one of the three central features of Laud's outlook 'his deep conviction that the Reformation had deprived clergymen of authority and influence that was essential to the health of religion, monarchy, and society'.[8] From this developed the political face of Laudianism, which consisted of policies designed to restore the power and place of the clerical estate. A bishop (Juxon of London) became Lord Treasurer; Laud himself was probably the most powerful of royal counsellors; the church courts were revitalized; attempts were made to restore the fabric and finances of the church.[9]

An aspect of this it has been claimed – the one most relevant to us – was a growing tendency to use the theological langauge of politics (divine right monarchism) in areas beyond the conventional Jacobean boundaries. The sermons of Sibthorpe and Manwaring are taken to have been the earliest signs of this. But this was a matter quite separate from Arminian theology (there is no evidence that Sibthorpe and Manwaring were Arminian), and even Calvinist bishops, most notably Joseph Hall, might share in the high view of the clerical estate taken by Laudians; equally, Calvinists like Thomas Morton were as capable of preaching against resistance theory in 1639 as Arminians.[10] This may well suggest that the supposed 'rise of Arminianism' was something rather more amorphous than that neat label suggests. What is perhaps the most striking feature of the period 1625–40 is the rise of clericalism, at least in the realm of political practice.

But 'clericalism' alone is not enough to capture the essence of this period either. Though there came from the pulpits isolated attempts to employ divine-right theory to defend the legitimacy of specific acts of government, much more important was the fact that there came also in the law courts and elsewhere attempts to use a specifically *legal* theory of the absolute prerogative in new ways. In both instances the linguistic boundaries of the Jacobean consensus were being crossed. Sibthorpe and Manwaring used theological political languages to answer questions that should have been answered in the language of common law; but few other clerics did so. Lawyers and counsellors, however, made the most of the place allowed by the common law to an absolute prerogative usually discussed in civil and natural law terms. It is a little awkward for the historian that these two theoretical avenues (divine right and legal absolutism) do not fit very neatly with one another. Clerical preaching in favour of the royal prerogative is generally taken to be linked to the rise of Arminianism/Laudianism (though in accepting this linkage we may well just be the latest to be taken in by the propaganda of Pym and his cohorts in the Long Parliament); yet (on the other hand) those active in giving legal expression to the important role of the absolute prerogative were not necessarily well disposed towards Laudianism. Sir Robert Heath, for example, was an active anti-Arminian Calvinist,[11] while in general terms there were virtually *no* doctrinal Arminians amongst the barristers of Caroline England,[12] even though a number of common lawyers were prominent agents of royal policy during these years.[13] Such royal servants as Sir John Banks (attorney-general following the death of Noye in 1634) and Sir John Finch (a Ship Money Judge who was to become Lord Keeper in 1640) have even been loosely classified as puritans.[14]

What all of this might suggest is that the reign of Charles I saw at least two quite *separate* – but at times overlapping – processes occurring. One was the rise of Laudianism, however we might characterize this phenomenon (and it may be that it was an illusion caused by the *decline* of Calvinism); the other was the increasing frequency with which the implementation of particular policies was defended with reference to the absolute prerogative of the crown, whether conceived of theologically or legally.

Let us examine this latter tendency, the following of new counsels, in greater depth. We have seen, with regard to Manwaring and Sibthorpe, that it is possible to identify precisely what was contentious in the way some of the clergy addressed political questions. Controversy lay not in their theories of divine right monarchy but in the way those theories were applied to settle practical political questions, which were properly matters of law. At least looking back from 1640, critics of Charles's reign did not think that Manwaring and Sibthorpe were isolated eccentrics (a way in which one could dismiss John Cowell). It may indeed be that a more significant example, in a number of ways, than either Sibthorpe or Manwaring was William Beale. His significance lies in the fact that he, unlike the other two, most emphatically *was* an Arminian, and the attacks made on him from the Short Parliament onwards were instrumental in linking Arminianism (and Laud himself) with the 'preaching up' of the royal prerogative. Unfortunately, the text of Beale's political sermon of 1635 has not survived, which probably explains why it has attracted so little attention. Nevertheless, his story is worth telling.

On 1 May 1640 John Pym brought to the attention of the House of Commons a sermon preached in Cambridge on 'the Kings Coronacion day', 1635. In this sermon Beale had said, according to Pym, that 'the King might constitute Lawes what, where, when, and against whom hee would'; that 'it is his [i.e. the king's] meere grace to admitt at all any consultation of parliaments'; and that taxes, subsidies, and tonnage and poundage were 'the Kings Absolutely'.[15] Beale was a prominent Cambridge figure, Master of St John's from February 1634 and Vice-Chancellor of the University. There can be little doubt about Beale's religious position: as Master of St John's he set about making the college, along with Peterhouse (in the hands of John Cosin), one of Cambridge's Arminian showpieces.[16] But the attack on him in the Short Parliament made only slight mention of this, and was narrowly directed at his political sermon of 1635. The same was no longer true after November 1640.

The Short Parliament was dissolved before it was able to take action against Dr. Beale. The House had voted, on 1 May, that Beale should be asked to come and explain himself;[17] dissolution intervened on 5 May. But Pym did not let the matter rest: in his great programmatic speech of 7 November 1640 – four days after the opening of the Parliament – he included Beale in his list of grievances ('Frequent preaching for Monarchy, Doctor Beale and others'), but this time the charge was made in the context of a general onslaught on 'the corrupt part of our clergie' and those who would support Popery if it meant their own advancement.[18] Beale had become – and was to remain – but one plank in the charge that Laudianism equalled Popery, and his case was particularly useful in demonstrating the link between Laudianism/Arminianism and clerical support for arbitrary monarchy. Consequently this made him of interest as much as a means of linking *Laud* to theories of arbitrary monarchy as in his own right. Proceedings were, nevertheless, instigated against Beale himself. On 6 August 1641 articles were introduced into the Commons that took up the campaign against him; but, whereas the attack in the Short Parliament had concentrated on one isolated political sermon, these new charges were much broader. In them Beale was accused of praising Papists and condemning Puritans, of support for Laudian altar policy, of interrupting the continuance of orthodox worship in his College chapel, of encouraging Cosin in the Arminianisation of Cambridge, and of corrupting the faith of the Cambridge student body. It was not forgotten, also, that 'he preached at St. *Maries* against the *Subjects* freedome and liberty'.[19] On December 21, 1641 the Commons finally ordered that the Committee for the Bill for Scandalous Ministers take over the proceedings against Beale.[20]

While, over the period May 1640 to August 1641 the charges against Beale were widened from an attack on a single, tactless political statement to a broad onslaught on his Laudianism, the same period also saw Beale being taken up as a stick with which to beat Laud. On 18 December 1640 the two Houses initiated proceedings for High Treason against the Archbishop.[21] The matter was then laid aside until 24 February 1641 when the Commons voted unanimously to impeach Laud, who was, a few days later, committed to the Tower by the Lords. There he remained until his trial in 1644.[22]

The twelve articles that made up the original charge against Archbishop Laud began with the claim 'that he hath traitorously endeavoured to subvert the fundamental laws and government of this kingdom; and instead thereof, to introduce an arbitrary and tyrannical Government against law'. In furtherance of this objective, Laud was charged by the second article with having 'advised and procured divers sermons, and other Discourses, to be preached, printed and published, in which the Authority of Parliaments, and the Force of the laws of this kingdom, are denied'.[23] In the Commons debate on these articles (24 February 1641) the example cited here was that of William Beale.[24] Again, in the actual trial of Laud, Beale's sermon was brought up, though not in the unconvincing hotch-potch of evidence related to the second article (which did, incidentally, charge him with allowing the reprinting of Cowell's *Interpreter* in 1638).[25] But, tucked away on the ninth day of the trial (16 May 1644) was the evidence given by Mr. Jenkins

> That seven years since Dr. Beal was Vice-chancellor of Cambridge; that in his sermon then he inveighed bitterly against the Power of Parliaments, and named some unsavory speeches of his, both concerning their persons and proceedings.

Laud replied to this that Beale was responsible for his own words, 'he is alive, let him answere for them'.[26] Beale was clearly useful: here was a man, clearly pro-Laudian, against whose political opinions at least some evidence could be found. But as his trial shows, there was not much else in support of the claims made against Laud. Beale's name was also introduced, in similarly gratuitous fashion, into the proceedings against John Cosin. On 15 March 1640 Rous presented, on behalf of the Commons, the articles of impeachment against Cosin to the Lords. Though the articles were all concerned

with Cosin's Arminianising policies, Rous's speech nevertheless
included a charge of 'political popery' levelled at Cosin:

> Our laws and popery cannot stand together; but either popery
> must overthrow our laws, or our laws must overthrow popery.
> But to overthrow our laws, they must overthrow parliaments;
> and to overthrow parliaments they must overthrow property;
> they must bring the subjects goods to be arbitrarily disposed,
> that so there may be no need of parliaments: This hath been
> done by Dr. Manwaring; (whom we find wanting, yet not in the
> Seats, but at the bar of the lords house) and the like by Dr. Beale:
> And I think it was the intention of the late Canons.[27]

This propaganda effort of the 1640s, using Beale to demonstrate
the links between Arminianism and political absolutism, has been
important in establishing the view – hard to document from the pre-
Civil War evidence itself – of a close linkage of this sort. There may
be two reasons – one narrow, one wide – for the efforts made after
1640 to show that Laudianism was politically, not just religiously,
unsound. The narrow one relates to events between the Short and
Long Parliaments, during which time the charges made against
Beale in May were taken up by High Commission. The evidence
relating to this suggests that an attempt was being made to use
High Commission to ferret out Beale's *opponents*, which may well
have provoked their further attacks after November 1640. In a letter
of 29 July 1640 to Beale and Cosin, Sir John Lambe finished with a
postscript: 'Though the matter were long since, yet the malignity,
it seems, continues, and it is fit in have an end, which I think is all
that is intended by those that wish you well'.[28]

Provocative though this may have been, it provides at best only
a partial explanation for the continuing animosity shown towards
Dr. Beale. More significant, perhaps, was that Beale was very
useful to those opposed to the Laudian church: by enabling them,
however loosely, to link Laud with absolutist doctrine, he also
encouraged the attempt to build a consensual base for the attack
on Arminianism. Religion was always a contentious issue in the
Long Parliament, but – in contrast – the attack during early-mid
1641 on the agents of Charles's so-called prerogative rule was able
to command wide support. Indeed, the attack was led by men who
were to become Royalists in the civil war, Viscount Falkland and Sir
Edward Hyde (later Earl of Clarendon), as well as Edmund Waller

(who was a Parliamentarian, but only just). If Arminianism could be shown to have intimate links with those 'new counsels' that had led to the crisis of faith in the common law then perhaps there was some chance of widening the support for an attack upon it. In other words, the widespread political opposition to Charles's rule may have encouraged some to think that it could be tapped for religious purposes also. Waller expressed the early consensus view that the law required immediate attention when he said of his emphasis on legal matters:

> not but that Religion ought to be the first thing in our purposes and desires, but that which is first in dignity is not alwaies to preceed in order of time: for well being supposed a being, and the first impediment which men naturally endeavour to remove, is the want of those things without which they cannot subsist.[29]

Those things, Waller indicated, were laws. This sense of the need to repair the laws that defined and held together the body politic was strong during 1641, and it does seem at least plausible that Beale's sermon, with its implicit undermining of the law, was the object of an attempt to deflect some of the strength of this feeling towards Laudianism.

Henry Parker, propagandist for the coalition of peers and gentry that came to control the Long Parliament, wrote in 1640 that 'the Prelates'

> preach an unlimitable prerogative, and condemne all law of liberty as injurious to Kings, and incompatible with Monarchy. *Manwarring* denies Parliamentary power and honour, *Cowel* denies propriety of goods, further then at the Kings discretion, and *Harrison* accuses Judge *Hutton* of delivering law against Gods Law, in the case of Ship-money.[30]

Parker's work was published to coincide with the opening of the Long Parliament, and his charge was perhaps the public version of the equivalent one made by Pym in the Commons on November 7. But it should be noted that the most significant feature of Parker's statement is how much difficulty he had in proving it. The only apposite example he could find was an isolated sermon from the 1620s (Manwaring). Cowell was, of course, not a cleric at all – though he was another isolated case; while Thomas

Harrison was a none-too-significant parson who was sued (twice) for calling Hutton, who found against the Crown in Hampden's case, a traitor.[31] In fact, the actual pre-1640 evidence for a fusion of the two developments of Charles's reign – Arminianism and new counsels – is surprisingly weak. As we have seen, neither Manwaring nor Sibthorpe was Arminian (though the former did gain preferment within the Laudian church), and the many other political sermons that we can find in Caroline England seldom strayed into areas not traversed by the Jacobean clergy, in both cases without arousing controversy.[32] Indeed, the number and array of sermons and clerical tracts in praise of divine right monarchy in Jacobean England seems greater than that to be found in Caroline England, in good part because many statements of this sort were generated by anti-papalism and formed part of James I's international propaganda effort against the indirect deposing power. Other than Manwaring and Sibthorpe, with whom we have dealt, the Caroline period has little to compare with such powerful statements of divine-right monarchism as John Buckeridge's sermon before the king in 1603, or William Dickinson's assize sermon of 1619.[33] Margaret Judson, who has given the fullest survey of early Stuart clerical political theory, has made two points (which do not fit altogether well with her own framework of analysis). Most of those clergy who wrote about the powers of the monarch 'did not discuss specifically his power in respect to the laws of the land' and were indeed 'surprisingly unconcerned with the great constitutional and political controversy of their own age'. And, second, the period 1630 to 1640 saw no political sermons comparable to those of Sibthorpe and Manwaring.[34] What this suggests is the substantial survival, in the clerical estate at least, of the Jacobean consensus. Divine right language was, generally, still not used to answer the questions best dealt with in legal terms, and there should be nothing 'surprising' in the clerical failure to address specific political issues: they knew this was not their function. There was, then, no such thing as Arminian/Laudian political thought. Laudian bishops said nothing not to be found expressed by their Jacobean, or even Elizabethan, predecessors.[35] Sibthorpe and Manwaring – Beale, too – were isolated cases of clergymen who transgressed rules for the uncontentious use of divine right theory that most accepted. The idea of the Caroline period as one in which the clergy began to hold and express political ideas that were innovatory in their royalism may well have been a propaganda construct of the early 1640s.

Propaganda though, can be very informative – provided one does not believe it. In this case, there is real significance in the attempt to link the Laudian prelates with political absolutism. The effort would not have been attempted had there not already existed a widespread feeling that the law and the liberties of Englishmen were under threat, not so much from the prerogative as from some bizarre interpretations of the prerogative. In 1640–1 it was the need to repair the law that united the opposition to Charles I, and it was to be the attack on the Laudian church that divided it.[36] The propaganda attempt to transfer unity into religious matters failed, but it remains testament to the extent of concern for the health of the common law in 1640 and 1641.

The nature of that concern will be investigated in the next section. Here we need to investigate what underlay it. There were two trends apparent in Caroline England – the growth of Laudianism and the advent of 'prerogative rule'. As we have seen, the connections between these two trends are at best contingent and limited, more practical than theoretical. For our purposes it was the second of the developments that was more important: the more frequent resort to 'new counsels'. Even more important than the new counsels themselves was their effect in causing the crisis of the common law.

Of critical importance in this was the use of the common law courts for purposes of – as it was perceived – subverting the common law itself. The chief area in which this occurred was the crown's attempt to use the courts to support its claims to non-parliamentary taxation. The result, in the words of one recent historian, was a 'continuum of constitutional concern in the Commons over arbitrary royal taxation extending back into the reign of James I'.[37] But this perhaps goes too far; we need to be more discriminating. The concern revealed by the end of the 1620s, and (especially) in the early 1640s, was different in character from much earlier concerns, which throws some doubt on the appropriateness of the word 'continuum'. And even within the Caroline period itself there was a tendency for older ways of thinking to persist, so that not all of the financial disputes of that period show the same characteristics. We need, above all, to be sensitive to the nuances of political discourse, for this can tell us when conflict does and when it does not fit within the Jacobean consensual paradigm. Looking back from 1641, MPs accorded key significance to the Shipmoney case, as we shall see, and this was undoubtedly the climactic political event of the pre-Civil War period. Of a comparable nature was some of the debate surrounding the Forced Loan and leading thence to the Petition of Right. But beyond these two brief periods of debate (1627–29, 1638–41) we should be mindful of overestimating either the innovativeness or the contentiousness of Charles's policies. These policies provided much to grumble about. Who wanted to pay forest fines, or to be distrained for some technicality concerning knighthood? But grumbling was neither new nor dangerous in itself. What was new was the coupling of this discontent over the exploitation of *particular* royal prerogatives with a general fear for the safety of the common law. It took more than forest fines and distraint of knighthood to generate those fears.

Another matter that does not feed directly into the fears about the common law, in spite of recent attempts to argue the contrary, was the 1629 dispute over tonnage and poundage. It has been argued that this issue, in spite of its 'narrowness' and 'legalistic' nature, was one of considerable constitutional significance. In the debates of 1629 'absolute royal power faced absolute property'.[38] But, though there were wider dimensions to the debate, the crown was generally careful in this instance to debate the matter within the bounds of the Jacobean consensus. There was no *general* confrontation of an absolute prerogative with absolute property at all, because Charles claimed in his explanation for the 1629 debacle, to be claiming tonnage and poundage on the basis of precedent. Essentially he believed it to be a legal, customary right (or prerogative) of the crown, collected with implicit, though in this case not explicit, parliamentary authority.[39] It was not claimed under the absolute prerogative. Charles's predecessors had collected it from the time of their accession, not from the time of its granting by parliament, and he would do the same.[40] This was a specific dispute about whether the law did, or did not, give the crown a particular right. By themselves, it is hard to see that much would have come from disputes of this sort.

But, of course, now they were not by themselves. While the whole *point* of the Crown's arguments on impositions (and tonnage and poundage) was the *avoidance of absolutism* by claiming such revenue as a specific part of the legal prerogative or as part of an extra legal prerogative that did not impinge upon property rights at all, there were other demands made by the crown in such a way as to cause more general alarm. It was these demands, or rather the arguments advanced in their defence, that undermined the working of the Jacobean consensus. One need only to contrast the arguments involved in the Five Knights' Case with those used in Bate's case to sense the carelessness or foolishness of what the crown was doing in 1627. Above all, it was the argument of Attorney-General Heath, putting the case for the Crown, and his subsequent actions, rather than the decisions given by the judges, that were of key importance.

The Five Knights' Case (sometimes called also Darnel's case) was not about non-parliamentary taxation. Sir Thomas Darnel, Sir John Corbet, Sir Walter Erle, Sir John Heveningham and Sir Edmund Hampden – the five knights – were imprisoned by order of the Privy Council for refusing to pay the forced loan. On 3 November 1627 the court of King's Bench awarded them writs of *habeas corpus*, which required that a cause for their imprisonment be given if they were not to receive bail.[41] After some prevarication the Council decided that the response to be given to the writs of *habeas corpus* was that the five knights were imprisoned 'by his majesty's special commandment'. The question at issue in the subsequent proceedings in King's Bench was whether or not this vague statement was adequate really to satisfy the demand that cause of imprisonment be shown. The Crown and the privy council obviously decided upon this response to avoid any judicial consideration of the forced loan itself, and it was this evasion of the issue that irritated many. In other circumstances the Crown might well have acted as it did quite without controversy;[42] but the use of argument based on 'reason of state' in circumstances where, many felt, the refusal to pay a forced loan was not illegal appeared dangerously like an attempt to use a royal prerogative (in itself possibly legal) to safeguard actions of more dubious legality from investigation. The decision given by the judges, as they later emphasized in parliament, was not a judgement in favour of the crown's right to imprison arbitrarily; indeed it was not a judgement at all, but a 'rule of court' that disallowed bail to the knights in this instance, pending further proceedings, but was not to be taken as approval of the Crown's claims, and could not be cited as a precedent.[43]

This decision may have been more readily treated as a possible compromise decision had it not been for Attorney-General Heath, and his royal master. In 1627 – as also in the Shipmoney case – the arguments put forward by the Crown's advocate were much more far-reaching than the decisions given by the judgement, but (in each case) a decision that *in practice* ended up being in the Crown's favour could be seen to allow a sort of victory for the arguments advanced for the king's position. Or, more to the point, perhaps the decisions revealed the inability of the common-law courts (and of the common law itself?) to stand against the sorts of arguments being used by the crown and to protect the property and liberty of the subject. In this way it contributed, as did nothing else, to the crisis of the common law.

Attorney-General Heath's argument for the crown in the Five Knights' case contains two crucial passages of interest to the historian of political thought.[44] The first, which contained the heart of Heath's legal argument, was an attempt to use the standard duplex theory of the royal prerogative. In saying that Darnel and the others were imprisoned by special command of the king, it was being stated that it was 'His Majesty's immediate act and will' that they be detained. In such circumstances the judges were to accept that the king had good reason for his command and did not specify the actual crime involved because it was 'a matter of State, and . . . not ripe nor timely for it to appear'. Behind this conclusion was the claim that

> The King cannot command your Lordship, or any other Court of Justice, to proceed otherwise than according to the laws of this kingdom, for it is part of your Lordship's oath, to judge according to the law of the kingdom. But my lord, there is a great difference between those legal commands and that *absoluta potestas* [absolute power] that a sovereign hath, by which a king commands. But when I call it *absoluta potestas*, I do not mean that it is such a power as that a king may do what he pleaseth, for he hath rules to govern himself by, as well as your Lordships, who are subordinate judges under him. The difference is, the king is the head of the same fountain of justice, which your Lordship administers to all his subjects. All justice is derived from him, and what he doth, he doth not as a private person, but as the head of the commonwealth, as *justiciarius regni*, yea, the very essence of justice under God upon earth is in him. And shall we generally, not as subjects only, but as lawyers, who govern themselves by the rules of the law, not submit to his command, but make enquiries whether they be lawful, and say that the King doth not this or that in course of justice?[45]

The crucial difference between this and the royal position on impositions is that now it was being argued that the king's absolute power could be employed in common-law proceedings. In Bates's case it was determined that the matter effectively lay beyond the territorial reach of the common law; but Heath in this instance was arguing that in a domestic matter (depriving a subject of his liberty) the king could use his absolute prerogative, and could cite that as his cause for acting in answer to a writ of *habeas corpus*. This seems to result in a dangerous mixing of absolute and legal prerogative. Politically, this might just have been acceptable, were it not for the fact that in this particular case the resort to absolute prerogative was designed to prevent any common-law consideration of the legality of forced loans. The position looked plainly duplicitous: everyone knew (except the judges, who were bound to act as if they did not know) what the 'matter of state' behind this case was, and that the only reason for not mentioning it was to prevent its legality being properly determined. The real problem, then, was that, suddenly, the royal absolute prerogative – inherently an accepted component of the crown's authority – was being used to shield actions many considered to be of dubious legality. The king insisted on protecting such actions by moving matters from his legal to his absolute prerogative. If he could get away with this – and whether he did or not is hard to say, given the carefulness of the judges' decision – then it might legitimately be asked what protection the common law really did provide for the subjects' liberty and property. To put the matter precisely, what was contentious in Heath's statement was not the view that the crown had absolute powers, but the way in which they were said to relate to the law and the legal prerogative. Above all, this was an attempt to deploy the absolute prerogative for uses not given to it by the Jacobean consensus. In the second important passage from his argument Heath said that when no specific cause of imprisonment was given by the crown the response of the courts should be

> to say there is no cause expressed, and therefore the matter is not ripe; and thereupon the courts of judicature have ever rested satisfied therewith; they would not search into it. My Lords, there be *arcana Dei, et arcana imperii* [mysteries of God, and mysteries of state]

and mysteries of state should not be inquired into. In short, Heath was arguing that where mysteries or reasons of state were involved neither the subject nor the law should pry. The king should be trusted: 'you will believe that there is great reason of state so to do, or else they would not do it'.[46] Which was all very well, except that in this instance the reasons were all too transparent and the mysteries quite unmysterious. Put crudely (and this, no doubt, is how many did put it), Charles, through his Attorney-General, was effectively using his absolute prerogative to frustrate the normal course of law. Behind it sheltered the imprisonment of men who refused to pay a loan not sanctioned by parliament.

The judges did not give their approval to Attorney-General Heath's theories (though the decision did contain the point that 'if no cause of the commitment be expressed, it is to be presumed to be for matter of state, which we cannot take notice of').[47] Indeed, it was not the theory that was problematic, but rather the circumstances in which, and the purposes for which, it was being deployed. Distrust of the king and his Attorney-General can only have been increased when it was revealed in the Commons in 1628 that Heath had attempted, feloniously, to pervert the record of the case so that it could be used in future as a firm legal precedent for the king's right to imprison without showing specific cause.[48] It is hard to express how shocking this must have appeared to contemporaries, and how fully it must have strengthened the fear that the crown was disregarding the law.

The law was under threat: was it strong enough to survive? That was the real question at issue in 1628. The debates on what was to become the Petition of Right show, I think, that fear and confusion were the predominant reactions to the experience of the early years of Charles I's reign. Fear and confusion were generated not because spokesmen for the king were putting forward new and innovative political theories, but because they were using theories of absolute prerogative, in themselves quite commonplace and uncontentious, in *contexts* that were inappropriate and for purposes that they ought not to have been made to serve. To be precise, there was an evident tendency by 1627–28 to use the theological or (much more commonly) civil law languages of absolute prerogative to answer questions of a common law nature. It was this that raised the question of the integrity and the adequacy of the common law. Central to this question was the problem of what meaning the law had. The early events of Charles's reign had brought home to many the fact that the law was *ambiguous*, and in its ambiguity lay the possibility that it would not, after all, serve the purposes that MPs had thought it would. It would not serve as a *secure* protection for the subject's rights. Peter Ball expressed the essence of the matter: 'The question is not whether the laws be in force or no, but for the meaning of them. What is *lex terrae*? We all agree what it is, but have the Lords and the judges so agreed?'[49] Ball was pointing to the erosion of consensus, and was – like many of his contemporaries – primarily concerned with the need to come to terms with the possibility that his king might see the law in ways very different from himself.

Could the law be given a definition so clear and so firm that it could not be used in the way that Charles had used it since 1626? Two episodes in the debates of 1628 reveal this to have been the major point at issue. First, on April 25 the Lords produced their own set of propositions in answer to the Commons' resolutions (3 April) against arbitrary imprisonment and related matters (these resolutions and proposals were effectively ancestor documents of the Petition of Right, but the story of the transmutation by which they became the Petition is a very complex one). The Lord's proposals included a clause 'saving' the royal prerogative. This stated that the prerogative was 'intrinsical to his sovereignty and entrusted to him from God', and it accepted the king's prerogative right to imprison, in some cases, for reason of state.[50] The proposition saving the prerogative was motivated by a perception that, as well as defending the liberties of the subject, it was 'fit and necessary also to preserve the just prerogative of the king'.[51] This raised the question of the relationship between prerogative and law. It was raised again on 17 May in the debates on the Petition itself when the Lords suggested that MPs should tell the king in the Petition of Right that they were acting 'with a due regard to leave entire that sovereign power wherewith your Majesty is trusted'.[52] This, our second episode, produced a debate in the Commons similar to that following the proposals of April 25.

A good number of prominent figures in the Commons, including Sir Edward Coke, were unhappy with each of the two suggestions from the Lords intended to show the king that parliamentary actions were not an attack on the royal prerogative. Their disquiet with the proposals could be interpreted as a sign that they really were attempting to reduce the royal prerogative and wished to deny the king *any* absolute prerogatives whatsoever. But this would be to go too far. The 1628 proceedings were designed to do two separate things: first, to state what MPs believed the law to be on such matters as arbitrary imprisonment and non-parliamentary taxation; and, second, to gain a statement from the king – preferably one of some legal force – that conveyed *his* acceptance of this interpretation of the law. The whole business of Heath's attempt to pervert the King's Bench records must have convinced many that the second of these claims required as unambiguous a statement as possible. A clear and powerful declaration of the illegality of arbitrary imprisonment was, therefore, needed not because the Commons wanted to make new law, but because they feared anything less than clear would not serve when dealing with a government capable of considerable duplicity. Consequently, the opposition to the Lords' attempts to make the parliamentary statements of 1628 into defences of both the royal prerogative *and* the rights of the subject took two main lines.

Edward Coke expressed the first of these most emphatically. The law needed positive definition, and the Lord's proposals introduced so much ambiguity into the matter that they negated the whole point of the exercise. 'Intrinsical' prerogative was not legally definable: '"Intrinsical" is no word of the law.' The Lords' statement mixed law and theology and ended up saying of the prerogative that 'it is due *jure divino*, and then no law can take it away'.[53] Later, on May 20, Coke made much the same point about the effort to add a clause saving the prerogative to the Petition itself. In it he stated

> I know that prerogative is part of the law, but 'Sovereign Power' is no parliamentary word. In my opinion it weakens Magna Charta, and all the statutes; for they are absolute, without any saving of 'Sovereign Power'; and should we now add it, we shall weaken the foundation of law, and then the building must needs fall . . . . If we grant this, by implication we give a 'Sovereign Power' above all laws.[54]

Coke's point – and this is particularly evident when his remarks are read in the context of other contributions to this debate – was that 'sovereign power' was legally *undefinable*, and to introduce it into a legal document such as the Petition of Right was to negate the effect of that document. It was to give *legal* recognition to the absolute prerogative, and thus to allow it a role in matters normally the province of the common law. The need was to give a firm definition of the law so that it really could secure liberties, but – as Alford said – accept the Lord's amendment and 'we shall acknowledge a regal as well as a legal power',[55] that is they would give the king's power (in its legal *and non-legal* aspects) a legal sanction and a place in law.

John Pym spoke to the same theme: 'All our Petition is for the laws of England, and this power seems to be another distinct power from the power of the law. I know how to add sovereign to the king's person, but not to his power'.[56] Sir Thomas Wentworth summed up the argument: 'these laws are not acquainted with "Sovereign Power"'.[57] This is a statement we should take literally: the law could not define 'Sovereign power', so the inclusion of the phrase in a legal document[58] had the effect of introducing into the law a principle that left it permanently uncertain, permanently in danger of being overridden.

The principle behind this position was expressed most clearly by Lord Saye and Sele in the debates in the Lords prior to the voting of the propositions of April 25.[59] Saye opposed the majority in favour of the proposals, arguing on April 22 that,

> Reason of State, [is acceptable] in tymes of necessitye, *etc.*, but not to rule the Lawe nor leave a gappe. But we are nowe to consider of the auncient liberties used in the best tymes of our Kinges. Better have the Lawe to be positive and absolute, then the reason of State; for the Lawe wyll in cases of Necessitye yeelde to reasons of State *prout*, in cases of fyre, Fortes, *etc.*, to pull downe howses and buylde on the owners grounds, *etc.* But wyll you not make the Lawe absolute, but leave the King power to pull downe howses, *etc.*, at all tymes.[60]

Only a positive and absolute definition of the law would serve the purpose of clarifying it sufficiently to enable it to preserve the liberty and property of the subject. But – as Saye made plain – this clarification was to ensure that no 'gappe' was left in the law, not to take away the absolute prerogative altogether. The latter still existed no matter how 'absolute' was the definition of the law. Later in the day Saye put his point more succinctly:

> Trust reposed in the King but not in Ordinary causes of Justice. Never fell any Inconveniences to the State bycause the Lawe is positive . . . . If this be rightly understood, noe inconvenience to the Kinge.[61]

The behaviour of Charles and Heath in 1627–28 convinced some of the need to make an 'absolute' statement of the law (by which they meant a clear one), for it was only if the law was defined with precision that it was any use. Behind this, surely, lay doubt. The obsessive insistence on clear definition in 1628 revealed the doubt that the government's actions raised about whether the law really was the bulwark of liberties that it had been taken to be.

Following neatly from this was the second major argument used against the Lords' wish to specify their acceptance of the royal prerogative. This, indeed, was the argument that eventually convinced the Lords. Put succinctly, it consisted in the claim that since the Petition of Right was a document about the subjects' liberties the matter of the prerogative had no place in it. John Selden, speaking in the Commons debate on the Lords' addition (May 22), cited examples of previous documents stating the liberties of the subject (including Magna Carta), and pointed out that none of them made reference to the prerogative. Such reference would at best be simply irrelevant, and at worst confusing. He went on:

> As to what we declared, by the mouth of our speaker, this parliament, that it was far from our heart to encroach on the king's prerogative; we then spake of the king's prerogative by itself, and we are bound to say so: but speaking of our own rights, shall we say, We are not to be imprisoned saving, but by the king's 'Sovereign Power'?[62]

The answer to which question was clearly no. Selden's point was re-emphasized in the Commons on May 22 by Robert Mason, who was replying to the Lords' attempt to justify their saving clause. The Petition was not intended to encroach on royal authority, Mason said:

> By our Petition, we only desire our particular rights and liberties to be confirmed to us; and, therefore, it is not proper for us to mention therein 'sovereign power' in general, it being altogether impertinent to the matter of the Petition.[63]

Mason was also, however, quite explicit about what the possible effects of this irrelevance might be. He was not perturbed by the theory of the royal prerogative used by the Crown in itself, but rather by the fear that this might be given legal *form*. If the contended clause were added to the Petition, then the most favorable construction will be, that the king hath an ordinary prerogative, and by that he cannot impose taxes or imprison; that is, he cannot impose taxes at his will, or employ them as he pleaseth: but that he hath an extraordinary and transcendent 'sovereign power', for the protection and happiness of his people; and for such purpose he may impose taxes, or billet soldiers as he pleaseth.[64]

The clause saving the royal prerogative was irrelevant to the matter of the Petition of Right. Further, the effect of adding the clause would be to negate the purpose of clarifying the law; it would give legal sanction and form to the absolute prerogative, thus enabling it to act in spheres normally reserved to the legal prerogative and the common law. In short, what Mason feared, was the confusion of the two parts of the duplex theory of royal prerogative. To keep them apart required careful definition. These points were put to the Lords by Glanville on May 23.[65] On May 26 the Lords agreed to accept the Petition of Right without the saving clause. Prominent in the debates leading to this decision was the Commons' argument that the prerogative was irrelevant to the matter of the Petition. As Clare was reported to have said (May 24), 'this peticion dwells only in the Region of the lawe, our birth right . . . . Neither cann this Peticion, nor any thinge ells we shall doe, hurte that prerogative'.[66] Clarifying the law *could* not impinge upon the royal prerogative, so the saving clause was quite irrelevant. The opposition to, and the defeat of this clause, came not necessarily because members did not accept that the king had an emergency prerogative, but because their major concern was with the law, and with fear for its integrity. The prerogative could look after itself, but the law needed to be clarified and defined if it was to remain of use. Its ambiguities had to be downplayed, and (above all) the last thing that could be afforded was to produce a *legal* document that seemed to give a *legal* role to the absolute prerogative. Perhaps, in other times, this would not have mattered so much, but Attorney General Heath's attempt to confuse absolute prerogative and law made the need for definition an urgent one. If definitional clarity was not forthcoming, then the common law ceased to be the sole (or at least hegemonic) language through which domestic political matters were to be discussed.

The Jacobean consensus, as we have seen, was a complex one. In some senses the king was above the law; in other senses the law was above the king. It all depended on what was being talked about, and who was being addressed. It is one of the more ominous features of the 1628 debates that they show this complexity giving way to simplicity and clarity. When definitions are needed trouble is at hand. On April 26 Sir Dudley Digges commented, 'So now there is a doubt whether the law be above the King, or the King above the law'.[67] It was precisely through the avoidance of such simple questions, and their simple answers, that consensus existed. Digges' question was a bad sign, perhaps, but on the whole it was an isolated one. The years from 1637 to 1641, however, saw something like a repetition of the events of 1626–28, and this time it was to prove more serious. Intervening events had made the crisis of the common law considerably more acute.

Before proceeding to an analysis of the years 1637 to 1641 a crucial question needs to be raised: what, in all of this, did Charles I think he was doing? Why was it that Charles behaved in such a way as to threaten the destruction of consensus? It is far from easy to give an answer to this, but if forced to provide a single-word response the best one might be 'impatience'. Charles was not, to say the least, a man overly possessed with political skills, and he seems to have found it difficult to believe that people could sincerely disagree with him on various matters. His conviction of his own rectitude made him impatient of the political process. Why couldn't people talk less and see that their king was right?[68] It was this character trait more than any political theory that made Charles look like an absolutist.[69] Indeed, recent historical work has probably over-emphasized the degree to which Charles's absolutism was of conviction rather than of temperament.[70] The political statements made by, or on behalf of Charles, were not in themselves particularly innovative in theoretical terms. There was nothing much new about theories of divine right or absolute prerogative. The problem with Charles was more that he was careless about the way in which he used these theories. He was, in brief, *impatient* of following legal forms and procedures. An analogy might be useful. The statements made by Charles and his agents were unproblematic theoretically, but nevertheless broke the ground rules of the Jacobean consensus. Their fault, we might say, lay not in *grammar* or *syntax*, but in *idiom*. Charles spoke the political languages of his day unidiomatically, and he did so largely because he was too unconcerned with detail ever to learn the rules of idiomatic usage. Now the problem with an unidiomatic speaker is not that he cannot be understood, but that he loses command over mood and nuance. Charles came across as an absolutist (whatever his intentions) because he insisted on ignoring the rules for the usage of languages of divine right and absolute prerogative. Unidiomatic speakers sound (and often are) foreign, strangers to the linguistic community in which they operate. Generally, one can tell what they are saying, but one can never be quite sure what overtones and implications they intend. Charles's statements sounded foreign to his subjects (so foreign that some came to accept the fiction that he was insane). He talked about divine right loosely, and *sounded* as if he was claiming arbitrary powers to take property and deprive subjects of their liberty. This was not a consequence of the theory he employed: his father had employed similar theories without ever sounding like Charles. It was a consequence of the unidiomatic use of those theories. The trouble, of course, is that it is impossible to be certain whether an unidiomatic speaker really *knows* what he is saying, at least in fine detail. And so we are left with Charles the Enigmatic. His mind will remain enigmatic because his words form, in part, a private language that only he could decipher fully.

A single example from 1628 might clarify some of this. On May 12 Charles sent a letter to the House of Lords. It can hardly have helped matters. The King sought to encourage the Lords to abandon the Petition of Right. Charles certainly indicated his willingness to preserve the liberties and rights of his subjects. But he also – whether he knew it or not – claimed a prerogative *jure divino* to override the law, even though he promised to use it only in moderation. He stated:

> That it is not in our heart, nor will we ever extend our royal power, lent unto us from God, beyond the just rule of moderation, in any thing which shall be contrary to our laws and customs; wherein the safety of our people shall be our only aim.[71]

Given his known implication in Heath's attempted felony,[72] and the general situation of 1628, it is hard to believe that Charles could have been so careless as to say this. It was hardly likely to satisfy his subjects to be told that the king promised to break the law only in moderation. Charles seems to have been unable to believe that his subjects might not trust his promise to break the law only in cases of necessity. Their lack of trust was, in his eyes, simple disobedience and disaffection, though in fact it was an understandable reluctance to allow the king by himself to define the requirements of necessity. Charles did not seem to

realize, as his father had, that in such matters as property rights
he ought to exercise his *legal* prerogative (however disingenuously).
Genuine necessity might create a situation in which kings' could
do otherwise without controversy, but a general statement of this
sort was quite unacceptable – because unidiomatic. It was Charles's
lack of any sense of when it was *appropriate* to use the languages of
absolute prerogative (and when it was not) that caused alarm in
his subjects. The *theory* of absolute prerogative was not the point
at issue.

These issues of prerogative and the claims of necessity were raised
again, even more pointedly, in the Shipmoney Case (Hampden's
Case) of 1637. The decision in this case, even more than that of a decade earlier, seemed to imply that the law was quite worthless as a
protection for the rights of the subject; and, like that earlier decision,
the Shipmoney judgement was very quickly questioned in Parliament. Two things made the discontent following the Shipmoney
verdicts more serious than the discontent that had followed the
verdict in the Five Knights' Case. By 1637 people had had a much
longer time to reach a verdict on their king, and the policies that he
had pursued in the intervening years (raising money by mercilessly
exploiting various antiquated legal rights that he possessed, and
above all the enforcement of Laudian church policy) did not win
Charles many friends. The issues raised by these policies were not
those of political theory. It was generally Charles's actions not his
theories (if we can exclude religion from this term) that were the
source of anxiety amongst his subjects. Furthermore, what gave the
opportunity for Charles's English subjects to express their dislike
of his religious and fiscal policies (as well as of the political theory
they saw underpinning the Shipmoney proceedings) was the crisis
occasioned by the Scottish revolt and the English defeat in the
Bishops' Wars. This, of course, was largely a product of Charles's
religious policy and its details are beyond our purview.[73]

Coming immediately before this general political crisis, the
Shipmoney case was not surprisingly seen in 1641 as the chief piece
of evidence for the claim that Charles's policies were frequently
illegal. The whole business of Shipmoney shows, once again, that
the matter was rather more complex than the men of '41 were usually
prepared to admit. It also shows again that the view of Charles as
a potentially arbitrary and absolute monarch arose in his subjects'
minds from the way in which his words seemed to threaten more
than he literally said. Most of Charles's subjects continued to think

and speak in terms of the rules of the Jacobean consensus – but Charles himself did not (wittingly or unwittingly). The problem then was that his utterances were interpreted *as if he was* following those linguistic rules, and consequently could only have looked like statements of an intention to govern arbitrarily.

Yet, although Charles's subjects still thought in the terms of the Jacobean consensus, by 1637 they clearly had some difficulty in doing so. Nowhere is this more apparent than in Oliver St John's argument for Hampden in the Shipmoney case. Once more, we have the Crown effectively attempting to translate an *extra*-legal claim into legal terms, and can see the claim calling forth a response that was itself highly problematic. St John was prepared to concede that the law gave to the king all power to command the defence of the realm, including leaving 'his majesty sole judge of dangers from foreigners, and when and how the same are to be prevented'.[74] He continued:

> the question will not be *de persona*, in whom the 'Suprema Potestas' of giving the authorities or powers to the Sheriff, which are mentioned in this writ [of Shipmoney], doth lie, for that is in the king: But the question is only *de modo*, by what medium or method this supreme power, which is in his majesty, doth infuse and let out itself into this particular.

The law entrusted the defence of the realm to the king; it also 'set down a method and known rules, which are necessarily to be observed'.[75] St John invoked the normal duplex understanding of royal authority: 'in his majesty there is a twofold power, *voluntas* or *potestas interna* or *naturalis*, and *externa* or *legalis*'. But he was forced, at this point, to argue in such a way as to discount completely the former of these powers. If the king acted through his 'internal will', rather than mediately through the law and other institutions, then he did not operate 'to the good and relief of the subject'.

> His majesty is the Fountain of Justice; and though all justice which is done within the realm flows from this fountain, yet it must run in certain and known channels.[76]

Thus, St John argued, usually the king would not sit in person in his own courts but was bound to act mediately, through the judges.

Similarly, in some matters (including the one that St John believed to be relevant here, taxation) it was not 'sufficient to do it without the assistance of his Great Council in parliament'.[77] Many things were done in the *name* of the king, but this should not mislead anyone into thinking that the king could do such things personally. In fact, 'without the assistance in parliament, his majesty cannot in many cases communicate either his justice or his power into his subjects'.[78]

So, St John recognized the duplexity of royal authority – only to confine one half of it to oblivion. But what else could he have done, in the circumstances? He could admit that the king had an absolute prerogative (though not in those terms), but no more than the Lords and Commons in 1628 could he afford to give legal form to that prerogative. Given that Shipmoney was, or could be seen to be, an attempt to shift a legal matter into the extra-legal sphere of absolute prerogative, given also that defence of the realm *was* traditionally the preserve of the prerogative (though taxation was not), and given that Charles insisted that the need for Shipmoney was one of urgency and necessity, St John had to develop a case that confined *all* acts of prerogative to legal forms. Throughout his reign Charles showed a tendency to exploit every loophole he could in traditional theories of prerogative. If he were allowed *any* prerogative outside of the law, it was felt that he would shift into its domain, as the whim took him, matters that should have been dealt with through the law. The Shipmoney example itself showed the Crown to be not at all particular about whether its claims of urgency and necessity had any plausibility. The only guard against this was to ensure that such claims could not be made, at least not in a court of law.

And there was the nub of the problem. Charles was not just claiming that the defence of the realm required ships so urgently that there was no time to call parliament to find them (and claiming it year after year!), he was now seeking a legal decision in favour of his power to do this.[79] Preceding events had made it clear what the crown's position was. In December 1635 Charles had secured a brief judicial statement which, though carefully worded, seemed to support the legality of Shipmoney. In February 1637 he sought a further judicial opinion which – in Gardiner's words – was 'not to enlighten himself but to hinder his subjects from arguing the disputed question'.[80] The judges eventually accepted the crown's position, answering in the affirmative the following questions put to them:

When the good and safety of the kingdom in general is concerned, and the whole kingdom is in danger; Whether may not the king, by Writ under the Great Seal of England, command all the subjects of this kingdom, at their charge, to provide and furnish such number of Ships, with men, victuals and munition, and for such time as he shall think fit, for the defence and safeguard of the kingdom from such danger and peril; and by law compel the doing thereof, in case of refusal or refractoriness? And whether, in such a case, is not the king sole judge, both of the danger, and when and how the same is to be prevented and avoided?[81]

This might have been quite uncontroversial had it not been the case that the 'sole judge' of 'danger and peril' was transparently using his power of judgement badly. A victory for the Crown in the Shipmoney case later in 1637 would mean that there were no legal barriers to a misuse of prerogative of this sort. Probably there could not have been such a barrier: the uncontroversial use of discretionary power relied on that use being appropriate to circumstances. It relied on the crown voluntarily using it in a sensible way. Charles's use was clearly inappropriate, but this was a failure in his abilities or judgement rather than an action straightforwardly illegal. Nevertheless, Charles's victory in November 1637 meant that it was made very apparent that the common law was *not* a barrier against this use of the absolute prerogative. It was not a guarantor of *meum* and *tuum*. Thus, the crisis of the common law was immeasurably deepened.

The judges in Hampden's Case gave judgement for the crown by the narrowest of majorities, seven to five. Deciding for the crown were Sir Francis Weston, Sir Edward Crawley, Sir Robert Berkeley, Sir George Vernon, Sir Thomas Trevor, Sir William Jones, and Sir John Finch (Lord Chief Justice of Common Pleas); deciding for Hampden were Sir George Croke, Sir Richard Hutton, Sir John Denham, Sir Humphrey Davenport (Chief Baron of the Exchequer) and Sir John Bramston (Chief Justice of King's Bench).[82] Examined in narrowly legal terms the judges, statements are less frightening, perhaps, than many took them to be. At the heart of the arguments of those who accepted the king's position was the view that Shipmoney was not a tax. It was a service owed to the king, in emergency, to enable him to carry out his duty to defend the realm; and, in consequence, the money taken on this pretext was not to be used for any purpose except the provision of a ship, or other related naval purposes. This comes through clearly in the tentative conclusion to Jones's verdict for the king:

> Mr. Hampden shall be charged with the 20s with this limitation and condition, that none of it comes to the king's purse, for if it do, my opinion is against it.[83]

This view, that Shipmoney was valid because it was *not* a tax,[84] is superficially reminiscent of the royal position on impositions. The judges were preserving the principle that subjects could not be taxed without their consent. Sir Robert Berkeley, for instance (often taken to be an extremist on the king's side, rather unfairly) was clear: it was not

> the question in this case, whether the king may at all times, and upon all occasions, impose charges upon his subjects in general, without common consent in parliament? If that were made the question, it is questionless, That he may not.[85]

But the similarity between this and the royal position on impositions should not be over-stressed. It is true that in both cases the legal argument in the case tended to preserve the principle of taxation by consent, but the differences are perhaps more important. First, the royal case for impositions did more than accept parliamentary taxation: it accepted also the inviolability of English property rights (by arguing that customs duties were imposed on foreign rather than English goods). Furthermore, royal spokesmen on the subject were careful to ensure that this point was always apparent. As Bacon said, the matter raised by impositions 'is not . . . touching any taxes within the land, but of payments at the ports' concerning goods from 'foreign ports'.[86] But Shipmoney, on the contrary, was an infringement of property rights: the whole case swung on the question of whether the king could infringe his subjects' (individual) property rights for the common (collective) good.[87] Crawley, indeed, made explicit the view that the king could in cases of necessity use his absolute prerogative, founded on the *jus gentium*, to override individual property rights:

> in these cases of necessity and danger, the king, *jure gentium*, may charge the subject, without his consent in parliament, by his regal

prerogative; for in the king there are two kinds of prerogatives, *regale et legale*, which concern his person, lands and goods.[88]

The idea that one's 'person, lands and goods' were under the sway of the king's *regal* power (i.e. of his absolute prerogative) was one that even James I would have found odd. Shipmoney may not have been a tax, but it still entailed a power, exercisable by the Crown, to override common-law property rights.

A second difference between the case of impositions and the case of Shipmoney lay in the surrounding political rhetoric and the circumstances in which it was employed.[89] Victory in a court case is likely to give credence to the views expressed by the victorious party, even when (as in this case) the judges do not entirely accept them. Those presenting the crown's case in Shipmoney (especially the Attorney-General, Sir John Banks) were nowhere near as circumspect as James's spokesmen on impositions. Banks recognized that the king had an ordinary and an absolute prerogative, and began his argument by attempting to demonstrate that the law *gave* the king his prerogative to act for the defence of the realm.[90] However, Banks also argued that the king's power to command his subjects to contribute to defence was 'innate in the person of an absolute king': 'All magistracy . . . is of nature, and obedience, and subjection'.[91] It was not altogether clear how Banks reconciled the argument that Shipmoney was grounded on the king's legal prerogative with the argument that it derived from a natural law right inherent in kings. He eventually came to tackle St John's claim that the king certainly *had* the power to demand the means to defend his kingdom, but that it must be used 'according to the institution of the laws of the realm', which was to say with parliamentary consent. At this point Banks appears to argue that the kings case rested on his absolute rather than his legal prerogative: 'for kings were before parliaments, and then surely they might have done it'. Originally kings ruled by 'natural equity', and this power remained inherent in them.[92] These positions came close to arguing that the king had an absolute prerogative, based on natural rather than positive law, which enabled him to override the common law (including property rights) for the common good – of which he was the sole judge. The victory for the crown in the case can only have increased the fear that the law was powerless before claims of this sort: the king had only to announce an emergency to be able to walk over the legal barriers before him. Some evidence for this can be found from

Kent, where Sir Roger Twysden reported that some thought that 'if the king's councell could make this good by law, the subject could not say he had property in ought'.[93] This was in February 1637: within a year or so Shipmoney had indeed been made 'good by law'. Twysden's report is also evidence that Shipmoney was perceived as a *tax*, whatever the legal pretexts, and as different in kind from previous ways of raising money. It involved 'nue [i.e. new] lawes', in contrast to 'that which tyme, use, and approbation' had sanctioned.[94] Archbishop Laud commented in May 1638 that, not only did the lukewarm verdict for the crown hinder the payment of Shipmoney, but it also

> puts thoughts into wise and moderate men's heads, which were better out; for they think if the Judges, which are behind, do not their parts both exceeding well and thoroughly, it may much distemper this extraordinary and great service.[95]

Laud also remarked that the 'faction' behind the Shipmoney trial, referring perhaps to Lord Saye and Sele and the Providence Island Company,[96] were much emboldened by the result.

But, of course, what really aroused disquiet about the whole matter of Shipmoney was that it was raised upon a pretext of necessity that was clearly false. Perceptions of this might well have been *heightened* by the judges' verdict. The verdict of Baron Weston, for example, actually tackled this matter directly, with a result that was possibly more unsettling than a studied silence on the matter would have been. Weston said, on the point that Charles should have called a parliament to deal with his financial needs:

> But you say he may call a parliament, and they will give him means wherewith to do it. It is true, this thing in question, if it had been done by parliament, it had been done by the happiest means; but because he might have it by parliament, must he therefore have it no other ways? The question now is, Whether what is done, may be done without a parliament or no? What is done, is done by the great seal, which is the next authority to a parliament. What if an enemy had come before the parliament had met, or before they had granted any aid, should the safety of the kingdom depend upon such contingencies? God forbid. Will you have forces on both sides, and restrain the king to his power

by parliament, which may be so dilatory, that the kingdom may be lost in the mean time?[97]

The remarks read almost like a calculated criticism of the Crown. They emphasized that the whole business would be better dealt with in parliament, and then tackled the theme of the 'dilatoriness' of the institution in a way that can only have made it apparent how inappropriate the argument was in the circumstances of 1637–8 (especially given that Shipmoney had become a regular, annual exaction, when no signs of an enemy at the door were apparent). But worse was to follow:

Next they object, That if this course be admitted, the king may pretend a danger when there is none; or a great danger, when it is but small: and so may raise a great sum of money, and the subject shall have but little benefit thereby . . . 1. If this power be in the king, and that power be just and equal, then it is not to be taken from him, because he may misemploy his power. If he misuse his power the fault is his. 2. This objection cannot be made unless you suppose injustice in the king: make what laws you will, if the king be unruly, he will break through them.[98]

This should remind us of a feature of the Shipmoney trial that ought never to be forgotten: the judges – on both sides – showed evident discomfort at being asked to handle the matter of Shipmoney. They did not appreciate being made to give legal shape to the king's absolute prerogative – particularly when it was being employed on specious grounds that they were bound to ignore – and, here, Weston makes the point plain. Blame the king for what is happening, not the law. But he made apparent also another point: the common law could be no barrier against an 'unruly' king [i.e. one who did not obey rules or laws]. What then of the widespread view that the English polity was a self-regulating balanced polity, with prerogatives and liberties equally enshrined by law?

The political thinking revealed in the Shipmoney case is not sharply dichotomous. It was not a clash of absolutists and constitutionalists. Rather, we are witnessing increasingly divergent interpretations of a commonly accepted framework. Charles and his agents were not introducing wildly new or innovative political theories. There was nothing in the political thought of Laudian divines, or of Attorney-General Banks, that was particularly unusual. Nor was there anything in these theories that was *inherently controversial*. But controversy did arise, and it arose from the fact that these theories, or languages, were being used unidiomatically by Caroline government. They were used not generally but in support of specific policies; absolute prerogative was used in such a way as to infringe *English* property rights. Above all, there was a patent dishonesty in Charles's actions. Emergency powers might be acceptable – but not when they were used to raise money when no emergency could be seen even on the distant horizon. Charles seems to have believed – not without cause – that his subjects ought to contribute the material to enable him to serve the common good, and was probably genuinely convinced that in consequence actions necessary to acquire that material were *ipso facto* legal. But he was careless in the way in which he went about defending this position. He infringed the rules of the Jacobean consensus, and so his view of his absolute prerogative (quite unremarkable in itself) sounded foreign and unEnglish in his subjects' ears.

Even more alarming to his subjects, however, was the implication of the events of the decade or so to 1638 for the common law. Weston had virtually said that the law was powerless against a king determined to take no notice of it. There was no legal barrier against a king who used his absolute prerogatives in unaccustomed ways. The result, clearly apparent in 1641, was the *crisis of the common law*. Charles's actions raised, above all else, fear and doubt about the adequacy of the law. For many it was the Shipmoney trial that brought the lesson home. It was not a clash in theories of government that was evident in 1641, but the almost universal fear that the king had a different interpretation of the relationship of law and prerogative from his subjects, and that the law was powerless to hold him to what (they believed) was the right interpretation. Was the law fatally ambiguous? Had too much trust been placed in it?

The root cause of all this was not sharp theoretical or ideological divergence, but simply the fact that the king was (many thought) cynically exploiting the tensions within a *common* framework. Even at this stage consensus, though decayed, had not disappeared. Yes, the king had an absolute prerogative – but could he use it in this way? Yes, the king had extra-legal powers, as well as legal ones – but could he use them to break the law itself? Yes, the common law preserved the subjects' property rights – but were they inviolable in *all* circumstances? By exploiting these ambiguities within the Jacobean consensus Charles puzzled and frightened his subjects.

In essence, he confused the languages of civil law/divine right and common law, and did so in ways that seemed to threaten the integrity of the latter. The consequence has never been expressed more clearly than by Clarendon:

> Imminent necessity, and public safety, were convincing persuasions; and it might not seem of apparent ill consequence to them [Charles's subjects], that upon an emergent occasion the regal power should fill up an hiatus, or supply an impotency in the law. But when they saw in a court of law, (that law that gave them title and possession of all that they had) apothegms of state urged as elements of law, judges as sharp-sighted as secretaries of state, and in the mysteries of state; judgement of law grounded upon matter of fact, of which there was neither inquiry or proof; and no reason given for the payment of the thirty shillings in question, but what concluded the estates of all the standers-by; they had no reason to hope that that doctrine, or the preachers of it, would be contained within any bounds.[99]

It mattered little when a John Cowell muddled common and civil law languages, especially when he was condemned by his king; it mattered perhaps a little more when Sibthorpe and Manwaring did much the same thing, in order to support a forced loan; but it certainly mattered when Manwaring continued to find royal favour, even after his errors had been pointed out, and when the crown itself used similar arguments in a court of common law. The problem was not Charles's absolutism, but his impatience with the forms of common law and the rules of consensus followed by his father. Very probably he never understood those rules, never understood that politics was a messy business requiring that you fit your actions to your words and your words to the expectations of your audience. Charles's view of his own position was not 'wrong' in seventeenth-century terms, it was just too simple and too unpolitical. For this he paid a very high price indeed.

8

Epilogue: The Crisis
of the Common Law

How might we summarize the changing patterns of political discourse in early Stuart England? Like most complex societies, England in the early-seventeenth century was characterized by complicated and subtle structures of discourse. It is only at our peril
that we attempt to read particular uses of the political languages
of the period without first uncovering the structures that helped to
give them meaning. Part II of this book has attempted to sketch a
model of these structures. Like all models it simplifies and abstracts
from reality. It also tends, by the very nature of being reduced to
writing, to convert unspoken, internalized conventions into written
rules, and to make the whole look too schematic. But the real test
of a model must be whether it goes with, or cuts against, the grain
of the reality it attempts to model. If it does the former then it will
prove enlightening, whatever its simplicities.

We began by examining the 'Jacobean consensus', which used
three languages to discuss a duplex theory of kingship. Each of those
languages could, and normally was, used quite uncontentiously.
Divine right theory was quite happily used to stress the absolute
duty of subjection. There was nothing controversial about this, nor
was it seen as contradicting the idea that kings must do at least
some things legally, provided (a) that the language was used
non-specifically, without reference to particular questions of law;
and (b) that it was used to an appropriate audience. Similarly, civil
law language (including reason of state) could be used to discuss the
kings powers *outside* of England and of the common law (for example in Ireland or over international commerce), without arousing
controversy. The third language, that of the common law, possessed
hegemonic status. It defined the appropriate sphere within which
other languages operated. Above all, it was the primary (not quite

the sole) language used for the discussion and resolution of *domestic* political conflict. There was, in short, no conflict between the divine right of kings and the common law, or theories of government by consent: they were used to address different problems in different contexts.

After 1625 this model began to dissolve (though we should not overemphasize either the speed or extent of this dissolution). It dissolved under the impact of a king who did not govern his utterances by the unspoken conventions that have just been summarized. We need to be specific about what was entailed in this. It was not the case that Charles's government resorted to innovative divine right theories: with rare exceptions political sermons and writings of Caroline England contained nothing that was new or controversial. There is nothing unusual in the political thought of the Arminian clergy, and much of the linkage made between them and 'absolutism' may have been a myth generated by their enemies. Nor was there, in Caroline England, a straightforward clash between rival theories of government. The area of conflict had little to do with philosophical theories about the origins of government, and the conflict took place between people who agreed (by and large) on two things: (a) that the king possessed an emergency prerogative of some sort; and (b) that the law protected the property rights of the subject. The actions that undermined confidence in Charles's government related to the relationship between these two propositions. Central to this was the unidiomatic deployment of the conventions of political discourse made by Charles and his spokesmen. It was not that Charles's theory of his absolute prerogative was new or innovative. But it was the case that he utilized that theory in inappropriate circumstances. It would never have been challenged had not Charles used it in ways that suggested to his subjects a cynical attempt to deprive the subject of his or her liberty and property. Emergency powers should only be used in emergencies if they are to remain unquestioned. Unlike his father, Charles made only the most unconvincing claims to be ruling by the law. They were unconvincing – in seventeenth-century terms – because Charles muddled the language of absolute prerogative with that of the common law. He raised, implicitly, the question of how far his prerogative could *override* the law – which meant also the question of how far the law was an adequate barrier to misgovernment. The answer suggested by the events of 1637–38 was not very far at all.

It was the raising of this latter issue that marks off Caroline politics (before the Civil War) from Jacobean. The real issue was not the prerogative, or 'absolutism', but the adequacy of the law. Certainly, there were continuities over the whole period 1603 to 1641, above all in the fact that Charles's subjects rather more than himself continued to attempt to think in 'Jacobean' terms until forced out of the habit by their king. Margaret Judson has commented on the continuity of 'royalist' argument across the three legal cases of the period most involving constitutional issues (Bate's case, the Five Knights' case, and Hampden's case),[1] and there are undeniably continuities to be found. But there is a crucial discontinuity also: the arguments used by the Crown in Charles's reign were much less careful to preserve English property rights, and much less careful to argue that the role of absolute prerogative was outside and not above the law. This discontinuity is most evident, not in royalist argument, but in the reaction to such argument of 'the common law mind'. Conrad Russell, with reference to the Commons debates of 1628, puts the matter well. In order to gain some weapon against royal policies arising from the forced loan, Coke was forced to adopt a harder attitude than previously to the relationship of law and prerogative. His arguments amounted to the 'rejection of legal *adiaphora*' and resulted in the claim 'that the common law could control, or . . . admeasure . . . prerogative'. As Russell remarks, this 'was very different from the claim made in 1610 that the common law laid down the limits within which the prerogative could operate'.[2] In 1628 the members – above all the common lawyers, usually most active – of the Commons argued that no 'saving' could be given to prerogative in the Petition of Right without giving away all that was being sought. The line between the lawful and the unlawful needed to be clearly drawn so that unlawful acts of prerogative could be seen clearly for what they were. St John's argument in the Shipmoney case was an extension of the same principle: the king had to accept that his prerogative was to be exercised through lawful channels. Calling an unlawful act an act of prerogative did not make it lawful. In both cases the firm unwillingness to recognize that prerogative could in some instances act against normal law was a reaction to the actions (more than the words) of the Crown. It was a position based on a fear for the sufficiency of the common law when faced with a king who seemed too impatient to follow customary forms.

This fear, the crisis of the common law, was central to political debate in 1640–41. It was a fear common to both those who would become Royalists and those who would become Parliamentarians. (We have already come across one expression of it from a Royalist pen – Clarendon's.) When the Long Parliament, on 14 January 1641, voted formal thanks to those who had given 'great Service' in dealing with Shipmoney and Lord Keeper Finch (the first scapegoat for the legal abuses of Charles's reign), it named St John, Bulstrode Whitelocke, Viscount Falkland and Sir Edward Hyde: two Parliamentarians and two Royalists.[3] The articles of impeachment against the common law judges, all of whom were charged with upholding Shipmoney (those who found against the Crown in Hampden's case were charged with subscribing to the extra-judicial opinion in favour of the levy in 1635), were presented to the Lords on 6 July 1641.[4] Those presenting the charges were Edmund Waller, Edward Hyde, John Crewe and William Pierrepont, a nice mixture of Royalists and Parliamentarians.[5] This very unanimity on legal issues meant, of course, that these were not the issues over which the Civil War came to be fought. The significance of the crisis of the common law was not as a cause of the English Civil War, except perhaps indirectly.

During its brief existence the Short Parliament began the parliamentary reaction to the Shipmoney verdicts (so similar to the 1628 reaction to the *habeas corpus* verdicts). Shipmoney was much discussed, particularly on 30 April, and in the debate on supply on May 4. This was initiated by a message from the king indicating his willingness to abandon Shipmoney in return for twelve subsidies, which – as a number of speakers pointed out – was scarcely much of a bargain if Shipmoney was illegal in the first place.[6] Sir John Culpepper (another future Royalist) summed up the essence of the concerns on May 4: 'that the Legallity & not the present pressure is that which troubles us'.[7] It was the implication of the judges' decision that Shipmoney was legal, or at least not contrary to law, rather than the exaction itself that was troubling. As Charles Jones put it (May 2): 'this was a Lawe created not declared'.[8] The central difficulty with the judgements was that they failed to define the law with the clarity necessary for it to do its job. Sir John Glanville, consequently, stated bluntly: 'Let us have noe dispute about it, but declaire it illegal absolute, Tis better live under a knowne lawe than an uncertaine'. The consequence of not defining clearly would be that 'the declaration wee shall make will take a way all'.[9]

Jones diagnosed the root of the problem as the fact that 'a generation of men . . . have rayzed a doctrine that the Common lawe wants reazon: parlament too strong, to Hygh, too populous'.[10] It was in reaction to this perceived threat to the common law (which was in reality a practical rather than a directly theoretical challenge) that common lawyers developed the sorts of extremist positions that Russell found in 1628. The clearest example of this in the Short Parliament was probably Oliver St John's statement 'that all taxes and levies made by [th]e King, alledging case of necessity to be voide, unles such necessity be allowed of in parliament'. It was a claim for the highest common law court, Parliament, to supervise the use of the discretionary prerogative.[11]

The most forceful statements of the worries engendered by Shipmoney came, however, from a much less well known figure, George Peard. As early as April 23 he made a controversial speech on the subject. When it came to the granting of supply, he remarked that 'slaves . . . did but restore; but free men give'. The question raised by Shipmoney was, in fact, whether Englishmen had any property to give, or were but slaves. 'Shippmoney hee said invaded the propertye of o[u]r goods and that it was necessarye to settle the poynte whether he had any thinge to give or not'. If it was allowed to become a firm precedent Shipmoney would be a burden to future generations. So 'hee held it therefore necessary first to determine the propertye of goods and soe take away [tha]t abominacion of Ship money'.[12] In a later speech (April 30), Peard homed in on the central concern, in a tone of breathless paranoia if Aston's report is any judge: 'If Kings ordayned to protect our goods they cannot despose. Common lawe appoynts a Certainty . . . . Common lawe cleare'. He commented, also, 'the Common lawe not for time but for perpetuity'. If the law was not clear, certain and defined, then there was no security of property. The consequences of this Peard outlined in a rousing climax:

> . . . if wee have noe property, noe man will marry that cannot leave his estate, noe man industrious if not sure to enjoy his labours, noe man sowe he may reape, but not sure to sowe. Noe may provid for a daughter, nor bring up a sonne at university, but must pay shipmoney. Noe man eate but in danger to have his meate taken away or to be taken away from his meate.[13]

Peard's adamant statement of the certainty of the law looks rather like whistling in the dark. It reflected a fear that the opposite was really the case. The same fear continued to be expressed strongly during the first year of the Long Parliament, with the redoubtable George Peard now prepared to pursue the Judges who had found for the Crown to their sick beds.[14] The major expression of discontent with Shipmoney and related matters in the Long Parliament was probably the impeachment, first of Lord Keeper Finch, then of a high proportion of the common law judges.[15] The attack on these men was a way, albeit an extreme way, of ensuring that the view of the nature of legal government prevalent in the Commons became the accepted one amongst the judiciary and officers of state as well. Finch was accused of

> having traitorously and wickedly endeavoured to subvert the fundamental laws and established government of the realm of England, and instead thereof, to introduce an arbitrary tyrannical government against law.[16]

Prominent in the particular articles charged against Finch were his activities in supporting the legality of Shipmoney. Indeed he seems to have been seen as the prime-mover amongst the judges in this matter. In Falkland's words (as reported by D'Ewes), since 'hee had been the Sollicitor and persuader to this business of shippmonie . . . hee should have the honour to bee the first in the punishment'.[17]

But Finch was to escape this punishment. On about 22 December 1640 he fled to the Hague, and his impeachment took place in his absence. On the same day as Finch's flight the first sign of the impending attack on the common law judges was seen.[18] The judges were pursued at a leisurely pace, with the articles against them not being transmitted to the Lords until 6 July 1641.[19] Things moved even more slowly thereafter.[20] In the articles Sir Robert Berkeley was accused, in words identical to those used of Finch, of subverting fundamental laws and established government. The most prominent charges in the particular articles against all six judges concerned their involvement with Shipmoney, whether in Hampden's case or the extra judicial opinions of 1635 and 1637.[21] Slightly more rapid progress was made on the statutory declaration of the illegality of Shipmoney (17 Car. I cap. 14) (to which the king assented on 7 August 1641) than on the impeachments. The primary purpose of this act was to annul the proceedings that had found Shipmoney legal. It 'declared and enacted' that the Shipmoney judgements (including the extra-judicial opinions) 'were and are contrary to and against the laws and statutes of this realm, the right of property, the liberty of the subjects, former resolutions in Parliament, and the Petition of Right'.[22] Thus the Lords and Commons were able to take advantage of Charles's considerable need for money in mid-1641 to gain his assent to a legal measure that ought, once and for all, to ensure that the law was clearly defined in this regard.

Impeachment and statute were the means of asserting a particular definition of the law. Of rather more interest to us are the arguments used to demonstrate the need for the employment of those means. A number of speeches relating to the impeachments of Finch and the judges were printed,[23] and they together present strongly the crisis of the common law. Falkland, speaking on 7 December 1640, argued that the judges ought to be punished for making uncertain what ought to be certain:

> the constitution of this Common-wealth, hath stablisht, or rather endeavoured to establish to us, the security of our goods, and the security of those Lawes, which should secure us, and our goods, by appointing for us *Judges*, so setled, so sworne, that there can be no oppression, but they of necessity must be accessary.[24]

Clearly, accessary was what the English judges were. They had acted in such a way as to remove that security that all thought they had. They had told the king that he could *legally* 'doe what he pleased'.[25] One did not have to accept William Prynne's view that the subject 'hath as absolute a property in his goods by the Common Law, as he hath in his Lands',[26] to find this threatening to customary ways of doing things. The central problem was one that Prynne discerned clearly enough:

> there is a vast and infinite difference in one and the self-same act, in times of Warre, and of Peace; that the same Act may be lawfull in times of Hostilitie, and yet utterly unlawfull in dayes of Peace.

All of the valid precedents for Shipmoney 'being onely in times of Warre, is no argument of the lawfulnesse of this Tax of Ship-money, nor yet of pressing Ships'.[27] It was not so much the use of an emergency prerogative that caused worry, but much more the pretence that it was being used in a wartime emergency – and the fact that the behaviour of the judges seemed to make the law blind to that pretence.

On 14 January 1641 the Commons presented the articles of impeachment against Lord Keeper Finch to the Lords at a Conference. Speaking on that occasion, Oliver St John argued that the decisions on Shipmoney meant that 'there is a surrender made of all our legall defence of property'; this in turn meant 'that the fundamentall laws of the Realme concerning our property, and our persons are shaken'.[28] It is interesting that in his full analysis of this shaking St John reminded the Lords of their attempt to add a clause 'saving' the royal prerogative to the Petition of Right. He reminded them, too, of why the Commons rejected this clause. The proposition about sovereign power was, he suggested, true in itself, but if added to the Petition would have made it *'Felo de se,* and wholly destructive to it selfe'. It would have done what could not be afforded: give legal form to the absolute prerogative. The consequence would have been that, though the Petition of Right said the king could not tax without consent, the addition would mean:

> It is true, it cannot be done by the Kings ordinary power, but it may be done by that Soveraign power wherewith the Law hath intrusted his *Majestie* for the protection, safety, and happinesse of the people.[29]

The Shipmoney verdicts did the same thing: they undermined the security and certainty that the law ought to have provided by allowing the king to override it upon any pretext of acting for the public good. They fatally confused common law language with the languages of absolute prerogative. The laws which were supposed to guarantee the property of the subject were being used for 'a contrary end to that, for which they were ordained': they were becoming an 'instrument of taking from us, all that we have'.[30]

The sense of confusion, of the destruction of old certainties, the sense almost of bewilderment, comes through many of the speeches of 1641. Falkland, also speaking in the Conference of 14 January, talked of the way in which 'the Meeres and bounders between the liberties of the Subject and Soveraigne power' were being broken down. He spoke, too, of the way in which Finch 'turned our Guard into a destruction, making Law the ground of Illegality'. That is 'he used this Law not only against us, but against it selfe, making it as I may say, *Felo de se'*.[31] Similar sentiments were apparent in the speeches delivered in the Conference of 6 July, 1641, which presented the articles of impeachment against the six judges to the Lords. Edward Hyde spoke of the confusion to the law that resulted from the judges' sophistry, as well as the destruction of 'the sweet harmony betweene the Kings protection and the subjects obedience'.[32] Edmund Waller mentioned, in relation to arguments from necessity, 'the confusion which necessity produces', and warned that it was as harmful to the king as to his subjects. The king's 'Royall State' was, after all, defined by the law. The judges – in particular Crawley – 'declar'd the dissolution of the Law' and so 'changed our reall propriety into the shadow of a propriety'.[33] Denzil Holles told of how,

> the laws (which should be the bars of our gates, to protect and keep us, and all that is ours, in safety) [were] made weak and impotent, to betray us into the hands of violence; instead of props to support us, [they had] become broken reeds to deceive us.[34]

The illness was perhaps best diagnosed by William Pierrepont when he examined the view that Justice Berkeley had given 'his opinion . . . how the lawes . . . may be broken'. He remarked that 'a judge is not to determine what may be done by the king, or what may be done by the subject in a case of imminent danger, or in any other where the lawes set no rule'.[35] The problem lay in giving legal form to extra-legal powers – literally, in making *regular* that which should be irregular. The result, like adding the clause on sovereignty to the Petition of Right, was to make the law act against itself.

In this perception that the law was confused and uncertain lay the crisis of the common law. In order to regain certainty and definition, and thus enable the law to perform its proper function, men resorted to dramatic measures in 1640 and 1641. They took judicial action in parliament against those guilty of creating the confusion, and they did their best to banish confusion and reintroduce clarity by statute. None of this was a direct cause of the English Civil War. It was not fought over the issues we have examined here, and those most active in dealing with legal grievances in 1641 included both future Royalists and future Parliamentarians. The issues dividing these two groups were largely religious. There was no deep polarity in theories of government before the Civil War, and so it is not surprising that fundamental differences over constitutional theory were not instrumental in dividing Royalists from their opponents. Of course theoretical differences of a sort did develop over the 1640s as each side sought the rhetorical and argumentative tools that would best win them support, but the importance of even this can be exaggerated.

However, this does not mean that the crisis of the common law can tell us nothing of use about the 1640s. It can. It provides at least part of the explanation for the prevalence in the 1640s of a pattern of political discourse very different from that of the pre-Civil-War period. Charles's actions before 1640, and the unidiomatic use he made of the different modes of political discourse available to him, raised in his subjects' minds the question of the certainty and sufficiency of the law. In order to counter his claims – in 1628, in 1640–41 – they were forced themselves to adopt more rigid and starker definitions of the law. By 1642 they were showing signs of accepting that positive law, by itself, was not enough. Charles's actions, and the ensuing crisis of the common law, had in some cases successfully undermined confidence in the law. It was not enough to have the law known: one needed to have a king who would take notice of it. In developing this point thinkers began to explore modes of political thinking that were not related to the common law at all. In the process the hegemony of the common law as a political language was destroyed. This is why it makes some sense to think that the person most responsible for the development of the view that subjects could disobey their legal king in some circumstances was Charles I. It was he who did most to point out, or to reveal, the inadequacy of the traditional trust in the law and the security it provided. Charles's subjects eventually came to believe him when he said that necessity knew no law.[36]

In order to find some way of dealing with a king whom they could not trust to obey the law, some came to realize the need themselves to override law. On Tuesday, 8 February 1642, the Commons received a letter from John Hotham (son of Sir John) announcing that he had 700 men at Hull. The people of Hull did not want them billeted, and it was reported of Hotham that he commented: 'He hope the house will not stand upon nicety of the law nor lawyers but that they may be billeted'.[37] It was in 1642 that the question was posed: the impeachments of 1641, the legislation of 1641, had made clear what the law was, and had made clear which actions of the king were not in accord with the law, but was that clear definition a sufficient barrier to misgovernment? Or was it the case, as Weston had said in Hampden's case, that the law was insufficient to restrain an 'unruly' king? It is fair to say that in 1642 the Parliament continued to give a variety of answers to the question just posed. When in April and May they came to justify the refusal to surrender the town of Hull into the king's hands[38] they tried to argue both that it was legal to resist the king, and that necessity was not bound by legal precedent.

But it is the latter position that is interesting. At least some men, who as little as two years ago were condemning the king's resort to 'necessity' to override the law, were in 1642 prepared not to 'stand upon nicety of the law'. The king's pragmatic refusal to follow customary forms of action could only in the end be countered by a similar refusal on the part of his opponents. This was, indeed, the diagnosis made by Clarendon (if due allowance is made for his heavily biased language). The actions of the judges under Charles led to the undermining of 'the dignity, reverence, and estimation of the laws themselves'. He continued:

> And no question, as the exorbitancy of the house of commons this parliament hath proceeded principally from their contempt of the laws, and that contempt from the scandal of that judgment [in Hampden's case]; so the concurrence of the house of peers in that fury can be imputed to no one thing more, than to the irreverence and scorn the judges were justly in.

It was the judges (and implicitly the king) who *first* 'thought themselves excused for swerving from the rules and customs of their predecessors'. Clarendon's further diagnosis of this situation is also of considerable relevance to the theme of this book. He pointed out that the problem of Charles's reign was not prerogative government. In previous reigns 'the prerogative went highest, (as very often it hath been swoln above any pitch we have seen it at in our times)'. But – the crucial difference – in the past kings had been careful not to use the judges and the law as the agents of their acts of prerogative. High-handed use of the prerogative could be acceptable – provided that the law remains apart from it and subjects could trust that though the king 'might sometimes make sallies upon them by the prerogative, yet the law would keep the people from any invasion of it'.[39] Thus a case could be made for seeing the illegalities embarked upon by parliament in 1642 as a trick they had learnt from their enemies.

This case would be strengthened by an examination of the Declaration of the two Houses on their taking up of 'defensive Arms' to protect themselves from the king (2 August 1642). The Declaration pointed out the the events of the 1630s had meant that 'the laws were no defence nor protection of any man's right; all was subject to will and power'. The Declaration, however, went on to use the same justification for Parliamentary actions that the king had employed earlier:

> This necessity brought on this parliament; and the same necessity gave it, in the beginning, power to act with more vigour and resolution than former parliaments had done.[40]

What happened in 1642 – in this Declaration and in many other statements – was that Parliament claimed to be acting not for the law as such but for the ends for which the law existed, the liberty of the subject and true religion. In emergencies (i.e. in necessity) the two Houses had the authority to preserve those ends even by means that were, at least in the narrow sense, illegal. Sometimes they would talk of 'fundamental law' to indicate the existence of principles justifying attempts to act against the letter of the law in order to preserve its essence or final cause. Fundamental law seemed to entail doing whatever was in the interest of the subject's liberties or of the true faith. Thus the Parliament argued, with respect to the militia ordinance, that 'being agreeable *to the scope and purpose* of the law, [it] cannot, in reason, be adjudged contrary to it'.[41]

This amounted to an abandonment of the idea that the language of common law – the language of the ancient constitution – provided a sufficient means for the discussion of all domestic political questions. Nowhere is this more apparent than in the Remonstrance of both Houses concerning Sir John Hotham's refusal to surrender Hull to the king (26 May 1642). This document considered an obvious objection to the position Parliament was taking:

> And as for 'the duty and modesty of former times, from which we are said to have varied, and to want the warrant of any precedents therein, but what ourselves have made': if we made any precedents in this parliament, we have made them for posterity; upon the same or better grounds of reason and law than those were, upon which our predecessors first made any for us. And as some precedents ought not to be rules for us to follow, so

none can be limits to bound our proceedings, which may and must vary according to the different condition of times.[42]

This was a rejection of the common law mind, and a rejection of the power of custom. Inherited rules might no longer be sufficient for the governing of the present. This was, I have argued, a position into which the crown's opponents were forced by 1642 if they were to deal adequately with the situation before them. What Charles had created by the end of 1641 was the fear in his subjects' minds that the common law, or the ancient constitution, was powerless before a ruler who would not voluntarily respect it. It was this crisis of faith in the common law that produced a statement like that of 26 May 1642: the law we have inherited might *not* preserve our liberties, but we are justified in taking whatever other steps are necessary to do so.

In terms of political discourse, then, the consequence of the crisis of the common law was the destruction of the hegemony of common law language. With it came the destruction of the 'common law mind' as a *mentalité*. The opening chapter of Part II of this book raised the question of 'move versus *mentalité*': was the common-law mind just a language for making political 'moves', or was it a genuine *mentalité* which to some degree confined thought and shaped the discourse of all? The answer to this question that has been suggested here is that the common law as a mode of discourse began the seventeenth century as a *mentalité*. It ceased to be one for Charles I in the late 1620s, and this left his subjects in a difficult position: they operated with a common law *mentalité* that was unable to cope with the cynicism of those who used common-law language as merely a way of making moves in a political game. By 1642 many of Charles's opponents themselves treated the common law as a facilitator of moves. This is not to say that they abandoned it, but rather that it became one of a variety of rhetorical modes they might employ to make a particular political case. It has been said that Professor Pocock exaggerated the speed with which the common law mind gave way to political 'rationalism' in the 1640s ('the shift from a past centred idiom of political discourse to one of natural rights was depicted as too abrupt and clear cut'),[43] and there is undoubtedly some truth in the claim.[44] A better way of characterizing the change that occurred in the 1640s might be in terms of the collapse of a *hegemonic* common law language and its replacement not with any simple alternative but with a system of discourse that was fundamentally rhetorical and polemical in character. Appeals to the past as a legitimating device did not disappear from the thought of the 1640s – as we have seen they were found in the writings even of such groups as Levellers and Diggers – but they were no longer hegemonic. The common law provided but one of many rhetorical strategies. It was employed for polemical purposes when it could be, but usually with the admission that it was not the full story.

Thus the period 1625–42 in the history of English political discourse is marked by the transition between two systems of discourse. The first – the Jacobean consensus – was dominated by a hegemonic common law. The common law provided a *mentalité* within which men thought of liberty and property, though this did not exclude them thinking also of divine right and conquest in other areas. Under the pressure of Charles's attempt to use the law as a weapon for his own battles there developed a crisis of the common law. This breaking of confidence in the law also destroyed the hegemony of common law discourse and the 'common-law mind' as *mentalité*.

In the 1987 additions to *The Ancient Constitution and the Feudal Law* Pocock has himself delineated the beginnings of this process. He remarks with regard to the 1628 Commons debates that:

> What was happening was that common law (which had a history) was failing to bind prerogative (which had none); the common-law argument was failing because it had reached the limits of its own strength. It was not that one reading of history was being countered by another; a historical discourse had exhausted itself and was giving way to discourse of another kind.[45]

It needs to be emphasized that the force generating this process (which intensified in the early 1640s) was the *failure* of the common law. Those thinking within its structures, those for whom the common law was a *mentalité*, were unable to deal fully with the arguments put forward by Charles's government. This sense of failure was what destroyed the hegemonic status of common law discourse.

In consequence, appeal both to the past and to the common law became one of several types of political discourse available in the 1640s. No longer was (domestic) politics discussed almost entirely in such terms. Those who did use these appeals were seldom committed to them fully and used them as tools to persuade when they might be effective, but were equally content to abandon them when they were not. We have seen the remarkable parliamentary declaration of 26 May 1642. Many others made the same statement, that they would be bound by the past, by the ancient constitution, only so far as that was consistent with pursuing the right goals. Gerrard Winstanley might at times appeal to an ideal past, but he was careful not to be trapped into particular historical debates about whether his view of the past was correct. He made it very clear that anti-Normanism, of his variety at least, was more than just an attempt to restore an ideal Saxon constitution:

> The Reformation that England now is to endeavour, is not to remove the Norman Yoke only, and to bring us back to be governed by those laws that were before William the Conqueror came in, as if that were the rule or mark we aime at: No, that is not it; but the Reformation is according to the word of God, and that is the pure Law of righteousnesse before the fall, which made all things, unto which all things are to be restored: and he that endeavours not that is a Covenant-breaker.[46]

Arguments from the past here exist in close tension with abstract arguments about what is right, and in much of Winstanley's writing it is obvious that he used common law sources for purely polemical purposes. His point was: *even* your *corrupt* law allows us this right. In general, it was reason and equity not age that mattered in determining whether a law was good.[47] Winstanley could indeed be quite scathing about the ancient constitution: 'ancient Laws, that will serve any Master'. 'Burn your old Law-Books', he urged, ' . . . set up a Government upon your own Foundation: do not put new Wine into old Bottles; but as your Government must be new, so let the Laws be new'.[48] The past survived as a rhetorical strategy, but it was subservient to more abstract reasoning.

The same pattern characterizes the Levellers too.[49] They could make *polemical* use of the past, of the ancient constitution, and of common law; but in the last resort it was not the past itself that provided legitimacy but some abstract ideal.[50] Thus, they too were eloquent on the limits of ancient law, and of the past. In Richard Overton's words, addressed to the Commons:

yee were chosen to worke our deliverance, and to Estate us in naturall and just libertie agreeable to *Reason* and common *equitie*; for whatever our Fore-fathers were; or what ever they did or suffered, or were enforced to yeeld unto; we are the men of the present age, and ought to be absolutely free from all kinds of exorbitancies, molestations or *Arbitrary Power*.[51]

Men of the present age did not need the legitimation of the past, or its laws. 'The Lawes of this Nation are unworthy a Free-People, and deserve from first to last, to be . . . reduced to an agreement with common equity, and right reason'.[52] William Walwyn was making a similar point when he advised Lilburne not to base his argument upon Magna Carta and the common law but upon 'reason, sense, and the common Law of equitie and justice'.[53] People would be better making themselves a new charter than in arguing about old ones.[54] Of course, as Seaberg has pointed out, equity and reason were terms used by common lawyers as well, but (as we saw in Chapter 3) the Levellers used them rather differently. Lilburne, for example, defined the law of England as consisting of

the ancient constitutions, and modern acts of Parliament, made by the States of the Kingdome: but of these onely such as are agreeable to the word of God, and law of Nature, and sound Reason.[55]

It was clear that for Lilburne only a subset of existing laws passed this test, whereas for the common lawyer the whole body of existing law was rational because it was customary. Lilburne's view of reason resembled much more that of the civil lawyer Hayward than it did the views of common lawyers. Reason was external to the law and a judge of it. 'Reason is demonstrable of it self, and every man (less or more) is endued with it'; thus every man could be his own judge of the law.[56] Reason and equity were the guiding considerations for the Levellers, not antiquity or legality as defined by positive law alone. Thus Walwyn was able to argue that on some matters the principles of the ancient constitution were positively pernicious. For example, they justified episcopal church government, when in fact the church and religion could not be tied to particular human forms, ancient or new. Freedom of conscience was an inherent right overriding even the ancient constitution.[57]

The clearest indication of the gap between Levellers and common

lawyers is to be found in the record of Lilburne's trial (on a charge of
high treason) in 1649. One of his judges, Philip Jermin gave, early in
the trial, a definition of English law that might be termed the 'classic'
common lawyer's view:

> you must know that the law of England is the law of God; and
> if there be anything in the law of England, but what was by
> admirable constitution and reason, we would not meddle with
> it. But I pray know this, that the law of England is no written
> law: It is the law that hath been maintained by our ancestors, by
> the tried rules of reason, and the prime laws of nature; for it does
> not depend upon statutes, or written and declared words or lines.
> And this is our laws, that have been maintained by our ancestors,
> and is subordinate to the law and will of God: Therefore I say
> again, the law of England is pure primitive reason, uncorrupted
> and unpolluted by human humours, or human corruptions, wits,
> or wills: That is the law of England.[58]

This statement would appear to mean no more than that the existing
body of law should be taken to have the sanction of God. A little
later in the trial Lilburne tried to exploit the point:

> upon your own grant, which is, That the laws of God are the laws
> of England, I desire to have the privilege of the law of God, which
> you yourself said is the law of England; and I am sure the law of
> God is, That you should 'do as you would be done to'.

Lilburne, however, was not saying the same thing as Jermin had
said. Between the statements that the law of England was the law
of God, and that the law of God was the law of England there was
a world of difference. Lilburne was arguing that whatever the law
might actually prescribe, one should follow the principles laid down
in the gospel. One judge replied to Lilburne that the laws of God,
of reason, and of England 'are all joined in the laws that you shall
be tried by'; and Jermin himself asked rhetorically whether these
three laws might not 'be consonant to each other'.[59] And that was
the essential point distinguishing Levellers and common lawyers:
for the latter common law was, almost by definition, consonant
with reason, nature and God's law; for the Levellers there always
remained alive the possibility of severing these things, and judging
common law to be wanting upon abstract grounds. Which is to say

that for the Levellers the language of common law was at best only one polemical weapon available to them – a set of moves rather than a *mentalité*. They might use it where they could; but when it suited them they were equally prepared to demonstrate its inadequacies. In this the Levellers were typical of the 1640s. This was an age of polemical rhetoric brought about, in part at least, by the crisis of the common law which occurred in the early years of the decade. In the last resort most would come to agree with John Milton, "Tis not the common law nor the civil, but piety and justness that are our foundresses'.[60]

Milton wrote this in 1641, and it is to those years, 1641–42, that one must turn in order to explain the development of a new structure of political discourse in the 1640s. As with many other things, the Levellers may have learnt the idea that law could be judged by abstract reasoning that was external to it from their Parliamentarian betters.[61] There was a clear transition in Parliamentarian propaganda, visible for example in the writings of Henry Parker, over the years 1640–42 which goes a long way towards defining the structure of discourse for the rest of the 1640s.[62] In 1640 Parker attacked Shipmoney on grounds now familiar to us: it meant that 'such a prerogative hath been maintained as destroyes all other Law . . . if wee grant Ship-money upon these grounds, with Ship-money wee grant all besides'.[63] Naturally, given this, Parker wanted to argue that Shipmoney was simply illegal. In deciding whether it lay within the king's prerogative powers 'it is more just that wee appeale to written lawes', for prerogative must 'be deduced out of the written and knowne Lawes of the Kingdome'.[64] This in itself is evidence of the 'hardening' of attitudes that had occurred in the king's opponents since the late 1620s. There was now no allowance made for an extra-legal prerogative. But Parker went further than this and initiated the Parliamentarian habit of turning the king's arguments from necessity to their own purposes and defence:

> the supreame of all humane lawes is *salus populi*. To this law all lawes almost stoope, God dispences with many of his lawes, rather than salus populi shall bee endangered, and that iron law which wee call necessity it selfe, is but subservient to this law.[65]

On this basis Parker was able to argue that in necessity the *people's* welfare rather than the king's ought to be followed, even against law. This argument figured prominently in his most famous work, *Observations upon Some of His Majesties Late Answers and Expresses,* where he developed the argument that parliament and not the king was best fitted to serve the people's interests. There he was able to argue that to secure the common good the king was bound to consent to necessary measures proposed by his parliament, and if he did not then they could take extraordinary measures on their own initiative.[66] Necessity might require that one abandon the ancient constitution and act against the monarch – at least for the time being. This was a move away from 'ancient ways'. To counter the king's arguments required the development of similar ones on one's own behalf. Parker's position became standard fare in 1642 and beyond. As he said in 1643, laws 'themselves do require to be regulated by further Lawes'.[67] The statement was the polar opposite of the view held by the 'common law mind'. Laws were to be deemed good or bad not on the basis of their survival into the present, but on a judgement as to whether or not they served the right purposes. There might still be propaganda value in claiming to be respecting the ancient constitution, but if the law did not do what you wanted there were now arguments for setting it aside. In necessity, law might be superseded.[68]

This was an argument central to the 1640s. It was an argument that Charles taught his subjects – taught them not so much directly as by destroying their belief in the sufficiency of the common law and its concepts. By 1642 'legal' meant for many not 'warranted by the common law' but 'justifiable by some guiding principle that overrode particular laws in the interests of public welfare'. This was what John Marsh meant when he demonstrated the 'legality' of the militia ordinance.[69] Having begun by arguing that nothing could be done, except through the forms of the common law, the opposition to Charles ended by arguing that virtually anything could be justified as legal. As with so much else, Charles I had only himself to blame for this. In a real sense it was he who taught his subjects how they might justify putting him to death.

In the process he destroyed the common law mind, at least in its guise as a *mentalité*. The classic age of common-law political thought, of ancient constitutionalism, was thus remarkably short. It took shape in the Elizabethan period, went through its 'classic phase' in James's reign, and was gradually battered to death by his son. (The irony of this was that in the 1640s Charles himself, and his supporters – above all David Jenkins – were able to pose as friends of the ancient constitution and critics of parliamentary illegalities: an almost exact reversal of 1628 and of 1640).[70] It is sometimes said that in 1660 the ancient constitution was restored, along with Charles II. There is of course much truth in the remark, but the discourse of Restoration politics was, if only subtly, different from that of the pre-Civil-War period. Above all, there was no restoration of the common-law mind as a hegemonic *mentalité*. The past remained an important device of political legitimation, and there were some who did continue the traditions of the common-law thinkers of the early-seventeenth century (especially Sir Matthew Hale).[71] But Restoration political discourse was notably *broader* than that of the 1610s and 1620s, and it was now impossible to isolate the language of the common law from, and elevate it over, other political languages as had been done before. Its position was constantly under challenge from other modes of conceptualizing the political world. In particular the idea of an ancient constitution now became muddled with a legacy from the Civil War period, the idea of an original contract (this is particularly clear in the debates surrounding the Glorious Revolution).[72] In addition various other sets of ideas became entwined with those of the common law, Harringtonian civic humanism in the case of Henry Neville, a whole variety with Algernon Sidney.[73] After 1660 arguments from 'reason' and from 'history' were combined differently than they had been in the classic age of the common law mind. Then, history subsumed reason; in the Restoration period reason had its own independent sphere; though it was frequently recombined with history through the idea of original contract.[74] But the very idea was the direct opposite of immemoriality. The politics of the ancient constitution were, at the very least, fundamentally transformed by the crisis of the common law.

Notes

CHAPTER 1: ANCIENT CONSTITUTIONS – POLITICS AND THE PAST

1. J. G. A. Pocock, *The Machiavellian Movement: Florentine Political Thought and the Atlantic Republican Tradition* (Princeton, 1975), chpt. X.
2. The seminal work is J. G. A. Pocock, *The Ancient Constitution and the Feudal Law: A Study of English Historical Thought in the Seventeenth Century* (Cambridge, 1957; reissued with additional material 1987). See the use made of it in David Wootton's introduction to Wootton (ed.), *Divine Right and Democracy: An Anthology of Political Writings in Stuart England* (Harmondsworth, 1986), pp. 22–38; and Austin Woolrych, 'Political Theory and Political Practice', in C. A. Patrides & R. B. Waddington (eds), *The Age of Milton: Backgrounds to Seventeenth-Century Literature* (Manchester, 1980), pp. 34–42.
3. The phrase is Pocock's: *Ancient Constitution*, chpts II & III.
4. Ibid., p. 261. The following pages are based on chpts II & III of this work.
5. The description of English common law as 'custom' (or rather as akin to custom) probably arose from the difficulty of describing its principles in the categories of Roman law. It was not quite *lex* (because unwritten) and not quite *consuetudines* (because general rather than local). Hence Bracton's explanation of why it was still appropriate to call English common law a true type of law, even though unwritten: Ewart Lewis, *Medieval Political Ideas* (London, 2 vols, 1954), vol. I, pp. 39–40. See also F. Pollock & F. W. Maitland, *The History of English Law* (Cambridge, 2nd ed., 2 vols, 1911), pp. 174–78. An important new examination of the concept of custom has come to my attention since this chapter was substantially completed: Donald R. Kelley, '"Second Nature": The Idea of Custom in European Law, Society, and Culture', in Anthony Grafton & Ann Blair (eds), *The Transmission of Culture in Early Modern Europe* (Philadelphia, 1990), chpt. 4.
6. James I, 'The King's Proposals for an Union' in *The Parliamentary History of England from the Earliest Period to the Year 1803*, vol. I (1066–1625) (London, 1806), col. 1020: 'the fundamental laws, priviledges, and good customs of this kingdom, whereby only the king's princely authority is conserved, and the people's (both in general and particular) security of their lands, living, and priviledges, is maintained unto them.' Compare also James's comment, delivered to Parliament *via* Salisbury in 1610: 'the marriage between law and prerogative is inseparable and like twins they must joy and mourn together, live and die together, the separation of the one is the ruin of

the other' – Elizabeth R. Foster (ed.), *Proceedings in Parliament 1610*, (New Haven, 2 vols, 1966), vol. II, p. 50.
7. Bacon in Calvin's Case (1608): *State Trials*, vol. II, col. 580.
8. Coke in Calvin's case: ibid., col. 614. On Coke's theory of allegiance expressed in 1608 see David Martin Jones, 'Sir Edward Coke and the Interpretation of Lawful Allegiance in Seventeenth-Century England', *History of Political Thought*, vol. VII (1986), pp. 321–40.
9. Hedley in Foster (ed.), *Proceedings in Parliament 1610*, II, p. 191.
10. Popham in *State Trials*, II, col. 569.
11. Sir John Fortescue, *De Laudibus Legum Anglie* (ed. & trans. S. B. Chrimes) (Cambridge, 1949), chpt. XVII, p. 39.
12. Pocock has raised this matter in terms of what he calls the 'paradox' inherent on the concept of custom – Pocock, *Ancient Constitution*, p. 36.
13. The clearest indication of Selden's revision of Fortescue is a long passage about how successive conquerors of Britain, such as Saxons, Danes and Normans 'made a mixture' of the laws and customs they found in their newly-acquired lands with those they brought with them. Conquests 'bring always some alteration'. Selden then coolly concluded: 'By this well considered, That of the laws of this realm being never changed will be better understood' (John Selden, 'Notes on Fortescue', in Sir John Fortescue, *De Laudibus Legum Angliae* (trans. Robert Mulcaster) (London, 1616; reprinted 1672), pp. 6–8).
14. John Selden, 'Notes on Fortescue', pp. 17–18.
15. A. P. D'Entrèves, *The Medieval Contribution to Political Thought*, (Oxford, 1939), pp. 93–4.
16. Christopher St German, *St German's Doctor and Student* (ed. T. F. T. Plucknett & J.L. Barton) (London: Selden Society, 1974), First Dialogue, chpts v, vii–ix, esp. p. 69.
17. David Hume, *A Treatise of Human Nature* (1739–40), III, 1, 1; and Immanuel Kant. *Groundwork of the Metaphysic of Morals* (1785) Preface.
18. See George H. Nadel, 'Philosophy of History before Historicism', *History and Theory*, vol. 3 (1964), pp. 291–315.
19. The best introduction to historicism and its early history is Georg G. Iggers, *The German Conception of History* (Middletown CT, 1968, rev. 1983). For an excellent account of the effect of German 'historicism' on the assumptions of professional history see Peter Novick, *That Noble Dream: The 'Objectivity Question' and the American Historical Profession* (Cambridge, 1988).
20. The best source of information on early Stuart historical scholarship and writing is now D. R. Woolf, *The Idea of History in Early Stuart England: Erudition, Ideology, and 'The Light of Truth' from the Accession of James I to the Civil War* (Toronto, 1990). Unfortunately, it appeared too late to be used in the writing of this chapter.
21. Hugh G. Dick, 'Thomas Blundeville's *The true order and Methode of wryting and reading Hystories* (1574)', *Huntington Library Quarterly*, vol. 3 (1940), p. 161. (Blundeville actually took most of his material from standard Italian sources).

22. Ibid., p. 165.
23. An introductory comparison of the two disciplines can be found in Eric Cochrane, *Historians and Historiography in the Italian Renaissance*, (Chicago, 1981), chpt. 15. N.B. also Cochrane's demonstration that both historians and antiquarians aimed at discovering the 'truth', notwithstanding their commitment to the usefulness of knowledge of the past (p. 432).
24. For a useful overview, Philip Styles, 'Politics and Historical Research in the Early Seventeenth Century', in Levi Fox (ed.), *English Historical Scholarship in the Sixteenth and Seventeenth Centuries* (Oxford, 1956), pp. 49–72. Also invaluable on the political uses of antiquarian scholarship is Kevin Sharpe, *Sir Robert Cotton 1586–1631: History and Politics in Early Modern England* (Oxford, 1979), Part I and chpt. VII. (Sharpe brings out well how the historical attitudes of the antiquarians shared the preconceptions that I have outlined.) For introductions to antiquarianism see Joseph M. Levine, *Humanism and History: Origins of Modern English Historiography* (Ithaca NY, 1987), chpt. 3.; Arthur B. Ferguson, *Clio Unbound: Perception of the Social and Cultural Past in Renaissance England* (Durham NC, 1979), chpt. IV; F. Smith Fussner, *The Historical Revolution: English Historical Writing and Thought 1580–1640* (London, 1962), chpt. 4; and the suggestive remarks of Arnaldo Momigliano, *Studies in Historiography* (New York, 1966), chpt. 1.
25. Ferguson, *Clio Unbound*, p. 117. On the evolutionary character of antiquarian thought see Sharpe, *Sir Robert Cotton*, pp. 224–6.
26. On this subject see Mary F. Tenney, 'Tacitus in the Politics of Early Stuart England', *Classical Journal*, vol. 37 (1941), pp. 151–63; Alan T. Bradford, 'Stuart Absolutism and the "Utility" of Tacitus', *Huntington Library Quarterly*, vol. 46 (1983), pp. 127–55; F. J. Levy, 'Hayward, Daniel, and the Beginnings of Politic History in England', *Huntington Library Quarterly*, vol. 50 (1987), pp. 1–34; and David Womersley, 'Sir Henry Savile's Translation of Tacitus and the Political Interpretation of Elizabethan Texts', *Review of English Studies*, vol. 42 (1991), pp. 313–42.
27. Pocock, *Ancient Constitution*, pp. 17–18. Further material on the themes discussed here is in J. G. A. Pocock, 'The Origins of Study of the Past: A Comparative Approach', *Comparative Studies in Society and History*, vol. 4 (1962), pp. 209–46; Pocock, 'England', in Orest Ranum (ed.), *National Consciousness, History, and Political Culture in Early-Modern Europe* (Baltimore, 1975), chpt 4; and Pocock, 'English Historical Thought in the Age of Harrington and Locke', *Topoi*, vol. 2 (1983), pp. 149–62.
28. Pocock, *Ancient Constitution*, pp. 28–9 & chpt. III.
29. Ibid., pp. 30–1.
30. Cf. Pocock: 'there were myths of constitutional antiquity in French thought, but they were formed in other ways [than those in English thought]', ibid., p. 28.
31. George Huppert, 'The Renaissance Background of Historicism', *History and Theory*, vol. 5 (1966), pp. 50–1 & passim. The uncovering of

the 'historicism' of Renaissance legal scholars owes most to Donald R. Kelley, *The Foundations of Modern Historical Scholarship: Language, Law and History in the French Renaissance* (New York, 1970); and Julian H. Franklin, *Jean Bodin and the Sixteenth-Century Revolution in the Methodology of Law and History* (New York, 1963). Kelley has also published a large number of articles on various aspects of the matter, amongst which are 'Civil Science in the Renaissance: Jurisprudence Italian Style', *Historical Journal*, vol 22 (1979), pp. 777–94; 'Civil Science in the Renaissance: Jurisprudence in the French Manner', *History of European Ideas*, vol. 2 (1981), pp. 261–76; and 'The Rise of Legal History in the Renaissance', *History and Theory*, vol. 9 (1970), pp. 174–94. A useful overview is Kelley, 'The Theory of History' in Charles B. Schmitt & Quentin Skinner (eds), *The Cambridge History of Renaissance Philosophy* (Cambridge, 1988), chpt. 21.

32. Pocock, *Ancient Constitution*, chpts II & III; Donald R. Kelley, 'History, English Law and the Renaissance', *Past and Present*, No. 65 (1974), pp. 24–51.

33. Criticisms of the insularity thesis include Christopher Brooks & Kevin Sharpe, 'Debate: History, English Law and the Renaissance', *Past and Present*, No. 72 (1976), pp. 133–42; Hans S. Pawlisch, 'Sir John Davies, the Ancient Constitution, and Civil Law', *Historical Journal*, vol. 23 (1980), pp. 689–702; Pawlisch, *Sir John Davies and the Conquest of Ireland: A Study in Legal Imperialism* (Cambridge, 1985); and Louis A. Knafla, 'The Influence of Continental Humanists and Jurists on English Common Law in the Renaissance', in R. J. Schoeck (ed.), *Acta Conventus Neo-Latini Bononensis: Proceedings of the Fourth International Congress of Neo-Latin Studies, Bologna 26 August to 1 September 1979*, pp. 60–71. The Pocock/Kelley perspective is, on the whole, supported by C. P. Rodgers, 'Humanism, History and the Common Law', *Journal of Legal History*, vol. 6 (1985), pp. 129–56; and, from a different perspective, by Rodgers, 'Legal Humanism and English Law – The Contribution of the English Civilians', *The Irish Jurist*, vol. 14 new series (1984), pp. 115–36. For comment on the criticisms see Pocock, *Ancient Constitution*, pp. 262–64, 258; Kelley, 'A Rejoinder', *Past and Present*, No. 72 (1976), pp. 143–46; and Paul Christianson, 'Political Thought in Early Stuart England', *Historical Journal*, vol. 30 (1987), pp. 960–67 (esp. 966).

34. Zachary Sayre Schiffman, 'Renaissance Historicism Reconsidered', *History and Theory*, vol. 24 (1985), pp. 170–82; Schiffman, 'An Anatomy of the Historical Revolution in Renaissance France', *Renaissance Quarterly*, vol. 42 (1989), pp. 507–33; and Schiffman, 'Estienne Pasquier and the Problem of Historical Relativism', *The Sixteenth Century Journal*, vol. 18 (1987), pp. 505–17.

35. Schiffman, 'Renaissance Historicism Reconsidered', pp. 171–2.

36. Schiffman, 'Anatomy of the Historical Revolution', p. 516.

37. Hugo Grotius, *A Treatise of the Antiquity of the Commonwealth of the Battavers* (London, 1649), epistle dedicatory.

38. It should be recognised that Pocock was not without a precursor in this: Herbert Butterfield, *The Englishman and his History* (Cambridge,

1944). Cf. Pocock, *Ancient Constitution*, pp. vii–ix, xi, xiv.

39. Quentin Skinner, *The Foundations of Modern Political Thought* (Cambridge, 2 vols, 1978), vol. II, p. 310. See also Ralph Giesey, 'When and Why Hotman wrote the *Francogallia'*, *Bibliotheque d'Humanisme et Renaissance*, vol. 29 (1967), pp. 581–611; the editors' introduction to François Hotman, *Francogallia* (ed. Ralph Giesey & J. H. M. Salmon), (Cambridge, 1972); and Nannerl O. Keohane, *Philosophy and the State in France: The Renaissance to the Enlightenment* (Princeton, 1980), pp. 49–53.

40. Hotman, *Francogallia*, p. 333.

41. Ibid., p. 459.

42. Arthur H. Williamson, *Scottish National Consciousness in the Age of James VI* (Edinburgh, 1979), pp. 107–16; H. R. Trevor-Roper, 'George Buchanan and the Ancient Scottish Constitution', *English Historical Review*, Supplement 3, 1966; I. D. MacFarlane, *Buchanan* (London, 1981), chpts 11 & 12; and Skinner *Foundations*, vol. 2, pp. 339ff.

43. See the English translation *De Jure Regni apud Scotos, or A Dialogue, concerning the due Priviledge of Government in the Kingdom of Scotland* (transl. 'Philalethes') (London, 1680).

44. Simon Schama, *The Embarrassment of Riches: An Interpretation of Dutch Culture in the Golden Age* (Berkeley, 1988), pp. 69–93; I. Schöffer, 'The Batavian Myth during the Sixteenth and Seventeenth Centures', in J. S. Bromley & E. H. Kossmann (eds), *Britain and the Netherlands V* (The Hague, 1975), chpt. 5.

45. See the English translation by Thomas Woods, *A Treatise of the Antiquity of the Commonwealth of the Battavers* (1649).

46. Ibid., pp. 145–9. For the context see W. S. M. Knight, *The Life and Works of Hugo Grotius* (London, 1925), pp. 121–5; also E. H. Kossmann, 'The Development of Dutch Political Theory in the Seventeenth Century' in J. S. Bromley & E. H. Kossmann (eds), *Britain and the Netherlands I* (London, 1960), p. 94.

47. Schöffer, 'Batavian Myth', p. 93.

48. I am dependent here on Martyn P. Thompson, 'The History of Fundamental Law in Political Thought from the French wars of Religion to the American Revolution', *American Historical Review*, vol. 91 (1986), pp. 1121ff. (esp. 1123). This article has been of general use in understanding the background to English ancient constitutionalism; see also Harro Höpfl & Martyn P. Thompson, 'The History of Contract as a Motif in Political Thought', *American Historical Review*, vol. 84 (1979), pp. 919– 44.

CHAPTER 2:   THE ANCIENT CONSTITUTION OF ENGLAND

1. This chapter draws heavily on Glenn Burgess, 'Custom, Reason and the Common Law: English Jurisprudence 1600–1650', Cambridge PhD thesis, 1988, chpts 2 & 3.

2. This question is raised by M. I. Finley, 'The Ancestral Constitution'

in his *The Use and Abuse of History* (London, 1975, pbk. ed. 1986), chpt. 2.

3.   J. G. A. Pocock, *The Ancient Constitution and the Feudal Law: A Study of English Historical Thought in the Seventeenth Century* (Cambridge, 1957, new ed. with retrospect, 1987). In Chapter I of the 'Retrospect' Pocock comments on this misreading of his initial text.

4.   A number of specialized studies of Coke are referred to below. In addition to these, good general introductions are Stephen D. White, *Sir Edward Coke and the Grievances of the Commonwealth* (Manchester, 1979), esp. chpt. 1; and Louis A. Knafla, 'Die Theorie des "Common Law"', in *Grundriss der Geschichte der Philosophie: Die Philosophie des 17. Jahrhunderts, Band 3 – England* (Basel, 1988), pp. 517–27, 590–3. Both of these have extensive references to other materials. A useful short interpretative essay is Samuel E. Thorne, *Sir Edward Coke 1552–1952* (London, 1957); but the standard biography remains Catherine Drinker Bowen, *The Lion and the Throne: The Life and Times of Sir Edward Coke 1552–1634* (London, 1957). On more particular aspects of Coke's thought, excluding works referred to later, there is useful material in R. A. Mackay, 'Coke – Parliamentary Sovereignty or the Supremacy of the Law?', *Michigan Law Review*, vol. 22 (1924), pp. 215–47; S. E. Thorne, 'Courts of Record and Sir Edward Coke', *University of Toronto Law Journal*, vol. 2 (1937), pp. 24–49; S. E. Thorne, 'Dr. Bonham's Case', *Law Quarterly Review*, vol. 54 (1938), pp. 543–52; T. F. T. Plucknett, 'Bonham's Case and Judicial Review', *Harvard Law Review*, vol. 40 (1926–27), pp. 30–70; Charles M. Gray, 'Bonham's Case Reviewed', *Proceedings of the American Philosophical Society*, vol. 116 (1972), pp. 35–58; T. F. T. Plucknett, 'The Genesis of Coke's Reports', *Cornell Law Quarterly*, vol. 17 (1942), pp. 190–213; and J. H. Baker, 'Coke's Note- Books and the Sources of his Reports', *Cambridge Law Journal*, vol. 30 (1972), pp. 59–86.

5.   Sir John Davies, *A Report of Cases . . .* (Dublin, 1762), 'Preface Dedicatory', p. 4.

6.   There is a good discussion of Coke's views on legal change by Charles Gray in Sir Matthew Hale, *The History of the Common Law of England*, ed. Charles M. Gray (Chicago, 1971), 'Editor's Introduction', pp. xxiff.

7.   Sir Edward Coke, *The Second Part of the Institutes of the Laws of England* (London, 1671), 'Preface'. See also Coke, *The First Part of the Institutes of the Laws of England* (London, 1670), fol. 115b: Statues are 'for the most part are affirmations of the Common Law'. Compare these remarks with Coke's general recognition of the legal omnicompetence of parliament in the making and abrogating of laws, *First Part of the Institutes*, fol. 110.

8.   See, for example, Coke, *Second Part of the Institutes*, pp. 529, 540, and Coke, *First Part of the Institutes*, fol. 379 b.

9.   Coke, *Second Part of the Institutes*, p. 74.

10. Francis Bacon, *Maxims of the Law* in *The Works of Francis Bacon*, ed. James Spedding, Robert Leslie Ellis, and Douglas Denon Heath, vol. VII (Literary and Professional Works, vol. II) (London, 1859),

p. 370. I have incorporated a variant MS reading, supplied by the editors in a fn, into my quotation.

11.   Selden, quoted in Richard Tuck, '"The Ancient Law of Freedom": John Selden and the Civil War', in John Morrill, ed., *Reactions to the English Civil War 1642–1649* (London, 1982), p. 141.

12.   Ellesmere, 'The Speech of the Lord Chancellor of England, in the Exchequer Chamber, touching the *Post-Nati*' (1608) in Louis A. Knafla, *Law and Politics in Jacobean England: The Tracts of Lord Chancellor Ellesmere*, (Cambridge, 1977), pp. 223–4.

13.   Thomas Hearne (ed.), *A Collection of Curious Discourses written by Eminent Antiquaries upon several heads in our English Antiquities* (London, 2nd ed., 1771), vol. 1, p. 308. This group of 'discourses' on the history of parliament was printed first under the editorship of Sir John Doddridge (nephew of the Jacobean lawyer) under the title *The Several Opinions of Sundry Learned Antiquaries . . . touching the Antiquity . . . of The High-Court of Parliament in England* (London, 1658). These tracts also exist in numerous MS copies. Note should also be taken of the group of discourses on the antiquity of the law: in several places they explicitly reject any neo-Fortescuean notions of the immutability of English law. (See Hearne (ed.), *A Collection of Curious Discourses*, vol. 1, pp. 1–10, and for some similar views from Sir Henry Spelman, as well as a neat, brief summary of his historical approach to the law, see ibid., vol. II, pp. 369–75).

14.   Sir John Doddridge, 'A Breif Consideracion of the Unyon' in *The Jacobean Union: Six Tracts of 1604*, ed. Bruce R. Galloway & Brian P. Levack, Scottish History Society, 4th series, vol. 21 (Edinburgh, 1985), p. 146.

15.   *The Politics of Aristotle*, ed. and transl. Ernest Barker (Oxford, 1946, pbk. ed. 1958, repr. 1982), II, viii, 16–25 (pp. 72–3).

16.   Aquinas, *S. Theol.*, 1a, 2ae, qu 97, art 2. in *Aquinas: Selected Political Writings*, ed. A. P. d'Entrèves (Oxford, 1959), pp. 142/3– 144/5; Jean Bodin, *Six Books of the Commonwealth*, ed. M. J. Tooley (Oxford, 1955), Bk IV, chpt. 3, pp. 123–8. Machiavelli is a more complex case in that the whole of his work could be said to be a meditation on the difficulties and dangers of legal and constitutional innovation: for a brief example see Machiavelli, *The Discourses*, ed. Bernard Crick (Hardmondsworth, 1970, repr. 1985), I, 25, pp 175–6. For a fuller view of the matter see the interpretation of Machiavelli in J. G. A. Pocock, *The Machiavellian Moment: Florentine Political Thought and the Atlantic Tradition* (Princeton, 1975).

17.   See, for example, G. P. Gooch, *Political Thought in England: Bacon to Halifax* (London, 1914–15), pp. 22–34; and J. W. Allen, *English Political Thought 1603–1660*, Vol. 1, 1603–1644 (London, 1938), pp. 50–62. Margaret Judson aptly remarks that Bacon had 'a flexible mind', Judson, *The Crisis of the Constitution: An Essay in Constitutional and Political Thought in England 1603–1645* (New York, 1976, orig. ed. 1949), p. 168, and generally pp. 168–70.

18.   Francis Bacon, *The Essays*, ed. John Pitcher (Harmondsworth, 1985), pp. 104, 119.

19. Ibid., pp. 132–3.
20. Francis Bacon, 'Certain Articles or Considerations touching the Union of the Kingdoms of England and Scotland' (1604) in James Spedding, *The Letters and the Life of Francis Bacon*, vol. III (London, 1868), pp. 230–1.
21. John Hayward, *A Treatise of Union of the two Realmes of England and Scotland* (London, 1604), pp. 11–16.
22. Sir Henry Spelman, 'Of the Union', in *The Jacobean Union: Six Tracts*, ed Galloway & Levack, p. 181.
23. The tendency to assimilate the ideas of Davies to those of Coke derives, of course, from the powerful reading of Pocock, *The Ancient Constitution and the Feudal Law*, chpt. II. But important qualifications of Pocock's views are to be found in Hans Pawlisch, 'Sir John Davies, the Ancient Constitution, and Civil Law'. *Historical Journal*, vol. 23 (1980), pp. 689–702; and Pawlisch, *Sir John Davies and the Conquest of Ireland* (Cambridge, 1985).
24. Davies, *A Report of Cases*, 'Preface', p. 6, and for his view of custom, see pp. 3–4.
25. The *locus classicus* for Coke's historical views is his 'Preface' to *The Third Part of the Reports* in *The Reports of Sir Edward Coke*, ed J. H. Thomas and J. F. Fraser, 6 vols. (London, 1826), vol. II, pt III.
26. Pocock, *Ancient Constitution*, p. 36.
27. Thomas Aquinas, *Summa Theologiae*, 1a, 2ae, qu. 95, art 2, in *Aquinas: Selected Political Writings* (ed. A. P. d'Entrèves), pp. 128/129; Cf. *St. Thomas Aquinas on Politics and Ethics* (ed. Paul E. Sigmund) (New York, 1988), p. 53.
28. I am aware that this chapter does not do full justice to the thought of Fortescue, since its concern is not with reconstructing his ideas in their own context, but with later almost emblematic – uses of his works. The best introduction to his own ideas probably remains S. B. Chrimes, *English Constitutional Ideas in the Fifteenth Century* (Cambridge, 1936), esp. chpt. 4, but passim. Valuable on his legal thought, especially for seeing at as containing a fundamental tension between its hints of legal positivism and its natural-law integument, is Norman Doe, 'Fifteenth-Century Concepts of Law: Fortescue and Pecock', *History of Political Thought*, vol. X (1989), pp. 257–80. References to works on Fortescue's political theory will be given in Part II.
29. On St German see Chrimes, *English Constitutional Ideas*, pp. 203–14; Peter Stein, *Regulae Juris* (Edinburgh, 1966), p. 160; Richard Tuck, 'Natural Rights Theories before Locke', Cambridge PhD Thesis, 1976, chpt. 3; J. A. Guy, *Christopher St. German on Chancery and Statute* (London, Selden Society, 1985); and Alistair Fox & John Guy, *Reassessing the Henrician Age: Humanism, Politics and Reform 1500–1550* (Oxford, 1986), chpts. 5 & 8. On Hooker see Christopher Morris, *Political Thought in England: Tyndale to Hooker* (Oxford, 1953), chpt. IX; Peter Munz, *The Place of Hooker in the History of Thought* (London, 1952); F. J. Shirley, *Richard Hooker and Contemporary Political Ideas* (London, 1949); W. D. J. Cargill Thompson, 'The Philosopher of

the "Politic Society': Richard Hooker as a Political Thinker' in Cargill Thompson, *Studies in the Reformation: Luther to Hooker* (London, 1980), chpt. VI; Robert Eccleshall, *Order and Reason in Politics: Theories of Absolute and Limited Monarchy in Early Modern England* (Oxford, 1978), chpt. V; Robert K. Faulkner, *Richard Hooker and the Politics of a Christian England* (Berkeley, Calif., 1981); J. P. Sommerville, 'Richard Hooker, Hadrian Saravia, and the Advent of the Divine Right of Kings', *History of Political Thought*, vol. IV (1983), pp. 229–45; and Peter Lake, *Anglicans and Puritans? Presbyterianism and English Conformist Thought from Whitgift to Hooker* (London, 1988), chpt. 4.

30. Christopher St German, *St German's Doctor and Student* (ed. T. F. T. Plucknett and J. L. Barton) (London, Selden Society, 1974), p. 27. The book was first published in 1523 and has a very complex bibliographical history. Reference should be made to the fine critical apparatus of this edition, and to the editors' useful introduction. In all quotations I have removed the editors' markings, used to indicate which edition particular passages are from.

31. Ibid., pp. 31–3.

32. Chrimes, *English Constitutional Ideas*, p. 209.

33. *St German's Doctor and Student*, pp. 33–5.

34. Ibid., pp. 36–9.

35. I would like to acknowledge the very useful remarks on custom and reason in English law in A. W. B. Simpson, 'The Common Law and Legal Theory' in Simpson (ed.), *Oxford Essays in Jurisprudence* (Second Series) (Oxford, 1973), pp. 77–99, esp. pp. 92–3.

36. The other grounds of laws of England identified by St German were (1) the law of reason; (2) the law of God; (4) maxims; (5) particular customs; and (6) statutes.

37. *St German's Doctor and Student*, pp. 45–7. On the matter of custom and maxims it might be useful to compare Fortescue: 'In the laws, indeed, there is no matter and form as in physical things and in things artificially devised. But, nevertheless, there are in them certain elements out of which they proceed as out of matter and form, such as customs, statutes, and the law of nature, from which all the laws of the realm proceed as natural things do out of matter and form, just as all we read comes out of the letters which are also called elements. The principles, therefore, which the Commentator said are effective causes, are certain universals which those learned in the laws of England and mathematicians alike call maxims, just as rhetoricians speak of paradoxes, and civilians of rules of law. These principles, indeed, are not known by force of argument nor by logical demonstrations, but they are acquired, as it is taught in the second book of the *Posteriora*, by indication through the senses and the memory'. (Sir John Fortescue, *De Laudibus Legum Anglie* (ed. S. B. Chrimes) (Cambridge, 1949), p. 21). Fortescue's argument would appear to be much less subtle and nuanced than that of St German and later thinkers. In particular, although he seems to have thought that maxims came from custom, statutue or nature, he also seems to have believed that they were timeless axioms (like those of logic

or geometry). Consequently there was much less flexibility in his system, since the implication was that the basic principles of the law (maxims) are immutable. If this is so, then there is also little room for custom as an area of continual change or evolution. It is therefore easy to see why Fortescue can believe that English law, by which he probably meant its basic maxims, must have remained unchanged since the time of the Britons. (Pocock, *The Machiavellian Moment*, chpt. 1, pp. 9– 20, analyses the shortcomings in Fortescue's idea of custom but we should not attribute similar shortcomings to other lawyers from St German on. Cf. also Ferguson, *Clio Unbound*, pp. 230–41).

38. *St German's Doctor and Student*, pp. 55–7.
39. Ibid., p. 57.
40. Aquinas, *S. Theol.*, 1a, 2ae, qu. 95. art. 2, concl. in *Selected Political Writings* (ed. d'Entrèves), pp. 128/129; Richard Hooker, *Of the Laws of Ecclesiastical Polity*, Book I, chpt. x, para. 10 in *The Works of that Learned and Judicious Divine Mr. Richard Hooker* (ed. J. Keeble; rev. R. W. Church & F. Paget) (Oxford, 7th ed., 3 vols, 1888), vol. I, p. 248.
41. *St German's Doctor and Student*, pp. 57–9.
42. Ibid., p. 59.
43. Pocock, *Ancient Constitution*, p. 267. This is from the 'Retrospect' added to the 1987 edition. See generally pp. 265–70.
44. Ibid., p. 266.
45. *St German's Doctor and Student*, pp. 69–71.
46. Fortescue, *De Laudibus Legum Anglie* (ed. Chrimes), p. 39. (For the linking of customs and maxims see chpt. VIII).
47. Useful on this theme, and in broadening the context in which the idea of the ancient constitution can be seen, is J. P. Sommerville, *Politics and Ideology in England, 1603–1640* (London, 1986), chpt. 3, esp. pp. 92–5.
48. John Selden, 'Notes on Fortescue' in Sir John Fortescue, *De Laudibus Legum Angliae*, trans. Robert Mulcaster (London, 1616) pp. 17–18.
49. Sir John Fortescue, *De Laudibus Legum Anglie*, ed. S. B. Chrimes, (Cambridge, 1949), chpt. XVII.
50. ibid., p. 39.
51. Selden, 'Notes on Fortescue', p. 9.
52. See, e.g., John Selden, *The Historie of Tithes* (London, 1618), p. 484, where he talks of Saxon laws being 'abrogated' at the Conquest (though not by the *authority* of Conquest: they were abrogated either by Parliament or by gradual discontinuance, i.e. customarily).
53. Selden, 'Notes on Fortescue', p. 7.
54. Ibid., p. 17.
55. Exactly when this promulgation occurred has been the subject of some controversy. See the divergent opinions of Richard Tuck (in *Natural Rights Theories: Their Origin and Development* (Cambridge, 1979, pbk. ed. 1981), chpt. 5) and J. P. Sommerville ('John Selden, the Law of Nature, and the Origins of Government', *Historical Journal*, vol. 27 (1984), pp. 437–47). The latter denies the contention of the

former that there was a time before which human beings were not subject to the natural law.

56. Selden, 'Notes on Fortescue', p. 17.
57. Ibid., pp. 17–18.
58. William Noy, *A Treatise of the Principall Grounds and Maximes of the Lawes of this Kingdome* (London, 1641), p. 1.
59. Ibid., sig. A3, p. 1.
60. Ibid., chpt. 1.
61. Sir Henry Finch, *Law, or A Discourse Thereof* (London, 1627), p. 75. This is probably an early version of Finch's *Nomotechnia* (London, 1613). There is a translation of this latter work: see Finch, *A Description of the Common Laws of England* (London, 1759). (An equivalent passage to be the one quoted is here found on p. 52). For the complex bibliographical history of Finch's work see Wilfrid Prest, 'The Dialectical Origins of Finch's Law', *Cambridge Law Journal*, vol. 36 (1977), pp. 326–52.
62. John Doddridge, *The English Lawyer* (London, 1631), pp. 153–4.
63. Ibid., p. 191.
64. Ibid., p. 194. It should be noted that Doddridge goes on to indicate that custom is part of the law of reason: 'And of this sort in the Lawes of the Realme there are so many found, that some men have affirmed, that all the Law of the Realme is the Law of Reason: because they are derived out of the generall Customes, and Maximes, or Principles of the Law of Nature of Primary conclusions', ibid., p. 194.
65. Ibid., p. 242.
66. Finch, *Law, or, A Discourse Thereof*, p. 75.
67. This work was originally published with the *Use of the Law* under the title, *The Elements of the Common Law* (London, 1630). It was probably written c.1596–7.
68. Francis Bacon, *The Maxims of the Law* in *The Works of Francis Bacon*, ed. James Spedding, Robert Leslie Ellis, and Douglas Denon Heath, vol. VII (Literary & Professional Works, vol. II) (London, 1859), pp. 358–9.
69. Ibid., p. 360.
70. See J. G. A. Pocock, *The Ancient Constitution and the Feudal Law: A Study of English Historical Thought in the Seventeenth Century* (Cambridge, 1957, new ed. with retrospect, 1987), chpt. II; and David Wootton (ed.) *Divine Right and Democracy*, pp. 32–3, 129, 131–43. Pocock's views of Davies have been challenged in some respect by Hans Pawlisch, 'Sir John Davies, the Ancient Constitution, and Civil Law', *Historical Journal*, vol. 23 (1980), pp. 689–702; and Pawlisch, *Sir John Davies and the Conquest of Ireland*, (Cambridge, 1985). See also Pocock's remarks on Davies in J. G. A. Pocock, *Politics, Language and Time: Essays on Political Thought and History*, (London, 1972), p. 213.
71. Sir John Davies, *A Report of Cases . . .* (Dublin, 1762), 'Preface Dedicatory', p. 3.
72. Ibid., p. 4. (This passage immediately follows the long quotation from Davies cited in Pocock, *Ancient Constitution*, pp. 32–3, but

Pocock does not allude to it at all. It is included in Wootton (ed.), *Divine Right and Democracy*, pp. 131–2.)

73. Ibid., p. 9. (Again, the passage is not discussed by Pocock, but is found in Wootton (ed.), *Divine Right and Democracy*, p. 135). The metaphor of Lesbian rule is explained by Aristotle, *Ethics*, 1137b (Penguin ed., p. 200). The builders of Lesbos used a flexible leaden rule, and Aristotle commented that there were some situations in which an immutable law was unsuitable and needed to be supplemented by the flexibility of equity, just as the Lesbian builders found need for a flexible rule.

74. For some alternatives to Pocock's interpretation of Coke on artificial reason see Charles Gray, 'Reason, Authority, and Imagination: The Jurisprudence of Sir Edward Coke' in Perez Zagorin (ed.), *Culture and Politics : From Puritanism to the Enlightenment* (Berkeley, 1980), chpt. II, pp. 25–66; and John U. Lewis, 'Sir Edward Coke (1552–1633): His Theory of "Artificial Reason" as a Context for Modern Basic Legal Theory', *Law Quarterly Review*, vol. 84 (1968), pp. 330–42. Both contain some suggestive remarks.

75. Sir Edward Coke, *The First Part of the Institutes of the Laws of England* (London, 1670), fol. 97b. The other major discussion of the matter by Coke is in his remarks on Calvin's Case (this is used as the basis for Pocock's discussion – see Pocock, *Ancient Constitution*, p. 35) and can be found in *State Trials*, vol. II, col. 612.

76. Sir Edward Coke, *The Compleat Copy-Holder* (London, 1650, 1st ed. 1641), p. 70. See also Coke, *First Part of the Institutes*, fol. 115b.

77. Hobbes treated Coke's theory of artificial reason as if it were saying the same thing as Doddridge's, which it was not. Coke talked of the reason of the *law*, Doddridge of the *lawyers*. It is, nevertheless, interesting to note that Hobbes did clearly perceive the *purpose* of the theory, and agreed with it, though he wished to achieve the same effect by other means. For their different reasons, Hobbes and the common lawyers were agreed in wanting to produce a theory in which the civil laws of a state cannot be in conflict with natural law (i.e. reason). I refer above all to Hobbes's sentence, introducing his discussion of Coke: 'The Law can never be against Reason, our lawyers are agreed . . . And it is true . . . ', Thomas Hobbes, *Leviathan*, ed. C. B. Macpherson (Harmondsworth, 1968, repr. 1983), chpt. 26, p. 316. See also Hobbes, *Dialogue Between a Philosopher and a Student of the Common Laws of England*, ed. J. Cropsey (Chicago, 1971), pp. 53–57. Coke's formulation is, though, not quite as clear as I have made it: the passage Hobbes quoted does indicate the source of the concept in an idea similar to Doddridge's. Coke (in the long passage quoted in my text) did slide around between talking of the law as artificial reason, and of artificial reason as something lawyers get by studying diligently. Lawyers gained artificial reason 'by long study', and it was something different from 'every mans natural reason'. But it is implied (eventually) that artificial reason was contained in the laws and then passed on to those who study them deeply enough.

78. The text of this is in Elizabeth R. Foster (ed.), *Proceedings in Parliament 1610* (New Haven, 2 vols, 1966), vol. II, pp. 170–97. There is a briefer report of it in S. R. Gardiner (ed.), *Parliamentary Debates in 1610* (London, Camden Society, First Series, vol. 81, 1862), pp. 72–5. Cf. the discussion in Pocock, *Ancient Constitution*, pp. 270–6.
79. Foster (ed.), *Proceedings in Parliament 1610*, II, p. 174.
80. Ibid., pp. 173, 175.
81. Ibid., p. 175.
82. Ibid., p. 176.
83. Ibid., pp. 182, 176.
84. Ibid., p. 174.
85. Ibid., pp. 178–9.
86. Noy, *Treatise*, p. 20. For St German on particular or local customs see *St German's Doctor and Student*, pp. 71–3.
87. Noy, *Treatise*, pp. 1–18.
88. Finch, *Law, or, A Discourse Thereof*, p. 77.
89. Ibid., p. 77.
90. Ibid., p. 78.
91. Ibid., p. 76.
92. John Doddridge, *The English Lawyer*, p. 101.
93. Ibid., p. 101.
94. Ibid., p. 102.
95. Ibid., p. 153.
96. Charles Calthrop, *The Relation between the Lord of a Mannor and the Copy-holder his Tenant* (London, 1650; orig. ed. 1635), pp. 17, 23–4. (Printed with Edward Coke, *The Compleat Copy- holder*).
97. Ibid., pp. 18–19.
98. Davies, *A Report of Cases*, 'Preface', p. 6.
99. Ibid., p. 3.
100. Ibid., p. 4.
101. Ibid., pp. 5–6.
102. Finch, *Law, or A Discourse Thereof*, p. 75.
103. The best account of the humanist influences on common lawyers is Louis A. Knafla, 'The Influence of Continental Humanists and Jurists on English Common Law in the Renaissance', in R. J. Schoeck (ed.), *Acta Conventus Neo-Latini Bononensis: Proceedings of the Fourth International Congress of Neo-Latin Studies, Bologna 26 August to 1 September 1979*, pp. 60–71.
104. In general (apart from some of the works in the following note) see Neal W. Gilbert, *Renaissance Concepts of Method* (New York, 1960), pp. 93–8, and passim; Wilfred R. Prest, *The Inns of Court under Elizabeth I and the Early Stuarts 1590–1640* (London, 1972), pp. 143–9; Wilfred R. Prest, 'The Dialectical Origins of Finch's *Law*', *Cambridge Law Journal*, vol. 36 (1977), pp. 326– 52; and Richard J. Terrill, 'Humanism and Rhetoric in Legal Education : The Contribution of Sir John Dodderidge (1555–1628)', *Journal of Legal History*, vol. 2 (1981), pp. 30–44.
105. The major works are Donald R. Kelley, *Foundations of Modern Historical Scholarship: Language, Law, and History in the French Renaissance*

(New York, 1970); and Julian H. Franklin, *Jean Bodin and the Sixteenth-Century Revolution in the Methodology of Law and History* (New York, 1963). See also Eric Cochrane, *Historians and Historiography in the Italian Renaissance* (Chicago, 1981). Kelley has extended his treatment of the subject in numerous articles: see in particular Donald R. Kelley, 'The Rise of Legal History in the Renaissance', *History and Theory*, vol. IX (1970), pp. 174–94; Kelley, 'Civil Science in the Renaissance: Jurisprudence in the French Manner', *History of European Ideas*, vol. 2 (1981), pp. 261–76; Kelley, 'Clio and the Lawyers: Forms of Historical Consciousness in Medieval Jurisprudence', *Medievalia et Humanistica*, n.s., vol. 5 (1974), pp. 25–49; and on England, Kelley, 'History, English Law and the Renaissance', *Past and Present*, no. 65 (1974), pp. 24–51. (These articles are all reprinted in D. R. Kelley, *History, Law and the Human Sciences* (London, 1984).)

106. Besides the work of Tuck, *Natural Rights Theories*, chpt. 5; see also Martha A. Ziskind, 'John Selden : Criticism and Affirmation of the Common Law Tradition', *American Journal of Legal History*, vol. XIX (1975), pp. 22–39; and Paul Christianson, 'Young John Selden and the Ancient Constitution, ca 1610–18', *Proceedings of the American Philosophical Society*, vol. 128, (1984), pp. 271–315.

107. Kelley, 'History, English Law and the Renaissance' examines this matter carefully. The debate on this article between Christopher Brooks, Kevin Sharpe and Kelley (*Past and Present*, no. 72 (1976), pp. 133–146) seems to me to leave Kelley's argument more or less unscathed. See further Knafla, 'Influence of Continental Humanists'; Peter Stein, 'Continental Influences on English Legal Thought, 1600–1900' in Stein, *The Character and Influence of the Roman Civil Law: Historical Essays* (London, 1988), chpt. 15; and C. P. Rodgers, 'Humanism, History and the Common Law', *Journal of Legal History*, vol. 6 (1985), pp. 129–56.

108. Thomas Starkey, *A Dialogue Between Reginal Pole & Thomas Lupset*, ed. Kathleen M. Burton (London, 1948), written c.1532–3, pp. 29–36. The whole work is interesting in this regard.

109. Sir Thomas Smith, *De Republica Anglorum*, ed. Mary Dewar (Cambridge, 1982). For discussion of these Tudor humanists see Kelley, 'History, English Law, and the Renaissance', and Ferguson, *Clio Unbound*, chpt. VII.

110. Sir Henry Savile, 'Historicall Collections' in *The Jacobean Union: Six Tracts*, ed. Galloway and Levack, p. 199.

111. Ellesmere, 'Post-Nati' in Knafla, *Law and Politics*, p. 216. (For Ellesmere's humanist learning see chpt. I of Knafla's introductory material.)

112. Ibid., p. 218.

113. Ibid., p. 223

114. Sir Francis Bacon, 'A Proposition to his Majesty . . . Touching the Compiling and Amendment of the Laws of England' in James Spedding, *The Letters and the Life of Francis Bacon*, vol. VI (London, 1872); pp. 65–6. For a discussion of Bacon's legal thought see Paul Kocher, 'Francis Bacon on the Science of Jurisprudence' in Brian

Vickers (ed.), *Essential Articles for the Study of Francis Bacon* (London, 1972), pp. 167–194. It is also interesting to compare Bacon's humanism with that of his father, beautifully analysed in Patrick Collinson, 'Sir Nicholas Bacon and the Elizabethan *Via Media'*, *Historical Journal*, vol. 23 (1980), pp. 255–73, reprinted in Collinson, *Godly People: Essays on English Protestantism and Puritanism* (London, 1983), chpt. 5.

115. Bacon, 'Proposition' in Spedding, *Letters and Life*, VI, p. 67.
116. Ibid., pp. 68–70.
117. Sir Francis bacon, *Of the Dignity and Advancement of Learning* in *The Works of Francis Bacon*, ed. James Spedding, Robert Leslie Ellis, and Douglas Denon Heath, vol. V (Translations of the Philosophical Works, vol. II), (London, 1858), pp. 88–109. (Latin text in *Works*, ed. Spedding, Ellis, and Heath, vol. I (London, 1857), pp. 803–827).
118. Ibid., aphorisms 15, 22, pp. 91, 92.
119. Ibid., aphorism 63, p. 101.
120. Ibid., aphorism 76, p. 104.
121. Ibid., aphorism 82, p. 106.
122. Ibid., aphorism 85, p. 106.
123. Bacon, 'Proposition' in Spedding, *Letters and Life*, VI, p. 63.
124. The standard work on this is Samuel Kliger, *The Goths in England: A Study in Seventeenth and Eighteenth Century Thought* (New York, 1972; orig. ed. 1952). This book should be used with some care, as it considerably overstates its case, sometimes failing to distinguish carefully enough between Saxons and Britons. E.g. Kliger's argument that Celts and Celtic Druidism were seen as 'Gothic' (pp. 84ff.) seems to be taken by him as a licence to treat statements about the Celtic Britons as applicable to the Germanic peoples. This only seems to remove any clear sense of purpose from his argument. For example he argues in his key chapter on Gothic Parliaments (chpt. 2) that the tracts of Doddridge and other members of the Society of Antiquaries on the antiquity of parliament formed 'an anthology or primer of Gothic ideas', yet he also attributes to these tracts the creation of the myth of a *pre*-Saxon parliament (pp. 120–1). Again, he says of Coke that he 'was strong for the common law but he does not figure importantly as a Gothicist' (p. 122, n. 19). Pocock agrees with this argument (*Ancient Constitution*, pp. 56–7). The point about Coke is certainly true on Kliger's initial definition of what he means by Goths ('the Germanic invaders of Rome', 'the Germanic tribes' [p. 1]). But if one uses his later, looser sense of Gothic to include Celts and the Britons then Coke would fit the model. In other words there is a confusion on this point. Kliger's looser sense of Gothic would also make meaningless Pocock's verdict on the parliamentary debates of 1628: 'There is not much sign of the semi-alternative myth that the laws of England are of German or Gothic, rather than merely immemorial origin' (Pocock, 'The Commons Debates of 1628', *Journal of the History of Ideas*, vol. 39 (1978), p. 333. This article is a review of the Yale ed. of the debates). It will be apparent that I do not view Gothicism and immemoriality as being in conflict, nor do I see Gothicism as an alternative to common law ideas. Cf. the remarks of R. J. Smith, *The Gothic Bequest:*

Medieval Institutions in British Thought, 1688–1863 (Cambridge, 1987), pp. 6–7.

125. On the antiquarian movement that developed during the Elizabethan period and flourished through to the 1620s see Linda Van Norden, 'The Elizabethan College of Antiquaries', University of California at Los Angeles, PhD Dissertation, 1946; F. Smith Fussner, *The Historical Revolution : English Historical Writing and Thought 1580–1640* (London, 1962), chpt. 4; Kevin Sharpe, *Sir Robert Cotton 1586–1631: History and Politics in Early Modern England* (Oxford, 1979), Part I; Ferguson, *Clio Unbound*, chpt. IV; and Joseph M. Levine, *Humanism and History: Origins of Modern English Historiography* (Ithaca NY, 1987), chpt. 3.

126. William Lambarde, *A Perambulation of Kent* (London, 1596; orig. ed. 1576), epistle dedicatory.

127. Lambarde to Camden, July 1585, B. L. Cotton M. S., Julius, C.V.9, fol. 25. See also Wilbur Dunkel, *William Lambarde: Elizabethan Jurist, 1536–1601*, (New Brunswick, 1965), pp. 56–8; Retha M. Warnicke, *William Lambarde: Elizabethan Antiquary 1636–1601* (London, 1973), pp. 26, 33–4; and Richard J. Terrill, 'William Lambarde: Elizabethan Humanist and legal Historian', *Journal of Legal History*, vol. 6 (1985), pp. 157–78.

128. See Van Norden, 'Elizabethan College of Antiquaries' (chpt. III examines the membership lists in detail); and R. J. Schoeck, 'The Elizabethan Society of Antiquaries and Men of Law', *Notes and Queries*, vol. CXCIX, (1954), pp. 417–21. On Schoeck's figures (which are incomplete) up to thirty-seven out of forty-three members had legal connections.

129. For a summary of this matter see Hugh A. MacDougall, *Racial Myth in English History: Trojans, Teutons, and Anglo-Saxons* (Montreal, 1982), chpts. I–III; and, above all, T. D. Kendrick, *British Antiquity* (New York, 1950; reprinted 1970), esp. chpts. VII–VIII.

130. William Camden, *Britain, or A Chorographicall Description of the . . . Kingdomes, England, Scotland, and Ireland*, trans. Philemon Holland (London, 1637; orig. Latin ed. 1586), pp. 6–23.

131. Lambarde, *Perambulation of Kent*, p. 6.

132. Camden, *Britain*, p. 152.

133. William Lambarde, *Archeion or, A Discourse upon the High Courts of Justice in England* (ed. Charles H. McIlwain and Paul L. Ward) (Cambridge, Mass., 1957; orig. ed. 1635, written c.1590s), pp. 124–5.

134. Ibid., pp. 126–7.

135. Ibid., p. 133.

136. Ibid., pp. 133–4.

137. Selden, *History of Tithes*, p. 482.

138. Lambarde, *Archeion*, pp. 133–4.

139. Ibid., pp. 134–5.

140. Ibid., p. 12.

141. For an excellent account of Selden's work on English legal history, see Paul Christianson, 'Young John Selden and the Ancient Constitution, ca 1610–18', *Proceedings of the American Philosophical Society*, vol. 128, no. 4, (1984), pp. 271–315. A good brief introduction to

Selden's life and work is D. S. Berkowitz's entry on him in *Biographical Dictionary of British Radicals in the Seventeenth Century,* ed. Richard Greaves and Robert Zaller, vol. III (Brighton, 1984), pp. 153–60. More substantial is Berkowitz, *John Selden's Formative Years: Politics and Society in Early Seventeenth-Century England* (Washington, 1988), learned but dated in its historiographical perspectives.

142.   John Selden, *Ad Fletam Dissertatio* (ed. and trans. David Ogg), (Cambridge, 1925), p. 105.

143.   Ibid., p. 105.

144.   Ibid., p. 167.

145.   On these matters, particularly the latter, a fuller account of Selden's oscillations and subtleties is Christianson, 'Young John Selden'.

146.   John Selden, *Jani Anglorum Facies Altera* (London, 1610), 'Preface', translated as 'The Reverse or Back-face of the English Janus' in *Tracts written by John Selden of the Inner-Temple, Esquire,* trans. Redman Westcot, (London, 1683), sig. a3v–a4.

147.   John Selden, 'England's Epinomis' in Selden, *Tracts,* p. 8. Cf. Selden's defence of his reliance on Tacitus for an account of Saxon customs in 'Reverse or Back-face of the English Janus', p. 30, 'For though he treat in general of the Germans, yet nevertheless without any question, our Saxons brought over along with them into this Island very many of those things, which are delivered to us by those who have wrote concerning the Customs of the Germans'.

148.   Christianson, 'Young John Selden', pp. 293–5 (I emphasise different elements in Selden's account from those stressed by Christianson); Pocock, *Ancient Constitution,* pp. 288, 334.

149.   Sir Roger Owen, 'Of the Antiquity, Ampleness, and Excellency of the Common Laws of England', B. L. Harleian MS 6606, fol. 210b. Quoted from William E. Klein, 'Ruling Thoughts : The World of Sir Roger Owen of Condover', Johns Hopkins PhD dissertaton, 1987, p. 100.

150.   Selden, 'Reverse or Back face of the English Janus', p. 94.

151.   For a survey of opinions see E. Evans, 'Of the Antiquity of Parliaments in England: Some Elizabethan and Early Stuart Opinions', *History,* vol. 23, (1938–9), pp. 206–221. Also useful is Catherine Strateman (ed.) *The Liverpool Tractate: An Eighteenth Century Manual on the Procedure of the House of Commons* (New York, 1967: orig. ed. 1937), introduction, pp. xxx–lx.

152.   See, e.g., the variety of opinions expressed by the contributors to the debate of the Society of Antiquaries on the antiquity of Parliament, in Hearne (ed.), *A Collection of Curious Discourses,* I, pp. 281–310. (One M.S. copy of these tracts has an additional item which remained unprinted. It is attributed to Cotton, but is in fact a transcript of Lambarde, *Archeion,* ed. McIlwain & Ward, pp. 123–7, with the addition of the concluding phrase 'And soe I end'. See B. L. Egerton MS 2975, fols. 30–32b. Sharpe, *Sir Robert Cotton,* p. 164 accepts the ascription to Cotton at face value).

153.   Camden in Hearne (ed.), *A Collection of Curious Discourses,* I, p. 303.

154.   Ibid., I, p. 296.

155. Selden, 'Reverse or Back-face of the English Janus', p. 38.
156. Ibid., 'Preface', sig. a3v. Note the allusion to the Aristotelian prudential maxim discouraging legal change that was discussed at the beginning of this chapter.
157. Ibid., 'Preface', sig. a3v.
158. Ibid., p. 48.
159. Ibid., chpts. xx–xxi.
160. *Hooker's Ecclesiastical Polity: Book VIII* (ed. Raymond Aaron Houk), (New York, 1931), editor's introduction, pp. 6–7, 50.
161. Hooker, *Laws of Ecclesiastical Polity*, Bk IV, chpt. IV, para. 2, in *The Works of . . . Richard Hooker* (ed. J. Keble; rev. R. W. Church & F. Paget), vol. I, p. 430.
162. Sheldon Wolin, 'Richard Hooker and English Conservatism', *Western Political Quarterly*, vol. 6 (1953), p. 36. The whole of this article is most suggestive on the aspects of Hooker under discussion here.
163. Ibid., p. 39.
164. Hooker, *Laws*, I, v, 1; in *Works*, I, p. 215.
165. Wolin, 'Hooker and English Conservatism', p. 40; citing Hooker, *Laws*, IV, xiv, 2; V, ix, 1; in *Works*, I, pp. 481–2; II, pp. 36–8.
166. Hooker, *Laws*, I, viii, 11; in *Works*, I, pp. 235–6.
167. Hooker, *Laws*, IV, i, 3; in *Works*, I, p. 419.
168. For analyses of Spelman's work see F. M. Powicke, 'Sir Henry Spelman and the "Concilia"' in Lucy S. Sutherland, ed. *Studies in History: British Academy Lectures* (Oxford, 1966); Pocock, *Ancient Constitution*, Chpt. V; and Ferguson, *Clio Unbound*, pp. 303–11.
169. Sir Henry Spelman, 'Of the Ancient Government of England' in *Reliquiae Spelmanniae*, p. 49. (This is printed as *The English Works of Sir Henry Spelman Kt . . . Together with his Posthumous Works*, ed. Edmund Gibson (London, 2nd ed., 1727). The *Reliquiae* forms the second half and is separately paginated. The pagination is identical to the ed. of 1698).
170. Ibid., p. 49.
171. Sir Henry Spelman, 'Of Parliaments', *Reliquiae Spelmanniae*, pp. 57–8.
172. Ibid., p. 61.
173. William Hakewill, 'The Antiquity of the Laws of this Island' in Hearne, (ed.), *Collection of Curious Discourses*, I, p. 2.
174. Ibid., pp. 4–5.
175. Ibid., p. 6.
176. Ibid., pp. 6–7.
177. anon., *The Use of the Law* in *The Works of Francis Bacon*, ed. Spedding, Ellis, and Heath, vol. VII (London, 1859), pp. 451–504. See esp. pp. 465–6, 481–5. This tract was first printed with an unattributed fragment of Doddridge's *English Lawyer* as *The Lawyers Light* (London, 1629). The (highly unlikely) attribution to Bacon derives from the fact that its second manifestation was its appearance with Bacon's *Maxims* as Francis Bacon, *The Elements of the Common Lawes of England* (London, 1630).
178. Hayward, *Treatise of Union*, p. 11.
179. Bacon, 'Proposition' in Spedding, *Letters and Life*, VI, p. 63.

180. anon, 'Of the Antiquity of the laws of England', in Hearne, ed., *Collection of Curious Discourses,* I, p. 8.
181. Pocock, *Ancient Constitution,* chpts II & III; Ferguson, *Clio Unbound* chpt. VIII; Sommerville, *Politics and Ideology,* chpt., 3.
182. Sir Edward Coke, 'Report of Calvin's Case' in T. B. Howell, (ed.), *A Complete Collection of State Trials* (London, n.d.), vol. II. col. 612.
183. Sir Edward Coke, *The Second Part of the Reports,* 'Preface', pp. vii–viii, in Coke, *Reports,* ed. Thomas and Fraser, vol. I, pt. II.
184. Sir Edward Coke, *The Third Part of the Reports,* 'Preface', p. xii in Coke, *Reports,* ed. Thomas and Fraser, vol. II, pt. III.
185. Ibid., p. xiv.
186. Ibid., p. xiv.
187. Ibid., pp. xviii–xix.
188. Ibid., p. xxi ; Fortescue, *De Laudibus Legum Anglie* (ed. Chrimes), p. 39.
189. Sir Edward Coke, *The Sixth Part of the Reports,* 'Preface', pp iii–iv, in Coke, *Reports,* ed. Thomas and Fraser, vol. III, pt. VI.
190. Ibid., p. vi.
191. Sir Edward Coke, *The Eighth Part of the Reports,* 'Preface', p. iv, in Coke, *Reports,* ed. Thomas and Fraser, vol. IV, pt. VIII.
192. Ibid., p. xi.
193. Sir Edward Coke, *The Ninth Part of the Reports,* 'Preface', p. iii, in Coke, *Reports,* ed. Thomas and Fraser, vol. V, pt. IX.
194. Ibid., p. xi.
195. Ibid., pp. xiiff., xviii.
196. Ibid., p. xxv.
197. *Cobett's Parliamentary History of England,* vol. I (London, 1806), col. 1016. On the use of the term 'positive law' to mean legislation cf. Egerton's use of the term to cover proclamations and statutes: Sir Thomas Egerton, *A Discourse upon the Exposicion & Understanding of Statutes,* ed. Samuel E. Thorne (San Marino, Calif., 1942), pp. 103–4. And see p. 103 n. 1 for a discussion of the matter.
198. Michael Dalton, *The Countrey Justice* (London, 1618), p. 1.
199. George Saltern, *Of the Ancient Lawes of Great Britaine* (London, 1605), sig. B2.
200. Ibid., sig. B3.
201. Ibid., sigs. B4, C1.
202. Ibid., sig. C4v–D1.
203. Ibid., sig. E4.
204. Ibid., sigs. G2–G2v.
205. It should be noted that in the 'Retrospect' to the 1987 ed. of his work Pocock has moved towards some recognition of this point. He remarks, for example, that his thinking has moved in ways 'involving a partial shift of emphasis from Davies's "common custom of the realm" to Hedley's "time and reason", which enables us to see custom and reason . . . as existing in a Fortescuean symbiosis', Pocock, *Ancient Constitution,* p. 276. In the same place Pocock argues persuasively that even the original ed. of his book was never intended to say that common lawyers believed the law to be literally

immutable.
206. Useful in this regard is J. P. Sommerville, *Politics and Ideology,*
pp. 92–5; and also George L. Mosse, *The Struggle for Sovereignty in
England: From the Reign of Queen Elizabeth to the Petition of Right* (East
Lansing, Mich., 1950), chpt. VIII. However Sommerville's further
contention (pp. 105–8) that the common lawyers were natural law
theorists seems misleading. They did use the language of natural
law occasionally, but often in unusual circumstances (most notably
Calvin's Case which was concerned with Scotland as well as England
and so required consideration of more than just English law). In a
domestic English context, though, common lawyers, as has been
intimated, gave little place to a natural law exterior to and capable
of limiting the capacity of the common law. The 'classic' natural law
theorists believed that positive laws were subject to the judgement
of those (theologians and others) who were able to interpret natural
law; the common lawyers, in one way or another, subverted this
position. A classic natural law theorist, even such an unusual one as
Marsilius of Padua, believed that there was an external standard by
which positive law could be judged, which meant that the positive
law could be examined using natural reason alone (see *Defensor
Pacis*, I, x, 5, & II, xii, 9 – Gewirth ed. (Toronto, 1980), pp. 36,
191). See also Ewart Lewis, 'The "Positivism" of Marsiglio of
Padua', *Speculum*, vol. 38 (1963), pp. 541–82; and Cary J. Nederman,
'Nature, Justice and Duty in the *Defensor Pacis*: Marsiglio of Padua's
Ciceronian Impulse', *Political Theory*, vol. 18 (1990), pp. 615–37, esp.
628–32. For general introductions to the classic natural law tradition,
from a variety of perspectives, see A.P. d'Entrèves, *Natural Law: An
Introduction to Legal Philosophy* (London, 2nd. ed., 1970); Heinrich A.
Rommen, *The Natural Law: A Study in Legal and Social History and
Philosophy*, trans. Thomas R. Hanley (St Louis, Minnesota, 1947);
Paul E. Sigmund, *Natural Law in Political Thought* (Cambridge,
Mass., 1971); and Leo Strauss, 'On Natural Law' in Strauss, *Studies
in Platonic Political Philosophy* (Chicago, 1983), chpt. 6.

CHAPTER 3: PROBLEMS AND IMPLICATIONS

1. Full reference to the theses of Pocock and Kelley, and the arguments
of their critics can be found in fnn. 32 & 33 to Chapter 1.
2. Hans S. Pawlisch, *Sir John Davies and the Conquest of Ireland: A Study
in Legal Imperialism* (Cambridge, 1985), chpt. 9, esp. pp. 174–5,
166 (this chapter is reprinted as Pawlisch, 'Sir John Davies, the
Ancient Constitution, and Civil Law', *Historical Journal*, vol. 23
(1980), pp. 689–702); W. D. Hassell (ed.), *A Catalogue of the Library
of Sir Edward Coke* (New Haven, 1950) – this shows Coke to have
owned numerous civil-law works, and a considerable number of
political and historical writings, including works by Machiavelli,
Justus Lipsius, Bodin, Guicciardini, Pasquier, de la Popelinière, as
well as many English writers.

3. Louis A. Knafla, *Law and Politics in Jacobean England: The Tracts of Lord Chancellor Ellesmere* (Cambridge, 1977), chpt. I; David Sandler Berkowitz, *John Selden's Formative Years: Politics and Society in Early Seventeenth-Century England* (Washington, 1988), chpt. 3 & p. 69; Richard Tuck, *Natural Rights Theories: Their Origin and Development* (Cambridge, 1979), p. 83; Martha A. Ziskind, 'John Selden: Criticism and Affirmation of the Common Law Tradition', *American Journal of Legal History*, vol. XIX (1975), pp. 22–39.

4. Richard J. Terrill, 'Humanism and Rhetoric in Legal Education: The Contribution of Sir John Dodderidge (1555–1628)', *Journal of Legal History*, vol. 2 (1981), pp. 30–44; Wilfrid R. Prest, *The Inns of Court under Elizabeth I and the Early Stuarts 1590–1640* (London, 1972), pp. 143–9; and Prest, 'The Dialectical Origins of Finch's *Law*', *Cambridge Law Journal*, vol. 36 (1977), pp. 326–352.

5. Christopher Brooks & Kevin Sharpe, 'Debate: History, English Law and the Renaissance', *Past and Present*, No. 72 (1976), pp. 133–42; Louis A. Knafla, 'The Influence of Continental Humanists and Jurists on English Common Law in the Renaissance', in R. J. Schoeck (ed.), *Acta Conventus Neo-Latini Bononensis: Proceedings of the Fourth International Congress of Neo-Latin Studies, Bologna 26 August to 1 September 1979*, pp. 60–71. For some sense of the general European intellectual scene and the involvement in it of English scholars see Kevin Sharpe, *Sir Robert Cotton 1586–1631: History and Politics in Early Modern England* (Oxford, 1979), chpt. III.

6. Cf. Pocock, *The Ancient Constitution and the Feudal Law* (Cambridge, 1957; new ed. 1987), pp. 263–4 & p. 263 n. 11; Paul Christianson, 'Political Thought in Early Stuart England', *Historical Journal*, vol. 30 (1987), p. 900; see also Donald Kelley's reply to Brooks & Sharpe, in *Past and Present*, No. 72 (1976), pp. 143–6.

7. Compare the account of insularity – partly accurate, partly condescending – in A. B. Ferguson, *Clio Unbound: Perception of the Social and Cultural Past in Renaissance England* (Durham, NC, 1979), pp. 259–66.

8. The major contributions are Pocock, *Ancient Constitution*; Quentin Skinner, 'History and Ideology in the English Revolution', *Historical Journal*, vol. 8 (1965), pp. 151–78; John M. Wallace, *Destiny His Choice: The Loyalism of Andrew Marvell* (Cambridge, 1968; pbk. ed. 1980), chpt. 1; and Johann P. Sommerville, 'History and Theory: the Norman Conquest in Early Stuart Political Thought', *Political Studies*, vol. 34 (1986), pp. 249–61.

9. Pocock, *Ancient Constitution*, pp. 52–3.

10. Skinner, 'History and Ideology', pp. 156ff.; Wallace, *Destiny His Choice*, pp. 22ff.

11. Cf. Christianson, 'Political Thought in Early Stuart England', p. 957.

12. For Coke see Sommerville, 'History and Theory', pp. 252–3; John Selden, *The Historie of Tithes* (London, 1618), p. 482.

13. Robert C. Johnson, Mary F. Keeler, Maija J. Cole & William B. Bidwell (eds.), *Commons Debates 1628: Volume III – 21 April–27 May 1628* (New Haven, 1977), p. 528; Pocock, *Ancient Constitution*,

pp. 299–300; Sommerville, 'History and Theory', pp. 258–9. Curiously, Sommerville arrives at the (incorrect, in my view) reading that Mason denied the Conquest to have occurred and believed an ancient (pre-conquest) contract to be still in force. In fact, Mason was arguing that the post-Conquest Statutes were themselves tantamount to an original contract. Sommerville's reading is accepted by Christianson, 'Political Thought in Early Stuart England', p. 957.

14. Sir John Hayward, *The Lives of the III Normans, Kings of England,* (London, 1613), p. 96. (However, Hayward's overall verdict is not as harsh or unequivocal as the quotation suggests: see important qualifications on pp. 101–3, 122–4); Hayward, *A Treatise of Union of the two Realmes of England and Scotland* (London, 1604), p. 11.

15. William Fulbecke, *A Parallele or Conference of the Civill Law, the Canon Law, and the Common Law of this Realme of England* (London, 1601), 'To the courteous reader', sig. **1. On Fulbecke's background see *DNB*; and Brian P. Levack, *The Civil Lawyers in England 1603–1641: A Political Study,* (Oxford, 1973) pp. 136–7.

16. See Levack, *Civil Lawyers,* pp. 148–50. On Thomas Starkey, whom Levack sees as a precursor of the early-seventeenth century civilians, see the interesting background material in Thomas F. Mayer, *Thomas Starkey and the Commonweal: Humanist Politics and Religion in the Reign of Henry VIII,* (Cambridge, 1989), pp. 61–2; Thomas Starkey, *A Dialogue between Pole and Lupset* (ed. T.F. Mayer) (London, Camden Society, Series 4, vol. 37, 1989), pp. 77, 128–9.

17. *St German's Doctor and Student* (ed. T. F. T. Plucknett & J. L. Barton), (London, Selden Society, 1974), Prologue, pp. 2/3–4/5.

18. This aspect of St German's thought is well caught by John Guy, in Alistair Fox & John Guy, *Reassessing the Henrician Age: Humanism, Politics and Reform 1500–1550* (Oxford, 1986), pp. 102–3, 180–87; John Guy, *Christopher St. German on Chancery and Statute* (London, Selden Society, 1985), pp. 19–20, 64–94.

19. St German, *Replication of a Serjeant at the Lawes of England* (written c.1530–32) in Guy, *St German,* pp. 102–3 (for date and authorship see pp. 56–62).

20. Edward Hake, *Epieikeia: A Dialogue on Equity in Three Parts* (ed. D.E.C. Yale) (New Haven, 1953), p. 5.

21. Ibid., pp. 16, 55–6.

22. Fox & Guy, *Reassessing the Henrician Age,* p. 198; Hake, *Epieikeia,* pp. 121–6.

23. Some discussions of the varieties of *de facto* theory are John M. Wallace, *Destiny His Choice,* chpt. 1; Quentin Skinner, 'Conquest and Consent: Thomas Hobbes and the Engagement Controversy' in G. E. Aylmer (ed.), *The Interregnum: The Quest for Settlement 1646–1660* (London, 1972; rev.ed. 1974), chpt. 3; Tuck, *Natural Rights Theories,* chpt. 6; Glenn Burgess, 'Usurpation, Obligation and Obedience in the Thought of the Engagement Controversy', *Historical Journal,* vol. 29 (1986), pp. 515–36.

24. One scholar has remarked on the way in which the common lawyers conflated 'the actual and the ideal': Enid Campbell, 'Thomas

Hobbes and the Common Law', *Tasmanian University Law Review*, vol. I (1958), p. 31, n. 64. Even more significant is Robert Parsons' complaint about Coke, that though he has claimed to offer (in his remarks on Caudrey's Case) two types of argument, 'the first *De Jure*, the second *De facto*', in the end even when he embarks on the former arguments 'yet doth he nothing lesse then prosecute that kind of proofe, but rather slippeth to the second, which is *De Facto*, endeavoring to proove, that certaine Kings made certaine lawes, or attempted certaine factes sometimes and upon some occasions', Robert Parsons, *An Answere to the Fifth Part of Reportes lately set forth by Sir Edward Cooke* (London?, 1606), p. 63. By the standards acceptable to the Jesuit Coke did not have legal arguments because, as a common lawyer he tended to take as law not what should be done but what had been done (and was still done). For him, of course, long usage was *proof* of rationality and rightness, but Parsons' incredulity at the procedure should remind us of the oddity of such an argument when viewed from the perspective of classic natural law thinking.

25. Janelle Greenberg, 'The Confessor's Laws and the Radical Face of the Ancient Constitution', *English Historical Review*, vol. 104 (1989), p. 612.

26. Pocock, *Ancient Constitution*, chpt. VI (esp. pp. 125–7) and pp. 318–20; Quentin Skinner, 'History and Ideology in the English Revolution', pp. 161–2.

27. For introductions to this subject see S. Prall, *The Agitation for Law Reform during the Puritan Revolution, 1640–1660* (The Hague, 1966) and D. Veall, *The Popular Movement for Law Reform, 1640–1660* (Oxford, 1970).

28. For an interpretation of the Leveller critique of the existing order that implicitly draws on these views see Brian Manning, *The English People and the English Revolution* (Harmondsworth, 1978), chpt. 9.

29. Christopher Hill, 'The Norman Yoke', in his *Puritanism and Revolution: Studies in Interpretation of the English Revolution of the 17th Century*, (Harmondsworth, 1986; orig. ed. 1958), chpt. 3, pp. 58–125. See also H. N. Brailsford, *The Levellers and the English Revolution* (London, 1976; orig. ed. 1961), chpt. VII.

30. R. B. Seaberg, 'The Norman Conquest and the Common Law: The Levellers and the Argument from Continuity', *Historical Journal*, vol. 24 (1981), pp. 791–806.

31. Ibid., pp. 792–3.

32. Ibid., pp. 796–7, n. 13; 797–8.

33. I have attempted a (very preliminary) survey of the 1640s from this perspective in Glenn Burgess, 'The Impact on Political Thought: Rhetorics for Troubled Times' in J. S. Morrill (ed.), *The Impact of the English Civil War* (London, 1991), chpt. IV.

34. For Lilburne's citations from Coke and various other legal-historical sources see D. B. Robertson, *The Religious Foundations of Leveller Democracy* (New York, 1951), pp. 126–32.

35. Andrew Sharpe, 'John Lilburne and the Long Parliament's *Book of*

Declarations: A Radical's Exploitation of the Words of Authorities', *History of Political Thought*, vol. 9 (1988), pp. 19–44.

36. John Lilburne, *The Legall Fundamentall Liberties of the People of England* (London, 1649), pp. 1–18.

37. John Lilburne, *The Free-Mans Freedome Vindicated* (London, 1646), p. 3.

38. E.g. John Lilburne, *An Anatomy of the Lords Tyranny* (London, 1646), pp. 5, 13. See also the attack on the Lord's imprisonment of Lilburne: *A Pearle in a Dounghill* (London, 1646) in A. L. Morton (ed.), *Freedom in Arms: A Selection of Leveller Writings* (London, 1975), p. 82. (On the authorship of this tract see Jack R. McMichael & Barbara Taft (eds), *The Writings of William Walwyn* (Athens GA, 1989), p. 529.)

39. Lilburne, *Legall Fundamentall Liberties*, p. 44.

40. On the roots of Lilburne's anti-Normanism see Andrew Sharp, 'John Lilburne's Discourse of Law', *Political Science*, vol. 40 (1988), p. 31. On the divergence of immemoriality and anti-Normanism note the neat historiographical survey of R. J. Smith, *The Gothic Bequest: Medieval Institutions in British Thought 1688–1863* (Cambridge, 1987), pp. 4–6.

41. See e.g. John Lilburne, *The Just Mans Justification* (London, 2nd ed., 1647), p. 14. Cf. the reading in Seaberg, 'The Norman Conquest and the Common Law', p. 795 which is unbearably strained: I can see no grounds for thinking that Lilburne meant the phrase 'the mainstreame of our Common Law' to refer, contrary to its more obvious literal meaning, only to procedural law. It is not hard to find other statements of Lilburne's anti-Normanism that do not limit the innovations of the Conquest to procedural, as opposed to substantive, law: e.g. John Lilburne, *Regall Tyrannie discovered* (London, 1647), p. 92: 'here you have the true story of the subversion of the ancient manner of Parliaments, and the ancient Lawes and Liberties of Government of this Kingdome, and a Law innovated, and introduced, flowing meerly from the will of a Bastard, Thief, Robber & tirant'.

42. This paragraph is indebted to Sharp, 'John Lilburne's Discourse of Law'.

43. John Lilburne, *Londons Liberty in Chains Discovered* (London, 1646), p. 41.

44. John Lilburne, *Strength out of Weaknesse* (London, 1649), p. 14.

45. Ibid..

46. Cf. John Lilburne, *Free-Mans Freedome*, pp. 11–12.

47. E.g. Lilburne, *Legall Fundamentall Liberties*, pp. 51–2.

48. Edward Hare, *St Edwards Ghost: Or, Anti-Normanisme* (London, 1647 – written 1642), pp. 14–16 (quotation from p. 16).

49. Ibid., pp. 17, 19.

50. On whom see Christopher Hill, *The World Turned Upside Down: Radical Ideas During the English Revolution* (Harmondsworth, 1975), pp. 272–6.

51. John Warr, *The Corruption and Deficiency of the Laws of England Soberly Discovered* (1649) in David Wootton (ed.), *Divine Right and Democracy:*

An Anthology of Political Writing in Stuart England (Harmondsworth, 1986), p. 152.

52.　Ibid., p. 153.

53.　Ibid., p. 153.

54.　Ibid., pp. 154–6.

55.　For pertinent discussions of the concept of radicalism see J. C. Davis, 'Radicalism in a Traditional Society: The Evaluation of Radical Thought in the English Commonwealth 1649–1660', *History of Political Thought*, vol. 3 (1982), pp. 193–213; Davis, 'Radical Lives', *Political Science*, vol. 37 (1985), pp. 166–72; and, for an attempt to expunge the term altogether, Conal Condren, 'Radicals, Conservatives and Moderates in Early Modern Political Thought: A Case of Sandwich Islands Syndrome?', *History of Political Thought*, vol. 10 (1989), pp. 525–42.

56.　Clarendon, *The History* in *The History of the Rebellion and Civil Wars in England . . . Also His Life Written by Himself* (Oxford, 1843), p. 267.

57.　These remarks summarise Richard Tuck, '"The Ancient Law of Freedom": John Selden and the Civil War' in John Morrill (ed.), *Reactions to the English Civil War 1642–1649* (London, 1982), chpt. 6.

58.　*Table Talk of John Selden* (ed. Sir Frederick Pollock) (London, 1927), p. 137. For a different reading of this passage see Tuck, '"Ancient Law of Freedom"', p. 154.

59.　Selden, *Table Talk*, p. 137 (see also pp. 36, 65–6, 69).

60.　Greenberg, 'The Confessor's Laws', p. 614, n. 1 argues that immemoriality was compatible with theories of original contract on the grounds that 'immemorial' meant only before the date of legal memory (3 September 1189). I know of almost no evidence for the *pre*-Civil-War period to indicate that immemorial was taken to mean anything other than of unknown origin. The 1189 date was a later development, and may help to explain how after 1660 ancient constitutionalism did become mingled with theories of original contract. But this development marked the *end* of the 'classic' phase of ancient constitutionalism and was not a characteristic of it. (See also C. C. Weston & J. R. Greenberg, *Subjects and Sovereigns: The Grand Controversy over Legal Sovereignty in Stuart England* (Cambridge, 1981), pp. 132–3: Weston and Greenberg cite in support of their contention Alan Wharam, 'The 1189 Rule: Fact, Fiction or Fraud?', *Anglo-American Law Review*, vol. I (1972), pp. 262–79, but this article actually demonstrates persuasively that it was not until the *late* seventeenth century at the earliest that immemorial came to mean only prior to 1189.)

61.　What follows is indebted to Greenberg, 'The Confessor's Laws', esp. pp. 621–3, 624–7, but my estimate of the significance and implications of these works differs from hers. Milton, whom Greenberg places in much the same category as Bacon and Sadler, seems to me to be primarily a rhetorical user of the language of ancient constitutionalism.

62.　*DNB*, under 'Selden, John'. It seems the claim was supported by Chief Justice John Vaughan, one of the executors of Selden's estate.

63. Nathaniel Bacon, *An Historical Discourse of the Uniformity of the Government of England. The First Part* (London, 1647), chpt. 4, esp. pp. 15, 16.
64. Ibid., chpt. 16, esp. pp. 48–9.
65. Ibid., p. 50.
66. Ibid., p. 111.
67. Ibid., sig. A4.
68. Ibid., p. 115.
69. Ibid., pp. 116–17.
70. E.g. John Sadler, *Rights of the Kingdom; Or, Customs of our Ancestours* (London, 1649), pp. 21–22.
71. Ibid., pp. 34ff.
72. E.g., ibid., pp. 56–7, 73–6.
73. J. G. A. Pocock, 'England' in Orest Ranum (ed.), *National Consciousness, History and Political Culture in Early-Modern Europe* (Baltimore, 1975), pp. 105–6, 106ff.; and J. G. A. Pocock, 'The History of British Political Thought: The Creation of a Center', *Journal of British Studies*, vol. 24 (1985), pp. 290–1. Also Pocock, *Machiavellian Moment*, pp. 340–1.
74. On precedent in English law see C. K. Allen, *Law in the Making*, (Oxford, 7th ed., 1964), pp. 187–235.
75. Ibid., pp. 71–9.
76. Sir John Fortescue, *De Laudibus Legum Anglie* (ed. S. B. Chrimes), (Cambridge, 1949), chpts. XV–XVII.
77. Antiquarianism can be seen as a product of humanism, a case most cogently argued in Joseph M. Levine, *Humanism and History: Origins of Modern English Historiography* (Ithaca NY, 1987), chpt. 3. Also Ferguson, *Clio Unbound*, a general study of the impact of the Renaissance on English views of the past, but N.B. the review by G. R. Elton, *History and Theory*, vol. 20 (1981), pp. 92–100.
78. On Verstegan see T. D. Kendrick, *British Antiquity* (New York, 1970), pp. 116–20; on Saxonism more generally Samuel Kliger, *The Goths in England: A Study in Seventeenth and Eighteenth Century Thought* (New York, 1972).
79. The material on which this rests has been discussed in the previous chapter; but note that Selden also discussed the Britons in his notes to Michael Drayton's *Poly-Olbion* (1613). Here Selden was circumspect in his disagreement with a popular myth, but the implications of his remarks were unmistakable. See Michael Drayton, *Poly-Olbion . . . Being the Fourth Volume of his Works* (ed. J. William Hebel) (Oxford, 1961), pp. viii–xiv, 21–6.
80. On which see Retha M. Warnicke, *William Lambarde: Elizabethan Antiquary 1536–1601* (London, 1973), pp. 22–6.
81. Almost certainly the debates on this subject were a crucial catalyst to the development of 'mature' ancient constitutionalism. There were genuine fears in the first decade of James I's reign that Union would mean the complete destruction of the common law, so an argument that could demonstrate its perfect utility in coping with England's political needs was a valuable weapon for those who wished to

oppose legal union of the two kingdoms. See, on this, Brian P. Levack, *The Formation of the British State: England, Scotland, and the Union 1603–1707* (Oxford, 1987), chpt. 3 (also Levack's other writings on the subject, referred to in ibid., p. 244). A general introduction to the Jacobean debates is Bruce Galloway, *The Union of England and Scotland 1603–1608* (Edinburgh, 1986); useful in suggesting the importance of the Union issue for early Jacobean politics is Conrad Russell, 'English Parliaments 1593–1606: One Epoch or Two?', in D. M. Dean & N. L. Jones (eds), *The Parliaments of Elizabethan England* (Oxford, 1990), chpt. 8.

82. Guy, *St German*, p. 19.
83. E.g. John Selden, *Jani Anglorum Facies Altera*, transl. by Redman Westcot in *Tracts Written by John Selden* (London, 1683), pp. 27–8; Sir Edward Coke, 'Of the King's Ecclesiastical Law' [Caudrey's Case], in *Fifth Part of the Reports* (1605) (and N.B. the reply of Robert Parsons, *An Answere to the Fifth Part of Reportes lately set forth by Sir Edward Cooke* (London?, 1606), esp. pp. 92–165.); and Nathaniel Bacon, *Historical Discourse*, pp. 3–5. Note also William Camden, *Britain* (transl. Philemon Holland) (London, 1637), pp. 63, 67–8.
84. See F. J. Levy *Tudor Historical Thought* (San Marino, Calif., 1967), chapt. III, 'The Reformation and English History Writing', esp. pp. 114–22 for Parker and the historical defence of the Elizabethan Settlement.
85. This is a strong theme of the discussion of the subject by Coke in Caudrey's Case, essentially an attempt to deny any ecclesiastical jurisdiction independent of the monarchy.
86. See the modern edition, with a useful introduction, John Jewel, *An Apology of the Church of England* (ed. J. E. Booty) (Charlottesville, 1963); for further discussion see J. E. Booty, *John Jewel as Apologist of the Church of England* (London, 1963).
87. Jewel, *Apology* (ed. Booty), p. 84; *The Works of John Jewel D.D.*, (ed. R. W. Jelf) (Oxford, 8 vols, 1848), vol. II, pp. 67ff., & vol. IV, pp. 162ff.
88. Jewel, *Apology* (ed. Booty), p. 101.
89. Thomas Bilson, *The True Difference between Christian Subjection and Unchristian Rebellion* (Oxford, 1585), pp. 515–7.
90. For pertinent discussion see Peter Lake, *Anglicans and Puritans? Presbyterianism and English Conformist Thought from Whitgift to Hooker*, (London, 1988), pp. 132–5; and William Lamont, 'The Rise and Fall of Bishop Bilson', *Journal of British Studies*, vol. 5 (1966), pp. 22–32.
91. For the latest word on whom see Jane Facey, 'John Foxe and the Defence of the Elizabethan Church', in Peter Lake & Maria Dowling (eds.), *Protestantism and the National Church in Sixteenth Century England* (London, 1987), chpt. 7.
92. John Aylmer, *An Harborowe for Faithfull and Trewe Subjectes* (Strasburg [London], 1559), sigs H3–H4.
93. Some aspects of this have been pulled together in Patrick Collinson, 'The Monarchical Republic of Queen Elizabeth I', *Bulletin of the John Rylands University Library*, vol. 69 (1986–7), pp. 394–424.

CHAPTER 4: SOME HISTORIOGRAPHICAL PERSPECTIVES

1. For some discussion of 'revisionism', and further references, see Glenn Burgess, 'On Revisionism: An Analysis of Early Stuart Historiography in the 1970s and 1980s', *Historical Journal*, vol. 33 (1990), pp. 609–27.
2. Margaret Judson, *The Crisis of the Constitution: An Essay in Constitutional and Political Thought in England 1603–1645* (New York, 1976; orig. ed. 1949); and J. W. Allen, *English Political Thought 1603–1660*, (London 2 vols planned but only one appeared, 1938) – the one published vol. covers the period 1603–44.
3. This sort of feeling comes through some of J. P. Sommerville's work. See especially his essay 'Ideology, Property and the Constitution', in Richard Cust and Ann Hughes (eds), *Conflict in Early Stuart England: Studies in Religion and Politics 1603–1642* (London, 1989), chpt. 2.
4. Conrad Russell, 'Parliamentary History in Perspective 1604–1629', *History*, vol. 61 (1976), p. 18. Since this chapter was completed a considerable body of new work from Professor Russell has appeared. Most important to the subject of this book are his remarks on Sommerville in Russell, *The Causes of the English Civil War* (Oxford, 1990), chpt. 6, which seem broadly compatible with the case argued here. See also Russell's collected essays, esp. the introduction which also includes comments on the Sommerville thesis, published as Russell, *Unrevolutionary England 1603–1642* (London, 1990).
5. The word 'opposition' is a dangerous one, of course, because it implies a fixed group of people who oppose government policy on all points, and who are not themselves members of government. In the seventeenth century 'opposition' to particular policies was frequently conducted by those highly placed in court or political circles, and was a highly fluid phenomenon. See Russell, *Unrevolutionary England*, p. xiii. Cf. Robert Zaller, 'The Concept of Opposition in Early Stuart England', *Albion*, vol. XII (1980), pp. 211–34.
6. The emphasis on consensus has been strong in the work of Mark Kishlansky, *The Rise of the New Model Army* (Cambridge, 1979), chpt. 1, esp. pp.11ff. (See also Kishlansky, 'The Emergence of Adversary Politics in the Long Parliament', *Journal of Modern History*, vol. 49 (1977), pp. 617–40; and Kishlansky, *Parliamentary Selection: Social and Political Choice in Early Modern England* (Cambridge, 1986)). Just as Kishlansky has rejected polarised models of politics, so Kevin Sharpe has rejected them for cultural history. He has instead advanced a model of a shared world-view put to varying uses, 'a commonwealth of meanings'. The emphasis on a shared set of values (a consensus culture) underlying very different views about what those values entailed, closely matches the model of consensual politics in Kishlansky's work. (See Kevin Sharpe, *Politics and Ideas in Early Stuart England* (London, 1989), esp. chpt. 1; also Sharpe, *Criticism and Compliment: The Politics of Literature in the England of Charles I* (Cambridge, 1987).)
7. J. G. A. Pocock, *The Ancient Constitution and the Feudal Law: A Study*

of *English Historical Thought in the Seventeenth Century – A Reissue with Retrospect* (Cambridge, 1987), p. 262.

CHAPTER 5: THE ELEMENTS OF CONSENSUS IN JACOBEAN ENGLAND

1. Cf. J. P. Sommerville, 'Richard Hooker, Hadrian Saravia, and the Advent of the Divine Right of Kings', *History of Political Thought*, vol. 4 (1983), pp. 229–245.
2. J. P. Sommerville, *Politics and Ideology in England 1603–1640* (London, 1986), chpts. 1–3.
3. For some discussion of traditions see Quentin Skinner, 'Meaning and Understanding in the History of Ideas' in James Tully (ed.), *Meaning and Context: Quentin Skinner and His Critics* (Cambridge, 1988); and John G. Gunnell, *Political Theory: Tradition and Interpretation* (Cambridge, Mass., 1979), chpt. III.
4. For a useful introduction to 'languages' of political thought see Anthony Pagden (ed.), *The Languages of Political Theory in Early-Modern Europe*, (Cambridge, 1987), esp. chpt. 1 by Pocock.
5. For introductions see particularly Wilfrid Prest (ed.), *The Professions in Early Modern England* (London, 1987); and Wilfrid Prest (ed.), *Lawyers in Early Modern Europe and America* (London, 1981). For a critical word on the concept of profession see Michael Hawkins, 'Ambiguity and Contradiction in "the Rise of Professionalism": The English Clergy, 1570–1730', in A. L. Beier, D. Cannadine & J. M. Rosenheim (eds), *The First Modern Society: Essays in English History in Honour of Lawrence Stone* (Cambridge, 1989), chpt. 7.
6. Wilfrid Prest, *The Inns of Court under Elizabeth I and the Early Stuarts 1590–1640* (London, 1972), p. 23.
7. Thomas Wilson, *The State of England, 1600* in Joan Thirsk & J. P. Cooper (eds), *Seventeenth Century Economic Documents* (Oxford, 1972), p. 756.
8. Prest, 'Lawyers', in Prest (ed.), *Professions in Early Modern England*, pp. 72–5.
9. Levack, 'The English Civilians, 1500–1750' in Prest (ed.), *Lawyers in Early Modern Europe and America*, pp. 108–12.
10. Compare the chapter on common lawyers with that on the civilians in ibid., chpts 2, 3 & 5.
11. For an elaboration of the points made in these two paragraphs see my article, 'Common Law and Political Theory in Early Stuart England', *Political Science*, vol. 40 (1988), pp. 4–17.
12. See, e.g. J. G. A. Pocock, 'The Commons Debates of 1628', *Journal of the History of Ideas*, vol. 39 (1978), pp. 329–34. Also Conrad Russell, *Parliaments and English Politics, 1621–1629* (Oxford, 1979), chpt. VI, pp. 349ff., 363ff.; and Stephen D. White, *Sir Edward Coke and the Grievances of the Commonwealth* (Manchester, 1979), chpts. 6 & 7.
13. There is a good discussion of ecclesiastical jurisdiction in the early-seventeenth century in Louis A. Knafla, *Law and Politics in Jacobean*

England: The Tracts of Lord Chancellor Ellesmere (Cambridge, 1977), chpt. VI, esp. pp. 137ff. See also G. R. Elton, *The Tudor Constitution* (Cambridge, 1972), pp. 214–16, 152–3. Now see also R. M. Helmholz, *Roman Canon Law in Reformation England* (Cambridge, 1990), esp. chpts. 2 & 5.

14. For its business see Reginal G. Marsden (ed.), *Select Pleas in the Court of Admiralty* (London, Selden Society, 1894), vol. I, pp. lxv–lxxi.

15. Levack, 'English Civilians' in Prest (ed.), *Lawyers in Early Modern Europe and America*, p. 116; and at greater length, for all matters of the employment of civilians, Brian P. Levack, *The Civil Lawyers in England, 1603–1641* (Oxford, 1973), chpt. I

16. E.g., George L. Mosse, *The Struggle for Sovereignty in England* (East Lansing, 1950), p. 4; Francis D. Wormuth, *The Royal Prerogative 1603–1649*, (Ithaca, 1939), pp. 5–6, 26–7; and (though he does not make this point explicitly), J. P. Cooper, 'Differences between English and Continental Government in the Early Seventeenth Century' in Cooper (ed. G. E. Aylmer & J. S. Morrill), *Land, Men and Beliefs: Studies in Early-Modern History*, (London, 1983), chpt. 5, esp. pp. 107–8.

17. Peter Stein, 'Sir Thomas Smith: Renaissance Civilian', in Stein, *The Character and Influence of the Roman Law: Historical Essays* (London, 1988), chpt. 13, p. 193.

18. See the English translation of Cowell's work, John Cowell, *The Institutes of the Lawes of England, Digested into the Method of the Civill or Imperiall Institutions* (London, 1651). On these writers see Richard J. Terill, 'The Application of the Comparative Method by English Civilians: The Case of William Fulbecke and Thomas Ridley', *Journal of Legal History*, vol. 2 (1981), pp. 169–185; Peter Stein, 'Continental influences on English Legal Thought, 1600–1900' in Stein, *Character and Influence*, chpt. 15; and Levack, *Civil Lawyers*, chpt. IV. Also C. P. Rodgers, 'Legal Humanism and English Law – The Contribution of the English Civilians', *The Irish Jurist*, vol. 14 new series (1984), pp. 115–36.

19. Note for example how the writers grouped by J. W. Allen into his chapter on 'Theories of the Constitution and of Sovereignty' in Allen, *A History of Political Thought in the Sixteenth Century* (London, rev. ed., 1960), Pt II, chpt. X, are writers with a civil law rather than a common law background.

20. This account of Bodin is based particularly on Quentin Skinner, *The Foundations of Modern Political Thought* (Cambridge, 2 vols, 1978), vol. II, pp. 287ff., read in the context provided by Donald R. Kelley, *Foundations of Modern Historical Scholarship: Language, Law and History in the French Renaissance* (New York, 1970); and Julian H. Franklin, *Jean Bodin and the Sixteenth-Century Revolution in the Methodology of Law and History* (New York, 1963).

21. Cf. Julian H. Franklin, *Jean Bodin and the Rise of Absolutist Theory*, (Cambridge, 1973), p. 93.

22. Levack, 'English Civilians', in Prest (ed), *Lawyers in Early Modern Europe and America*, p. 125; Levack, *Civil Lawyers*, chpt. III.

23.   'That which naturall reason doth constitute among all men, is observed by all alike, and termed the lawe of Nations': John Hayward, *An Answer to the First Part of a Certaine Conference.* (London, 1603), sig. A4. Hayward is quoting Gaius from *Digest,* I, l, 9.

24.   Ibid., A4–A4v.

25.   Ibid., A4v–Blv.

26.   Levack, *Civil Lawyers,* pp. 136–40 – this is true in particular of Fulbecke and of Cowell.

27.   Ibid., pp. 131–40; Levack, 'English Civilians', in Prest (ed.), *Lawyers in Early Modern Europe and America,* p. 125; Stein, 'Continental Influences' in Stein, *Character and Influence,* pp. 211ff.; and Peter Stein, *Regulae Iuris: From Juristic Rules to Legal Maxims* (Edinburgh, 1966), chpt. IX.

28.   Levack, *Civil Lawyers,* pp. 131–3; G. R. Elton, *Reform and Renewal: Thomas Cromwell and the Common Weal* (Cambridge, 1973), pp. 138ff. See Thomas Starkey, *A Dialogue between Pole and Lupset* (ed T. F. Mayer) (London, 1989), pp. 128–9.

29.   Cowell, *Institutes* (1651 trans.), sigs a1–a2v.

30.   See above, chpt. 2; Bacon, 'A Proposition to his Majesty . . . Touching the Compiling and Amendment of the Laws of England', in James Spedding, *The Letters and the Life of Francis Bacon,* vol. VI (London, 1872), pp. 65–70. For the context of this document, Bacon's feud with Coke, see briefly Joel Epstein, *Francis Bacon: a Political Biography* (Athens, Ohio, 1977), pp. 109–15.

31.   Calybute Downing, *A Discourse of the State Ecclesiasticall of this Kingdome, in relation to the Civill* (Oxford, 1632), p. 31.

32.   J. F. Larkin & P. L. Hughes (eds), *Stuart Royal Proclamations, vol. I: Royal Proclamations of King James I, 1603–1625* (Oxford, 1973), pp. 1, 18.

33.   Elton, *Tudor Constitution,* p. 332; and Elton, *England Under the Tudors* (London 2nd ed., 1974), pp. 160ff. Also Walter Ullmann, '"This Realm of England is an Empire"', *Journal of Ecclesiastical History,* vol. 30 (1979), pp. 175–203; and the general discussion in John Guy, *Tudor England,* (Oxford, 1988), pp. 369–78.

34.   Larkin & Hughes (eds), *Stuart Royal Proclamations,* vol. I, p. 95. See also Brian P. Levack, *The Formation of the British State: England, Scotland, and the Union 1603–1707* (Oxford, 1987), pp. 51–2; & p. 2, n. 4. I am not convinced that the two meanings of 'imperial' discussed by Levack are quite as sharply distinguished as he implies.

35.   *State Trials,* vol. II, col. 589; also cols 633, 641 (Coke's Report); and 576 (Moore's Report). The maxim reads: 'cum duo jura concurrunt in una persona, aeguum est ac si essert in diversis'. Bruce Galloway, *The Union of England and Scotland 1603–1608* (Edinburgh, 1986), p. 151. Note Wheeler's remark that the anti-Unionist arguments were 'relying heavily on civil law maxims': Harvey Wheeler, 'Calvin's Case (1608) and the McIlwain-Schuyler Debate', *American Historical Review,* vol. 61 (1956), p. 589.

36.   Doddridge's 'A Brief Consideration of the Union of two Kingdoms'

is reprinted in Bruce R Galloway & Brian P. Levack (eds), *The Jacobean Union: Six Tracts of 1604* (Edinburgh, 1985).

37. Levack, *Formation of the British State*, pp. 73, 76–85. See also pp. 88ff. for some complications and complexities.

38. Hans S. Pawlisch, *Sir John Davies and the Conquest of Ireland: A Study in Legal Imperialism* (Cambridge, 1985), pp. 9–10.

39. Hans S. Pawlisch, 'Sir John Davies, the Ancient Constitution, and Civil Law', *Historical Journal*, vol. 23 (1980), p. 696; also in Pawlisch, *Sir John Davies and the Conquest of Ireland*, p. 168.

40. *State Trials*, vol. II, cols 578, 580.

41. Ibid., col. 577.

42. Ibid., col. 652.

43. Ibid., cols 613, 629.

44. Ibid., cols 629–633.

45. Galloway, *Union of England and Scotland*, p. 157.

46. For introductions see Charles H. McIlwain, 'Introduction' to *The Political Works of James I* (Cambridge, Mass., 1918), pp. xxxv–lxxx; J. P. Sommerville, *Politics and Ideology*, chpt. 6, esp. pp. 195–99, 203–208; and Peter Milward, *Religious Controversies of the Jacobean Age: A Survey of Printed Sources* (London, 1978), chpt. 3, esp. pp. 86–119, 128–131.

47. The text of the oath is in J. R. Tanner, *Constitutional Documents of the Reign of James I, 1603–1625* (Cambridge, 1930, reprinted 1961), pp. 90–1. The 1610 Act extending its scope is in ibid., pp. 105ff. See also Proclamations of 29 April 1608 and 2 June 1610 in Larkin & Hughes (eds), *Stuart Royal Proclamations*, vol. I, pp. 184–5, 245–50.

48. Though civil law references could crop up in it also – see, e.g. James I, *A Premonition* (1609) in McIlwain (ed.), *Political Works of James I*, p. 121.

49. For an introduction to the sorts of theories alluded to here see Ewart Lewis, *Medieval Political Ideas* (London, 2 vols, 1954), vol. II, chpts VII & VIII; Walter Ullmann, *Principles of Government and Politics in the Middle Ages* (London, 1961), Part II; and J. H. Burns (ed.), *The Cambridge History of Medieval Political Thought c.350–c.1450* (Cambridge, 1988), chpts 14–16.

50. The above is based on Rosemary O'Day, 'The Anatomy of a Profession: the Clergy of the Church of England' in Prest (ed.), *Professions in Early Modern England*, chpt. 2.

51. *Certaine Sermons or Homilies appointed to be read in Churches*, (London, 1623), title page. I have used in all citations of this the facsimile reprint: Mary Ellen Rickey & Thomas B. Stroup (eds), *Certaine Sermons or Homilies Appointed to be Read in Churches in the Time of Queen Elizabeth I (1547–1571): A Facsimile Reproduction of the Edition of 1623*, (Gainesville, Florida, 1968).

52. 'An Exhortation concerning good Order, and obedience to Rulers and Magistrates', *Certaine Sermons*, p. 69.

53. Ibid., pp. 70–1.

54. Ibid., p. 72.

55. Ibid., p. 75 (misnumbered 69). These points are elaborated at con-

siderable length in 'An Homilie against Disobedience and Wilfull Rebellion' in *The Second Tome of Homilies* (London, 1623), pp. 275–320, also reprinted in facsimile in Rickey & Stroup, *Certaine Sermons or Homilies.*

56.   Lancelot Andrewes, 'A sermon preached before the kings Majestie at Holdenbie, on the V. of August, A.D. MDCX.', in Andrewes, *XCVI Sermons* (London, 1629, 2nd ed., 1631), pp. 795–7.
57.   Ibid., p. 804.
58.   Samuel Ward, *Jethro's Justice of Peace. A Sermon Preached at a generall Assises held at Bury St Edmunds, for the Countie of Suffolke* (London, 1621), p. 34.
59.   Thomas Scot, *God and the King, in a sermon preached at the Assises holden at Bury S. Edmonds, June 13 1631* (Cambridge, 1633), p. 1.
60.   Edward Reynolds, *The Shieldes of the Earth. A Sermon preached . . . at the Assizes holden at North-hampton: February 25 1634* (London, 1636), pp. 6, 20.
61.   John White, *A Sermon Preached at Dorchester in the County of Dorcet, at the Generall assizes held the 7 of March, 1632* (London, 1648), pp. 3, 10.
62.   W. H. Greenleaf, *Order, Empiricism and Politics: Two Traditions of English Political Thought 1500–1700* (Westport, CT, 1980), p. 53.
63.   Ibid., p. 52. The position I allude to here is that of Greenleaf (esp. chpt. II). But it should be noted that even he found a puzzle in this: Aquinas had used order theory for constitutionalist purposes, so how could the same theory by used for the opposite ends in the seventeenth century? See W. H. Greenleaf, 'The Thomasian Tradition and the Theory of Absolute Monarchy', *English Historical Review*, vol. 79 (1964), pp. 747–60.
64.   For this reading of the political implications of order theory see James Daly, 'Cosmic Harmony and Political Thinking in Early Stuart England', *Transactions of the American Philosophical Society*, vol. 69, no. 7 (1979), esp. pp. 21–31; and Francis Oakley, *Omnipotence, Order and Covenant: An Excursion in the History of Ideas from Abelard to Leibniz* (Ithaca, 1984), chpt. 4.
65.   The standard discussion is Gordon Schochet, *Patriarchalism in Political Thought: The Authoritarian Family and Political Speculation and Attitudes, especially in Seventeenth-Century England* (Oxford, 1975). See also: Schochet, 'Patriarchalism, Politics and Mass Attitudes in Stuart England', *Historical Journal*, vol. 12 (1969), pp. 413–41; R. W. K. Hinton, 'Husbands, Fathers and Conquerors', *Political Studies*, vol. 15 (1967), pp. 291–300, and vol. 16 (1968), pp. 55–67; J. P. Sommerville, 'From Suarez to Filmer: A Reappraisal', *Historical Journal*, vol. 25 (1982), pp. 525–40; and Sommerville, *Politics and Ideology*, pp. 27–34.
66.   Edward Forsett, *A Defence of the Right of Kings* (London, 1624), p. 23. Forsett's work was, in fact, a contribution to the Oath of Allegiance controversy. Forsett's most famous work is also based on a complex analogical argument (the comparison is between natural and political bodies), but it is not primarily a work of patriarchal

theory: Edward Forsett, *A Comparative Discourse of the Bodies Natural and Politique* (London, 1606).

67. Laslett dated the composition of *Patriarcha* to around 1640, but more recently a variety of different estimates has been given. Richard Tuck has convincingly argued for the earlier date. See: Peter Laslett (ed.) *Patriarcha and Other Political Works of Sir Robert Filmer* (Oxford, 1949), p. 3; John M. Wallace, 'The Date of Sir Robert Filmer's *Patriarcha*', *Historical Journal*, vol. 23 (1980), pp. 155–65; and Richard Tuck, 'A New Date for Filmer's *Patriarcha*', *Historical Journal*, vol. 29 (1986), pp. 183–86. The matter is now authoritatively surveyed in a new edition of Filmer's works, Sir Robert Filmer, *Patriarcha and Other Writings* (ed. J. P. Sommerville) (Cambridge, 1991), pp. xxxii–xxxiv, which supports Tuck in general.

68. Filmer in Laslett (ed.), *Patriarcha and Other Politicial Works*, pp. 60–1.

69. For fuller discussion see Schochet, *Patriarchalism*, chpt. VIII; and James Daly, *Sir Robert Filmer and English Political Thought* (Toronto, 1979), chpt. 3.

70. Cf. Sommerville, 'From Suarez to Filmer', pp. 539–40.

71. *The Convocation Book of M DC VI., commonly called Bishop Overall's Convocation Book* (Oxford, 1844), pp. 2–3.

72. Ibid., p. 7 – also p. 8.

73. Ibid., Canon 6, p. 8.

74. Larkin & Hughes (eds), *Stuart Royal Proclamations*, vol. I, pp. 355–56.

75. Richard Mocket, *God and the King: or, A Dialogue shewing that our Soveraigne Lord King James, being immediate under God within his Dominions, Doth rightfully claime whatsoever is required by the Oath of Allegeance* (London, 1615), p. 6.

76. Ibid., p. 3.

77. Ibid., p. 31.

78. For an overview of some of this see R. Malcolm Smuts, *Court Culture and the Origins of a Royalist Tradition in Early Stuart England* (Philadelphia, 1987), Pt. I ('The Cults of Monarchy and the Wars of Religion').

79. Peter Lake, 'Constitutional Consensus and Puritan Opposition in the 1620s: Thomas Scott and the Spanish Match', *Historical Journal*, vol. 25 (1982), p. 807.

80. Ibid., p. 822.

81. Thomas Scott, *The High-Waies of God and the King . . . Delivered in two Sermons preached at Thetford in Norfolke, Anno 1620* (London, 1623), p. 67.

82. Ibid., p. 68.

83. Ibid., pp. 70–1.

84. Ibid., pp. 69–70, 67–8, 86–8.

85. The most notable exception was John Knight, imprisoned in 1622 for a sermon on resistance: *Calendar of State Papers Domestic, 1619–23*, pp. 379, 380, 386, 400. A letter was sent to the Universities condemning Knight – *Acts of the Privy Council, 1621–23*, p. 237. See also Thomas Cogswell, *The Blessed Revolution: English Politics and the Coming of War 1621–1624* (Cambridge, 1989), p. 31.

CHAPTER 6: MAKING CONSENSUS WORK

1. I have adopted this term from Conal Condren, *George Lawson's Politica and the English Revolution* (Cambridge, 1989), where the notion of duplexity is used to demonstrate the ambiguity of Lawson's views on resistance: men, as subjects, must obey; men, as citizens, might be able to resist – see pp. 108–16, 71–4. Condren also uses the concept of duplexity to analyse further terms in Lawson's political vocabulary – e.g. real sovereignty/personal sovereignty, rebellion/resistance, community/polity.

2. The crucial modern introduction to this theme is Francis Oakley, 'Jacobean Political Theology: The Absolute and Ordinary Powers of the King', *Journal of the History of Ideas*, vol. 29 (1968), pp. 323–46. Also Oakley, 'The "Hidden" and "Revealed" Wills of James I: More Jacobean Theology', *Studia Gratiana*, vol. 41 (1972), pp. 365–75; Oakley, *Omnipotence, Covenant, and Order* (Ithaca, 1984). In addition, Francis Wormuth, *The Royal Prerogative 1603–1649* (Ithaca, 1939), chpt. IV, esp. pp. 54ff.

3. G. W. Prothero (ed.), *Select Statues and other Constitutional Documents Illustrative of the Reigns of Elizabeth and James I* (Oxford, 4th ed., 1913), p. 341; *State Trials*, vol. II, col. 389.

4. J. P. Cooper (ed.), *Wentworth Papers 1597–1628* (London, Camden 4th Series, vol. 12, 1973), p. 74. Also Maija Jansson, *Proceedings in Parliament 1614 (House of Commons)* (Philadelphia, 1988), pp. 146–7, 156.

5. Cooper (ed.), *Wentworth Papers*, p. 67. Also Jansson, *Proceedings in . . . 1614*, p. 94.

6. S. R. Gardiner, *History of England from the Accession of James I to the Outbreak of the Civil War* (London, 4th ed., 1895), vol. II, p. 6. Gardiner also saw 1610 as the beginning of a struggle between the king and commons that continued to 1689 (ibid., p. 110).

7. S. R. Gardiner (ed.), *Parliamentary Debates in 1610* (London, Camden First Series, vol. 81, 1862), p. 41.

8. Prothero, *Statues and other Constitutional Documents*, p. 342; *State Trials*, II, col. 390.

9. Gardiner, *Parliamentary Debates in 1610*, p. 87.

10. Ibid., pp. 66, 71; *State Trials*, II, col. 395.

11. Gardiner, *Parliamentary Debates in 1610*, p. 72. There is a much fuller version of Hedley's speech in E. R. Foster (ed.), *Proceedings in Parliament 1610* (New Haven, 2 vols, 1966), vol. II, pp. 170–97. This reveals Hedley's awareness of the fact that the king possessed absolute powers outside of the law, but that these could not be used against the property rights of his subjects. The crucial step in the argument was the conclusion that ports, and thus impositions, lay within the jurisdiction of the common law and not outside it. See esp. pp. 183, 185, 188–9, 191, 194–5, 197. Hedley condemned the idea 'of an absolute power of the king and an unlimited or transcendent prerogative' only in the sense of a general power above law, not in the sense of some absolute prerogatives outside the law. The whole is a classic example of common law argumentation.

12. Gardiner, *Parliamentary Debates in 1610*, p. 89.
13. *State Trials*, II, col. 413; also Gardiner, *Parliamentary Debates in 1610*, pp. 79–80.
14. *State Trials*, II, cols 414–16.
15. Gardiner, *Parliamentary Debates in 1610*, pp. 112–115.
16. *State Trials*, II, col. 482.
17. Ibid., col. 483.
18. Gardiner, *Parliamentary Debates in 1610*, p. 93.
19. See for example the message from the king on 21 May 1610, where he promised to co-operate with parliament in the matter (Foster (ed.), *Proceedings in Parliament 1610*, I, pp. 88–9), and compare his statement of 21 November (ibid., II, pp. 340–1). Clearly James's willingness to compromise was always moderated by worry about his income and about insults to his honour.
20. J. P. Sommerville, *Politics and Ideology in England 1603–1640*, (London, 1986), pp. 37–8, also 162–3.
21. Sir John Davies, *The Question concerning Impositions, Tonnage, Poundage, Prizage, Customs, &c.* (London, 1656), p. 148.
22. Ibid., p. 30.
23. Ibid., p. 31.
24. Ibid., pp. 31–2.
25. Ibid., chpts II–VI.
26. Ibid., pp. 2–3.
27. Ibid., pp. 4–5, 8.
28. Ibid., pp. 17, 21, 23–4.
29. Ibid., pp. 27–8.
30. For a variety of opinions see Wormuth, *The Royal Prerogative*, pp. 15–16, 91–2; G. L. Mosse, *The Struggle for Sovereignty in England* (East Lansing, 1950), pp. 57–74; J. W. Allen, *English Political Thought 1603–1660*, vol. I (1603–1644) (London, 1938) pp. 4–6; W. H. Greenleaf, *Order, Empiricism and Politics: Two Traditions of English Political Thought 1500–1700* (Westport CT, 1980), pp. 60–3; Sommerville, *Politics and Ideology*, pp. 132–4. Wormuth is most inclined to recognise the conciliatory nature of James's speech; Mosse largely ignores it (significantly for it fits ill with his theme that James's concessions were purely verbal); Allen is bewildered; Greenleaf and Sommerville leave little room for seeing the speech as a serious attempt to mollify James's critics.
31. John Moore to Sir Ralph Winwood, quoted in Wallace Notestein, *The House of Commons 1604–1610* (New Haven, 1971), p. 282.
32. Cf. Sommerville, *Politics and Ideology*, pp. 132–3.
33. John Locke, *Two Treatises of Government* (ed. Peter Laslett), (Cambridge, 2nd ed., 1970), II, para. 200, pp. 417–8. N.B. Laslett's comment on the passage, which indictes that Locke used the passage from James I because it was still current in the debates of the Exclusion crisis period.
34. James I, 'A Speech to the Lords and Commons of the Parliament at White-hall, on Wednesday the XXI. of March. Anno 1609 [1610]', in C. H. McIlwain (ed.), *The Political Works of James I* (Cambridge, Mass.,

1918), pp. 306–7.

35.   Cobbett's *Parliamentary History* (London, 36 vols, 1806–20), vol. I, col. 1073; McIlwain (ed.), *Political Works of James I*, pp. 292–3, and contrast James's own explication of his intention in this speech, *Parliamentary History*, I, cols 1115–1119. Also B. P. Levack, *The Formation of the British State: England, Scotland, and the Union 1603–1707* (Oxford, 1987), pp. 71–2 & chpt. 3 generally; and B. Galloway, *The Union of England and Scotland 1603–1608* (Edinburgh, 1986), p. 165.

36.   There is an excellent account in Sommerville, *Politics and Ideology*, pp. 121–7. Also S. B. Chrimes, 'The Constitutional Ideas of Dr. John Cowell', *English Historical Review*, vol. 64 (1949), pp. 461–487; and Notestein, *House of Commons 1604–1610*, pp. 293–7.

37.   Chrimes, 'Constitutional Ideas of Dr. John Cowell', pp. 466–7.

38.   This was the opinion of Geoffrey Elton, 'The Rule of Law in Sixteenth Century England', in G. R. Elton, *Studies in Tudor and Stuart Politics and Government: Papers and Reviews 1946–1972* (Cambridge, 2 vols, 1974), vol. I, pp. 268–9. See the comment on this in Sommerville, *Politics and Ideology*, p. 125.

39.   Elton, 'Rule of Law' in *Studies*, I, pp. 265, 268.

40.   John Cowell, *The Interpreter: or Booke Containing the Signification of Words* (Cambridge, 1607), sigs Rrr 1–Rrr IV, Pp4V-Qqlv, Ddd3–Eee1, Aaa3–Aaa4. Key extracts reprinted in Chrimes, 'Constitutional Ideas of Dr. John Cowell', pp. 483–87.

41.   Cowell, *The Interpreter*, sig. Qq1.

42.   Ibid..

43.   Ibid., sigs Ddd3–Ddd3v.

44.   Gardiner, *Parliamentary Debates in 1610*, p. 23.

45.   J. F. Larkin & P.L. Hughes (eds), *Stuart Royal Proclamations, vol. I: Royal Proclamations of King James I, 1603–1625*, pp. 243–5.

46.   This is true of the accounts referred to above; but there are exceptions: e.g. Gardiner, *History of England*, vol. II, pp. 66–68. The starkest interpretation of James's motives as being less than straightforward is Mosse, *Struggle for Sovereignty*, p. 66.

47.   Useful here is the careful examination of the seventeenth century usages of the term 'absolute' in James Daly, 'The Idea of Absolute Monarchy in Seventeenth-Century England', *Historical Journal*, vol. 21 (1978), pp. 227–50. Daly demonstrates that before the 1640s the English monarchy was considered absolute in the sense of being irresistible and possessing unrestrained power in certain spheres, but not in the sense of having a general power to break the law. All were careful to avoid portraying the absolute monarchy of England in terms that would make it an *arbitrary* monarchy.

48.   Gardiner, *Parliamentary Debates in 1610*, p. 24.

49.   Ibid..

50.   McIlwain (ed.), *Political Works of James I*, p. 311.

51.   Elsewhere he remarked that in England 'fundamental law' was used 'of their Common Law' (ibid., p. 300), while in the 1610 speech he had already said (rather more ambiguously) that though he thought civil law had some role in England, he was 'reserving

ever to the Common Law to meddle with the fundamentall Lawes of this Kingdome' (ibid., p. 311).

52. Cf. *The Priviledge and Practice of Parliaments in England* (London, 1628), p. 40: 'And it is set downe for a rule; That if a King have a Kingdome by discent there, seeing by the Law of that Kingdome he doth inherit that Kingdome, He cannot change those Lawes of himselfe, without consent of Parliament'. (Also pp. 40–2 for a Fortescuean discussion of the absolute powers of the English king, which implied that kings were not always bound to follow the law; yet, since they ruled politically as well as regally, they could not *alter* the law without consent.) It is perhaps a sign of the changes in the political atmosphere by 1628 that this tract was given a substantial reply, 'A True Presentation of Forepast Parliaments', copies in British Library, Lansdowne MS 213 & Stowe MS 331. This aroused the interest of Secretary Windebank: S.P. 16/233/51; *Calendar of State Papers Domestic, 1631–33*, pp. 565–56.

53. McIlwain (ed.), *Political Works of James I*, p. 311.
54. Ibid., p. 310.
55. Ibid., p. 307.
56. Ibid., p. 309.
57. Ibid., p. 310.
58. Ibid., p. 311 (stress added).
59. Larkin & Hughes (eds), *Stuart Royal Proclamations*, vol. I, p. 243.
60. Ibid..
61. Ibid., pp. 495–6, 519–21.
62. Thomas Fuller, *The Church History of Britain* (ed. J. S. Brewer), (Oxford, 1845), vol. V, p. 556.
63. This is the thesis of Francis Oakley, developed most fully in his *Omnipotence, Order and Covenant*.
64. Forsett, *Comparative Discourse of the Bodies Natural and Politique*, (London, 1606), p. 20.
65. Ibid., p. 21.
66. *State Trials*, II, col. 482.
67. *Parliamentary History*, I, col. 1193.
68. Francis Bacon, 'Cases of the King's Prerogative' in *The Works of Francis Bacon* (ed. James Spedding, Robert Leslie Ellis, and Douglas Denon Heath), vol. VII (Literary and Professional Works, vol. II) (London, 1859), pp. 776–7.
69. Frank Smith Fussner, 'William Camden's "Discourse Concerning the Prerogative of the Crown"', *Proceedings of the American Philosophical Society*, vol. 101 (1957), p. 206.
70. Ibid., p. 210.
71. Ibid., pp. 211–12, 210.
72. Ibid., pp. 210–11.
73. Camden alludes to this view only in passing: 'Because they are called Gods will they think themselves so in all points of power over their subjects?', ibid., p. 209.
74. Sir Thomas Egerton, Lord Chancellor Ellesmere, 'A Coppie of a Wrytten Discourse by the Lord Chauncellor Elsemore concerning

the Royall Prerogative (c.1604)', in L. Knafla, *Law and Politics in Jacobean England: The Tracts of Lord Chancellor Ellesmere* (Cambridge, 1977), p. 197.

75. Ibid., p. 198.

76. I.e., the abortive canons now known as *The Convocation Book of MDCVI, Commonly Called Bishop Overall's Convocation Book* (briefly discussed in the previous chapter). Note that James refused to authorise these Canons because (he said) they argued 'that even tyranny is God's authority, and should be reverenced as such', and because they 'dipped too deep into what all kings reserve among the *arcana imperii*' (p. 8). Cf. Gardiner, *History of England*, vol. I, pp. 289–91, clearly somewhat bemused by the whole episode.

77. Fully discussed, especially with regard to medieval political thought, in Ernst Kantorowicz, *The King's Two Bodies: A Study in Medieval Political Theology* (Princeton, NJ, 1957). There is material on early modern England on pp. 7–41 which clearly demonstrates the use of this language in sixteenth and seventeenth century writings.

78. Sir John Fortescue, *De Laudibus Legum Anglie* (ed. S. B. Chrimes), (Cambridge, 1949), pp. 24–33; Fortescue, *The Governance of England: Otherwise called, The Difference between an Absolute and a Limited Monarchy* (ed. Charles Plummer) (Oxford, 1885, repr. 1926), pp. 109–10, *et seq.* For discussion S. B. Chrimes, *English Constitutional Ideas in the Fifteenth Century* (Cambridge, 1936), esp. pp. 309–24; and J. H. Burns, 'Fortescue and the Political Theory of *Dominium*', *Historical Journal*, vol. 28 (1985), pp. 777–97.

79. C. H. McIlwain, *Constitutionalism Ancient and Modern* (Ithaca, NY, 1947), p. 88.

80. Ibid., pp. 77–9.

81. Ibid., pp. 80–1.

82. Contrast his earlier interpretation in C. H. McIlwain, *The Growth of Political Thought in the West: From the Greeks to the End of the Middle Ages*, (London, 1932), pp. 354–63.

83. See particularly, Brian Tierney, 'Bracton on Government', *Speculum*, vol. 38 (1963), pp. 295–317.

84. Most generally, J. G. A. Pocock, *The Machiavellian Moment: Florentine Political Thought and the Atlantic Republican Tradition* (Princeton, NJ, 1975), pp. 19–30.

85. W. S. Holdsworth, 'The Prerogative in the Sixteenth Century', *Columbia Law Review*, vol. 21 (1921), pp. 554–71, esp. pp. 556–7. See also the largely identical account in W. S. Holdsworth, *A History of English Law* (London, 16 vols, 1903–66), vol. IV, pp. 190ff. (Holdsworth thought the absolute/ordinary distinction derived from discussions of the jurisdiction of the Lord Chancellor (pp. 557, 561) and on this needs to be corrected by the works of Oakley cited above, esp. 'Jacobean Political Theology', pp. 326–28, *et seq.*).

86. Cf. Knafla's remarks in his *Law and Politics in Jacobean England*, pp. 70–1.

87. For uses of Fortescue see Caroline J. Skeel, 'The Influence of the Writings of Sir John Fortescue', *Transactions of the Royal Historical*

Society, 3rd series, vol. 10 (1916), pp. 77–114; for the king's two
bodies, Kantorowicz, The King's Two Bodies, pp. 7–23.
88. Sir John Elliott, The Monarchie of Man (ed. Alexander B. Grosart),
(n.p., 2 vols, 1879), vol. II, pp. 39, 44.
89. Ibid., pp. 39, 64.
90. Ibid., pp. 69–72, 81.
91. McIlwain, Constitutionalism, chpt. VI.
92. Pocock, Ancient Constitution, p. 265.
93. Ibid., pp. 283–5; see the interesting reading of Selden in this context,
pp. 286–7.
94. McIlwain (ed.), Political Works of James I, p. 309.
95. See especially David S. Berkowitz, 'Reason of State in England
and the Petition of Right, 1603–1629', in Roman Schnur (ed.),
Staatsräson: Studien zur Geschichte eines politischen Begriffs (Berlin,
1985), pp. 165–212; and Brian P. Levack, 'Law and Ideology: The
Civil Law and Theories of Absolutism in Elizabethan and Jacobean
England', in Heather Dubrow & Richard Strier (eds), The Historical
Renaissance: New Essays on Tudor and Stuart Literature and Culture
(Chicago, 1988), pp. 220–41. Also, but with less focus on the
legal doctrines of prerogative, Sommerville, Politics and Ideology,
pp. 39–46; and R. Eccleshall, Order and Reason in Politics (Oxford,
1978), pp. 76–96.
96. Levack, 'Law and Ideology', pp. 232–3; Berkowitz, 'Reason of State',
p. 175.
97. See esp. Berkowitz, 'Reason of State', p. 176; and Levack, 'Law and
Ideology', pp. 234ff.
98. Fortescue, Governance of England (ed. Plummer), pp. 111, 110.
99. Fortescue, De Laudibus Legum Anglie (ed. Chrimes), pp. 24–7;
Chrimes, English Constitutional Ideas, pp. 310–11; Berkowitz, 'Reason
of State', p. 170.
100. Sir William Staunford, An Expocision of the Kinges Prerogative, (London, 1567), fol. 5; also fol. 85 for acknowledgement of the incom-
pleteness. Cf. G. R. Elton, The Tudor Constitution (Cambridge, 1960),
pp. 17–19.
101. Cf. Franklin Le Van Baumer, The Early Tudor Theory of Kingship
(New Haven, 1940), pp. 184–5; and chpt. V passim. At times
Baumer seems to confuse the issue (particularly, perhaps, with
his occasional remarks on the political implications of divine-right
theory), but he is surely right to insist that though the king had
certain discretionary rights he did not have a general power outside
and above the law.
102. Levack, 'Law and Ideology', pp. 234–5. See Bacon, 'Cases of the
King's Prerogative', in Works (ed. Spedding, Ellis & Heath), vol. VII,
pp. 776–77.
103. A full bibliography on these themes would be enormous. Perhaps
the easiest (though not always the most reliable) way of getting a
sense of the role these themes have played in recent historiography is
through summaries of them by their critics. For example, the editors'
introduction to R. Cust & A. Hughes (eds), Conflict in Early Stuart

England (London, 1989); Peter Lake, 'The Collection of Ship Money in Cheshire during the Sixteen-Thirties: a Case Study of Relations between Central and Local Government', *Northern History*, vol. 17 (1981), pp. 44–71; and Derek Hirst, 'The Place of Principle', *Past and Present*, no. 92 (1981), pp. 79–99.

104. I have stressed this factor more heavily in Burgess, 'Common Law and Political Theory in Early Stuart England', *Political Science*, vol. 40 (1988), pp. 4–17.

105. Thomas Cogswell, 'The Politics of Propaganda: Charles I and the People in the 1620s, *Journal of British Studies*, vol. 29 (1990), p. 190.

106. For an overview of this material see Richard Cust, 'News and Politics in Early Seventeenth-Century England', *Past and Present*, no. 112 (1986), pp. 60–90.

107. The practical political effect of puritanism was the result, in large part, of Apocalyptic anti-Catholicism. One scholar has in fact suggested that puritanism was really just anti-Catholicism by another name [Michael Finlayson, *Historians, Puritanism and the English Revolution: The Religious Factor in English Politics before and after the Interregnum* (Toronto, 1983), esp. chpt. 4], a claim that is probably just a bit too simple. Finlayson's detailed argumentation remains rewarding even where it is not convincing.

108. Cust & Hughes, *Conflict in Early Stuart England*, pp. 21ff.; K. Sharpe, *Politics and Ideas in Early Stuart England* (London, 1989), pp. 30–1.

109. This, of course, is a dramatic oversimplification of Whig historiography. Even the most extreme of Whig historians was capable of expressing some doubts about the simple equation of the Puritans and the Parliamentary opposition: see Williams M. Mitchell, *The Rise of the Revolutionary Party in the English House of Commons 1603–1629* (New York, 1957; reprinted Westport, CT, 1975), p. xi.

110. The key to this was 'anti-popery': the best introduction to the subject, and an up-to-date source of further references is Peter Lake, 'Anti-popery: the Structure of a Prejudice' in Cust & Hughes, *Conflict in Early Stuart England*, chpt. 3. The basic position that is being put forward here is also much indebted to the argument of William Lamont, *Godly Rule: Politics and Religion 1603–60* (London, 1969). I remain convinced that the history of English political conflict throughout the period 1603–1660 is best written, not in the terms of anti-authoritarianism, but in terms of the search for an authority that would faithfully serve God's purposes. See also my review article, 'Revisionism, Politics and Political Ideas in Early Stuart England', *Historical Journal*, vol. 34 (1991), pp. 465–78.

111. A thesis most closely identified with C. Russell, *Parliaments and English Politics 1621–1629* (Oxford, 1979), esp. pp. 70–84.

112. See e.g. P. Lake 'Constitutional Consensus and Puritan Opposition in the 1620s: Thomas Scott and the Spanish Match', *Historical Journal*, vol. 25 (1982), pp. 805–25; T. Cogswell, *The Blessed Revolution: English Politics and the Coming of War 1621–1624* (Cambridge, 1989); Cust & Hughes, *Conflict in Early Stuart England*; Richard Cust, *The Forced Loan and English Politics 1626–1628* (Oxford, 1987), esp. chpt. 3;

and L. J. Reeve, *Charles I and the Road to Personal Rule* (Cambridge, 1989).

113. Cf. some apposite remarks in Conrad Russell, 'The Foreign Policy Debate in the House of Commons in 1621', Russell, *Unrevolutionary England, 1603–1642* (London, 1990), chpt. 3.

114. A Jacobean example, difficult to discuss in detail since the sermon has not survived, is the preaching of Samuel Harsnett, Bishop of Chichester in 1610. It raised some fears in the Commons (see Foster (ed.), *Proceedings in Parliament 1610*, vol. II, p. 328). According to Abbot, writing in 1627 in the midst of the furore over his refusal to license Sibthorpe's sermon for publication, it was Harsnett's sermon that provided the immediate occasion for James I's 21 March speech: J. Rushworth, *Historical Collections* (London, 8 vols, 1659–1721), vol. I, p. 442; *State Trials*, vol. II, col. 1463. James commented very interestingly on the sermon in 1610, McIlwain (ed.), *Political Works of James I*, p. 308.

115. There is a good account of the facts of the matter in Sommerville, *Politics and Ideology*, pp. 127–31.

116. Ibid., p. 128; Cust, *Forced Loan and English Politics*, pp. 62ff.

117. Sommerville, *Politics and Ideology*, pp. 129–31; Cust's account of these sermons is much more guarded.

118. Mathew Wren, *A Sermon Preached before the Kings Majestie On Sunday the seventeenth of February last, at White-Hall* (Cambridge 1627), pp. 34, 27–8.

119. Isaac Bargrave, *A Sermon Preached Before King Charles, March 27, 1627. Being the Anniversary of his Majesties Inauguration* (London, 1627), pp. 5, 16–17.

120. Ibid., p. 18.

121. Robert Sibthorpe, *Apostolike Obedience* (London, 1627), p. 16.

122. Ibid., pp. 15, 17.

123. Roger Manwaring, *Religion and Alegiance: in two Sermons preached before the Kings Majestie* (London, 1627), first sermon, pp. 17–18.

124. Ibid., pp. 19–20, 26.

125. Ibid., pp. 28–33.

126. Rushworth, *Historical Collections*, vol. I, pp. 436, 443 (stress added).

127. Ibid., p. 444.

128. For the basics see DNB; and Harry F. Snapp, 'The Impeachment of Roger Maynwaring', *Huntington Library Quarterly*, vol. 30 (1966/67), pp. 217–232. Also useful is H. Schwartz, 'Arminianism and the English Parliament, 1624–1629', *Journal of British Studies*, vol. 12 (1973), esp. pp. 59–67.

129. *State Trials*, III, cols 336–7; R. C. Johnson, Mary Frear Keeler, M. J. Cole, & W. B. Bidwell (eds) *Commons Debates 1628*, vol. III (21 April–27 May 1628) (New Haven, 1977), pp. 261–2 (5 May); cf. Snapp, 'Impeachment of Roger Maynwaring', p. 221.

130. *State Trials*, III, col. 339.

131. Ibid., col. 337.

132. J. F. Larkin (ed.), *Stuart Royal Proclamations: Volume II Royal Proclamations of King Charles I 1625–1646* (Oxford, 1983), pp. 197–8.

133.   Snapp, 'Impeachment of Roger Maynwaring', pp. 229–30; *DNB.*

CHAPTER 7:   TOWARDS BREAKDOWN: 'NEW COUNSELS' AND THE DISSOLUTION OF CONSENSUS

1.   Russell, *Parliaments and English Politics 1621–1628* (Oxford, 1979), pp. 349–59.
2.   The idea that there was a 'crisis of parliaments' is, of course, associated with the work of Conrad Russell. See, for example, his *Parliaments and English Politics*, index entries for 'Parliaments, feared extinction of'; Russell, *The Crisis of Parliaments: English History 1509–1660* (Oxford, 1971), pp. 40–1, 296–7, and generally; Russell, 'Parliamentary History in Perspective 1604–1629', *History,* vol. 61 (1976), pp. 2–3. Also Kevin Sharpe, 'Parliamentary History 1603–1629: In or Out of Perspective?', introduction to Sharpe (ed.), *Faction and Parliament: Essays on Early Stuart History,* (Oxford, 1978). For a substantial critique of this line of interpretation see Thomas Cogswell, 'A Low Road to Extinction? Supply and Redress of Grievances in the Parliaments of the 1620s', *Historical Journal,* vol. 33 (1990), pp. 283–303.
3.   Richard Cust, *The Forced Loan and English Politics 1626–1628* (Oxford, 1987), p. 29; on 'new counsels' generally see pp. 5, 27ff.; and L. J. Reeve, *Charles I and the Road to Personal Rule* (Cambridge, 1989), chpt. 2. N.B. also Reeve's remark that he believes Cust to have exaggerated the speed with which a new pattern of politics was established after 1625 (p. 2, n. 3). Also, Richard Cust, 'Charles I, the Privy Council, and the Forced Loan', *Journal of British Studies,* vol. 24 (1985), pp. 208–35.
4.   S. R. Gardiner, *History of England from the Accession of James I to the Outbreak of the Civil War* (London, 4th ed., 1895), vol. VI, p. 110; L. J. Reeve, *Charles I and the Road to Personal Rule,* p. 13; Russell, *Parliaments and English Politics,* p. 306.
5.   R. Cust, *Forced Loan and English Politics,* p. 89.
6.   See Conrad Russell, 'Introduction' in Russell (ed.), *The Origins of the English Civil War* (London, 1973), p. 23; Nicholas Tyacke, 'Puritanism, Arminianism and Counter-Revolution', in Russell (ed.), *Origins,* p. 140; Tyacke, *Anti-Calvinists: The Rise of English Arminianism c.1590–1640,* (Oxford, 1987), pp. 157–9; and H. R. Trevor-Roper, 'Laudianism and Political Power' in Trevor-Roper, *Catholics, Anglicans and Puritans: Seventeenth Century Essays* (London, 1987), chpt. 2.
7.   Sharpe, *Politics and Ideas in Early Stuart England* (London, 1989), pp. 126–7; also G. W. Bernard, 'The Church of England c.1529–c.1642', *History,* vol. 75 (1990), pp. 201–2.
8.   J. Sears McGee, 'William Laud and the Outward Face of Religion', in Richard L. De Molen, *Leaders of the Reformation* (Selinsgrove, 1984), p. 323.
9.   Ibid., pp. 332–3; Christopher Hill, *Economic Problems of the Church:*

From Archbishop Whitgift to the Long Parliament (London, pbk. ed., 1968), chpt. 14; and Esther S. Cope, *Politics Without Parliaments 1629–1640* (London, 1987), pp. 66–76.

10. In the early 1640s Hall was the chief spokesman for *jure divino* episcopacy, yet in the 1630s he had opposed Arminian doctrine as well as the Laudian altar policy: see Tyacke, *Anti-Calvinists*, pp. 212–3; and the editor's introduction to Don M. Wolfe (ed.), *Complete Prose Works of John Milton*, vol. I (1624–1642) (New Haven, 1953), pp. 76–86. Morton was a veteran Jacobean opponent of the politics of Popery, promoted to the see of Durham by Charles in spite of his Calvinism. In 1639 he preached against the Scottish rebels, Morton, *A Sermon Preached before the Kings most Excellent Majestie, in the Cathedrall Church of Durham* (London, 1639). Compare his *An Exact Discoverie of Romish Doctrine in the Case of Conspiracie and Rebellion,* (London, 1605). The 1639 sermon was slightly tampered with before publication (S.P. 16/437/56), largely to remove citations of Calvin.

11. L. J. Reeve, 'Sir Robert Heath's Advice for Charles I in 1629', *Bulletin of the Institute of Historical Research*, vol. 59 (1986), pp. 215–24.

12. Wilfrid R. Prest, *The Rise of the Barristers: A Social History of the English Bar 1590–1640* (Oxford, 1986), pp. 213–4.

13. Ibid., p. 257; W. J. Jones, *Politics and the Bench: The Judges and the Origins of the English Civil War* (London, 1971), pp. 84ff. But note also W. R. Prest, *The Inns of Court under Elizabeth I and the Early Stuarts 1590–1640* (London, 1972), pp. 215–16. Probably the most discussed of the common lawyer agents of Charles's policies of the early 1630s was William Noye, on whom see W. J. Jones, '"The Great Gamaliel of the Law": Mr. Attorney Noye', *Huntington Library Quarterly*, vol. 40 (1977), pp. 197–226. Noye was accused, probably maliciously by the maliciously-minded Anthony Weldon, of being 'a great papist if not an atheist': Prest, *Rise of the Barristers*, p. 213, n. 10.

14. Prest, *Inns of Court*, p. 213.

15. The account here conflates the reports in E. S. Cope & W. H. Coates (eds.), *Proceedings of the Short Parliament of 1640* (London, Camden Fourth Series, vol. 19, 1977) pp. 185–6; and Judith Maltby (ed.), *The Short Parliament (1640) Diary of Sir Thomas Aston* (London, Camden Fourth Series, vol. 35, 1988), p. 112.

16. Tyacke, *Anti-Calvinists*, p. 194; Trevor-Roper, 'Laudianism and Political Power', pp. 82–9.

17. The debate on what to do with Beale is best followed in Aston's *Short Parliament Diary* (ed. Maltby), pp. 112–115; the clearest account of the whole matter is in Rossingham's newsletter in *Calendar of State Papers Domestic* [hereafter *CSPD*], 1640, p. 109.

18. Wallace Notestein (ed.), *The Journal of Sir Simonds D'Ewes from the Beginning of the Long Parliament to the Opening of the Trial of the Earl of Strafford* (New Haven, 1923), p. 8.

19. *Articles Exhibited in the Parliament, against William Beale . . . August the 6th 1641* (London, 1641), p. 2 & passim.

20. *Journals of the House of Commons* [herefter *CJ*], vol. II, p. 353; W. H.

Coates (ed.), *The Journal of Sir Simonds D'Ewes from the First Recess of the Long Parliament to the Withdrawal of King Charles from London* (New Haven, 1942), p. 333. For Beale's subsequent fate see *DNB*.

21.   Notestein (ed.), *Journal of D'Ewes*, pp. 169–70; H. R. Trevor-Roper, *Archbishop Laud 1537–1645* (London, 3rd ed., 1988), pp. 403–4 (chpt. 12 of this work provides a useful account of Laud's last years, and basic information is taken from this source unless otherwise indicated).

22.   In addition to Trevor-Roper, see Gardiner, *History of England*, vol. IX, pp. 249, 296–8.

23.   *State Trials*, vol. IV, col. 326.

24.   Notestein (ed.), *Journal of D'Ewes*, p. 366, n. 8 (diary of John Moore).

25.   *State Trials*, vol. IV, cols 371–2.

26.   Ibid., col. 446; *The Manuscripts of the House of Lords*, vol. XI (new series) (London, 1962), p. 407.

27.   *State Trials*, vol. IV, col. 26 – the articles of impeachment are at cols. 23–6. In his speech on episcopacy (8 Feb. 1641), Falkland also cited two examples of individuals who illustrated his claim that the bishops, who had once excommunicated the violators of Magna Carta, were now encouraging the breach of it – Manwaring and Beale: J. Rushworth, *Historical Collections* (London, 8 vols, 1659–1721), vol. IV, p. 185.

28.   *CSPD*, 1640, p. 532. See also further correspondence in ibid., 518–9, 519, 550. High Commission ordered 'the promoters of the complaints against him [Beale]' to appear before them on 15 October: *CSPD*, 1640–1, p. 385.

29.   Edmund Waller, *A Worthy Speech Made in the House of Commons, this present Parliament, 1641* (London, 1641), p. 6, datable by its place in the Thomason collection to March 1641. The speech has been thought to date from 22 (or 23?) April 1640, but it seems probable that it was never delivered. Its *publication* in mid-1641 served the needs of that time rather than of the period of the Short Parliament, hence its value as evidence for the mood in 1641 not 1640. (See Cope (ed.), *Proceedings of the Short Parliament*, pp. 306–8).

30.   Henry Parker, *The Case of Shipmoney briefly discoursed* (London, 1640), pp. 33–4.

31.   Jones, *Politics and the Bench*, p. 127.

32.   For overviews of the evidence see M. Judson, *The Crisis of the Constitution: An Essay in Constitutional and Political Thought in England 1603–1645* (New York, 1976), chpt. V; and Godfrey Davies, 'English Political Sermons, 1603–1640', *Huntington Library Quarterly*, vol. 3 (1939), pp. 1–23. N.B. the verdict of J.W. Allen, *English Political Thought 1603–1660*, vol. I (1603–1644) (London, 1938), p. 101 – 'There are but very few traces in English writings before 1642 of any theory of royal absolutism by divine right'. For further detail see my 'The Divine Right of Kings Reconsidered', *English Historical Review* (forthcoming).

33.   John Buckeridge, *A Sermon Preached at Hampton Court before the Kings*

Majestie . . . *1603* (London, 1606); and William Dickinson, *The Kings Right, Briefly set downe in a Sermon preached before the Reverend Judges at the Assizes held in Reaching* . . . *June 28, 1619* (London, 1619).

34. Judson, *Crisis or the Constitution*, pp. 195–6, 209.
35. This view is implicit in the work of J. P. Sommerville (though he has rather different uses for it than mine); it is probably most apparent in J. P. Sommerville, 'The Royal Supremacy and Episcopacy "Jure Divino", 1603–1640', *Journal of Ecclesiastical History*, vol. 34 (1983), pp. 548–58.
36. This is *not* to say that 'constitutional' issues were more important than 'religious' ones in 1640–1, or that some actions taken against the Laudian church could not command very wide support; nevertheless the attack in the Long Parliament on the 'illegalities' of Charles's rule did command a consensual support lacking for much religious policy, and the issues of episcopacy and other (wider) religious issues did help to divide Royalists from Parliamentarians by 1642. For background see J. S. Morrill, 'The Religious Context of the English Civil War', *Transactions of the Royal Historical Society*, 5th Series, vol. 34 (1984), pp. 155–78; Morrill, 'The Attack on the Church of England in the Long Parliament, 1640–1642' in Derek Beales and Geoffrey Best (eds), *History, Society and the Church: Essays in Honour of Owen Chadwick* (Cambridge, 1985), pp. 105–24. Cf. Sheila Lambert, 'Committees, Religion, and Parliamentary Encroachment on Royal Authority in Early Stuart England', *English Historical Review*, vol. 105 (1990), pp. 60–95, esp. pp. 90–5 where evidence is given for thinking that the Long Parliament never was united against the Laudian church, *pace* Morrill.
37. Linda S. Popofsky, 'The Crisis over Tonnage and Poundage in Parliament in 1629', *Past and Present*, No. 126 (1990), p. 45.
38. Ibid., p. 73, quoting Sommerville, *Politics and Ideology*, p. 151.
39. This is my interpretation of the phrase indicating that tonnage and poundage was known 'to have been had and enjoyed by the several Kings, named in those acts, time out of mind, by authority of Parliament', even before the formal granting of it, S. R. Gardiner, *The Constitutional Documents of the Puritan Revolution, 1625–1660* (Oxford, 3rd ed., 1906), p. 88.
40. Charles I, 'The King's Declaration showing the Causes of the late Dissolution', in Gardiner, *Constitutional Documents*, pp. 86–88. (For tactical reasons the Crown pulled back from even these claims during 1629, Popofsky, 'Crisis over Tonnage and Poundage', pp. 64, 72.)
41. For the proceedings in King's Bench, and discussion of them in the 1628 parliament, see the masterly account by J. A. Guy, 'The Origins of the Petition of Right Reconsidered', *Historical Journal*, vol. 25 (1982), pp. 289–312. Most details below are taken from this source. See also Linda S. Popofsky, 'Habeas Corpus and "Liberty of the Subject": Legal Arguments for the Petition of Right in the Parliament of 1628', *The Historian*, vol. 41 (1979), pp. 257–75 which also discusses prior events. For background see Cust, *Forced Loan*

and English Politics, pp. 55–62, 236–8; and Reeve, *Charles I and the Road to Personal Rule*, pp. 14–15, and chpt. 2 generally.

42. Cf. the legal background discussed in F. W. Maitland, *The Constitutional History of England* (Cambridge, 1908), pp. 271–5, 313–4.

43. On this point see Guy, 'Origins of the Petition of Right', pp. 292–6, 300–1; Popofsky, 'Habeas Corpus and "Liberty of the Subject"', pp. 263–4.

44. Most useful on the arguments in the case, especially on their political rather than legal implications, is Paul Christianson, 'John Selden, the Five Knights' Case, and Discretionary Imprisonment in Early Stuart England', *Criminal Justice History*, vol. 6 (1985), pp. 65–87. For the legal aspects see Guy, 'Origins of the Petition of Right'.

45. Gardiner, *Constitutional Documents*, pp. 60–1; *State Trials*, vol. III, cols 36–7.

46. *State Trials*, vol. III, cols 44–5; Gardiner, *Constitutional Documents*, pp. 62–3, with ellipses. The issue of trust in the king was crucial in the years 1627–30: see Reeve, *Charles I and the Road to Personal Rule*, passim, but esp. 24ff., and chpts 3 & 6.

47. Gardiner, *Constitutional Documents*, p. 64; *State Trials*, vol. III, col. 57.

48. This has been demonstrated by Guy, 'Origins of the Petition of Right'.

49. *Commons Debates 1628* (Vol. III: 21 April–27 May 1628), ed. R. C. Johnson, M. F. Keeler, M. J. Cole, and W. B. Bidwell (New Haven, 1977), p. 452.

50. For the Commons' Resolutions see Cobbett's *Parliamentary History*, (London, 36 vols, 1806–20), vol. 2, cols 259–60; *Commons Debates 1628*, II, (17 March-19 April 1628), p. 276; for the Lords' Propositions, *Parliamentary History*, vol. 2, cols 329–30 (which has 'incident' for 'intrinsical'); *Commons Debates 1628*, III, pp. 74–5.

51. *Parliamentary History*, vol. 2, col. 329; *Commons Debates 1628*, III, pp. 55, 56.

52. *Commons Debates 1628*, III, p. 452; *Parliamentary History*, vol. 2, col. 355.

53. *Commons Debates 1628*, III, pp. 94–6, 100.

54. Ibid., pp. 495, 502–3; *Parliamentary History*, vol. 2, col. 357 (I have used the latter source).

55. *Commons Debates 1628*, III, p. 494; *Parliamentary History*, vol. 2, cols 356–7.

56. *Commons Debates 1628*, III, p. 494; *Parliamentary History*, vol. 2, col. 357. (The speaker may have been Mr. Pyne).

57. *Commons Debates 1628*, III, pp. 488ff. records no speech by Wentworth in this debate; *Parliamentary History*, vol. 2, col. 357 (from Rushworth).

58. Useful contributions on the question of exactly what legal status the Petition of Right had, or was intended to have, are E. R. Foster, 'Petitions and the Petition of Right', *Journal of British Studies*, vol. 14 (1974), pp. 21–45; and L. J. Reeve, 'The Legal Status of the Petition of Right', *Historical Journal*, vol. 29 (1986), pp. 257–77. On the actual decision to proceed by petition, after the king effectively blocked the

possibility of preceding by bill, see Michael B. Young, 'The Origins of the Petition of Right Reconsidered Further', *Historical Journal*, vol. 27 (1984), pp. 449–52.

59. On the political differences between Saye (and his allies) and some of the Commons leaders (including Coke), see the useful remarks in Christopher Thompson, 'The Origins of the Politics of the Parliamentary Middle Group, 1625–1629', *Transactions of the Royal Historical Society*, 5th series, vol. 22 (1972), pp. 71–86, esp. pp. 82–6.

60. Frances H. Relf (ed.), *Notes of the Debates in the House of Lords* . . . *of the Parliaments*, A.D. *1621, 1625, 1628* (London, Camden Society 3rd ser., vol. 42, 1929) p. 124. Cf. Russell, *Parliaments and English Politics*, p. 370 commenting on Saye's speech: 'any formal saving of the King's discretionary power in response to the Commons' case would be a big change, in that it would give a clear legal recognition to a power which had previously only existed on sufferance'. This was the crux of the matter.

61. Relf, *Notes of the Debates*, p. 130.

62. *Parliamentary History*, vol. 2, col. 358; *Commons Debates 1628*, III, p. 534.

63. *Parliamentary History*, vol. 2, col. 362; *Commons Debates 1628*, III, p. 530.

64. *Parliamentary History*, vol. 2, col. 361; *Commons Debates 1628*, III, p. 529.

65. *Parliamentary History*, vol. 2, cols 363–66; *Commons Debates 1628*, III, pp. 560–71.

66. Relf, *Notes of the Debates*, p. 203; *Parliamentary History*, vol. 2, cols 371–2, for the Lords' final position.

67. *Commons Debates 1628*, III, p. 98: 'It is our unhappiness', Digges added.

68. Very good on these aspects of Charles's character is Reeve, *Charles I and the Road to Personal Rule*, pp. 173ff, esp. p. 176.

69. Cf. Charles Carleton, *Charles I: The Personal Monarch* (London, pbk ed., 1984), p. 109, also pp. 343–4, 84–5.

70. I have in mind here the work of Richard Cust and L. J. Reeve in particular.

71. *Parliamentary History*, vol. 2, col. 352; *Commons Debates 1628*, III, p. 372. Cf. p. 189 where Secretary Coke told the Commons they could make laws that ran against the requirements of necessity.

72. Guy, 'Origins of the Petition of Right', p. 300; Relf, *Notes of the Debates*, p. 93: Buckingham told the Lords (12 April 1628) that Heath 'had a check from the Kinge' for not ensuring that the decision in the Five Knights' Case was entered as a firm *judgement* in favour of imprisonment at the royal discretion.

73. See Conrad Russell, 'The British Problem and the English Civil War', *History*, vol. 72 (1987), pp. 395–415,

74. *State Trials*, vol. III, cols 860–61.

75. Ibid., col. 361.

76. Ibid.

77. Ibid., col. 362.

78. Ibid., col. 363.
79. For accounts of the case see Gardiner, *History of England*, vol. VIII, pp. 271–80; and D. L. Keir, 'The Case of Ship-Money', *Law Quarterly Review*, vol. 52 (1936), pp. 546–74. The best analysis of the judgements is Conrad Russell, 'The Ship Money Judgments of Bramston and Davenport', *English Historical Review*, vol. 77 (1962), pp. 312–18.
80. Gardiner, *History of England*, vol. VIII, pp. 94, 206–8. (Quotation from p. 207.) For further background discussion see Cope, *Politics Without Parliaments*, pp. 106–21.
81. *State Trials*, vol. III, col. 844.
82. Judgements in ibid., cols 1065–1251; also S. R. Gardiner (ed.), 'Notes of the Judgment Delivered by Sir George Croke in the Case of Ship-Money', *Camden Miscellany*, vol. 7 (London, Camden Society, n.s., xiv, 1875); and *The Autobiography of Sir John Bramston* (London, Camden Society, 1st series, xxxii, 1845), pp. 77–81 (This Sir John Bramston was the son of the Shipmoney judge).
83. *State Trials*, vol. III, col. 1191.
84. The foregoing analysis is indebted to Russell, 'Ship Money Judgments of Bramston and Davenport', passim.
85. *State Trials*, vol. III, col. 1090.
86. Ibid., vol. II, col. 395.
87. See for example the treatments of this issue by Weston (*State Trials*, vol. III, col. 1075), Berkeley (ibid., cols 1102–3), and Jones (ibid., cols 1184–5).
88. *State Trials*, vol. III, col. 1083.
89. Most valuable on the political aspects of Hampden's case is Michael Mendle, 'The Ship Money Case, *The Case of Ship Mony*, and the Development of Henry Parker's Parliamentary Absolutism', *Historical Journal*, vol. 32 (1989), pp. 513–36, esp. pp. 516–20.
90. *State Trials*, vol. III, cols 1016, 1019ff.
91. Ibid., col. 1019.
92. Ibid., cols 1025–6.
93. Kenneth Fincham, 'The Judges' Decision on Ship Money in February 1637: the Reaction of Kent', *Bulletin of the Institute of Historical Research*, vol. 57 (1984), p. 234.
94. Ibid., p. 235.
95. *The Works of the Most Reverend Father in God, William Laud, D.D.*, ed. W. Scott & J. Bliss (Oxford, 1847–60), vol. VI, p. 524 (Laud to Wentworth, 14 May 1638). Further insight into the popular reaction to the Shipmoney trial can be found in the diary of Robert Woodford, extracts in *Historical Manuscripts Commission Ninth Report*, Appendix, Pt II, pp. 496–99. Cf. John Fielding, 'Opposition to the Personal Rule of Charles I: The Diary of Robert Woodford, 1637–1641', *Historical Journal*, vol. 31 (1988), pp. 769–88.
96. See Nelson P. Bard, 'The Ship Money Case and William Fiennes, Viscount Saye and Sele', *Bulletin of the Institute of Historical Research*, vol. 50 (1977), pp. 171–84.
97. *State Trials*, vol. III, col. 1075.
98. Ibid., col. 1076.

99. Edward Hyde, Earl of Clarendon, *The History of the Rebellion and Civil Wars in England . . . Also His Life Written by Himself* (Oxford, 1843), pp. 28–9.

CHAPTER 8: EPILOGUE: THE CRISIS OF THE COMMON LAW

1. M. Judson, *The Crisis of the Constitution: An Essay in Constitutional and Political Thought in England 1603–1645* (New York, 1976), pp. 127, & ff.
2. C. Russell, *Parliaments and English Politics 1621–1629* (Oxford, 1979), pp. 352 n. 4, & 353.
3. *Journals of the House of Commons* [hereafter *CJ*], vol. II, p. 68.
4. *Journals of the House of Lords* [hereafter *LJ*], vol. IV (1628–42), p. 303.
5. Bramston, *The Autobiography of Sir John Bramston* (London, Camden Society, 1st series, xxxii, 1845), p. 77. Their future allegiances can most conveniently be checked in the listing of D. Brunton & D. H. Pennington, *Members of the Long Parliament* (London, 1954), pp. 225–45.
6. Esther S. Cope & Willson H. Coates (eds), *Proceedings of the Short Parliament of 1640* (London, Camden Society, 4th series, xix), pp. 193–7.
7. Aston, *The Short Parliament (1640) Diary of Sir Thomas Aston* (ed. Judith Maltby) (London, Camden Society, 4th series, xxxv), p. 130.
8. *Proceedings of the Short Parliament* (ed. Cope & Coates), p. 192.
9. Aston, *Short Parliament Diary* (ed. Maltby), p. 132.
10. Ibid., p. 133.
11. *Proceedings of the Short Parliament* (ed. Cope & Coates), p. 209. There is some interesting material on St John's position in the years 1640–41 in William Palmer, 'Oliver St John and the Legal Language of Revolution in England, 1640–1642', *The Historian*, vol. 51 (1989), pp. 263–82.
12. *Proceedings of the Short Parliament* (ed. Cope & Coates), p. 172.
13. Aston, *Short Parliament Diary* (ed. Maltby), pp. 101–2.
14. W. Notestein (ed.), *The Journal of Sir Simonds D'Ewes from the Beginning of the Long Parliament to the Opening of the Trial of the Earl of Strafford* (New Haven, 1923), p. 117.
15. On the proportion note the remarks of W. J. Jones, *Politics and the Bench: The Judges and the Origins of the English Civil War* (London, 1971), p. 139: excluding Croke, all the judges involved in Hampden's case were either dead or impeached in 1641. Finch, it should be remembered, was only appointed Lord Keeper in January 1640 and had been Chief Justice of Common Pleas in 1637.
16. *The Accusation and Impeachment of John Lord Finch, Baron of Fordwich, Lord Keeper of the Great Seal of England, by the House of Commons*, printed in *Somers Tracts*, vol. IV, p. 130.
17. Notestein (ed.), *Diary of D'Ewes*, p. 117. See also the printed version of the speech, Falkland, *The Lord Falkland His Learned Speech in*

Parliament, in the House of Commons, Touching the Judges and the late Lord Keeper (London, 1641), pp. 7–8. The speech was delivered on 7 December, 1640.

18.   Notestein (ed.), *Diary of D'Ewes*, p. 178.
19.   See also the debate of 12 February 1641 in ibid., pp. 352–4.
20.   Jones, *Politics and the Bench*, pp. 142–3; see also *DNB* entries for the six judges concerned.
21.   *Articles of Accusation, exhibited by the Comons House of Parliament now assembled, Against Sir John Bramston . . . Sir Robert Berkley . . . Sir Francis Crawley . . . Sir Humphrey Davenport . . . Sir Richard Weston . . . and Sir Thomas Trevor* (London, 1641). Also *The Manuscripts of the House of Lords*, vol. XI (new series) (London, 1962), pp. 263–73.
22.   S. R. Gardiner, *The Constitutional Documents of the Puritan Revolution 1625–1660* (Oxford, 3rd ed., 1906), p. 191.
23.   On the printed parliamentary speeches of this period a most useful guide is A. D. T. Cromartie, 'The Printing of Parliamentary Speeches November 1640–July 1642', *Historical Journal*, vol. 33 (1990), pp. 23–44.
24.   Falkland, *The Lord Falkland His Learned Speech*, p. 3.
25.   Ibid., p. 6.
26.   William Prynne, *An Humble Remonstrance against the Tax of Ship-money*, (London, 1643), p. 7. This tract was written (according to its title page) in 1636, which may well mean early 1637, and published in an unauthorised edition in 1641.
27.   Ibid., p. 31.
28.   Oliver St John, *The Speech or Declaration of Mr. St-John . . . Concerning Ship-Money* (London, 1641), pp. 26, 12. Also Notestein (ed.), *Diary of D'Ewes*, pp. 253–5.
29.   St John, *Speech . . . Concerning Ship-Money*, pp. 16–18.
30.   Ibid., p. 2.
31.   Falkland, *The Speech or Declaration of the Lord Falkland . . . against the Lord Finch* (London, 1641), pp. 4, 6.
32.   Edward Hyde, *Mr. Edward Hydes Speech . . . At the Transmission of the severall Impeachments against the Lord Chiefe Barron Damport, Mr. Barron Trevor, and Mr. Barron Weston* (London, 1641), pp. 11–12, & passim.
33.   Edmund Waller, *Mr. Wallers Speech in Parliament, At a Conference of both Houses in the painted Chamber, 6 July 1641* (London, 1641), pp. 4–5, 9.
34.   *LJ*, vol. IV, p. 303.
35.   William Pierrepont, *A Speech delivered by the Honourable William Pierrepont . . . against Sir Robert Berkley* (London, 1641), reprinted in *Somers' Tracts*, vol. IV, p. 305.
36.   See, for example, a document crucial in the events resulting in Charles's trial and execution: 'The Humble Remonstrance of his Excellency the Lord General Fairfax, and his General Council of Officers, held at St. Albans, Nov. 16 1648', in Cobbett's *Parliamentary History* (London, 36 vols, 1806–20), vol. 3, cols 1078–1127.

37. Willson H. Coates, Anne Steele Young & Vernon F. Snow (eds.), *The Private Journals of the Long Parliament 3 January to 5 March 1642* (New Haven, 1982), p. 322.
38. S. R. Gardiner, *History of England from the Accession of James I to the Outbreak of the Civil War* (London, 12 vols, 4th ed., 1895), vol. X, pp. 192–3. Anthony Fletcher, *The Outbreak of the English Civil War* (London, 1981), pp. 232–8, 312–16, 389–91 usefully puts the events of Hull into the context of Yorkshire politics and local politics generally. But, though it was perhaps only one of a series of events that contributed to the untidy and piecemeal division of the country in 1642, one should not forget the importance of the conflict over Hull as a spur to the development of political ideas.
39. Edward Hyde, Earl of Clarendon, *The History of the Rebellion and Civil Wars in England . . . . Also His Life Written by Himself* (Oxford, 1843), p. 29.
40. *Parliamentary History*, vol. 2, col. 1435.
41. Ibid., col. 1356 (stress added).
42. Ibid., cols 1299–1300.
43. Conal Condren in *Parergon*, new series, No. 7 (1989), p. 164.
44. J. G. A. Pocock, *The Ancient Constitution and the Feudal Law*, (Cambridge, 1957, new ed. 1987), chpt. VI, esp. pp. 125–7.
45. Ibid., p. 304.
46. Gerrard Winstanley, *To the Lord Fairfax, Generall of the English Forces, and his Councell of War* (June 9, 1649), in George H. Sabine (ed.), *The Works of Gerrard Winstanley* (Ithaca NY, 1941), p. 292.
47. See, for all of this, Winstanley, *A Watch-word to the City of London, and the Army* (August 26, 1649), in ibid., pp. 321–2.
48. Winstanley, *A New-years Gift for the Parliament and Armie* (January 1, 1650), in ibid., p. 358.
49. See also the discussion of Leveller uses of the common law above, chapter 3.
50. Cf. R. B. Seaberg, 'The Norman Conquest and the Common Law: The Levellers and the Argument from Continuity', *Historical Journal*, vol. 24 (1981), pp. 791–806; Diane Parkin-Speer, 'John Lilburne: a Revolutionary Interprets Statutes and Common Law Due Process', *Law and History Review*, vol. 1 (1983), pp. 276–96; and Andrew Sharp, 'John Lilburne and the Long Parliament's *Book of Declarations*: A Radical's Exploitation of the Words of Authorities', *History of Political Thought*, vol. 9 (1988), pp. 19–44.
51. Richard Overton, *A Remonstrance of Many Thousand Citizens* (London, 1646), pp. 4–5.
52. Ibid., p. 15.
53. William Walwyn, *Englands Lamentable Slaverie* (London, 1645), p. 5 & passim.
54. Ibid., p. 4.
55. John Lilburne, *Londons Liberty in Chains discovered* (London, 1646), p. 41.
56. John Lilburne, *Strength out of Weaknesse* (London, 1649), p. 14.
57. Walwyn, *Englands Lamentable Slaverie*, pp. 4–5.

58.   *State Trials,* vol. IV, cols 1289–90.
59.   Ibid., col. 1307.
60.   John Milton, *Complete Prose Works,* vol. I (ed. Don M. Wolfe) (New Haven, 1953), p. 605.
61.   Cf. David Wootton, 'From Rebellion to Revolution: The Crisis of the Winter of 1642/3 and the Origins of Civil War Radicalism', *English Historical Review,* vol. 105 (1990), pp. 654–69.
62.   Most illuminating on Parker's thought at this time is Michael Mendle, 'The Ship Money Case, *The Case of Ship Mony,* and the Development of Henry Parker's Parliamentary Absolutism', *Historical Journal,* vol. 32 (1989), pp. 513–36. The standard account, Wilbur K. Jordan, *Men of Substance: A Study of the Thought of Two English Revolutionaries, Henry Parker and Henry Robinson* (Chicago, 1942), is unsatisfactory. I am indebted to Mr. Howard Moss for many discussions of Henry Parker.
63.   Henry Parker, *The Case of Shipmony* (London, 1640), p. 2.
64.   Ibid., pp. 5, 14.
65.   Ibid., p. 7.
66.   Henry Parker, *Observations upon Some of His Majesties Late Answers and Expresses* (London, 2nd ed., 1642), pp. 5, 16 & passim.
67.   Henry Parker, *The Contra-Replicant, His Complaint to His Majestie,* (London, 1643), p. 6.
68.   See Parker's statement to this effect in his debate with Judge David Jenkins (1647) quoted in F.D. Wormuth, *The Royal Prerogative 1603–1649,* (Ithaca NY, 1939), p. 113.
69.   John Marsh, *An Argument or, Debate in Law: Of the Great Question concerning the Militia* (London, 1642), p. 7: 'by reason of the necessity, it is warranted by the Law for them to do it at this time'.
70.   There is no satisfactory study of Jenkins' thought: some useful material is in Robert Ashton, 'From Cavalier to Roundhead Tyranny, 1642–9' in J. S. Morrill (ed.), *Reactions to the English Civil War 1642–1649* (London, 1982), chpt. 8.
71.   On whom see Pocock, *Ancient Constitution,* pp. 170–81; 337–41; Richard Tuck, *Natural Rights Theories: Their Origin and Development* (Cambridge, 1979), pp. 113–8; 132–9; Sir Matthew Hale, *The History of the Common Law of England* (ed. Charles M. Gray) (Chicago, 1971), esp. editor's introduction.
72.   Well surveyed in Mark Goldie, 'The Revolution of 1689 and the Structure of Political Argument', *Bulletin of Research in the Humanities,* vol. 83 (1980), pp. 473–564.
73.   See J. G. A. Pocock, *The Machiavellian Moment: Florentine Republican Thought and the Atlantic Republican Tradition* (Princeton, 1975), chpt. XII; Caroline Robbins (ed.), *Two English Republican Tracts* (Cambridge, 1969); James Conniff, 'Reason and History in Early Whig Thought: The Case of Algernon Sidney', *Journal of the History of Ideas,* vol. 43 (1982), pp. 397–416, which demonstrates the introduction of original contract into views of the past, a view sharply different from pre-Civil War ideas, though arguably an alternative way of fusing reason and history; and Jonathan Scott, *Algernon*

Sidney and the English Republic 1623–1677 (Cambridge, 1988), esp. chpt. 2.

74. Martyn P. Thompson, 'A Note on "Reason" and "History" in Late Seventeenth Century Thought', *Political Theory*, vol. 4 (1976), pp. 491–504. See also Thompson, 'The History of Fundamental Law in Political Thought from the French Wars of Religion to the American Revolution', *American Historical Review*, vol. 91 (1986), pp. 1103–1128; and Harro Höpfl & Martyn P. Thompson, 'The History of Contract as a Motif in Political Thought', *American Historical Review*, vol. 84 (1979), pp. 919–44.

Index

The index excludes the names of modern historians, and does not include all incidental references to individuals mentioned frequently. However, it should be noted that it can an serve as a select bibliography. The references under the sub-entries 'bibliography' give further secondary reading on some of the more important individuals and concepts discussed in this book. Other than this, though, material in footnotes is not indexed unless it could not be traced through references to the main text. In a few cases where the number of entries is large, the most important references are given in **bold**.